DECENTRALIZATION POLICIES IN ASIAN DEVELOPMENT

DECENTRALIZATION POLICIES IN ASIAN DEVELOPMENT

Editors

Shinichi Ichimura

Kyoto University, Japan

Roy Bahl

Georgia State University, USA

World Scientific

NEW JERSEY • LONDON • SINGAPORE • BEIJING • SHANGHAI • HONG KONG • TAIPEI • CHENNAI

Published by

World Scientific Publishing Co. Pte. Ltd.
5 Toh Tuck Link, Singapore 596224
USA office: 27 Warren Street, Suite 401-402, Hackensack, NJ 07601
UK office: 57 Shelton Street, Covent Garden, London WC2H 9HE

British Library Cataloguing-in-Publication Data
A catalogue record for this book is available from the British Library.

DECENTRALIZATION POLICIES IN ASIAN DEVELOPMENT

ISBN-13 978-981-281-863-8
ISBN-10 981-281-863-4

Typeset by Stallion Press
Email: enquiries@stallionpress.com

Printed in B&Jo Enterprise Pte. Ltd.

Preface

This volume deals with the important subject of *Political and Fiscal Decentralization,* which is now under discussion and reform by governments in many Asian countries including Japan, India, Indonesia, and China. The progress with fiscal decentralization in Asia has attracted much attention from policy makers and scholars around the world as they consider their own reform programs.

In the early stage of economic development and nation-building, the concentration of power and resources was undoubtedly a necessity to politically unite the nation and to make the economic takeoff possible. As a result, the political system of a new nation-state was usually organized under an authoritarian central government. With economic development, however, civil society and the business sector demanded that the government offer better public services and utilities as well as better opportunities for employment and business development. Particularly as the regional disparities in living conditions kept widening, the people and businesses in outer regions desired governments to be closer and more responsive to them and demanded *decentralization* of political and fiscal administration. Recognizing this, bureaucrats and politicians began to seriously search for the ways and means of political and fiscal decentralization. For instance, in Indonesia even in the 1970s and the 80s, to talk about the possibility of federal system was a taboo for the newly borne nation. Now, as one article in this book shows, Indonesia has adopted a decentralized political and fiscal system.

After World War II most East Asian countries not only achieved political independence but also, in a few decades, reached the middle income country level over US$1,000 in per capita GDP. The ensuing demand for decentralization has been prevalent in almost all of the countries in Asia. For many years, however, decentralization was more discussed than acted on. *De facto* these countries were all victims of concentration and urbanization. The country papers in this book will clarify the reasons for the gap between arguments and realities.

Japan has been no exception. Very recently, however, the popular Prime Minister, Junichiro Koizumi, brought up this issue as the central theme of his government (2001–2006). In his election campaigns, he made wise use of two slogans: "from Center to Local" and "from Government to Private." *Decentralization* and *privatization* have become the timely key words for Koizumi to capture the trendy desires of the Japanese public at the time of Centennial change. Particularly after the success of Thatcher-Reagan liberalization and deregulation and following the end of the Cold War, *privatization* became extremely popular in Japan and actually enhanced the political interest in *decentralization.* Clearly the Japanese public wanted the government policies to be closer to them, and they wanted less intervention in private businesses from the governments at the same time. Three Japanese papers in this volume will explain the most recent practice of decentralization policies in Japan.

The experiences of Socialist countries, China and Vietnam, are different from those mentioned above. The articles on these two countries show the differences in institutional arrangements and the serious problems associated with large-scale privatization of State-Owned Enterprises as well as with decentralization of administration. It may be pointed out here that transition from Socialist planned economy to Capitalist market economy were started by the initiatives of Deng Xiao Ping in China in 1979, long before Gorbachov took the office of Secretary in the Soviet Union in 1985. Even in Vietnam the *Doi Moi* reform toward market economy started in 1986. By the end of the 20th Century, the success of *Socialist Market Economy* and *Doi Moi* had put the two Socialist economies at an almost equal place in the mixed economy as the rest of East Asia. Needless to say, there are many important problems about *privatization* as such to consider, besides *decentralization*. I have treated them in another book: *Transition from Socialist to Market Economies: comparison of European and Asian experiences*, edited with T. Sato and W. James (Palgrave and Macmillan). Fundamentally, however, the essays in this book show that China and Vietnam are facing many of the same issues in *decentralization* as are other Asian countries. In Japan the two reforms: *privatization and decentralization* have progressed in parallel. Arguments on political decentralization had been going on since the pre-war days, but in 1981 the government committee on Local Administration supported continuing the discussions, with no commitment to immediately implement the political and administrative decentralization. Again, however, the Committee on Local Administration Reform was set up in the Prime Minister's Office for 1989–92 and recommended passing a law to allow merger of prefectures. That law was in fact enacted in 2004. This opened the way for the long- debated "Do-Shu Sei" (Province-State System), so that political and administrative reforms to merge several prefectures is now legally possible. On the other hand, the Nakasone Cabinet (1982–87) succeeded in privatizing the National Railroad and opened the way to the next privatization of NTT (National Telephone and Telecommunication Public Enterprise) and most recently the Japan Post in 2007. These policies had some aspects of decentralization, because they subdivided the National Railway Corporation into several companies in different regions, and NTT and The Japan Post into several private companies.

It may be surprising to find few comprehensive studies on the subject of decentralization in Asia. Serving as directors of the research institutes at Kyoto University, Osaka International University and the International Center for the Study of East Asian Development (ICSEAD), Kitakyushu about forty years, I have long recognized the importance of these two subjects, but could undertake only a large project on transition economies, leaving the theme of decentralization in Asia utterly untouched. The difficulty was to mobilize an international team of economists and political scientists to undertake such studies.

In 2002 when the Mayor of Kitakyushu City, Mr. Koichi Sueyoshi, initiated a series of international conferences on Asia. I immediately suggested the subject of *Decentralization Policies*. He strongly supported it, probably because it was an urgent and controversial problem in Japanese politics then as well as now. Since, however, my knowledge and experiences in this area were limited, I decided to hold a preparatory workshop first. Inviting academic experts in Japan and Asia, the authorities of the World Bank (Vice President Yukio Yoshimura, Tokyo office) and the Asian Development Bank (Dr. Jung-Soo Lee, Tokyo office head), I asked them how to organize such a conference. Thanks to their enthusiastic support and help, we could identify many experts in Asia and the US and successfully organize the first Asian Development Conference in November 2003.

At the Conference 22 papers, including a keynote Speech by Prof. Roy Bahl, Georgia State University, were presented by the experts of Asian countries and the World Bank. In addition, an especially important panel discussion by three Japanese practitioners of Decentralization was held. They were: Governor Hiraku Kajiwara (Chairman of the Governors Association), Mayor Koichi Sueyoshi, Secretary General Keiji Araki (the Reform Committee for Promotion of Decentralization, Prime Minister's Office) and Prof. Tatsuo Hatta (The University of Tokyo). The details of the program and the summary reports are given in the Appendix to this book. The Proceedings of the Conference: *Development and Decentralization in Asia*, were made available in English and Japanese by Kitakyushu City and ICSEAD in 2004. The panel discussion report mentioned above is available only in the Japanese edition. In this book, however, Chapter II by H. Ikawa not only covers the main points of their discussions but up-dates the development of decentralization policies in Japan.

This book is, however, not just an outcome of the conference. Five years have passed since the time of first ADC. Decentralization policies have been implemented in various ways in almost all Asian countries. The authors have revised their papers to give even more up-to-date information on their country situations and to evaluate the recent progress with decentralization. All the papers have been carefully edited and re-edited by the two editors.

We are very pleased to have completed this book. We hope that this book will open up further discussions on many issues of *decentralization* like those related to urbanization, industrial location, and environmental problems. I regret that some experts from Korea and China could not join us due to the inconvenient timing. I must also apologize for the delay in editing and publishing this volume. I sincerely hope that the volume will still satisfy the needs for the academic discussions of the subject and make a modest contribution to decentralization policies in Asia as well as in the world. Lastly, I express my hearty gratitude for Dr. Sadayuki Takii's help in my editorial work in telecommunication from ICSEAD all the time.

March 30, 2008

Shinichi Ichimura

Contents

Detailed Table of Contents

List of Figures and Tables

Chapter XII Local Public Finance in Taiwan: Reform and Trend 281

Editors and Authors

Roy W. Bahl: Regents Professor of Economics, the Andrew Young School of Policy Studies, Georgia State University, Atlanta, GA, USA.
E-mail: rbahl@ gsu.edu

Shinichi Ichimura: Professor Emeritus, Kyoto University; Kyoto; Honorary Counselor, International Center for the Study of East Asian Development, Kitakyushu, Japan.
E-mail: s-ichimura@mub.biglobe.ne.jp

Hiroshi Ikawa Professor, National Graduate Institute for Policy Studies, Tokyo, Japan.
E-mail: ikawa@grips.ac.jp

Toshihiro Ihori Professor of Public Finance, Graduate Faculty of Economics, University of Tokyo, Tokyo, Japan.
E-mail: ihori@e.u-tokyo.ac.jp

Xue-Jin Zuo Vice Director, Shanghai Academy of Social Sciences, Shanghai, China.
E-mail: xjzuo@sass.org.cn

M. Govinda Rao Director, National Institute of Public Finance and Policy, Member, Economic Advisory Council to the Prime Minister, New Delhi, India.
E-mail: mgr@nipfp.org.in

Jay N. Shih	Professor, Department of Public Administration, National Cheng-Chi University, Taipei, Taiwan. E-mail: njshih@nccu.edu.tw
Benjamin E. Diokno	Professor, Faculty of Economics, University of the Philippines, Manila, the Philippines. E-mail: benjamin.diokno@up.edu.ph
Dana Weist	The World Bank, Washington, D. C., USA. E-mail: Dweist@worldbank.org
Charas Suanmala	Professor of Public Finance, Chulalongkorn University, Bangkok, Thailand. E-mail: scharas@chula.ac.th
Nguyen Khac Hung	Vice Rector, Dai Nam University, Ministry of Education and Training, Hanoi, Vietnam. E-mail: nkhung2001@yahoo.com
Wofgang Fengler	Senior Economist, Jakarta Office, The World Bank, Jakarta, Indonesia. E-mail: wfengler@worldbank.org
Bert Hofman	Country Director, Manila Office, The World Bank, Manila, the Philippines. E-mail: Bhofman@worldbank.org
Shin Saito	Professor of Public Finance, Graduate School of Economics, Osaka University, Osaka, Japan. E-mail: saito@econ.osakau.ac.jp
Hideo Yunoue	Assistant Professor, Graduate School of International Public Policies, Osaka University, Osaka, Japan. E-mail: yunoue@osipp.osaka-u.ac.jp

Chu-Wei Tseng	Professor of Public Finance, Graduate Faculty of Economics, National Cheng Chi University, Taipei, Taiwan. E-mail: chuwei@nccu.edu.tw
Hsien-Feng Lee	Professor of Public Finance, Department of Economics, National Taiwan University, Taipei, Taiwan. E-mail: leehsf@ntu.edu.tw
Azmi Setapa	Senior Staff, Ministry of Higher Education, Putrajaya, Malaysia. E-mail: drazmi@mohe.gov.my
Yee Siew Lin	Research staff, Malaysian Institute for Economic Research, Kuala Lumpur, Malaysia.
Rosario Manasan	Philippine Institute of Development Studies, Manila, the Philippines. E-mail: rmanasa@mail.PIDS. gov.ph
Hiroko Kudo	Professor, Faculty of Law, Chuo University, Tokyo, Japan. E-mail: hirokokd@tamacc.chuo-u.ac.jp
Motohiro Sato	Professor, Graduate Faculty of Economics, Hitotsubashi University, Tokyo, Japan. E-mail: satom@econ.hit-u.ac.jp
Hidehiko Tanimura	Professor, Graduate School of Social System Studies, University of Kitakyushu, Kitakyushu, Japan. E-mail: tanimura@gol.com

Chapter I

Promise and Reality of Fiscal Decentralization

ROY BAHL

Georgia State University

The growing interest in fiscal decentralization in Asia is part of a worldwide pattern. Most developing countries have long ago placed the strengthening of sub-national government on their development policy agenda. Decentralization is an important part of the transition strategy for many former socialist countries. Some industrialized countries are retuning their fiscal decentralization (Canada) while others have introduced major new initiatives in recent years (Japan, Spain).

In this paper, we consider the costs and benefits of fiscal decentralization, trends in the practice of decentralizing budgets, and the policy interventions that are being used to strengthen the financial position and the financial autonomy of sub-national governments. In particular, we examine inter-governmental transfers, local taxation and hard budget constraints as key policy issues. The focus in this paper is on developing countries. The process areas that are taken up have to do with comprehensive design of a decentralization reform, sequencing and politics. In outlining these issues, we draw heavily from the experiences of Asian countries, some of which are discussed in detail in the chapters in this volume.

1. The Benefits[1]

What are the major advantages to be gained from investing more fiscal powers in provincial and local governments? This is the fundamental question that sometimes gets lost in the political debate about fiscal decentralization. The most important benefit is the welfare gain that comes from moving governance closer to the people. This is the economic efficiency argument that drives the thinking of most economists who work on this subject (Oates, 1972). The argument is straightforward. Let us assume that people's preferences for government services vary, e.g., because of religion, language, ethnic mix, climate, economic base or just because of the inclinations of the local political leadership. Let us assume further that people have sorted themselves so that those with similar preferences live in the same region. If sub-national governments respond to these preferences in structuring their budgets, decentralization will result in variations in the package of services delivered in different regions. The voters will see to this in a system where there is downward accountability. People will get what they want and so the welfare of the population will be enhanced. Under the same circumstances, but with a centralized system, accountability will be upward to a higher level of government, service provision will be more uniform and people in different regions will get less of the service mix that they want. The more heterogeneous the country, the greater will be the welfare costs of uniformity.

If governance is properly decentralized, two good things can come to pass. One is that there will be more accountability on the part of government officials because they are held responsible for the quality of services delivered to the local population that elected them. If the makeup of local public services is determined by the center and paid for by the center, sub-national government officials can largely escape taking responsibility for the quality of services provided. The other benefit from a well-functioning decentralization is that there will be more willingness on the part of the local population to pay for services, because they get what they want. If one advocates fiscal decentralization, one must believe this story, because it is the primary argument.

[1] For more lengthy discussions of the pros and cons of fiscal decentralization, see Bahl and Linn (1992), Bahl and Wallace (2005), Litvak, Ahmad and Bird (1998), Bird and Vaillancourt (1998), Tanzi (1995) and Dillinger and Webb (1999).

True believers can point out that successful fiscal decentralization at once attacks several of the problems that face most developing and many transition countries: economic development, revenue mobilization, innovation in public service delivery, accountability of elected officials, capacity development at the local government level, and grassroots participation in governance.

Whether or not fiscal decentralization actually leads to accountability downward, however, depends on many things. Certainly there must be elections. Local governments must have the power to control their employees, and there must be enough accurate information available so that voters can evaluate the fiscal decisions of their local governments. In many developing countries, one or more of these conditions is not met.

A second important benefit of fiscal decentralization is the promise of increased revenue mobilization. This happens because decentralization can broaden the overall tax base. That is, if sub-national governments are more directly involved in taxation, a greater share of GDP might be reached by the tax system. If this hypothesis is correct, increases in sub-national government tax revenues would not be offset by equal amount reductions in central government tax revenues. In addition, the claim of sub-national governments on central revenues via inter-governmental transfers could be reduced by increased revenue mobilization at the sub-national government level.

The argument behind this hypothesis is that sub-national governments have the potential to reach the traditional income, consumption and wealth tax bases in ways that the central government cannot. Typically, central governments rely on a combination of company income tax, individual income tax, value added tax, excise and customs duties. All of these taxes, however, have a high entry threshold in most developing countries. Small firms, most individuals and owners of immovable property are "under-represented" in the tax base. In fact, local governments can broaden the overall tax base with a variety of tax instruments and administrative measures, and they do so in many countries. These instruments include payroll taxes, levies on the sales of assets of firms, licenses to operate, betterment charges and various forms of property taxation.[2] As we discuss below, few Asian countries have acted on this comparative advantage in local taxation.

---

[2] A good review of local tax practices in developing countries is in Bird (1999).

2. The Costs

There also are significant costs to fiscal decentralization, at least in the eyes of central governments, and perhaps this is why all countries do not embrace this policy route with the same degree of enthusiasm. Heading the list of costs is the loss of macro-economic control.[3] Central governments would argue that they should have the flexibility to respond quickly to changes in national economic conditions, for example, to raise taxes, cut expenditures or limit credit in order to deal with a deficit. There also are external pressures on developing country governments to implement an effective stabilization policy. The pressures from the IMF and World Bank for more austere economic policy to bring about internal or external balance usually requires holding the fiscal deficit to an acceptable level and limiting the level of domestic credit.

In a truly decentralized governance system, stabilization policy is more difficult to implement than in a centralized system. One reason is because the central government may not be able to control sub-national government spending so as to reduce an overall deficit. If the lower levels of government have their own resources — either significant own source revenues or a guaranteed share of national government collections — they may set their own level of spending. In many decentralized countries, sub-national governments do not face a hard budget constraint, and a more serious challenge to macroeconomic stability can emerge. In India, the deficits of the state and local governments rose to 10 percent of GDP in the late 1990s, and in Japan local government debt outstanding increased to a level equivalent to about 40 percent of GDP in 2003. (Rao, 2008; Ikawa, 2008). In the Philippines, the growing share of national tax collections earmarked for local governments compromised the budgetary position of the central government (Diokno, 2008).

Even when the central government does not tie the vertical share of grants to national tax collections, it may not have the flexibility to cut subsidies (conditional grants) to local governments. These subsidies can be sticky downward, especially in cases where they support public employee salaries or direct payment to needy individuals, and where their champions include powerful central government ministries.

[3] More detailed discussions of this may be found in Bahl and Linn (1992), Prud'homme (1995), Ter-Minassian (1997), Tanzi (1995) and Spahn (1997).

This "cost" of decentralization to the central government, however, may not be seen the same way when viewed from the provincial or local level. Where central governments are able to control the budgets of sub-national governments, for example because the budget law does not clearly define expenditure assignments, central deficits have sometimes been offloaded on to regional and local governments. For example in the 1990s, Russia transferred expenditure responsibility for certain infrastructure and social welfare services to regional governments without assigning additional revenue responsibility (Martinez-Vazquez *et al.*, 2006).

A second cost of decentralization to the central government is that it could lose some control over infrastructure development in cases where sub-national governments have discretionary spending power. The net result of fiscal decentralization will be a shift of resources from central governments that have higher rates of capital spending to provincial and local governments who spend at a greater rate on consumption goods and services. Fiscal decentralization, therefore, could lead to a lower overall rate of spending on infrastructure, and national growth could be slowed. Fiscal decentralization also may lead to a shift in the composition of public capital investments. This is because national priorities for capital investment are not the same as sub-national government priorities. The national government is interested in investments in infrastructure that have regional and national benefits, for example, large scale irrigation projects, national (inter-state) roads, and power. State (provincial) and local governments will be focused more on capital investments with provincial and local benefits.

Central governments have tried to resolve this problem in a number of ways. The most used remedy is to provide local governments with conditional grants that require expenditures in certain functional areas (e.g., local infrastructure) and often carry conditions as to the nature of the expenditures (e.g., construction standards, pay scales etc.). From the point of view of the sub-national governments, however, this approach compromises their discretion and leads to sub optimal uses of resources because of the failure to recognize local conditions.

In some countries there is movement away from conditional grants. Indonesia replaced its Inpres, a large number of specific grants for purposes ranging from re-greening to the construction of public markets, with a general purpose grant allocated by formula (Fengler and Hofman, 2008). Japan is moving away from conditional subsides to local taxes (Saito and Yunoue, 2008).

A third cost of fiscal decentralization is that it is not an inherently equalizing economic development policy. In fact, depending on how the system is designed, there may be little in it for poorer and rural provincial and local governments. Certainly revenue centralization gives a greater *potential* for equalization. In countries where the claim of sub-national governments on the overall tax base is small, the central government can create a larger pool of funds for allocation among local governments on an equalizing basis. However, just because the central government has more funds to allocate, it does not necessarily follow that they will allocate these funds on an equalizing basis. In fact, countries vary widely in terms of the amount of equalization that is done through their grant systems.

If fiscal decentralization takes the path of heavy reliance on own source revenues, a decided advantage is given to sub-national governments with a greater fiscal capacity. This would include, for example, industrial provinces and large cities where there is a larger tax base that is easier to reach and a better chance of developing the administrative capacity to collect taxes. This part of the equation alone suggests less equalization in the system. The way to address this, in a context of fiscal decentralization, is with a program of equalization grants that takes into account the weaker fiscal capacity of some regions/local governments. An example of this approach is South Africa, where the large cities raise over 90 percent of revenues from own sources and rural local governments are supported by an equalizing grant program (Reschovsky, 2003).

Finally, fiscal decentralization can be costly relative to the benefits gained. Sub-national governments may not have the administrative skills to deliver decentralized services efficiently or to collect taxes efficiently. In both areas, there may be duplication of services with the central government. If local governments attempt to improve their tax collections or service delivery efficiency to central government levels, the cost could be prohibitive. This comparative advantage is what leads many to argue to keep collection of major taxes at the central government level. This argument is reinforced by the observation that sub-national governments are often assigned "difficult" taxes, i.e., those that would be costly to collect at any level of government. Compounding these cost problems, according to some, is that decentralization can lead to increased corruption.[4]

Advocates would argue that fiscal decentralization need not be a more costly system to administer. Part of the tax administration costs could be reduced if tax assignment is more reasonable and if tax base sharing were adopted (central administration but local rate setting) (McLure, 1997). On the service delivery side, it is true that the learning curve for sub-national governments can be steep, even for functions that are properly assigned to lower-level governments, but eventually the responsiveness to the demands of citizens can outweigh these costs.

3. The Practice

One might test the hypothesis that the benefits of decentralization outweigh the costs, by looking for evidence on the growing fiscal importance of sub-national governments. In fact, countries around the world have moved only slowly toward the adoption of more decentralized inter-governmental fiscal systems. Based on IMF *Government Finance Statistics*, which is about the only comparable data source available, one can observe that the sub-national government share of public expenditures has remained at about 13 to 14 percent in developing countries over the last three decades.[5] The rather remarkable stability in the sub-national government expenditure share (which also holds in OECD countries) is reported in Table 1.

These averages hide a great deal of intercountry variation, which several analysts have tried to explain. Bahl and Wallace (2005) find that the sub-national government expenditure share is significantly higher in countries with a higher per capita GDP, a larger population size and

---

[4] Empirical work on the relationship between decentralization and corruption is inconclusive. Fisman and Gatti (2002), for example, find that corruption is lower in more decentralized countries; Treisman (2000) finds corruption to be higher in federal than in unitary countries.

[5] We measure decentralization here as the sub-national government share of total government expenditure in the country, i.e., sub-national government expenditures as the numerator, and total central plus sub-national government expenditures as the denominator. This is a flawed measure of fiscal decentralization because it does not indicate whether the sub-national government has any significant influence over how the money will be spent.

Table 1. Fiscal Decentralization Indicators

	1970s		1980s		1990s		
	Developing Countries	OECD Countries	Developing Countries	OECD Countries	Developing Countries	OECD Countries	Transition Countries
Sub-national Government Tax as a share of Total Government Tax	10.44 (43)	18.71 (22)	7.70 (35)	18.75 (22)	9.27 (28)	19.13 (20)	16.59 (14)
Sub-national Government Expenditure as a share of Total Government Expenditure	13.01 (48)	33.78 (22)	13.24 (43)	32.27 (23)	13.78 (54)	32.41 (23)	26.12 (23)

Note: Sample sizes are in parenthesis.
Source: *Government Finance Statistics Yearbook*. International Monetary Fund.

a lower degree of corruption. This more or less matches the findings in other studies.[6]

4. Policy Instruments for Decentralization

There are many fiscal policy instruments used in implementing decentralization systems. Three of the most important, and controversial, are sub-national government taxes, inter-governmental transfers, and the requirement of a hard budget constraint.

4.1. *Sub-national Government Taxes*

Voters will hold their elected officials more accountable if local public services are financed to a significant extent from locally imposed taxes and charges, as opposed to the case where financing is primarily by central government transfers. The local tax must be visible to local voters, large enough to impose a noticeable burden, and the burden must not be easily exported to residents outside the jurisdiction.[7] Minor taxes and nuisance taxes will not measure up to all of these requirements.

Reliance on own source taxes also has the advantage of imposing fiscal discipline on the sub-national government. A greater share of financing from own sources drives up the tax price of public services and reduces the upward pressure on sub-national government expenditures. Reliance on inter-governmental transfers has the opposite effect.

Significant tax assignment to sub-national governments is common practice in many industrial countries. At one extreme, US State governments and Canadian provinces have almost complete autonomy in choosing any tax base, so long as there is no interference with interstate commerce. In Denmark and Sweden, local taxes account for nearly one-half of local government spending (Owens and Norregaard, 1991). Revenues from sub-national government taxes in Switzerland are greater in amount than revenues received from grants. Japan has lagged other industrialized countries in the assignment of taxes to local governments but is now introducing a new inter-governmental reform that shifts local government finance significantly toward local taxation (Ikawa, 2008).

---

[6] For a good literature review, see Letelier (2005).

[7] A tax may be considered "local" if the sub-national government sets the tax rate.

In most developing and transition countries, however, central governments have been reluctant to release taxing powers to sub-national governments. As may be seen in Table 1, the sub-national governments tax share in developing and transition countries is about 10 percent, in comparison to 20 percent in industrialized countries. Public financing in low income countries is still primarily through the transfer system.

One common reason for a low level of taxation by sub-national governments in Asia is the unwillingness of central governments to share the productive tax bases. In many cases the taxes passed down are notoriously difficult to administer. For example, Pakistan gives its provincial governments the right to tax agricultural income, the consumption of services and property transfers. The result is a level of sub-national government tax revenue that is less than one percent of GDP (Bahl *et al.*, 2008).

The Philippines is a country where about one-third of sub-national government revenues are raised from own source revenues. This is a high share by comparison with most developing countries. In addition to the property tax, the principal revenue source is a business tax on gross receipts. However, Philippine local governments are limited in terms of their ability to set tax rates, and tax revenues fall well short of the level of devolved expenditures (Manasan, 2008). Sub-national governments in Cambodia, China and Vietnam all raise less than 5 percent of total revenues from own sources. (Taliercio, 2005).

4.2. *Inter-governmental Transfers*

No policy instrument of fiscal decentralization is more discussed, or more often reformed, than inter-governmental transfers. On the one hand, transfers are preferred to local taxation in most developing and transition countries because they recognize the superior tax administration capabilities of the central government and because they allow a greater measure of central control. On the other hand, transfers are an object of criticism precisely because of the central control, and in some countries because they discourage local revenue mobilization, are not adequately equalizing, and are not transparent. Reform in most countries has concentrated on finding a middle ground between central control and the goals of decentralization.

In fact, there are many different kinds of inter-governmental transfer systems in use, and each has a potentially different impact on sub-national government finances and a different implication for central control. Some stimulate local government spending, some are substituted for local government revenue effort, some are equalizing, and some lead to more local government fiscal autonomy than do others. The policy mistake most often made, and perhaps the reason why grant systems remain under review, is that countries often enter into grant design without fully exploring the alternatives available and their differential impacts. One might begin such an analysis by considering that inter-governmental transfers have two dimensions: the size of the divisible pool, and the distribution of this pool among eligible local government units. Some have referred to the divisible pool dimension as having to do with the *vertical fiscal balance* between the central and sub-national governments, and the allocation dimension as having to do with *horizontal fiscal balance*. Both dimensions must be part of the policy design.[8]

We present a taxonomy of inter-governmental transfers in Table 2, with the vertical sharing arrangements shown in the column heads and the distribution arrangements shown in the rows. The cells in the table show the different grant types. To demonstrate how different the outcomes of these systems can be, we might focus on the Asian experience with three grant types: unconditional transfers to sub-national governments, conditional grants and *ad hoc* transfers.

Unconditional grants are probably most consistent with the local autonomy goals of decentralization. If they are based on defined shares of national taxes (see Column 1 of Table 2), they give sub-national governments access to an elastic tax base as well as relative certainty about the amount they will receive. Asian countries vary widely in terms of their vertical sharing arrangements, but the shared tax option — which would tend to be favored by countries with a greater commitment to decentralization — is common. The Philippines, India, Indonesia and Pakistan all guarantee a percent of national taxes to sub-national governments, but the vertical shares differ. Indonesia shares 25 percent of actual collections, and India allocates about 30 percent of tax collections to the divisible pool for Finance Commission transfers. The Philippines shares 40 percent of internal revenue collections in the third previous year, and Pakistan shares 41 percent of total tax collections.

[8] Bahl and Linn (1992, Chapter 13).

Table 2. How Should the Grant System be Structured?

Alternative Form of Inter-governmental Grant Programs			
	Method of Determining the Total Divisible Pool		
Method of Allocating the Divisible Pool Among Eligible Units	Specified Share of National or State Government Tax	*Ad Hoc* Decision	Reimbursement of Approved Expenditures
Origin of collection of tax	A	NA	NA
Formula	B	F	NA
Total or partial reimbursement of costs	C	G	K
Ad hoc	D	H	NA

Source: Bahl and Linn (1992).

With respect to the distribution across eligible local government units, the revenue sharing method may be by origin of collections (China's income tax or VAT sharing) or by formula (as is done in Japan, Taiwan and Philippines). A derivation-based distribution (an "A" grant in Table 2) favors higher income provinces, where taxable capacity is greatest. Formula-based systems (B grants) can vary greatly in their impacts, depending on the formula used. In fact, formulas usually are driven by what a country wants to achieve with its grant system but are constrained mightily by politics and by "expediency". This is because data on provincial and local governments are so limited that formulas are driven more by what is available than by the objectives of the grant program. The following are some examples of formulas now in use in Asia.

- In the Philippines, the distribution formula for the IRA grant is based on population size, land area and equal shares. It is transparent but has no explicit element that rewards local revenue mobilization.[9]

[9] Diokno (2008) argues that the increased vertical share of the IRA grant has dampened local government revenue mobilization.

The equal shares allocation, which favors smaller governments, reflects an equalization concern.

- Pakistan distributes its National Finance Commission awards based on population size. This is transparent, and a compromise solution that has been accepted by the four provinces. This formula recognizes expenditure needs in a broad way, but does not recognize taxable capacity, nor does it provide an incentive for the four provinces to increase tax effort (Bahl *et al.*, 2008).
- Thailand uses a formula based on population size, land area, equal shares and revenues raised. The inclusion of revenues raised (inverse) effectively penalizes increased tax effort. The equal shares element in the formula arguably adds an equalization component.
- The grant component of Finance Commission transfers in India is distributed according to a formula that includes population, land area, the inverse of income level, and measures of both expenditure needs and tax efforts (Rao, 2008). While the system is equalizing, the weight attached to tax effort probably is not large enough to stimulate increased revenue mobilization.

Many have argued that a proper equalization grant would recognize both expenditure needs and fiscal capacity. Japan's local allocation tax grant attempts to do this, by distributing grants according to the difference between "standard expenditure" and "standard revenues". Taiwan more or less follows the same system as Japan. A similar approach is taken in Vietnam, which is judged to result in a strong equalization effect (Hofman and Guerra, 2005). Indonesia distributes grants with a formula that includes measures of both revenue capacity and expenditure needs. None of these programs, however, provides an incentive for increases in revenue mobilization by sub-national governments. The systems in Japan and Vietnam would appear to provide a disincentive.

Are inter-governmental transfers in Asia equalizing? If the criteria are whether per capita expenditure disparities are reduced by transfers, Hofman and Guerra (2005) conclude that there is some degree of equalization in the systems in China, the Philippines, Thailand and Indonesia, and a stronger equalization in Vietnam. Bahl, Wallace and Cyan (2008) find a slight degree of equalization in Pakistan, using the same criteria. Rao (2008) concludes that India's finance commission transfers reduce the disparity between higher and lower income states. Saito and Yunoue

(2008) find evidence of equalization in the Japanese transfer system. Tokyo, for example, receives a near zero amount from the local allocation tax transfer.

Another form of grant on which countries rely heavily is conditional grants i.e., grants that permit the central government to control the direction of spending, presumably toward functions where there are positive externalities and/or income distribution benefits. The vertical shares are most often determined on an *ad hoc* basis by the central government, or are based on estimated costs of providing the subsidized service (Columns 2 and 3 of Table 2). The similarity ends there. The distribution of conditional grants among eligible recipients can be done in many ways, though most commonly it is a reimbursement of some standard cost for a prescribed function, for example, teacher's salaries or payments to indigent families (G or K grants in Table 2).

Conditional grants usually are successful in diverting sub-national government spending toward the target functions. If the target functions lead to higher expenditures that generate spillover benefits, the conditional grants programs can be welfare enhancing. But, conditional grants are roundly criticized by sub-national governments and even by some central governments. Such grants are nationally uniform and do not give adequate consideration to local conditions, and they cause sub-national government spending patterns to deviate from local preferences. And, because both the line ministries and the local government ministry lobby for these subsidies, they can contribute significantly to expenditure growth at the local government level.

Asian countries also rely on *ad hoc* distributions of inter-governmental transfers. These are grants where either the vertical share or the horizontal share is determined by political considerations (D or H grants in Table 2). From the point of view of parliament, this approach offers a great deal of flexibility (though there is a tendency toward "incremental-ism"), but from a point of view of good public policy this approach is not transparent and lacks objectivity. Nevertheless, there is some degree of *ad-hoc*-ism in virtually every system of inter-governmental transfers. In Asia, both China and Thailand allocate their grants partially on an *ad hoc* basis, and this creates budget uncertainty at the local level (Charas and Weist, 2008).

A particularly difficult issue is the coordination of inter-governmental transfer policy among various Ministries and agencies. For example, in India, transfers are awarded by all of the national Finance Commission, the Planning Commission and the line ministries (Rao, 2008). All have different objectives and all use different allocation methods. Under this arrangement, some offsetting effects would be expected.

4.3. *Hard Budget Constraints*

Just as important as taxes or grants as instruments for implementing fiscal decentralization is the requirement of a hard budget constraint for sub-national governments. A hard budget constraint means that sub-national governments must balance their budgets without recourse to any end-of-year (ex post) assistance from the central government. Borrowing can co-exist with a hard budget constraint regime for sub-national governments, but only if the borrowing is used to finance long-lived capital assets, and only if it is understood that central government bailouts on unpaid debt obligations will not occur. Sub-national governments must have reason to believe that they are "on their own" in paying for their fiscal decisions. Otherwise, they will game the system by over-borrowing or under-taxing, in order to shift the burden of financing local services on to the center.

An issue here is the definition of a current budget deficit for a sub-national government. One working definition is that budget balance exists when all recurrent expenditures are covered by current revenues, with the latter defined to include only tax and non tax revenues of the sub-national government and "regular" inter-governmental transfers. In the case of developing countries, this measurement is not as easy as it might seem. Accounting systems are often not uniform, and accounting practices may be haphazard, especially for smaller local governments (Sethi, 2004). There also may be problems with the flow of expenditures during a fiscal year and cash balances often play a major role in expenditure policy. Finally, central governments do not always disburse grant entitlements in full and on time. So, a relatively simple concept, as the hard budget constraint seems to be, may not be so simple when it comes to implementation. As Rodden, Eskeland, and Litvack (2003, p. 4) point out, the question may be less whether the budget constraint is hard or soft, but whether there are weak spots that soften the budget constraint to a point where it alters the expectations and behavior of sub-national governments.

Soft budget constraints may be built into inter-governmental fiscal policy, i.e., sub-national government deficits may be an expected part of the system. Some central governments hold to a paternalistic approach to inter-governmental fiscal relations. In these cases, the policy frame implicitly allows for a soft budget constraint. The underlying problem may be an over-assignment of expenditure responsibility relative to revenue access, the failure of the central governments to pay full grant entitlements to sub-national governments, unfunded mandates, or an unconstrained access to credit. Under this scenario, the sub-national government begins the fiscal year with a projected imbalance between expenditures that it plans to make and revenues it expects to receive. A year-end budget deficit is, in effect, planned, and various forms of deficit grants are a guarantee that local governments may come to depend on. Enemies of the hard budget constraint rule include central government measures such as the following:

- Deficit grants, i.e., year-end grants to cover revenue shortfalls;
- Bailouts on delinquent debt; and
- Direct coverage of year-end shortfalls on certain items of expenditure.

Japan is a case where soft budget constraints on local governments have resulted from open-ended grants from the center, little local government taxing power, access to credit by local governments, and successful political lobbying. The predictable result is that total central government budget revenues have come to be viewed as "a common pool for local governments" (Ihori, 2008, p. 2).

5. Design must be Comprehensive

The crucial first step toward implementing a fiscal decentralization system is to have a plan or blueprint that spells out the strategy and the objectives that are to be achieved. It is crucial that this design address all of the major issues relevant to gaining a sustainable fiscal decentralization. In this connection, inter-governmental fiscal relations must be thought of as a system, and all the pieces in this system must fit together.[10] Implementation should begin with the design of a

[10] *Inter-governmental fiscal relations* is a term that refers generally to the division of fiscal powers and responsibilities among levels of government. *Fiscal decentralization* refers to an inter-governmental system where the balance of power moves more toward the sub-national government sector than has been the case.

comprehensive system, and should lay out the plan for each element of the system.

A little reflection will lead one quickly to the conclusion that fiscal decentralization involves a lot more than fiscal matters. In fact, the electoral system, the civil service arrangements and the public administration in general are arguably as important as the taxing and spending components.[11] Other key pieces are sub-national government revenue raising power, borrowing powers, expenditure assignment, and budgetary discretion. A "one-off" piecemeal reform, encompassing only one element of the system (e.g., revenue sharing), is not likely to lead to success.

Consider the following four examples which are suggestive of the complications that arise when important inter-governmental issues are not part of the design. Indonesia's big-bang decentralizations of the 2000s did consider both expenditure assignment and revenue assignment, but the planning was done by two different ministries with little coordination (Alm, Aten and Bahl, 2001). While the expenditure decentralization transferred nearly 40 percent of the public expenditure budget and 2 million employees to the local governments, little was done by way of assignment of taxing powers to the local governments. The result is very much an expenditure decentralization. The Indonesian decentralization can be rightly thought of as a very successful decentralization that was comprehensive (Fengler and Hofman, 2008), but the failure to address the issue of sub-national government taxation has led to a challenge that is yet to be resolved. A similar imbalance was realized in the Philippines (Manasan, 2008), and in Thailand (Charas and Weist, 2008).

In India, the National Finance Commission allocates inter-governmental transfers and shared taxes among the states, to try and achieve some budgetary balance. However, a national pay commission sets central government wage levels that roll out to the states and in recent years has dramatically compromised state budget balance. The lesson here is that in cases such as India, the determination of public sector wage rates and employment levels must be part of the decentralization design.

A comprehensive "trinity" reform in Japan is simultaneously considering revision of conditional grants, the general purpose grant and

---

[11] For a good discussion of the need for public administration reform as a component of decentralization, see the discussion of the Vietnam case in Hung (2008).

the assignment of taxing powers to local governments (Ikawa, 2008; Ihori, 2008). The intent is to design a revenue neutral reform that would impose a hard budget constraint on local governments. While the three major elements of local government finance are part of the package, some analysts have argued that a borrowing strategy should also have been included to insure achieving the hard budget constraint goal.

Finally, there is the interesting case of China, where responsibility for financing social welfare and public pensions has been assigned to local governments. This component of the fiscal decentralization, however, has given local governments an incentive to limit the migration of workers from rural areas (Zuo, 2008). Such actions may not be consistent with China's interest in increasing domestic demand for its consumer products.

6. Sequencing Fiscal Decentralization[12]

The success or failure of fiscal decentralization in developing countries depends on implementation as well as on program design. In particular, when introducing decentralization policies and administration, sequencing is a key to the transition to this different approach to governance.

Bahl and Martinez-Vazquez (2006) argue that there is an optimal pattern of sequencing. Even before beginning the implementation, two prerequisites are important for success: a rule of law and an existing de-concentration of public service delivery. The former makes it possible for sub-national governments to protest violations of the decentralization law, even those committed by the central government. The Supreme Court in the Philippines ruled that the central government could not hold back on the entitlements of local governments to IRA transfers (Diokno, 2008). The latter makes it possible to shift central government employees to local status without having to train a new force of local public employees. It is arguably true that an existing de-concentration was a primary reason why Indonesia's big-bang expenditure decentralization was accomplished without disruptions in service levels.

The sequencing of decentralization should begin with two important steps (Fig. 1). The first is to hold a national debate about decentralization,

[12] This section draws heavily from Bahl (forthcoming) and from Bahl and Martinez-Vazquez (2006).

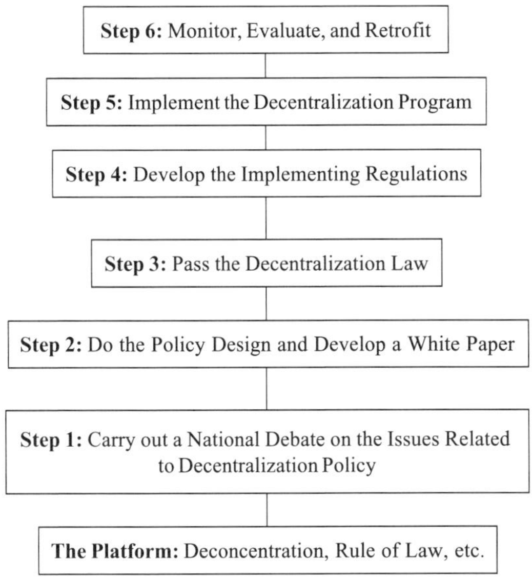

Source: Bahl and Martinez-Vazquez (2006)

Fig. 1. Sequencing Fiscal Decentralization: A Normative Approach

possibly in the context of an election or the report of a national commission. The national discussion should culminate in a policy paper on fiscal decentralization that lays out the goals of the program and the strategy for achieving it. These steps make up the road map for the decentralization program. The policy paper would include matters such as the assignment of expenditure responsibilities, the nature of the inter-governmental transfer system, and the revenue-raising powers of sub-national governments. The White paper cannot be limited to policy. It must address some key issues related to the public administration in the country, such as whether local government administrations will be subordinate to their elected leadership or to higher level line ministries. Vietnam is currently grappling with this difficult issue of dual subordination (Hung, 2008). Going forward without a policy and general administrative guideline would be tantamount to adopting a "make it up as we go" strategy.

Based on this road map, the decentralization law can be written. This key document of the program should guide all else that is done in the implementation process. Although the law must contain the key features of the program, it must not be too specific because legal drafting cannot accommodate all the realities of administration that will arise, nor can it anticipate changes in the country that will come with development. This process of gradual reformulation underlines the reason why it is dangerous to include too much detail about decentralization in the constitution. Charas and Wiest (2008) discuss the need for two changes in the Thai constitution within a decade.

The administrative phase begins with developing the implementing regulations to accompany the decentralization law. For example, the law may specify an equalizing grant program, but the implementing regulations will specify the exact formula to be used in distribution. The implementing regulations must conform to the decentralization law. If there are no implementing regulations, or if they are not clearly written, policy making could implicitly fall into the hands of bureaucrats.

A final step in the process is to provide for monitoring and evaluation. Fiscal decentralization programs emerge and change over time, sometimes due to poorly formulated policy and sometimes due to the changing needs of the country. It is important to have in place a process for fine-tuning the structure, and in general for measuring the success of the program. There is a mixed record on this count. Indonesia has put in a good data base to track local government finances, but in the Philippines — 10 years after enactment of its local government code — no monitoring system is in place (Diokno, 2008).

One problem with the stepwise approach to implementing decentralization in the way proposed here is that it makes the process very transparent and vulnerable to criticism. It also requires time, especially at the stage when the program is being formulated. Advocates will argue that this gives the opposition enough time to organize their objections and their constituency. Their approach would be to push ahead before opponents can get organized and to get the law written and adopted. The hope in this strategy, as was the case in the big-bang decentralization in Indonesia, is that once the law is written, there will be no turning back. Democrats, on the other hand, will argue that policies that touch everyone, as decentralization clearly is, should be debated widely before they are adopted.

Some will point out that the kind of approach outlined here is unrealistic, and ignores the politics of getting a fiscal decentralization in place. The main thing, it might be argued, is to "get on with it" while there is an opportunity. Fengler and Hofman, 2008 describe the highly successful Indonesian experience, which started with a drafting of the law, even before a policy design was in place.[13] On the other hand, the lack of clarity in expenditure assignment and inadequate tax assignments remain as important constraints to the Indonesian fiscal decentralization. As White and Smoke have observed in tracking the success of decentralization in Asia, a key message is the need for focused attention on policy design and legislative development (White and Smoke, 2005, p. 20).

7. The Politics of Fiscal Decentralization

Fiscal decentralization is about shifting the balance of power, both between levels of government and between ministries in the central government. It also has to do with shifting political risks, e.g., decentralization of taxing powers and hard budget constraints can put subnational government politicians in a more difficult position in terms of their accountability to local voters. Financing sub-national government budgets with inter-governmental transfers is an easier way to go for local politicians and is a concession that many central governments are all too willing to make. The result of all this is that fiscal decentralization has relatively few strong champions. This may be why, to date, fiscal decentralization has been much more rhetoric than action.

Decentralization should be a grassroots movement where voters and elected politicians, including the President, will be the natural champions. Voters see themselves gaining control over their governance, and Presidents count voters. It is a natural alliance. However, if decentralization conflicts with macroeconomic stabilization policy, as was the case in the Philippines in the 1990's, the President will advocate pulling back transfers to local governments (Diokno, 2008). Or, if the President is too closely aligned with the line ministries, his/her support for fiscal decentralization will be less firm. There also may be a concern that decentralization could strengthen the hand of governors who might oppose Presidential policies or who might become more formidable political rivals. Some have argued that the transfer of the Taiwan Provincial government to the central administration was a concern with the vote-getting power of the local governor (Shih, 2008).

[13] For an interesting summary of how the decentralization policy in Indonesia developed, see Rasyid (2004).

Parliament (Congress) often will embrace programs that voters embrace, and therefore is a potential champion of decentralization. However, members of Congress usually are most interested in how programs benefit their own constituency; hence they will be less enthusiastic than policy analysts about the need for transparency and for programs that are designed in the national vs. the local interest. Especially the more powerful members of Parliament might even favor *ad hoc* grants in hopes that they might direct more resources to their home districts. In the aftermath of the big-bang decentralization in Indonesia, Congress was fervent about overriding the results of the new grant formula to hold the grant revenues of each local government harmless at pre-reform levels. Manasan (2008) reported that this reluctance of congressmen toward decentralization in the Philippines was lessened by fraternal relations with local government politicians. She points out that it is not uncommon "to find sites (or provinces) where the mayor (or governor) is the congressman's wife (or brother/sister/father/son)."

The Ministry of Finance, the keeper of the tools to address instability, will not want to give up control over the major fiscal tools. If this Ministry is on record as favoring decentralization, it will tend to be a controlled form of decentralization. One might look for the following features in such a program:

- Limited freedom for sub-national governments to set tax rates for any major taxes;
- Strictly controlled borrowing powers, often including central government approval.
- Centrally controlled wage and salary rates for local government employees.

Giving sub-national governments a guaranteed share of national taxes compromises the flexibility of the Ministry of Finance, but the popularity of revenue sharing makes it hard to defy this policy. In many cases the MOF has not only accepted a shared tax version of intergovernmental transfers, but it has championed this approach. Apparently, it is a more palatable policy than the alternative of giving up taxing power to sub-national governments.

The Ministry of Economy or planning could be a significant opponent of fiscal decentralization. This Ministry will be interested in a system that allows central rather than local direction of investment.

If investment decisions are decentralized to any significant extent, it could compromise national planning on the distribution of capital expenditures by function and by location.

The line ministries often will oppose decentralization on grounds that seem more paternalistic. Their view is that the local governments (particularly rural local governments) do not have the technical capacity to deliver services or to plan resource allocation; hence there must be strong central direction. Another explanation is that the line ministries stand to lose significant bureaucratic power and some share of the central budget if conditional transfers are replaced with general purpose grants to sub-national governments. Line ministries, if they are persuaded on fiscal decentralization, will be more comfortable with a regime of conditional grants and mandated expenditure requirements.

The Ministry of Local Government (Ministry of Home affairs, Ministry of Interior) will be an advocate of directing more funds to local government budgets. Usually this Ministry will argue for more control over the expenditures in local government budgets, e.g., determination of wages, hiring and firing of employees, oversight on expenditure processes, etc. It also can be an effective lobbyist for increased central government subsidies to local governments, as has been the case in Japan.

The sub-national governments generally will favor decentralization, but the rich and poor will have very different views about what is the best version of decentralization. Generally, sub-national governments will argue for increased fiscal discretion on the expenditure side of the budget. On the revenue side of the budget, there is not likely to be too strenuous an argument for more taxing powers, so long as the flow of inter-governmental transfers is adequate. Increased taxation implies incurring the wrath of local voters, especially those with significant tax-paying capacity. The rural local governments will be primarily interested in a redistributive system based on a guaranteed revenue flow.

In fact, all sub-national governments will agree that they are entitled to a greater share of total national tax collections. But when it comes to the distribution of this pool among local governments, considerable disagreement will arise and the politics will force some kind of compromise. The constitution in Pakistan requires that all four provinces agree on the allocation formula. The result, predictably, is that no agreement can be reached and the allocation formula (an equal per capita sharing) is made by Presidential decision (Bahl *et al.*, 2008).

Finally, some of the external donors and advisors will champion fiscal decentralization. The World Bank, ADB (Usui, 2007) and the Inter-American Development Bank (1997) see decentralization as part of a development strategy that will lead to a more satisfactory and balanced growth, and promote decentralization as a country-wide strategy. USAID is also an advocate of decentralization, and is heavily influenced by the democracy aspects. The IMF takes a more cautious and qualified view because of its concern with any policy that might promote fiscal instability. The external advisors play an important catalytic role. When they bring funding as the carrot, their main contribution is that they oftentimes catch the attention of government officials and stimulate the government to begin to look harder at the decentralization issue. But unless the government itself is enthusiastic, the harder look will not lead to meaningful policy reform and in fact will be quickly forgotten when the external support money is gone. The implementation stage is never reached.

8. Conclusion

Fiscal decentralization has not emerged as the groundswell economic development strategy that many expected. The advantages of centralization and the political power of the centralists have been too strong. But the world has changed, and decentralization is becoming a more irresistible strategy. Its progress may be slowed by politics and by an unstable world economy, as most new policies will be, but its time may have come. Governments around the world are increasingly elected, and sooner than later, a platform of citizen participation in governance; economic development has eroded some of the advantages of fiscal centralization; and the service delivery capabilities of sub-national governments have improved dramatically. Moreover, much of the world has come to see that granting some form of local autonomy is better than separatism as a policy direction. The major roadblock to success now may be poorly conceived decentralization policies. Design must match objectives, and implementation must face up to the many dimensions of decentralization. This paper is an attempt to stimulate that discussion.

References

Alm, J, R Bahl, and R Aten (2001). Can Indonesia decentralize successfully? Plans, problems and prospects. *Bulletin of Indonesian Economic Studies*, 37(1), pp. 83–102.

Bahl, R (2008). Opportunities and Risks of Fiscal Decentralization: A Developing Country Perspective. In *Fiscal Decentralization and Land Policies*, G Ingram and Y-H Hong (eds.), Cambridge, Mass: Lincoln Institute of Land Policy.

Bahl, R W and J F Linn (1992). *Urban public finance in developing countries*. New York: Oxford University Press.

Bahl, R and J. Martinez-Vazquez (2006). Sequencing fiscal decentralization. World Bank Policy Research Working Paper 3914, Public Sector Governance Group. Washington, DC: World Bank.

Bahl, R, S Wallace, and M Cyan (2008). Pakistan: Provincial government taxation. ISP Working Paper. Atlanta: International Studies Program, Georgia State University.

Bahl, R and S. Wallace (2005). Public Financing in Developing and Transition Countries. *Public Budgeting and Finance*, Silver Anniversary Issue, pp. 83–98.

Bird, R M and F Vaillancourt (eds.) (1998). *Fiscal decentralization in developing countries*. Cambridge: Cambridge University Press.

Dillinger, W and S B Webb (1999). Decentralization and fiscal management in Colombia. Policy Research Working Paper 2122, Latin American and Caribbean Division. Washington, DC: World Bank.

Fisman, R and R Gatti (2002). Decentralization and corruption: Evidence across countries. *Journal of Public Economics*, 83, pp. 325–345.

Hofman, B and S C Guerra (2005). Fiscal Disparities in East Asia: How Large and Do they Matter? In *East Asia Decentralizes*, P Smoke and R White (eds.), Washington DC: World Bank.

Inter-American Development Bank (1997). *Latin America after a decade of reforms*. Washington, DC: Inter-American Development Bank.

Letelier, L (2005). Explaining Fiscal Decentralization. *Public Finance Review*, 33(2), pp. 155–183.

Litvack, J, J Ahmad, and R Bird (1998). *Rethinking decentralization*. Washington, DC: World Bank.

Martinez-Vazquez, J, A Timofeev, and J Boex (2006). Reforming Regional-Local Finance in Russia. Washington DC: World Bank Institute.

McLure, C E (1997). Topics in the Theory of Revenue Assignment: Gaps, Traps and Nuances. In *Macroeconomic Dimensions of Public Finance*, M Blejer and T T-Minassian (eds.), London: Routledge.

Oates, W E (1972). *Fiscal federalism*. New York: Harcourt Brace Jovanovich.

Owens, J and J Norregaard (1991). The Role of Lower Levels of Government: The Experience of Selected OECD Countries. In *Local Government: An International Perspective*, J Owens and G Panella (eds.), Amsterdam: North Holland, pp. 3–54.

Prud'homme, R (1995). The dangers of decentralization. *World Bank Research Observer*, 10(2), pp. 210–226.

Reschovsky, A (2003). Intergovernmental Transfers: The Equitable Share. In *Restructuring Local Government Finance in Developing Countries: Lessons from South Africa,* R Bahl and P Smoke (eds.), Cheltenham, UK: Edward Elgar Publishing, pp. 173–236.

Rodden, J, G Eskeland, and J Litvack (eds.) (2003). *Fiscal decentralization and the challenge of hard budget constraints*. Cambridge: The MIT Press.

Sethi, G (ed.) (2004). Fiscal decentralization to rural governments in India. Washington D.C.: The World Bank.

Spahn, P (1997). Decentralized government and macroeconomic control. Infrastructure Notes FM-12. Washington, DC: World Bank.

Taliercio, R (2005). Sub-national Own-Source Revenue: Getting Policy and Administration Right. In *East Asia Decentralizes: Making Local Government Work*. Washington: The World Bank, pp. 107–128.

Tanzi, V (1995). Fiscal federalism and decentralization: A review of some efficiency and macroeconomic aspects. In *Annual World Bank Conference on Development Economics*, M Bruno and B Pleskovic (eds.), Washington, DC: World Bank, pp. 295–316.

Ter-Minassian, T (ed.) (1997). *Fiscal federalism in theory and practice*. Washington, DC: International Monetary Fund.

Treisman, D (2000). *Decentralization and the quality of government.* Washington, DC: International Monetary Fund.

Usui, N (2007). Critical Issues of Fiscal Decentralization. ERD Technical Note No. 21. Manila: Asian Development Bank.

White, R and P Smoke (2005). East Asia Decentralizes. In *East Asia Decentralizes*, P Smoke and R White (eds.), Washington DC: World Bank.

Part A

Political Decentralization in Asia: Case Studies/A Review of Decentralization

Chapter II

Trinity Reform of Local Fiscal System in Japan

HIROSHI IKAWA[1]

National Graduate Institute for Policy Studies

1. Introduction

The fiscal relations between the central and local governments in Japan have been under reform mainly to improve the administrative efficiency and the autonomy of local governments. The reform has been carried out as a package consisting of three parts so that it was called *trinity reform* (*Sanmiittai Kaikaku* in Japanese). The goals were, first, to reform the transfer of tax revenue sources from the central to local governments; second, to reform the *national treasury subsidies and obligatory shares*, and third, to reform the *local allocation tax*.

The paper seeks to give an exposition of this reform and an evaluation of its results. We begin by explaining first, the recent conditions of public finance of local governments and their problems. This will clarify the necessity for trinity reform. Then, an overview of the experiences of trinity reform from 2003 to 2005 is provided by examining the

[1] This paper was originally written in March, 2007 and rewritten in February, 2008. The original title was "Recent Local Financial System Reform (Trinity Reform)". It was published as "COSLOG Up-to-date Documents on Local Autonomy in Japan No. 2." by the Institute for Comparative Studies in Local Governance(COSLOG) of National Graduate Institute for Policy Studies (GRIPS) and the Council of Local Authorities for International Relations (CLAIR). The author expresses his gratitude for all the assistances provided to the previous work and the permit of modified republication.

performance of *Basic policies for economic and fiscal management and structural reform* and the corresponding budget compilations. Lastly, an evaluation is offered on the results of the trinity reform to date and the unresolved problems.

2. The Recent Conditions and Problems of Local Public Finance

2.1. *Important Roles of Local Public Finance in Japan*

1) *Major Expenditures of Local Governments*

Japanese local governments consist of prefectures and municipalities (cities, towns and villages) that perform a variety of functions in providing administrative services for the daily living of their residents. The role of local public finance in the national economy is very important. The share of local governments in Gross Domestic Expenditure is about three times as much as that of the central government. For example, in the fiscal year 2005, local governments accounted for 12.1% (60.8 trillion yen) of GDE (503.4 trillion yen), whereas the central government and social security funds accounted for 4.2% (21.2 trillion yen) and 6.5% (32.9 trillion yen) respectively. The net aggregate expenditure[2] of the central and local governments in fiscal year 2005 was 150.6 trillion yen, and if it is divided between the central and local governments, they account for 61.2 trillion yen (40.6% of the total) and 89.4 trillion yen (59.4%) respectively.[3]

Local governments perform a variety of activities that directly affects the quality of people's lives, such as education, police and fire protection, welfare, medical services, public health, garbage disposal, and public financial assistance. Figure 1 shows the expenditure responsibilities of the central and local governments. The point here is the great importance of fiscally healthy local governments.

---

[2] The net aggregate of expenditure is obtained by subtracting the overlap from the total expenditure of the central government (net budget of both the general account and ten special accounts) and local governments (ordinary accounts). The amount of overlap consists of the amount of local allocation tax, national treasury disbursements for local governments, and so on.

[3] Ministry of Internal Affairs and Communications ed.: "White Paper on Local Public Finance, FY2007 Edition", National Printing Bureau, April, 2007, pp. 1–5.

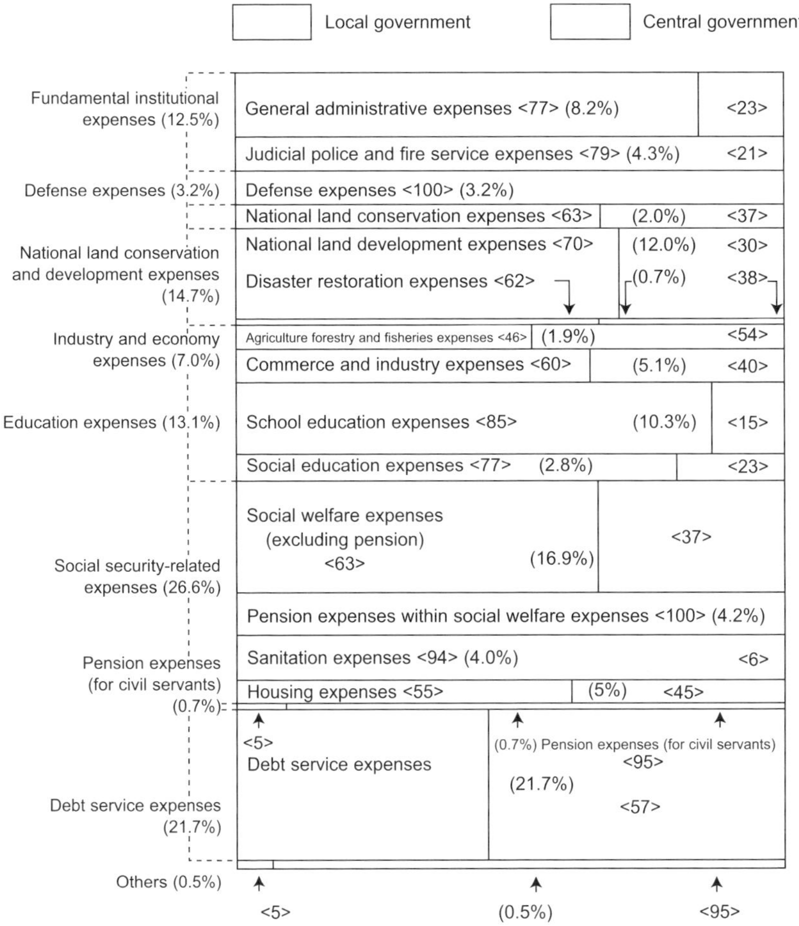

Notes:

1 Source: Ministry of Internal Affairs and Communications ed.: "White Paper on Local Public Finance FY2007 Edition", National Printing Bureau, April, 2007, p. 2.

2 Figures in ( ) indicate the constituent percentage of expenses on a function basis.

3 Figures in < > indicate the percentage share of the central and local goverments respectively in expenses on a function basis.

4 Expenses indicate in the left side of the Figure are expenses by a group of similar functions. For example, "Fundamental institutional expenses" consists of "General administrative expenses" and "Judicial, police and fire service expenses."

Fig. 1. Central and Local Government Percentage Share of Main Expenditures by Function (Settlement of FY 2005)

2) *Major Revenues of Local Governments*

Table 1 shows the major revenues of local governments: namely, local taxes, local allocation tax, national treasury disbursements, and local government loans.

Local taxes are collected from residents and companies in each region by local governments in accordance with the provisions of the Local Tax Law and bylaws.[4] Local taxes account for about one-third of revenues.

The *local allocation tax* is the principal inter-governmental transfer in the system. It is distributed by the central government to equalize the difference in fiscal resources due to diversity in economic situations and to try and ensure the provision of the standard level of services by all local governments. It is a general revenue with no restriction on usage and in that respect is similar to local taxes. The total amount of local allocation tax is set at about 30 percent of collections from five national tax revenues, including income tax, corporate

Table 1. Annual Revenue of Local Government (Fiscal 2005) (hundred million yen, %)

Category	Revenue Settlement	Constituent Ratio
Local taxes	348,044	37.4
Local transfer taxes	18,490	2.0
Special local grant	15,180	1.6
Local allocation tax	169,587	18.2
Sub total (general revenue sources)	551,301	59.3
National treasury disbursements	118,889	12.8
Local government loans	103,763	11.2
Others	155,412	16.7
Total	929,365	100.0

Source: Ministry of Internal Affairs and Communications ed.: "White Paper on Local Public Finance, FY2007 Edition" National Printing Bureau, April, 2007, p. 11.

[4] The standard local tax rates and the tax bases are determined by the laws prepared by the central government. Local governments can change the standard by their own regulations but have hardly done so in practice.

income tax and consumption tax. At present, local fiscal resources are thought to be insufficient, so that the amount of local allocation tax has been increased. An extra amount is added from the national general account. The amount allocated to each local government is determined according to the provisions of the Local Allocation Tax Law approximately as the balance between *standard fiscal needs* and *standard fiscal revenues*.

The *national treasury disbursements* are granted on the condition that they are used for specific projects or specific administrative purposes. They consist of national treasury obligatory shares, national treasury subsidies, and so on. The national treasury obligatory shares, such as a national treasury obligatory share of compulsory education, are disbursed to local governments based on the central government's obligations and responsibilities. On the other hand, the national treasury subsidies are granted to local governments to promote specific policies or to provide financial assistance for them.

Local government debt is borrowing for a period exceeding a single fiscal year. It is used normally as a financial resource for such purposes as building elementary schools, which requires a large amount of initial expenditure but gives benefits for a long period.

Other revenues include the local transfer taxes that fundamentally belong to local tax category but are first collected by the central government and then transferred to local governments. Examples are the rent collected for the use of school facilities or the fees for the issuance of residency cards.

3) *Public Finances of Local Governments*

Both the central and local governments are financially in a bad shape, and have relied increasingly on debt finance. The data in Table 2 show the outstanding long-term debt of both levels of government. At the end of fiscal year 2006, the national and local governments held long-term debt of 600 trillion yen and 201 trillion yen respectively. Compared to 1995, the outstanding long-term debt of the central government doubled and that of local governments increased by 1.6 times. The total debt outstanding almost doubled and is now 1.5 times as much as the GDP. According to the OECD, the ratios of *general governments' gross debt* to the GDP of major countries in 2007 are 0.5 (U.K.), 0.6 (U.S.), 0.7 (Germany),

Table 2. Outstanding Long-term Debt on the Part of Central Government and Local Governments (unit: trillion yen)

Category	End of Fiscal1995 <Settlement>	End of Fiscal2000 <Settlement>	End of Fiscal2005 <Settlement>	End of Fiscal2006 <Revised>	End of Fiscal2007 <Budget>
Central government	297	491	590	600	607
Local governments	125	181	201	201	199
Overlap between the central & local gov.	▲12	▲26	▲34	▲34	▲33
Total debt	410	646	758	767	773
Share of gross domestic product	82.6%	128.1%	150.6%	150.2%	148.1%

Notes:
1. *Source*: "Highlights of the Budget for FY2007" Ministry of Finance, December, 2006, p. 11.
2. GDP for FY2006 is estimated, GDP for FY2007 is forecast.

0.7 (France) and 1.2 (Italy). By comparison, the Japanese ratio over 1.7 is conspicuous.[5]

The outstanding long-term debt of local governments was 39 trillion yen in 1980, 57 trillion yen in 1985 and 67 trillion yen in 1990, all in fiscal years. The increases were more dramatic in the 1990s: 125 trillion in 1995 and 181 trillion in 2000. The amount had almost tripled in ten years.[6] The balance of local public finance deteriorated because tax revenues showed no large increase after the burst of the bubble economy and local governments undertook many public works in partnership with the central government.

2.2. *Problems in the Local Fiscal System*

The challenge to the local public finance was how to overcome the critical financial situation and recover the independent management of local governments. For this purpose, reforms of local fiscal system are considered to be essential. The first was the reform of *the national treasury subsidies and obligatory shares system*; the second was the requirement of central government approval for the issuance of local government debt; and the third was the reform of *the local allocation tax system.* Above all, the subsidy system has come under heavy attack, because it impedes the autonomy and independence of local government and hinders the effective and efficient local administration.

These subsidies have advantages from the view-point of the central government since they are conditional. From the view-point of local governments, however, the subsidies posed problems: (1) the uniform conditions imposed for delivering subsidized services do not always fit local conditions, (2) projects with a lower priority for local communities are implemented by local governments, because they can be carried out with lower general revenue sources of local governments, (3) the troublesome and costly application procedures that must be taken to acquire the subsidies and obligatory shares — including the formulation and submission of the application, and the review and inspection of projects — impose significant compliance costs on local governments, and, (4) the

[5] Ministry of Finance: "Highlights of the Budget for FY2007", December, 2006, p. 16. (http://www.mof.go.jp/english/budget/e20061224a.pdf)

[6] Study group on local allocation tax system, ed.: "Overview of local allocation tax in 2006", Institute of Local Finance, April, 2006, p. 70.

autonomous local administrations that have the advantage of familiarity with local conditions are by-passed and creative initiatives of local governments are impeded.

Therefore, many people believe that the *national treasury subsidies and obligatory shares* should be reduced and radically rationalized. This is, however, only one side of the problem. The other side is the shortage of tax revenues of local governments. The ratio between the central government and local governments is 3:2 in expenditure and 2:3 in revenue. In this inverted structure, a major need is to strengthen local taxation. Local taxes account for about one-third of the gross total revenue of local governments. To better accomplish the goals of fiscal decentralization, access to additional tax revenue sources should be transferred from the central to local governments to better establish self-governing local public finance.

3. Necessity and Objectives of Trinity Reform

3.1. *Local Public Finance Needs Fundamental Reform*

Ever since the Shoup Report of 1949, the Local Government System Research Council and other provisional research councils have repeatedly pointed out the need for reform, reduction and rationalization of *the national treasury subsidies and obligatory shares system*. Some improvements have been made by: (1) reducing the amount of such subsidies and increasing general revenue sources like local taxes and the local allocation tax; (2) simplifying the conditions for subsidies and grant procedures; and (3) eliminating the "extra financial burden" imposed on local governments due to the inappropriate criteria embedded in subsidy policy. The reform, however, remains incomplete.

In April 2000 a large-scale decentralized program was introduced, aiming at an expansion of the autonomy of local governments, by enacting the "Law on the amendments of related laws to promote decentralization (the Omnibus Decentralization Law)." In this law, (1) the roles to be shared by the central and local governments were defined, (2) delegated agency functions imposed upon local governments were abolished, (3) the central government's commitment to local government administration was toned down, and (4) some additional authority was transferred to local governments. This primary reform of decentralization, however, was mainly with the administrative system rather than the local public finance, except for the approval process for local government debt.

Then, on June 14, 2001 the Decentralization Promotion Committee announced that the secondary decentralization innovations should be implemented to narrow the gap between local government tax revenue and local government current expenditures. The guiding principle would be "revenue neutrality." This calls for both the *national treasury subsidies and obligatory shares* and the local allocation tax to be reduced and for tax resources equal to the reduced amounts to be transferred to local governments.

On June 26, 2001 the Koizumi cabinet endorsed the first *Basic policies for economic and fiscal management and structural reform of economic society*. In this policy, the *national treasury subsidies and obligatory shares* were restricted to the "tasks advantageous to all of Japan or wide areas, and to the maintenance and establishment of necessary administrative services that shall be guaranteed by the central government." The policy also stated that, "the subsidies and obligatory shares shall be rationalized, local allocation tax shall be revised, and the allocation of tax sources shall be revised and examined from the standpoint of basic principles." (see Table 3 for the chronology of local fiscal reform.)

3.2. *Start of the Trinity Reform*

In May, 2002, Mr. Katayama, then Minister of Internal Affairs and Communications, issued a document entitled "Structural reform of local public finance and transfer of tax revenue sources" (Katayama draft policy) and proposed the "trinity reform". The basic idea of the proposal was to achieve a 1 to 1 ratio between national and local taxes by transferring 7 trillion yen or half of the difference between national and local taxes (14 trillion yen) to the local tax revenues. Katayama planned to enlarge local tax sources first by reducing the national treasury disbursement of 5.5 billion yen and transferring financing of these functions to local taxes, and second by replacing the local allocation tax with locally raised taxes and improving the balance of revenue and expenditure.

On June 25, 2002, Prime Minister Koizumi made a Cabinet decision, "Basic policies for economic and fiscal management and structural

Table 3. Chronology of Local Financial Reform

June, 1993:	Resolutions about the promotion of decentralization were made (in both the House of Representatives and House of councilors).
July, 1995:	Decentralization Promotion Law was executed and the Decentralization Promotion Committee was inaugurated.
April, 2000:	Omnibus Decentralization Law was executed.
June, 2001:	Final report from the Decentralization Promotion Committee was published. "Basic policies for economic and fiscal management and structural reform of economic society (Basic policies for 2001)" was endorsed by a Cabinet decision.
July:	Council for Decentralization Reform was inaugurated.
May, 2002:	"Structural reform of local public finance and transfer of tax revenue sources" (Katayama draft policy) was published.
June:	"Basic policies for economic and fiscal management and structural reform 2002 (Basic policies for 2002)" was endorsed by a Cabinet decision. (Reform promoted by the trinity method was decided for the first time.)
October:	"Opinions about the ideal state of clerical works and projects" was reported by Council for Decentralization Reform.
June, 2003:	"Basic policies for 2003" was endorsed by a Cabinet decision. (4 trillion yen of subsidy and obligatory share reform was decided.)
April, 2004:	Aso, Minister of Internal Affairs and Communications published the "Local financial reform for the promotion of decentralization."
June:	"Basic policies for 2004" was endorsed by a Cabinet decision. (Local governments were requested to prepare specific reform plans aiming to achieve a 3 trillion yen transfer of tax revenue sources.)
August:	A reform plan by the six associations of local governments was proposed to the government.
September:	Conference of central and local government on trinity reform was inaugurated.
November:	The government and ruling parties came to an agreement over "Trinity reform."

(Continued)

Table 3. (*Continued*)

June, 2005:	"Basic policies for 2005" was endorsed by a Cabinet decision. (Decisions were taken on activities to ensure a steady implementation of the trinity reform by fiscal year of 2006.)
November:	The government and ruling parties came to an agreement over "Trinity reform."
June, 2006:	The six associations of local governments submitted the "Report on the promotion of decentralization."
July:	"Basic policies for 2006" was endorsed by a Cabinet decision.

reform 2002", which stated the government's aim as "to discuss the pattern that should be achieved through trinity reform in terms of the national treasury subsidies, the local allocation tax, and the allocation of tax sources including transfer of tax revenue sources, and to prepare a reform proposal including the most desirable outcome and a specific reform schedule for achieving it within one year." Furthermore, the *Basic policies for 2002* aimed at (1) Finalizing, within one year, a plan for the abolition and/or reduction of the national treasury subsidies on the basis of the research carried out by the Council for Decentralization Reform, (2) reducing *national treasury subsidies and obligatory shares* by several trillion yen by the fiscal year 2006, (3) re-evaluating the financial guarantee functions of the local allocation tax and achieving a reduction by 2006.

In October, 2002, the Council for Decentralization Reform, (successor to the Decentralization Promotion Committee) submitted a research paper that did not fully support the proposals discussed above. There also was resistance from the local governments. In this situation, a budget for the fiscal year 2003 was drawn up. The result was a reduction of about 560 billion yen in *national treasury subsidies and obligatory shares*, including those related to public works and the obligatory share of compulsory education expenses. This was the beginning of the trinity reform (see Table 4).

3.3. *The Intentions and Objectives of Trinity Reform*

The trinity reform pursued in an integrated manner the transfer of tax revenue sources to local governments, reform of *national treasury*

Table 4. National Treasury Subsidies and Obligatory Shares Reform and Transfer of Tax Revenue Sources (unit: hundred million yen)

Category	Total Amount	Breakdown of Figures Shown on the Left			
		Fiscal2003	Fiscal2004	Fiscal2005	Fiscal2006
1. Amount of national treasury subsidies and obligatory shares reform	52,286	5,625	10,314	36,347	
1.1 Amount related to the transfer of tax revenue sources (part of above figure)	31,176	2,344	4,749	Amount related to the agreement between the government and ruling parties in 2004 17,539 Amount related to the agreement between the government and ruling parties in 2005 6,544	
1.2 Amount related to other reform (part of above figure)	21,110	3,281	5,565	6,441	5,823
1.2.1 Streamlined amount (part of above figure)	13,167	3,281	4,235	3,011	2,640
1.2.2 Amount converted to grants (part of above figure)	7,943		1,330	3,430	3,183
2. Amount of transfer of tax revenue sources	30,094	(Fis-2006)			

Source:
Study group on local allocation tax system (ed): *Overview of local allocation tax in 2006*, p. 110, April, 2006, Institute of Local Finance.
Study group on local allocation tax system (ed): *Overview of local allocation tax in 2004*, p. 84, April, 2004, Institute of Local Finance.

subsidies and obligatory shares, and revision of the local allocation tax. Opinions differed, however, in choosing which of the three items would be given priority.

The final report of the Decentralization Promotion Committee and the Katayama draft policy took the position to "reduce subsidy and obligatory share as the first priority". Officials at the local administration and the Ministry of Internal Affairs and Communications attached a high value to increasing the autonomy of local governments by re-allocating the tax sources from the central to local governments, whereas officials in the Ministry of Finance and people in business attached a heavier weight to achieve sound public finance for the central and local governments by reducing the amount of *national treasury subsidies and obligatory shares* and the local allocation tax.

Thus, the trinity reform had two objectives. One was the promotion of the decentralization of power and the expansion of autonomy of local governments in local public finance. The other was to establish a more sound system of Japanese public finance. The objective is to encourage reductions in the size of the central and local government expenditures. Consequently, any evaluation of the success of the trinity reform depends on which objective is given a higher weight.

4. Evolution of the Trinity Reform

4.1. *Trinity Reform in Fiscal Year 2003*

In *Basic policies for 2002*, the government aimed at completing a reform plan within one year, but was unable to do so even in 2003. Finally after receiving directives from Prime Minister Koizumi, the government offices reached some conclusions. On June 27, 2003, the policy document, *Basic policies for economic and fiscal management and structural reform 2003* was endorsed by a Cabinet decision. It set a specific action plan, as follows:

(1) to carry out measures to reduce the *national treasury subsidies and obligatory shares* by about 4 trillion yen:
(2) to carry out an overall revision and reduction of the local allocation tax;
(3) to carefully examine and revise individual projects and set a target for the transfer of tax revenue sources to local governments

sufficient to cover about 80 percent of costs (100 percent for mandatory projects) by fiscal year 2006.

Thereafter, there was no significant development in the plan to implement the reform.

In October and November, 2003, the Japan Association of Mayors submitted a list of subsidy abolitions amounting to 5.9 trillion yen and the National Governors' Association submitted a similar list amounting to 8.9 trillion yen. Koizumi then directed the reduction of subsidies by one trillion yen in the fiscal 2004 State Budget and accelerated the budgetary process. The central government side (the Ministry of Health, Labor and Welfare, etc.) proposed to lower the subsidy and share levels, such as that of livelihood protection payments and the Ministry of Finance proposed to transfer the tobacco tax to local governments. Local governments and the Ministry of Internal Affairs and Communications, however, objected to these proposals, alleging that reductions in these subsidies would not expand the autonomy of local governments and that the transfer of tax revenue sources should include broad-based taxes like the income tax.

To resolve such confrontations, Koizumi and the leadership decided:

(1) to reduce national treasury disbursement by 1,030 billion yen through conversion to a permanent general revenue source (244 billion yen), to convert the national treasury obligatory share of compulsory education expenses to a temporary general revenue source (231 billion yen) and to cut back national subsidies related to public works (about 550 billion yen); (see Table 4)
(2) to grant a special revenue source (656 billion yen) to local governments as a transitory measure before carrying out a full-scale transfer of tax revenue sources.

Local governments were favorable to the 2004 state budget that contained (1) the reduction of 1 trillion yen in the national treasury disbursement, and (2) the retention of the subsidy level for livelihood protection payments and the withdrawal of the proposed tobacco tax transfer. They critically pointed out, however, that the general revenue source was smaller than the reduction in national treasury disbursement, and that the plan *rebalanced* fiscal resources in favor of the central government by reducing the fiscal resources of local governments.

Especially the local governments with small amounts of local taxes had no choice but to depend heavily on the local allocation tax.

The total amount of local allocation tax was reduced by 1.2 trillion yen (6.5%) in fiscal year 2004. In addition to this, the total amount of an extraordinary financial measure loan, which is a local governments special debt (borrowing) approved by the Ministry of Internal Affairs and Communications as an alternative revenue source to local allocation tax, was reduced by 1.7 trillion yen (28.6%). Consequently, the total amount of substantial local allocation tax was reduced by 2.9 trillion yen (12 percent) (see Table 5). Many criticized the reform that forced them to compile inappropriate budgets due to the insufficient general revenue.

4.2. *Trinity Reform in Fiscal Year 2004*

In April, 2004, on the basis of criticisms by local governments, Mr. Aso, Minister of Internal Affairs and Communications published *the local financial reform for the promotion of decentralization (trinity reform)* and argued that the central government should transfer about 3 trillion yen of tax revenue sources to the local governments. The Ministry of Finance objected to this and maintained that the amount of tax revenue sources to be transferred should be determined only after knowing the amount by which *national treasury subsidies and obligatory shares* would be reduced.

On June 4, 2004, however, Koizumi directed the Cabinet to endorse the document, *Basic policies for economic and fiscal management and structural reform 2004*. In this policy document, the government set out its plan: (1) to transfer tax revenue sources of approximately 3 trillion yen (transfer from income tax to individual inhabitant tax[7]), (2) to request local governments to prepare specific plans for national treasury disbursement reform amounting to about 3 trillion yen, and (3) to decide in 2004 on the complete picture of reform for the period up to fiscal 2006.

---

[7] Individual inhabitant tax is levied by both prefectures and municipalities. It is imposed on inhabitants an aggregated amount of the "Per Capita Rate" tax and "Income Rate" tax. "Per Capita Rate" tax is assessed on individual taxpayers in same amount, regardless of their net income. "Income Rate" tax is imposed on the basis of the net income earned in the previous year.

Table 5. Transition of Amount of Local Allocation Tax and Amount of Local Public Finance Program (On the Basis of the Original Plan) (unit: hundred million yen)

	Amount of Local Allocation Tax		Extraordinary Financial Measures Loan		Amount of Substantial Local Allocation Tax		Amount of Local Public Finance Program		Amount of Local Taxes	
Category	①	Rates of Increase (%)	②	Rates of Increase (%)	(① + ②)	Rates of Increase (%)	—	Rates of Increase (%)	—	Rates of Increase (%)
Fiscal2000	214,107	2.6	—	—	214,107	2.6	889,300	0.5	350,568	▲0.7
Fiscal2001	203,498	▲5.0	14,488	—	217,986	1.8	893,071	0.4	355,810	1.5
Fiscal2002	195,449	▲4.0	32,261	122.7	227,710	4.5	875,666	▲1.9	342,563	▲3.7
Fiscal2003	180,693	▲7.5	58,696	81.9	239,389	5.1	862,107	▲1.5	321,725	▲6.1
Fiscal2004	168,861	▲6.5	41,905	▲28.6	210,766	▲12.0	846,700	▲1.8	323,231	0.5
Fiscal2005	168,979	0.1	32,231	▲23.1	201,210	▲4.5	837,687	▲1.1	333,189	3.1
Fiscal2006	159,073	▲5.9	29,072	▲9.8	188,145	▲6.5	831,508	▲0.7	348,983	4.7

Notes:

1. *Source*: Study group on local allocation tax system, ed.: "Overview of local allocation tax in 2006", p. 116, April, 2006, Institute of Local Finance, etc.
2. The amount of local taxes is based on the local public finance program.

Six associations of local governments including the National Governors' Association drew up their reform plans for the national treasury subsidy and other local fiscal system reforms at the request of the central government, and submitted these to Koizumi on August 24. In these reform plans, the six associations of local governments requested the establishment of a consultative body for the central government and local governments. They proposed also to implement the trinity reform with a first phase introduced by 2006 and a second phase from 2007 to 2009. A total of 8 trillion yen of tax revenue sources would be transferred and national treasury disbursements of 9 trillion yen would be reduced. They requested in the first phase to reduce the national treasury disbursement by 3.23 trillion yen, including 850 billion yen of the national treasury obligatory share of compulsory education expenses, and 260 billion yen of private nursing center operation subsidies. They also requested that livelihood protection payments should be eliminated from "transferred national treasury disbursement" and that financial resources of local governments should be secured by means of the local allocation tax.

Many ministries expressed concern over these proposals by the six associations of local governments. The Ministry of Education, Culture, Sports, Science and Technology reacted sharply against the abolition of the national treasury obligatory share for compulsory education expenses. The Ministry of Health, Labor and Welfare requested a reduction in the level (percentage) of obligatory share of livelihood protection payments. The Ministry of Land, Infrastructure and Transport and Ministry of Agriculture, Forestry and Fisheries demanded reform of the *national treasury subsidies and obligatory shares*, not by abolition but by conversion to grants with a reduced central government involvement. Meanwhile, the Ministry of Finance and expert members of the Council on Economic and Fiscal Policy insisted on reductions in the local public finance program and on the promotion of local allocation tax reform.

At the newly established conference between the central government and local governments, the government ministries concerned and the six associations of local governments consulted each other but found no room for compromise. Under these circumstances, the government and the ruling parties in the Diet proposed the entire program of the trinity reform up to 2006. On November 26 the government and the ruling parties finally came to an agreement which set out a plan in 2005 and 2006 to abolish or reduce the national treasury disbursement up to about 3 trillion yen and to transfer tax revenue sources of about 3 trillion yen from income taxes to the individual inhabitant tax. The parties decided to reduce the national treasury obligatory share of compulsory education expenses provisionally by 850 billion yen and to reduce it by 425 billion yen in 2005 as a stop-gap measure. They decided also to reduce the national treasury obligatory share by 700 billion yen with the introduction of a new system of prefectural disbursement into National Health Insurance which was operated by municipalities. This was a new obligatory expenditure imposed on prefectures, which was not proposed by the six associations. In addition, they decided to reach a conclusion in 2005 about the revisions of the State liability in relation to livelihood protection payments, child rearing allowances, and the handling of the expenses for public educational facilities.

In accordance with the agreement between the government and the ruling parties, the fiscal 2005 State budget proposed reform of 1,768 billion yen of national treasury disbursements. It was also proposed to transfer 1,116 billion yen in tax resources. The local allocation tax in the 2004 State budget was significantly reduced, which invited heavy attack from local governments. In 2005 however, it showed a 0.1% increase over the previous year. The reduction of the amount of substantial local allocation tax was only about one trillion yen (4.5%) even when the extraordinary fiscal measures loan was included (see Table 5).

4.3. *Trinity Reform in Fiscal Year 2005*

There were a number of problems that needed to be solved including the national treasury obligatory share of compulsory education expenses (tentative measure) and livelihood protection payments.

On June 21, 2005, the Cabinet endorsed the policy document *Basic policies for economic and fiscal management and structural reform 2005*. In this document, the government set out its plans

(1) to continue the reform based on the agreement between the government and the ruling parties in 2004;
(2) to transfer tax revenue sources up to about 3 trillion yen from income tax to individual inhabitant tax by flattening the tax rate of individual inhabitants tax;
(3) to reach a conclusion on the remaining problems regarding national treasury disbursement reform by autumn, 2005.

The problems pointed out in the basic policies for 2005 were resolved by an agreement about Trinity reform on November 30, 2005 between the government and the ruling parties. The national obligatory share of compulsory education expenses as a stop-gap measure was reduced by 850 billion yen by lowering the ratio of State liability from 1/2 to 1/3, not by abolishing the national treasury obligatory share of compulsory education expenses for junior high schools. The level of the national treasury obligatory share was maintained for livelihood protection payments. The subsidy percentages for the child-rearing allowance and child allowance were lowered from 3/4 to 1/3 and from 2/3 to 1/3 respectively.

As shown in Table 4, the total sum of the *national treasury subsidies and obligatory shares* reform related to the transfer of tax revenue sources amounted to about 3 trillion yen. This includes 234.4 billion yen by the 2003 reform, 474.9 billion yen by the 2004 reform, 1,753.9 billion yen by the November, 2004 agreement, and 654.4 billion yen by the November 2005 agreement.

The 2006 State budget was prepared on the basis of the same agreement, and the plan was to make the 3 trillion yen transfer of tax revenue sources permanent by cutting the income tax for 2007 and flattening the individual inhabitant tax rate (a 10 percent proportional rate for individual inhabitant tax). It was scheduled that the prefectural tax rate of 2 and 3 percent in 2005 was to be increased to 4 percent and the municipal tax rate of 3 percent, 8 percent and 10 percent in 2005 was to be changed to 6 percent in 2007. In 2006, a provisional measure was taken to give the sum of 2,179.4 billion yen to prefectural governments and the sum of 830 billion yen to municipalities as local transfer taxes (income transfer tax).

5. Results and Problems of Trinity Reform

5.1. *Up-to-date Results of the Reform*

The results of trinity reform up to 2006 show that a sum of 4,666 billion yen in national treasury disbursements was abolished or converted to grants from 2004 to 2006 (see Table 4). If the reform effect amounting to 563 billion yen in the budget of 2003 is added, the total amounts to 5229 billion yen. This is more than 40 percent of the total amount of 11.9 trillion yen of national treasury disbursements in 2005 (see Table 1). Within this amount, the amount of *national treasury subsidies and obligatory shares* reform categorized as being related to the transfer of tax revenue sources was 3,118 billion yen. The remaining 2,111 billion yen was generated by the reduction in national treasury disbursements not related to the transfer of tax revenue sources or "the conversion to grants", which means the reform of subsidies by simplifying the conditions and grant procedures. Out of 2,111 billion yen, 1,317 billion yen was generated by streamlining and 794 billion yen by conversion to grants with the reduced commitments of the central government.

The amount of the transfer of tax revenue sources was about 3 trillion yen. All transferred amounts (3,009.4 billion yen) were to be covered by income transfer tax in 2006. For most of the subsidy reductions categorized as being related to the transfer of tax revenue sources, 100 percent of the amount of the reductions was to be transferred. For facilities subsidies, such as subsidies for public school facilities covered by the construction bonds, tax revenue sources for 50 percent of the abolition and reductions will be transferred.

As shown in Table 5, the amount of local allocation tax, including the extraordinary financial measures loan, was significantly reduced from 23.9 trillion yen (the fiscal 2003 budget) to 18.8 trillion yen (the fiscal 2006 budget), i.e., a reduction of 5.1 trillion yen (21.3%). This amount was partially offset by the increase in local tax revenues during the period (an increase of 2.7 trillion yen from 32.2 trillion yen to 34.9 trillion yen). However, the most significant impact was the reduced scale of the local public finance program, which is closely related to the total amount of local allocation taxes. The scale of the local public finance program was reduced over a period of five straight years from its peak in fiscal 2001. The amount was 83.2 trillion yen in fiscal 2006, indicating a reduction of 3 trillion yen compared to fiscal 2003 (86.2 trillion yen) and a significant reduction of 6.1 trillion yen compared to fiscal 2001 (89.3 trillion yen).

The parties concerned tried to correct the gap between the local public finance program and its accounting. The too complicated calculation of local allocation tax has been simplified. The number of local governments receiving no local allocation tax increased, and the calculation method was revised to provide incentives in administrative and fiscal reform.

5.2. *Local Governments' Evaluation of the Reform*

All local governments did not give high marks to the trinity reform. A questionnaire survey was administered to governors by Jiji Press Co.

Its findings showed that as for the agreement of November 2005 between the government and ruling parties, no governor gave a high evaluation; 13 governors considered it as *satisfactory*, 20 governors as *less than satisfactory*, and 5 governors *nonsense*. Clearly the majority gave a very low score.[8]

The reason for the dissatisfaction was the reform did not increase the autonomy of local government management as much as was expected. Actually the reduction of national treasury disbursements did not increase their degree of freedom in forming and implementing policies. On the contrary, the general revenue source conditions placed on local governments in executing the subsidized projects increased. In addition, as the reform is practiced, the scale of local public finance programs and the total amount of local allocation tax (including the extraordinary financial measures loan) have been significantly reduced.

Some evaluate the reform more favorably, however, because of (1) the 3 trillion yen transfer of tax revenue sources to local governments, (2) the establishment of a forum for discussions between the central and local governments, and (3) the consolidation and rationalization of national treasury disbursements such as the abolition of facility subsidies.

Although the central government had originally requested the six associations of local governments to prepare the reform plan, it largely ignored all their input. As the total amount of local allocation tax was significantly reduced, some criticized that the trinity reform did not focus its target on furthering the decentralization of authority but only on reallocating resources to the central government. Local governments have not given a strong positive evaluation of the trinity reform.

5.3. *Basic Policies for 2006 and Sound Fiscal Administration*

On July 7, 2006, the Cabinet endorsed a document, *Basic policies for economic and fiscal management and structural reform 2006*. Implementation was proposed for three phases; the first, up to the end of 2006, the second, from 2007 to the beginning of the 2010s, and the third, from the beginning of the 2010s. The proposal is to restore the positive balance of basic fiscal revenue and expenditure in 2011. In the

[8] Kancho Sokuhou (Government Office Flash News), Jiji Press, December 6, 2005.

third phase, the goal is to decrease the ratio of outstanding long-term debt to the GDP. They estimate the amount required to restore the positive balance of basic fiscal revenue and expenditure to be as much as 16.5 trillion yen by fiscal 2011, and to achieve this, the required amount of expenditure reduction will be between 11.4 trillion yen and 14.3 trillion yen.

The basic policies for 2006 in local public finance were to reduce expenditures: (1) to reduce the total number of employees (by 5.7%) to the same level as that of the central government employees within five years, (2) to reduce investment expenditure and (3) to suppress general administrative expenditure to the level of fiscal 2006.

As for local allocation tax, the cabinet argues to "secure the total amount of the general revenue sources including local taxes and local allocation tax required for the stable management of public finance."

The cabinet document has strengths and weaknesses. A certain degree of understanding has been shown about the need to secure the total amount of necessary resources. On the other hand, too little attention has been paid to the reform of national treasury disbursements. There is only brief mention of a "plan to reduce or abolish national treasury disbursements". In addition, the basic policy promises some efforts to review the method of calculating local allocation tax, to review the legal framework for appropriate fiscal reconstruction, and to establish new guidelines for local administrative reform with an emphasis on sound local public finance.

In the trinity reform, however, emphasis seems to be shifting from decentralization of authority to sound fiscal administration. As a first step, local governments have carried out their own administrative and fiscal reforms such as reduction of the number of employees and revision of the enforcement of policy. What is important for local governments now is to manage fiscal operations more efficiently.

5.4. *Future Challenges to the Local Public Finance*

There are several major challenges in moving ahead with reform of the local public finance system. First, national treasury disbursements must be revised so as to truly contribute to the decentralization of authority. The six associations of local governments proposed an overall idea of trinity reform in August, 2004. They estimated that the abolition of 9 trillion yen in national treasury disbursements was required.

In June, 2006, they proposed a reduction of half of the total number of *national treasury subsidies and obligatory shares* in a document, *Report on the promotion of decentralization*. Using these reform plans as a basis, what they must do now is, while anticipating strong opposition from the central government's ministries and agencies, push for a drastic reduction of national treasury disbursements so as to enhance the autonomy of local governments.

The second important problem is the reform of the local allocation tax. The Ministry of Finance has stated that there is a need (1) to reduce the amount of the local allocation tax because local governments' finance is more stable than the central government's, and (2) to review the structure of the local allocation tax because guaranteed fiscal resources are a blanket protection and a hindrance to efficient fiscal administration.

In response to these assertions, those involved in local administration argue that (1) Local governments are constantly engaged in reducing expenditures and cannot absorb further budget cuts. (2) There are large differences in fiscal capability among local governments, and some must be guaranteed financial support from the local allocation tax. (3) The more serious problem for efficient local government operation is not the local allocation tax but the *national treasury subsidies and obligatory shares*. Before reducing the local allocation tax rate, it is necessary to eliminate the large deficit in local public finance.

Report on the promotion of decentralization mentioned above proposes that the name *local allocation tax* should be changed to *local common tax* so as to clarify its function as an indigenous fiscal resource for local government. The methods used to calculate the local allocation tax have also been pointed out to be controversial. The Ministry of Internal Affairs and Communications has proposed to introduce a new local allocation tax with a distribution among local governments based on population size and land area, and some indicators that would take account of administrative and financial reform efforts.

The third problem is the trends in the reform of the local public finance other than the reforms in national treasury disbursements and local allocation tax. In July 2006, the round-table conference established by the former Minister of Internal Affairs and Communications, Dr. Heizo Takenaka produced a report about the present state of decentralization. The report pointed out the need to achieve the "full-freedom of local government borrowing" and to review the "Collapsed

Reconstruction Law". In fact, a *New Local Financial Reconstruction Law* was drawn up, and it was enacted in June, 2007. This report also proposed that the draft of *New Omnibus Decentralization Law* should be submitted to lawmakers within three years so as to review and reform the authority and responsibility of the central government. The six associations of local governments also requested, in their *Report on the promotion of decentralization* that a *New Decentralization Promotion Law be enacted.*

In October, 2006, the draft of a *New Decentralization Promotion Law* was finally presented to lawmakers, and it was enacted in December, 2006. It specified the basic ideas for promoting decentralization and proposed the necessary committees. Attention should to be paid on how decentralization and autonomy of local governments is going to be promoted through the execution of these laws.

6. Conclusion

The government has shifted the main emphasis of the trinity reform from decentralization of authority to sound fiscal administration by local governments. Nevertheless, the *national treasury subsidies and obligatory shares* have not been revised enough from the viewpoint of improving the freedom of local governments to make their own fiscal decisions. More attention needs to be devoted to the reform of *national treasury subsidies and obligatory shares*, and to the reconstruction of the local fiscal system, so that local governments will have more autonomy in fiscal decision making.

Some would argue that the role of the local allocation tax in guaranteeing fiscal resources is too strong, so its function should be diminished. However, fiscal capacity of local governments is weak and differs greatly among them. Therefore fiscal resources must be guaranteed for local governments. We should consider the necessity of "even" and "unbiased" policies of different local governments and discuss the ideal way to guarantee the fiscal resources for them. Still, the methods to calculate local allocation taxes must be reconsidered. This might include the introduction of a new and simplified local allocation tax that would be consistent with the larger goals of increased revenue mobilization, local government autonomy and equalization.

The public finances of both the central and local governments are in crisis. Sound fiscal administration is an essential part of the way out of this problem. However, autonomy is indispensable to enable them to execute the kinds of policies that would bring about more efficient operations and better service delivery. Thus, decentralization of authority and sound local government finance must be part of the same policy agenda.

References

References other than those shown in the text.

Ikawa, H. Responsibility of the central government and secure of revenues, for policies of local governments I, II, *Jichi kenkyu (Journal of Local Governance Studies)*, Vol. 82, No. 10, No. 11, October, November, 2006, Dai-ichi Hoki Co. Ltd.

Komuro, Y. Verification and reconstruction of trinity reform — Reduction of regional differences by subsidy, etc., *Jichi kenkyu*, Vol. 82, No. 11, November, 2006.

Okamoto, M. Evolution of trinity reform — Evaluation and Challenges (1), (2), (3) and (4), *Chihou Zaimu* (Local Fiscal Affairs), Vol. 602, 603, 612, 625, August, September, 2004, June, 2005, July, 2006, Gyosei Corporation.

Yano, K. *Local government finance system*, rev. 8, October, 2007, Gakuyo Shobo.

Chapter III

Political Decentralization and Fiscal Reconstruction in Japan

TOSHIHIRO IHORI

University of Tokyo

This paper investigates inter-governmental financing and political decentralization during the fiscal reform process in Japan using the concept of soft budget constraints. We briefly explain the Japanese inter-governmental fiscal system and review some historical background of political and fiscal decentralization. The existence of some inter-governmental transfer programs induces a free-riding behavior on the part of local governments, resulting in deficits. It is shown that an increase in the portion of local taxes compared with national taxes will not have desirable effects. On the contrary, an increase in local and/or national taxes may be desirable for fiscal reconstruction to some extent although this policy cannot attain the Pareto-efficient outcome.

1. Introduction

This paper investigates positive and normative implications of inter-governmental financing and political decentralization during the fiscal reconstruction process in Japan. We focus on the problem of soft budget constraints, which has been useful in explaining inefficient, money-losing behavior of public enterprises (Kornai, 1979). A good example of soft budget constraints is inter-governmental financing. The Japanese inter-governmental transfer programs induce free-riding behavior on the part of local governments, thereby encouraging deficits.

In fiscal 2003, total central and local government deficits reached 7.7% of GDP, a very high level by industrial country standards. There are a number of reasons why the government deficits increased rapidly during the 1990s. First, local governments receive significant transfers from the central government mainly in the form of public works grants. These conditional grants to local governments are awarded by the center in an *ad hoc* way and are politically driven. In some cases they effectively fill a financing gap caused by overspending on the part of local governments. Second, Japanese local governments have little independent taxing power; hence they are heavily dependent on transfers from the central government. If they overspend, they cannot fall back on local source financing. The central government provides support to local governments amounting to about 5 percent of the GDP, in part because of the influence brought by powerful interest groups in rural regions.

Given this situation, the central government has tried to play a leading role in balancing local finances by providing guidelines for cost-cutting and rationalizing expenditures, a process which is referred to as "fiscal reconstruction". The central government still provides a financial guarantee to allow local governments to cope with the political pressure to enhance the welfare of the community and develop and maintain the infrastructure. It is this guarantee that ultimately leads to the soft budget constraint.

Technically, the central government makes grants to local governments, but it is more accurate to add that local governments play a role in determining the amount of inter-governmental transfers that they receive. Many local governments seek to obtain more money from the central government through a variety of lobbying activities, and they succeed. The existence of open-ended inter-governmental transfer programs without a fixed overall limit on the local government entitlement (i.e., no defined vertical share) makes total central government budget revenues a common pool for local governments. This encourages overspending and generally "softens" budget constraints.

It is well recognized in Japan that reforming the system of inter-governmental finance is a key element of fiscal reconstruction. Many believe that one promising way to promote political and fiscal decentralization, and to alleviate the fiscal crisis, is to transfer part of the tax base from the central to local governments. However, the problem of the soft budget constraint has not been properly factored in to this solution. In this paper, we show that an increase in the local government share of national taxes will not have desirable effects on fiscal discipline or fiscal condition so long as a hard budget constraint is not imposed on local governments. On the contrary, we show that an increase in local and/or national taxes cannot lead to a Pareto-efficient outcome. Raising taxes has an effect similar to that of an increase in GDP.

The organization of the paper is as follows. Section 2 summarizes Japan's local finance system. Section 3 reviews the historical background of Japan's political and fiscal decentralization. Section 4 investigates the soft budget constraint problem caused by the current inter-governmental financing system, using a theoretical model of rent- seeking behavior of local interest groups. Section 5 discusses some current issues. Finally, section 6 concludes the paper.

2. Local Finance System

2.1. *Local Finance Law*

There are three levels of government in Japan: the central, prefectural, and municipal (see Fig. 1). The prefecture and municipal governments are the *local* governments in Japan.

The central and local governments are expected to perform their functions based on a formal division of responsibilities and an attitude of mutual cooperation. The financial and political relationship between the central and local governments is specified in the Local Finance Law: "The central government shall endeavor to promote the self-dependence and soundness of local finance, and refrain from any action prejudicial to the financial autonomy of local government or from shifting its burden upon local governments" (Local Finance Act, Article 282). Under this article, financial and political intervention by a higher level of government is conceptually limited to the purpose of maintaining the sound operation of public finance. However, in reality, the financial relationship among the different levels of government is becoming increasingly complex, due in part to national economic conditions and to the political pressures brought by local governments for more resources.

The division of expenditure responsibilities is determined by the law or by cabinet order. Tax revenues (inter-governmental transfers)

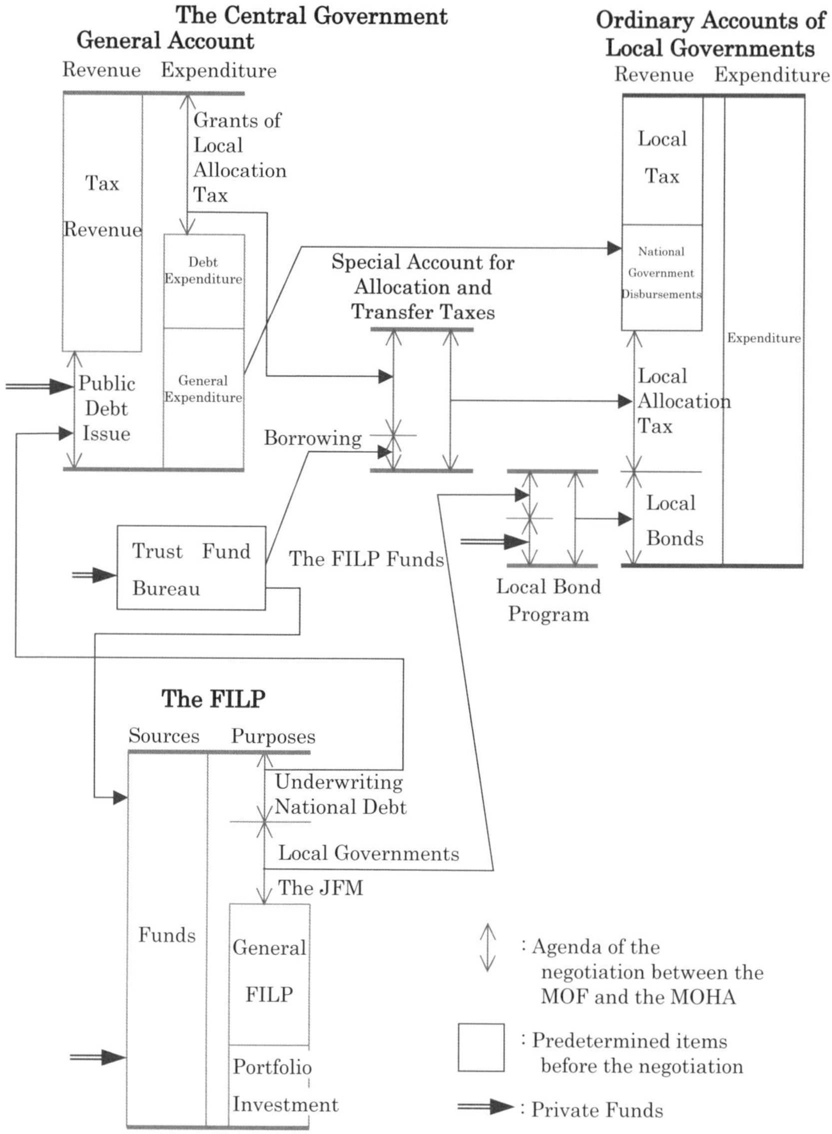

Fig. 1. Relationship between the National Budget and Local Public Finance

are distributed between the different levels of government so that each level of government can perform these tasks in a proper way. Ideally, the central government may grant subsidies to local public bodies only if such subsidies are found especially necessary for national welfare. In reality, under the existing soft budget constraint model, many local governments seek to overspend and then cover their deficits by obtaining more money from the central government through a variety of lobbying activities. In the 1990s the government deficits in Japan increased rapidly, even though local governments received significant amounts of central transfers in the form of local allocation taxes and public works grants.

The present system of inter-governmental revenue distribution consists of the following four parts:

(1) Taxes are divided into national and local taxes, imposed by the central and local governments, respectively.
(2) Revenues from a number of national taxes are transferred (in whole or in part) to local government.
(3) National disbursements are paid to local governments to finance a part of or all of the expenses related to specific expenditure programs.
(4) Payments are made by local governments to the national government to finance a number of special programs run by the central government.

There are five transfers from the national government to local governments: the local allocation tax, national government disbursements, local transfer taxes, special traffic safety grants, and the transfer as a substitution of fixed property tax. The local allocation tax and national government disbursements account for almost all of the transfers from the central government to local governments.

The local allocation tax is a general purpose grant made to local governments to enable them to finance those services they are required to provide. National government disbursements are the largest transfer category, and include over one thousand programs. These conditional grants cover almost all fields of local government activities including education, social welfare, public works, transportation, and regional development.

2.2. *Comparison Between Central and Local Governments*

Central and local government expenditures totaled 153.3 trillion yen in 2001. A significant portion of local government expenditures is financed by transfers from the national government.

The ratio of national taxes to local taxes is approximately 2 to 1, but in order to match up with expenditure responsibilities, a fixed percentage of national taxes is assigned as local allocation tax grants to local governments for unrestricted use. In addition, the central government uses subsidies to make disbursements to local governments for specific purposes. Consequently, the final ratio of direct expenditures (central-to-local) is about 1 to 2.

In a purely decentralized system, and assuming away the problems of externalities and fiscal capacity differences, the expenditures of a local government should be covered by local sources of tax revenue collected by that government. However, in reality, taxable capacity varies widely across local governments, so there must be a system to guarantee adequate financial resources to provide for local budgets. This is why the local tax allocation system was established as an inter-governmental transfer.

The central government not only plans and drafts proposals for local public corporation systems but also arranges financing for them and provides support and advice. These corporations provide essential services like clean water, transportation, hospital management, and sewage. As of fiscal 2001, there were 12,611 such units. Final account balances for these corporations total 21.2 trillion yen, or a little more than 20 percent of total general account expenditures for local public organizations.

In total, the amount of the local allocation tax grant is equivalent to a certain percentage of national tax revenues, as stated in the Local Allocation Tax Law. The central government collects these taxes on behalf of local governments because of advantages in assessment and collection. The entitlement of the local governments from these central collections is 32 percent of the revenue from the personal income tax and the liquor tax, 35.8% of the revenue from the company income tax 29.5% of the revenue from the consumption tax, and 25 percent of the revenue from the tobacco tax. Because local governments can play no role in setting the tax rates or determining the tax bases, these are more properly viewed as inter-governmental transfers than as local government taxes. The total amount of these components is transferred from the general account of the central government to the special account for grants of allocation tax and transfer taxes.

2.3. *The Local Public Finance Program*

Each year the national government must make an official estimate of expenditures and revenues of all local governments (Article 7 of the Local Allocation Tax Law). These estimates of revenues and expenditures are considered "ideal" or "standard" targets based on officially approved criteria. The national government policies and distributions based on this estimate are consolidated into the local public finance program. This program seeks to guarantee sufficient financial revenues to local governments and to provide guidelines for local governments to manage their financial affairs.

According to the conventional view (see, for example, Shibata (1991), the function of the local public finance program can be summarized as follows:

(1) Guarantee sufficient local financial resources to local governments. Prefectural and municipal governments are required by law to bear responsibility for a number of tasks, and are expected to provide a certain level of services regardless of the amount of tax revenues available. The local public finance program helps the central government determine whether the local allocation tax rate should be revised, or whether any reform in local public finance is necessary.
(2) Coordination of central and local public finance policies. Local and central government public finance plays an important role in the national economy. In order to establish a consistent national budget policy, proper coordination is essential. The issue came to the fore in the 1990s, when local governments increased spending on public works by issuing local bonds to stimulate the aggregate demand.
(3) Setting guidelines for local government financial management. National policies that would regulate and attempt to impose fiscal discipline on local governments are stated in the local public finance program.

In reality, the demand for local public services, and the political support for recognizing this demand, has been increasing in recent years. This has made it necessary for the central government to guarantee greater amounts of financial resources to the local governments. When there is a gap between revenue and expenditure estimates for a fiscal year, ex-post measures to cover the deficit are implemented. This gives rise to the soft budget constraint at the local level.

2.4. *Local Government Bonds*

Local government bonds are an acceptable means of financing long-lived assets, i.e., in cases where it is considered desirable that future residents should share in the costs incurred. It may also be acceptable in cases where a major emergency expenditure is necessitated by some natural disaster. In Japan, the central government plays a role in determining the aggregate amount of local government bonding by drafting plans for, determining the expected amounts, and giving final approval to bond issues. In theory, it should be possible to hold local governments to acceptable levels of borrowing and to acceptable uses of debt finance.

In reality, the use of debt finance has not followed these golden rules, in large because of the financial crisis that local governments have faced. Most of Japan's 3,300 local public organizations are financially weak, particularly those located in the rural areas. The shortage of financial resources for local governments has been rapidly increasing since 1994, due to a drop in local tax revenue combined with national tax cuts designed to stimulate the economy. The fiscal year 2003 shortfall was more than 17 trillion yen. This has led to an issuance of local government bonds to compensate for reduced revenues, and increased expenditures to stimulate the stagnant economy. It is estimated that total local government debt will reach 199 trillion yen by the end of fiscal 2003 (see Fig. 2). This is equivalent to 40 percent of GDP; 2.8 times more than in 1991, and an increase of 129 trillion yen.

The problem of deficit finance at the local government level arises in spite of the safeguards against unwise borrowing practices. In Japan, issues of local public bonds are legally controlled by the central government. (In fact, all local government revenues are managed by the central government.) Though basically they cannot freely issue local bonds in Japan, local governments did significantly increase their issuance of local bonds in the 1990s. Local governments must obtain the permission for issuing local bonds from the central government. Strictly speaking, prefectures and designated cities (12 big cities) must obtain permission from the Ministry of Public Management, Home Affairs, Posts and Telecommunications (MPHPT; the former Ministry of Home

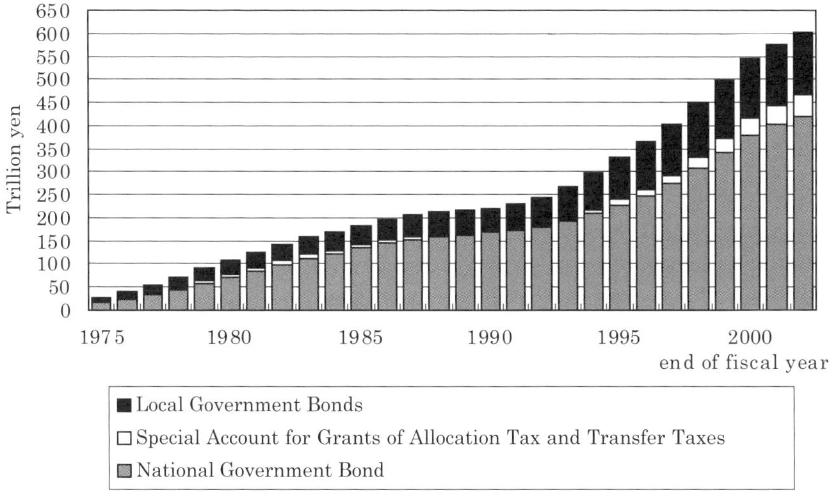

Fig. 2. Outstanding of Government Bonds

Affairs (MHA)), and municipalities must obtain permission from the prefectural governor.

In practice, the policy on local borrowing is primarily determined by the MPHPT. Local bonds permits are not merely permission for issuing local bonds but include the decisions of underwriters of the bonds. The MPHPT, which receives applications from local governments for permission, negotiates with the Ministry of Finance (MOF), and decides the extent to which their Funds will purchase local bonds. As Doi and Hoshi (2002) pointed out, postal savings and pension funds under-wrote about 60 percent of total issuance of local bonds in the 1990s. Private financial institutions hold about 30 percent of total of local bonds (see Fig. 3). Since the underwriters are determined by the MPHPT, no local governments pay for underwriting their own bonds. This neither encourages them to improve their fiscal situation nor fully disclose their fiscal information.

The result is that local governments depend on loans to finance a portion of their recurrent expenditures. Local officials might see such loans as being repayable in the future, after their term of office is over. Hence, there is no incentive to reduce the issuance of local bonds as long as the central government grants permission to borrow and places the bond issue. This practice is an enemy of fiscal discipline at the local level. Local bonds may be redeemable in the future with the help of the

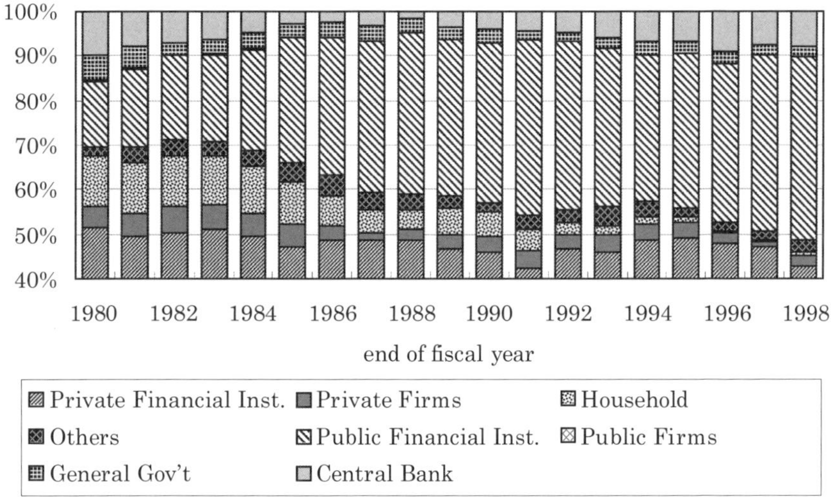

Fig. 3. Holding Ratios of National and Local Government Bonds

central government, but this worsens the fiscal position of the central government. A classic case of moral hazard is introduced by this feature of the inter-governmental fiscal system.

3. Historical Background

Before WWII, Japanese local governments were controlled by the central government. Governors were appointed by the central government, and local governments were simply regarded as agents of the central government in the highly centralized system. After WWII the movement toward fiscal decentralization began. Local autonomy is guaranteed by the constitution, in chapter VIII on local-autonomy clearly states. The Local Autonomy Law, the basic statute concerning the local government system, contains provision for local tax and finance administration.

3.1. *Reform Towards Fiscal Decentralization (1945–1954)*

In 1947 the Local Autonomy Law was implemented and the Ministry of Internal Affairs was reformed as the Ministry of Home Affairs (MHA).

The control of the central government over local governments was weakened and movements towards fiscal and political decentralization began. From the political viewpoint, voters were able to choose their own governors and in the first local election, four left-wing governors were actually chosen. In 1949, an economic advisory group headed by Professor Carl S. Shoup of Columbia University visited Japan to conduct studies, which resulted in recommendations for the restructuring of the Japanese tax system. The Shoup reforms pursued an "idealistic" fiscal decentralization. Namely, the central government would not intervene in fiscal decision making at the local government level.

However, the revenue sharing from the national taxes was not sufficient to cover assigned expenditures. Many administrative duties such as elementary education and police were transferred to the local governments, and the private sector could not pay sufficient taxes to local governments to support these services. As a result, the local governments faced revenue shortfalls, and fiscal crises resulted in many local governments. In 1951, 15 prefectures and 145 municipal governments were in deficit. In 1954 the situation worsened and 35 prefectures, which corresponded to 70 percent of all the prefectures and 1,644 municipal governments, which were about 40 percent of all the municipal governments, were in deficit. Local governments asked the central government for additional financial support to cover this deficit. The idealistic fiscal and political decentralization reform had not produced a good outcome.

This failure of the decentralization experiment induced the central government to reconsider the monitoring system with respect to local governments. The central government established a large amount of its own agencies in all prefectures during this period, in order to strengthen its control over local governments. Conceptually fiscal and political decentralization was still pursued, but in reality dual governance by the central and local governments emerged.

The central government also supported local governments financially by implementing the Fiscal Reconstruction Act for Local Governments, which is still the only legal basis to rescue local governments in the emergency situation. According to this law, the central government can offer a bailout, but it should be accompanied by cuts in public spending and the implementation of austerity programs under the control of the central government. Simultaneously, departments of the central government strengthened their monitoring power over local governments. Thus, when the local governments faced deficits, the inter-governmental structure changed from the idealistic decentralization system to the more centralized system. We may say that political decentralization failed to lead to sound fiscal management on the part of many local governments.

3.2. *Expansion of Local Administration (1955–1980)*

During this period, local governments were under tight control from the central government. When a local government undertook an agency-delegated function, it became an agent of the central government and executed functions as directed. Agency-delegated functions are essentially the responsibility of the central government but are delegated to local governments for administrative convenience. The number of agency-delegated functions increased significantly during this period. For example, more than half of the functions performed by the prefectural governments were agency-delegated.

The central government also tried to control functions other than agency-delegated functions. For almost all activities of local governments, it set guidelines, standards, and regulations, even for functions which were the responsibility of local governments. Various inducements were also provided. In this respect, the central government disbursements for specific purposes became the most important fiscal discipline instrument for the central government. These disbursements were distributed on condition that the recipients follow the directives issued by the central government. On the other hand, many local governments tried to convert these disbursements to general purpose grants since local residents were not taxed to provide the service in question.

A basic principle that underlined central government control seemed to be uniformity throughout the country. The central government intended to standardize local taxation as well as the distribution of public services. As a policy, the central government tried to treat all local governments equally. When a department of the central government distributed a specific-purpose disbursement, it took great care not to treat any local government different from the others. The question of "what do we mean by equal?" would soon become an important question.

The local allocation tax also played a very important role in standardizing the level of public services among local jurisdictions. This program equalized the fiscal capacity among local governments by supplementing the shortage of tax revenue. The allocation tax enabled local governments to provide public services at the level prescribed by the central government.

Several departments of the central government increased subsidies to local governments during this period. By doing so, the control by the central government of local government spending decisions, through legal and financial methods, was established. This governance mechanism did not give an incentive for local governments to reduce public spending, and hence took another step away from a hard budget constraint. Interestingly, however, since tax revenue automatically increased with rapid economic growth, this shortcoming did not cause serious financial problems until mid-1970s.

Rent-seeking behavior by local interest groups in terms of distribution of public works became common at this time. This was partly because GDP rose rapidly in the urban areas and the income gap between the urban and rural jurisdictions increased rapidly. Conservative local governments, whose heads were dominantly from the MHA, became popular in many rural regions.

In late 1960s the negative side effects of high-economic growth, such as environmental pollution, became visible. Politically left-wing governors were elected in major urban prefectures including Tokyo and Osaka as the second era of progressive local governments arrived. However, in the early 1970s, after the first oil shock, the economic growth rate declined significantly. During this period, many local governments faced a second fiscal crisis due to the tax reduction brought on by the economic slowdown. Since progressive governors were reluctant to reduce welfare-related spending, the fiscal crisis erupted and fiscal reconstruction of local governments became an important political issue.

During this period, central agencies did not cooperate with one another in their control of local governments' finances. Namely, the MHA reflected the interests of local governments and demanded more subsidies from the central government, whereas the MOF was against such political pressures. (Asako *et al.*, 1991). This non-cooperative political structure did not lead to restraining public spending. The public finance authorities of local governments lost their control of managing public finance. Since fiscal reconstruction was not avoidable in the long run, such governance structure was not sustainable either.

3.3. *Fiscal Reform/Regional Development Promotion (1981–1992)*

During this period, fiscal reconstruction became the top priority and the important step was the establishment of the *ad hoc* Council on Administrative Reform (*Rincho*) in 1981. With the support of PM Nakasone and the MOF, *Rincho* submitted five reports from July 1981 to March 1983 and recommended a number of important reforms to trim overly expanded portions of the government bureaucracy. The privatization of three major public corporations, and cuts in spending on public works were among the most important. Rincho also promoted fiscal reconstruction and administrative reforms in central and local governments. The proposed central-local governance reforms were regarded as the top priority by the leadership of PM Nakasone. This stronger financial leadership by the MOF caused conflict with the conventional governance by the MHA and other departments, which wanted to raise local are l spending as much as possible.

After the Japanese economy recovered from the oil shock and experienced a "bubble-boosted" expansion in mid-1980s, local governments did manage to avoid fiscal crisis for a time. The administrative reform changed its target from fiscal reconstruction to the promotion of regional development by using "third sector" (half-public, half-private) corporations, where the local government and private firms invested heavily. This method, however, had no clear legal basis. When the bubble economy burst, it resulted in fiscal deficits that were usually covered by issuing local bonds.

The MHA had the role of promoting regional development by local governments, as well as monitoring these local governments. The MHA established a number of agencies to support this objective. In 1980s each local government received a one-time award of 100 million yen as the "hometown" promotion project, irrespective of population size. This was a huge lump-sum transfer to small jurisdictions. Also, in order to promote regional development, several other measures were financed by the local allocation tax and by local borrowing.

All the influential parties, except for the communist party, joined the ruling party as advocates for the expansion of local governments. Most citizens considered the management ability and good relationship with the central government as the top priority of the Governor. Hence, the number of governors from the MHA increased. Interestingly, this would also result in reduction of the political concerns among voters, which in turn caused a drop in the voting turnover rate.

Local allocation taxes are transferred from the central government to most local governments as unconditional transfers. The system works as follows: The central government reserves a certain percent of national tax revenue in the general account as a common fund for local governments. It distributes funds to each local government according to their fiscal needs and capacity, based on a detailed equation determined by the national government. Hence, the total amount that local governments were to receive as the local allocation tax grants (the demand for transfer) was often greater than the amount the central government could transfer (the supply of transfer), resulting in deficits in the special accounts for allocation and transfer taxes, as Fig. 1 shows. This special account may be regarded as a *hidden deficit* of the public sector in Japan, because it was financed not by issuing national or local bonds but by a loan from the private banks. As a result, the statistics of public debt outstanding does not include this part of deficit.

In the second half of 1980s, national and local tax revenues increased, therefore the total amount of local allocation tax grants increased automatically. If the calculation of the basic financial needs and the basic financial revenue was not revised to reflect increased transfers, shortfalls of local governments, that is, the difference between the basic financial needs and the basic financial revenue would have decreased. In fact, the MHA revised the calculation to increase only the basic financial need. This is another aspect of the soft-budget constraint problem.

During this period, two factors were important: The weak fiscal condition of local governments and changes in local politics. The MHA had two objectives; to establish sound fiscal management of local government and to induce local governments to advance regional development by providing money for projects such as enhancing information technology and international interaction. When the fiscal situation became severe after the bubble was burst, these objectives did not coexist easily. For example, in early 1990s local bonds were issued in significant amount in order to stimulate regional development. This effort did not meet much success (Ihori and Kondo, 2001 and Ihori *et al.*, 2002). Eventually, this policy resulted in more severe fiscal deficits, and set the stage for further changes in the control of central governments over local governments.

3.4. *Fiscal Decentralization and Fiscal Reform (1993–Present)*

In the 1990s, national tax revenues decreased and the total amount of local allocation tax revenues decreased automatically. Because as the MHA did not revise the calculation of the basic financial needs, and the basic financial revenue did not increase, shortfalls of the special account for grants of allocation tax and transfer taxes increased. The central government (the MOF and MHA), however, increased the total amount of local allocation tax grants by an increase in borrowing in the special account, as shown in Fig. 2. This *hidden debt* accumulated significantly in the 1990s.

During the Hosokawa coalition government, decentralization became one of the main issues of central government policy, and reforms towards political and fiscal decentralization gained much popularity. The Council for Decentralization Promotion recommended a reform in subsidies from the national government to local governments, and in 2000 the Decentralization Act was implemented to reform administrative duties.

In particular, the Koizumi administration intended to introduce a comprehensive package of decentralization reforms. The *Plan on the Reform of the Three Major Policies* was promoted to realize the fundamental objective of local autonomy, allowing the local government authorities to make its own decisions and weakening the central government' control over local governments. At the same time, enterprising departments would lose power and the MHA would gain power since the MHA is supported by local governments. However, fiscal decentralization has proceeded slowly. Although the idea of structural reforms is very popular among politicians and business people, the actual structure of inter-governmental financing has not changed much. We now turn to the question of why structural reforms of inter-governmental financing have been delayed.

4. Local Interest Groups and Soft-Budget Problem

4.1. *Local Interest Groups in Japan*

In the 1990s, the government deficits in Japan increased rapidly because local interest groups in rural and agricultural areas received significant transfers, mainly conditional grants for public works.

Investment in agriculture-related infrastructure, fishing ports, measures for flood control, and conservation of forests have been stimulated, perhaps excessively, because of the lobbying activities of local interest groups. In addition to the concern that the accumulation of public debts may well be unsustainable, the expansionary fiscal policy in the 1990s brought another problem. Continuing budget deficits are harmful for the economy in the sense that excessive deficits today mean higher political privileges tomorrow, which results in the delay of restructuring the fiscal system in the long run.

In Japan, the central government provides heavy financial support to local governments, amounting to about 5 percent of GDP every fiscal year due to the soft-budget problem in the inter-governmental financing. Many local business interest groups and the politicians supported by them seek to obtain more money from the central and local governments through a variety of lobbying activities. They may be regarded as one of the most powerful business interest groups in Japan. The data on Japanese public works seem to show in comparison with those in other countries that the influential role of the interest groups related to public works is stronger and giving the local residents larger privileges than in other countries.

Under the Japanese fiscal system, the central government distributes local transfer taxes, local allocation tax grants, and national government disbursements to local governments. Therefore, representatives of the Diet appeal to the cabinet or the central bureaucrats to distribute more to their own regions. Getting more grants is thought to be an important factor in being re-elected. As a result, the allocation of region-specific privileges in the form of subsidies from the central government has been mainly determined by political factors.

It should be noted that there is a fiscal redistribution among regions that operates through the inter-governmental fiscal system. Kanto, Tokai, and Kinki regions account for about 60 percent of the population of Japan, and people and firms in these regions pay about 75 percent of national taxes in each year. However, they receive less in grants than people in the rural regions: Hokkaido and Tohoku, Hokuriku and Koshin'etsu, Chugoku and Shikoku, and Kyushu.

One reason why the central government distributes the grants in this way is that the rural regions hold more seats in the ruling party (the LDP for the post-war period) than do the urban regions. This rural interest is felt when the ruling party exerts an influence on decisions about the national budget and about the local public finance program. The result is that grants are distributed more heavily to the rural regions. For this reason, it is important to incorporate the political influence of local interest groups explicitly into the analytical framework.

Although the central government can impose the ceiling constraint on some public spending for fiscal reconstruction, it cannot easily restrain region-specific transfers. Decentralization normally means less inter-regional transfers by the central government, which would hurt most of the local governments in the rural regions. The empirical evidence (Ihori, Doi and Kondo, 2001; Doi and Ihori, 2002) indicates that lobbying activities of local interest groups was exaggerated in the 1990s. That was the main reason why fiscal reconstruction did not perform very well and the speed of decentralization was not high in the 1990s.

4.2. *Theoretical Model*

Following Ihori and Itaya (2001 and 2002), we develop a simple politico-economic model of inter-governmental financing. There are many ($n \geq 2$) symmetric interest groups (local governments) in a small open economy. Each of them enjoys a group-specific privilege of higher subsidies, which may be used for local expenditures L_i. The utility of local government i (or representative agent of region i) is assumed to be strictly increasing in private consumption c_i, local expenditures L_i and central public consumption or amenity G, which is common to all groups and may be viewed as a pure central public good. It is further assumed to be a twice-continuously differentiable and strictly quasi-concave function, which is expressed by

$$U = U(c_i, L_i, G)$$

where subscript (or superscript) i means local government i. Given the instantaneous utility function, the inter-temporal utility function of local government i over an infinite-horizon starting at time 0 is given by

$$\int_0^\infty U(c_i(t), L_i(t), G(t))e^{-\rho t}dt \qquad (1)$$

where ρ (> 0) is the constant discount rate, which is common to all local governments.

Public consumption of the central government good G at each point in time is determined according to

$$G(t) = G^* - rB(t) \tag{2}$$

where G^* is an exogenously given ceiling level, r is the exogenously given world interest rate, and B is government debt. Equation (2) means that central government spending on public consumption and interest payments is fixed at the level of G^* through time, so that higher public consumption is possible only by reducing the debt outstanding B.

During the fiscal reconstruction process Japan has actually imposed the ceiling constraint on certain types of government spending (mainly public consumption) in order to prevent a further deterioration in budget deficits (see Fig. 4). Equation (2) formulates such a ceiling rule. The strict ceiling rule of (2) (i.e., constancy of G^*) is adopted only for simplicity.

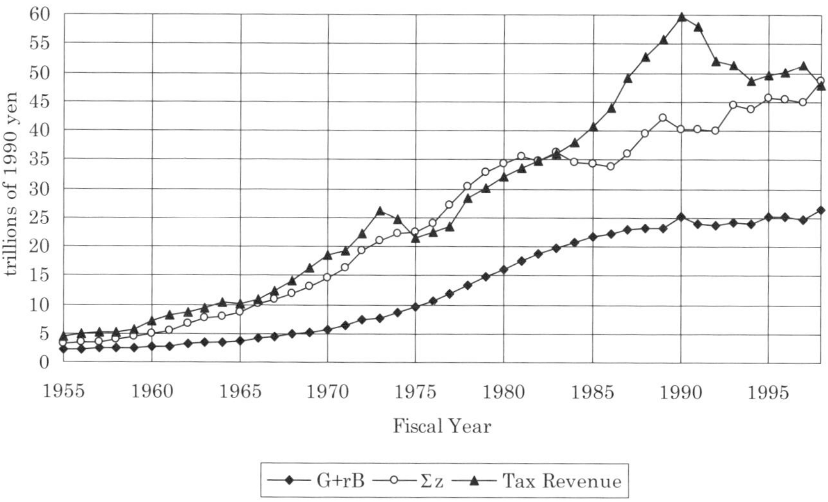

Notes: G is public spending by the central government including national agencies, national defense, disposition of external affairs, and education and culture rB is interest payment. Z is public investment and privileges to regions, including the remaining expenditures.

Fig. 4. Real National Government Expenditures and Revenues

A representative individual in region i will face the following budget constraint.

$$Y_i = c_i + \omega Y_i + \tau Y_i \tag{3}$$

where Y is exogenously given income common to all individuals (or regions), ω is the common local income tax rate, and τ is the common national income tax rate. To focus on the problem at hand, Y is assumed to be fixed over time. Local governments do not have any freedom to set their own tax rates.

The amount of local allocation tax (hereafter LAT) is given as

$$z_i - 0.8\omega Y_i,$$

where z_i is the level of standard (targeted) fiscal needs. The difference between standard fiscal needs and 0.8 of own local taxes will be given by the central government as LAT. The budget constraint of the local government is given as

$$(z_i - 0.8\omega Y_i) + \omega Y_i + H_i = L_i \tag{4}$$

H_i means local debt finance. Inter-governmental financing is "soft" in the sense that local governments can effectively set the local expenditure L (i.e., H_i).

Financing of LAT comes from two parts. One is the certain portion of national taxes $\varepsilon\Sigma\tau Y_i$ and another is debt finance, A in the special account for allotment of LAT.

$$\varepsilon\sum \tau Y_i + A$$

where ε is the portion of national taxes that is to be transferred as LAT. Hence, the budget constraint with respect to LAT is given as

$$\sum (z_i - 0.8\omega Y_i) = \varepsilon\tau\sum Y_i + A \tag{5.1}$$

The deficits in the special account of LAT as well as local governments $A + \Sigma H_i$ are eventually transferred to the central government, which reflects the soft-budget constraint. Thus, the general account budget constraint of the central government is given as

$$\dot{B} = G + rB + A + \sum_{j=1}^{n} H_j - (1-\varepsilon)\tau \sum_{j=1}^{n} Y_j \tag{5.2}$$

From (5.1,2) the public debt, B, will change over time, following the integrated government budget constraint.

$$\dot{B} = G + rB - \sum_{j=1}^{n} g_j \tag{6}$$

where g_i is net payment of taxes provided by agent i. More precisely, g_i is defined by the local and national tax payment applied to all agents $0.8\,\omega Y + \tau c_i$ minus region-specific standard fiscal needs (e.g., subsidies to local government i that benefits only region i) and local debt finance $z_i + H_i$.

$$g_i \equiv 0.8\omega Y + \tau Y_i - z_i - H_i \tag{7}$$

The central government (more precisely, fiscal authorities) may be "strong" enough to impose the ceiling constraint (2). However, the central government cannot directly reduce region-specific transfers (standard fiscal needs and local debt finance), so that they could be restrained only with the voluntary acceptance of the associated local governments. In this sense, the central government is "weak" in that fiscal reconstruction can be thought of as an outcome of voluntary concession on how the increases in net taxes g_i are to be apportioned between various local governments, which reflect the free-riding behavior of local interest groups.

From (2) and (6) we have

$$\dot{G} = r\sum_{j=1}^{n} g_j - rG^* \tag{6'}$$

Considering (3) (4) and (7) we have

$$L_i + g_i = (\tau + \omega)Y \tag{8}$$

$$c_i = (1 - \omega - \tau)Y \tag{9}$$

(9) means that private consumption is exogenously fixed.

Let us investigate the open-loop strategies. This type of Nash equilibrium concept presumes that the voluntary contribution to net tax revenue made by each local government (or mean voter) in the fiscal reconstruction process at each point in time is only conditioned on the initial stock of public debt and hence the initial level of national public goods, $G(0)$, and that each local government recommits itself to the entire path of region-specific transfers chosen at the outset of fiscal reconstruction.

The optimization problem of local government l is formulated as follows: Maximize its inter-temporal utility subject to (6′), (8), (9) and the exogenously given $G(0)$ and $g_j(t), j \neq i$, at time 0.

An increase in r would lead each local government to co-operate more willingly with fiscal reconstruction since the marginal return on doing so (i.e., saving interest payments) rises. Ihori and Itaya (2001) demonstrated that a higher r accelerates the adjustment speed of G at the open-loop solution in the similar context of fiscal reconstruction. From (8) and (9) an increase in τ or ω has the same effect as an increase in Y so that it raises total tax revenues of the public sector.

4.2. *Implications*

4.2.1. *Transferring the Tax Base from Central to Local Governments*

We now investigate the implications of fiscal decentralization, i.e., of attempts to transfer part of the tax base from central to local governments. It is widely recognized in Japan that this policy is one important way to achieve better fiscal discipline (and hence better reconstruction). In our analytical framework such a movement may be represented in two ways: (1) an increase in ω, the local income tax rate, with a decrease in τ, the national income tax rate, or (2) an increase in ε, the portion of national taxes to be transferred as local taxes.

Since the sum $\omega + \tau$ appears but either of ω, τ, or ε does not appear in (8), and (9), changes in ω, τ, ε will not affect the dynamic behavior of real equilibrium, so long as $\omega + \tau$ is fixed. An increase in ω or ε can reduce the amount of subsidies from the central government, H, but it does not have any other real effects. This is because the reduction of H will completely be offset by an equal-amount decrease in tax revenues in the central government budget account. The dynamic paths of G, g_i, L_i and c_i are therefore all independent of the redistribution parameter

ε. Since each local government knows exactly the integrated government budget constraint (6′), it is concerned only with the net payment of taxes, g_i (i.e., L_i), which is only a relevant choice variable to the local governments. So long as inter-governmental financing is "soft" in the sense that local governments can effectively set the local expenditure L (i.e., H_i), any policy measures taken towards decentralization do not improve the overall financial state of the government sector (i.e., the level of B) at all.

Furthermore, a revenue-neutral increase in local taxes accompanied by a decrease in national taxes will not affect the real equilibrium either. Finally, a change in the adjustment co-efficient 0.8 of LAT will not have any real effects.

So long as local governments effectively set the standard fiscal needs of LAT, none of the above measures improves the overall financial state of the central government. It is also easy to see that the tight restriction of local debt finance by the central government does not work effectively. Namely, a reduction in H will lead to an equal amount increase in z (and hence A), so that L will not change.

4.2.2. *Raising Taxes*

Equations (6) and (8) mean that the overall tax rate $\omega + \tau$ can affect the fiscal reconstruction process only through changes in each region's disposable income. Thus, an increase in the tax rate implies an income transfer from the private sector to the public sector and thus raises the total tax revenue of the central government. Because of the normality assumption of L and G, the increased tax revenues raise local expenditures L (through the increase in H) and central public spending G via (6) but reduce public debt B via (1) at the expense of private consumption.

If private consumption is initially too high compared with local spending ($U_L > U_c$), an increase in the income tax improves the welfare of the representative resident in each region; otherwise, this increase has a negative welfare effect and a Pareto-efficient outcome cannot be achieved. Nevertheless, raising income taxes is unambiguously desirable for fiscal reconstruction, even with the "soft" budget constraint of local governments, since B is decreased, although it cannot lead to a Pareto-efficient outcome in the long run.

5. Current Political Issues

5.1. *Strengthening Financial Base of Local Governments*

It is true that Japan needs to promote further decentralization for increasing the freedom and independence of local governments in terms of both revenue and expenditure. However, in order to improve the current state of public finance, which is in an extremely severe situation, local governments must increase their tax effort and reduce their dependency on borrowing (see Fig. 5).

It is also crucial to reduce the total amount of the local allocation tax and simplify the method of calculating the local allocation tax. By reforming the local allocation tax system so that each local government is encouraged to collect taxes to finance its own spending, the soft budget constraint problem may be solved. Then, the central government might be able to better restrain lobbying activities of local political groups.

5.2. *Promotion of Municipal Mergers*

In order to promote fiscal and political decentralization, the Japanese central government encourages municipal mergers. The central government

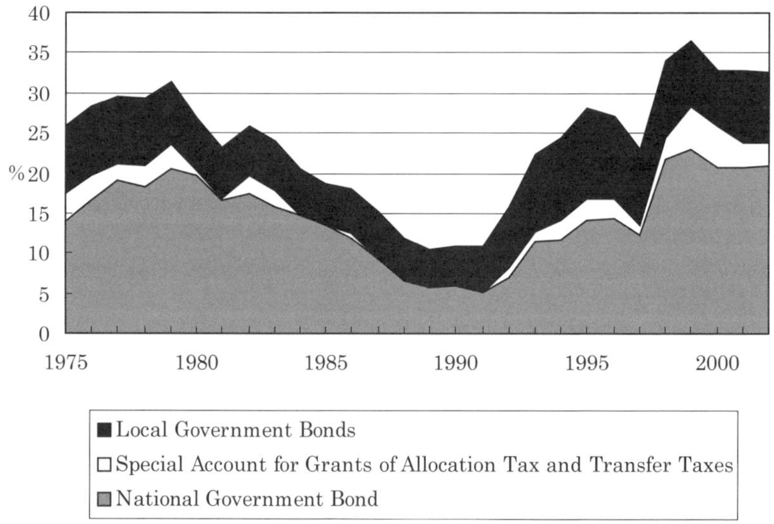

Fig. 5. Bond Dependence Ratio

financially supports such mergers by the Special Municipal Merger Law, which provides money for various projects for a few years (expansion of local financial measures, priority selection and priority investment in public work projects, elimination of various obstacles relating to merger, etc.).

Certainly, mergers have benefits. They can enable local planning from an area-wide perspective. Administrative and financial affairs will be made more efficient, because it will be possible to increase efficiency in the management sector and distribute human resources and budget more appropriately.

However, so long as the soft-budgeting mechanism exists, mergers will not always result in a good outcome. On the contrary, it might simply raise wasteful public spending in local governments since administrative services and salaries may rise to the levels that exist in the highest spending municipality.

6. Concluding Remarks

This paper investigates inter-governmental financing and political decentralization during the fiscal reconstruction process, using the concept of soft budget constraints as an integrating theme. It briefly explains the Japanese inter-governmental fiscal system and reviews some historical background of political and fiscal decentralization. The existence of soft-budgeting inter-governmental transfer programs induces free-riding behavior of local governments and results in deficits.

A brief review of the recent reform of Japan's local fiscal system is presented to conclude. In June 2003 the Council of Economic and Fiscal Policy (CEFP) created the *Trinity Reform Package*. It is one of the main reform schemes launched by the Koizumi government. As the name implies, it involves three factors: local taxes, Local Allocation Tax (LAT) grants, and national government disbursements. These and local bonds are the sources for local government spending.

The Trinity reform is desirable because Japan currently has an excessively centralized governance structure.

The Trinity Reform Package was implemented in stages. For fiscal 2003 to 2006, matching grants were reduced by about 5.2 trillion yen, about 3 trillion yen in tax revenue was shifted from the central government to local governments, and LAT grants were reduced by

3.6 trillion yen. The reform began after the start of the fiscal year, so that most of the matching grant reduction came in fiscal 2004–06 — some 4.7 trillion yen in total. The revenue transfer was achieved by reducing the personal income tax at the national level while increasing it by the same amount at the local level.

The central government is deeply involved in local government finance, and the present centralized governance system has created obstacles for the Trinity reform. There are a number of conflicts of interest among local governments, the Ministry of Internal Affairs and Communications (MIC), and the MOF. Local governments want stable and productive revenue sources because they have a large amount of local bonds and a difficult financial condition. The MOF wants to retain national tax revenue and reduce national subsidies in order to reduce government indebtedness. The MIC does not want to lose its authority over local fiscal affairs. Other government departments also hesitate to reduce the subsidies for which they are responsible.

Not surprisingly, conflicts about the nature and extent of decentralization have resulted in arguments among these stakeholders. There has been little consensus about how to proceed, and this has crippled reform efforts. Reform plans unwanted by many of those who must implement them seldom materialize.

To achieve the ultimate purpose of decentralization, all parties involved must have a mutual interest in solving the problem. In this case, the problem is lax fiscal administration at the local government level. Both the local government and MIC sides must agree to solve this problem. In the short term, the process should focus on preventing unwanted or universe spending. Such spending problems can result when there is a gap between those who benefit from the service provided and those who pay the taxes that finance those services. This gap can be eliminated with the full-fledged devolution of power from the central government to local governments.

Local government debt has been increasing rapidly since the mid 1990s. The outstanding total was about 27 trillion yen at the end of fiscal 2006. In addition to their own bonds, local governments need to partially repay local public enterprise bonds and borrowing that was used to fund LAT grants from the central government to the enterprises. Further, if local governments are also obliged to take on the debts of joint public-private ventures or local public corporations, they will face an even larger outstanding debt. This heavy debt obligation may be attributed to the lax spending that has routinely exceeded debt-repayment ability.

What is a proper local fiscal system to capture the merits of decentralization? Central Government should limit bond issuance by local governments that have insufficient repayment ability and abolish the LAT grant scheme. These two reforms are necessary to truly decentralize the current fiscal framework. The overall evaluation of the Trinity Reform Package is positive for three reasons. First, the existing revenue guarantee system is being fully revised and scaled down to reduce reliance on LAT grants. In particular, the ex-post addition of local bond-service expenditure to standard financial need has been eliminated. Second, taxation authority at the local level is being expanded to provide localities with a more sufficient base of tax revenues. Third, subsidies are being reformed.

However, the Trinity package has some shortcomings. First, it does not clearly set out local bond financing reforms, and neglecting problems in this area will result in unsuccessful decentralization. Many local governments receive LAT grants to repay their bonds. Thus, they effectively impose a bond-repayment burden on the national government. Solving this requires to enhance the taxation ability of local governments so as to let them repay the debts with their own tax revenue. It is also necessary to reduce reliance on national subsidies and to significantly scale down LAT-grant benefits. In other words, decentralization reform should involve four factors rather than three: local tax, LAT grants, national government disbursement, and local bonds.

The reform package specifies reform of LAT grants. However, it also states that "general revenue sources (that is, local taxes, local transfer taxes, LAT grants, and special local grants) should steadily account for a larger percentage at the local level." This entails preserving the LAT-grant scheme. In particular, because the special local grant is an exceptional measure to compensate for tax cuts at the national level, there is no need to change it. There is no necessity to enhance the general revenue of localities, including this subsidy. The reform package should involve raising the share of local taxes in total local revenue, rather than raising the share of general revenue. The latter might lead to half-hearted reform efforts regarding LAT grants.

Many argue that the decentralization process should include horizontal equality among regions. However, consideration of this type of equality is not important in the long run in seeking a proper local fiscal system. This is because equality among regions should be evaluated in terms of utility rather than in simple financial terms.

Because people seek higher utility levels by freely choosing a place to live, utility levels are equalized among regions in the long run, independently of the fiscal system's design. Residents obtain utility from non-monetary elements (for example, love for their home district) as well as monetary elements (for example, income and consumption). According to economic theory, even if there are differences in regional income, residents in low-income communities are compensated by their high utility from their love for their home district. So, if moving to another community means decreased utility, they will stay in the same community despite a lower income level. If moving will increase utility, they will move. Even if regional income differences appear, utility levels are actually equalized. This equality comes from voluntary migration, not from artificial fiscal measures.

Beyond maintaining the national minimum, equalizing revenue sources for every local government leads to inefficiency. If the government abolishes LAT grants, and successfully transfers necessary revenue sources to keep national-minimum services, there is no need to additionally adjust revenue sources among regions.

Still, policy-makers should not completely stop income re-distribution measures. However, such measures should focus on the circumstances of individual people, rather than on regions or industries. This is because income differences are, ultimately, a personal problem. There often is a correlation between personal income and an industry or region. A person in a depressed industry has a lower income, while a worker in a growing industry enjoys a higher income. However, policy-makers should avoid prioritizing industry- or region-based income redistribution measures over family or person-based redistribution.

Administrative costs are lower when focused on industries or regions. The central government provides generous LAT grants to Okinawa, where per capita income is the lowest. As a result, even rich Okinawa residents enjoy benefits. On the other hand, the central government does not provide funds to Tokyo, which has the highest per capita income. That means Tokyo residents making a small fraction of what some Okinawa residents make, receive no benefits. Such fiscal transfers have significantly pernicious effects, including a significant loss in economic welfare.

References

Asako, K, T Ito, and K Sakamoto (1991). The rise and fall of the deficit in Japan. *Journal of the Japanese and International Economies*, 5, pp. 451–472.

Doi, T and T Ihori (2002). Fiscal reconstruction and local interest groups in Japan. *Journal of the Japanese and International Economies*, 16(4), pp. 492–511.

Doi, T and T Hoshi (2002). Paying for the FILP. National Bureau of Economic Research Working Paper No. 9385. In *Structural Impediments to Growth in Japan*, M Blomström, J Corbett, F Hayashi and A Kashyap (eds.), University of Chicago Press.

Ihori, T, T Doi, and H Kondo (2001). Japanese fiscal reform: Fiscal reconstruction and fiscal policy. *Japan and the World Economy*, 13(4), pp. 351–370.

Ihori, T and J Itaya (2001). A dynamic model of fiscal reconstruction. *European Journal of Political Economy*, 17, pp. 779–797.

Ihori, T and J Itaya (2002). Fiscal reconstruction and local government financing. *International Taxation and Public Finance*, 17, pp. 1057–1097.

Ihori, T and H Kondo (2001). Efficiency of disaggregate public capital provision in Japan. *Public Finance and Management*, 1, pp. 161–182.

Ihori, T, T Nakazato, and M Kawade (2003). Japan's fiscal policies in the 1990s. *The World Economy*, 26, pp. 325–338.

Kornai, J (1979). Resource constrained versus demand constrained systems. *Econometrica*, 47, pp. 801–819.

Shibata, T (ed.) (1993). *Japan's public sector: How the government is financed*. University of Tokyo Press.

Chapter IV

China's Decentralization and Its Impact on Urbanization

XUEJIN ZUO

Shanghai Academy of Social Sciences

1. Introduction

Decentralization and central-local government relations have been the major theme of China's reform since its commencement in the late 1970s. The evolution of decentralization and central-local relations can be roughly divided into three phases.

Fiscal decentralization during early 1980–1993.

During this period, the major reform measures were to decentralize economic management from the government to the enterprises (then dominated by the state-owned enterprises), and from the central to local governments.[1] The rationale for decentralization was to promote growth in output and revenues by empowering the enterprises and local governments with greater autonomy and financial incentives. The decentralization strategy adopted was consistent with Deng Xiaoping's

[1] China's government hierarchy consists of five levels: the central government and the four levels of local governments, including provinces (provincial-level municipalities and autonomous regions), prefectures (prefecture-level cities), counties (county-level cities), and townships or towns. Therefore, "local" can be used interchangeably with "sub-national." This classification is somewhat different from that of the US government, which consists of federal, state and local governments.

strategy of "allowing some households and some regions to prosper first."[2] This new development strategy was based on the understanding that it would be difficult and inefficient, if possible at all, for China to carry out a more or less egalitarian and balanced development strategy.

Prior to the early 1980s, the fiscal system was highly centralized. All taxes and profits were remitted to the central government and then transferred back to the provinces according to expenditure needs approved by the Center. Fiscal decentralization allowed the local governments to share tax revenues with the center based on the case-by-case negotiated sharing scheme between the center and the provinces.[3] Similar sharing arrangements were also negotiated between the provincial-level and prefecture-level governments, between the prefecture-level and county-level governments, and between the county-level and township-level governments.[4]

The implementation of these revenue sharing schemes resulted in "two declines", that is, the decline of government revenues as a percentage of the GDP, and the decline of central revenues as a percentage of total government revenues.

Fiscal re-centralization during 1994–2002.

In order to reverse the undesired trend of central revenue decline, the Center initiated a new tax-sharing reform in 1994. The primary design of the new tax assignment system was to simplify the tax structure by reducing the number of taxes and using more unified tax rates, and to strengthen the Center's fiscal position. The Center assigned to its revenue 75 percent of the value-added tax (VAT) and 100 percent of

[2] Deng Xiaoping first mentioned in 1978 the strategy of allowing some regions and some people to prosper first, and then encourage their neighborhood households and regions to follow them to achieve common prosperity. This strategy was re-stated in his talks later.

[3] Fiscal decentralization was first introduced to 1980–1984, when a revenue-sharing system between the central and provincial governments was adopted for 15 provinces and autonomous regions. The sharing scheme was updated for 1985–87 and 1988–93 respectively. The last scheme was originally designed for the period 1988–90. It was extended to 1993 with some modifications since the center was not able to find a satisfactory replacement of the scheme. In spite of these modifications, the basic principle of these sharing schemes remained unchanged until the new tax-sharing reform in 1994.

[4] For more detailed description about China's fiscal decentralization, see Bahl and Wallich (1992), Wong (1995) and Wong, Heady and Woo (1995).

consumer tax, in addition to custom duties, and income taxes of central government-owned enterprises etc. The local fixed revenues included business taxes, corporate income tax of local-owned enterprises and their remitted profits, personal income taxes, and several categories of insignificant local taxes, *plus* 25 percent of VAT. Furthermore, to overcome the avoidance behavior of local governments, the new system instituted the central tax bureaus to collect the center's own revenue.

This reform was effective as the share of central revenue in the total revenues gradually expanded, eventually stabilizing at a level of over 50 percent in recent years (see Table 1). However, as the local expenditures accounted for nearly three quarters of total expenditures, there has been a growing vertical fiscal imbalance between the Center and the local governments. Note from Table 1 that in 2005 local governments accounted for nearly three quarters of expenditures but less than half of revenues. Inter-governmental transfers have not filled the financing gap in every case. It was quite common that in poor rovinces, local governments, especially at the lower levels such as county-level and township-level governments, suffered from fiscal deficits.

While this period emphasized fiscal re-centralization, the local governments continued to enjoy adequate autonomy in promoting growth, carrying out industrial and urban development projects, and attracting investments including foreign direct investment (FDI).[5] Some argued that the active involvement of local governments in economic development was one of the most important explanations for China's sustained high growth (Hong and Cao, 1996; Qian and Weigast, 1997). However, these growth-oriented policies led to the disparities between urban and rural areas, coastal and hinterland regions, the social and economic dimensions of development, and production and environmental protection. This has led the central government to direct its development strategy toward more balanced growth.

---

[5] In addition to budgetary funds, local governments also received "extra-budgetary funds", which were not subject to sharing, and "off-budgetary funds", which were not even reported in the fiscal statistics. For instance, proceeds from the lease of land are usually controlled by the local "Development and Reform Commission" rather than the financial bureau.

Table 1. Central and Local Revenues and Expenditures, Selected Years 1978–2005

	Revenues			Expenditures		
Year	Nation (Y billion)	Central (%)	Local (%)	Nation (Y billion)	Central (%)	Local (%)
1978	113.23	15.5	84.5	112.21	47.4	52.6
1980	115.99	24.5	75.5	122.88	54.3	45.7
1985	200.48	38.4	61.6	200.43	39.7	60.3
1989	266.49	30.9	69.1	282.38	31.5	68.5
1990	293.71	33.8	66.2	308.36	32.6	67.4
1991	314.95	29.8	70.2	338.66	32.2	67.8
1992	348.34	28.1	71.9	374.22	31.3	68.7
1993	434.90	22.0	78.0	464.23	28.3	71.7
1994	521.81	55.7	44.3	579.26	30.3	69.7
1995	624.22	52.2	47.8	682.37	29.2	70.8
1996	740.80	49.4	50.6	793.76	27.1	72.9
1997	865.11	48.9	51.1	923.36	27.4	72.6
1998	987.60	49.5	50.5	1079.82	28.9	71.1
1999	1144.41	51.1	48.9	1318.77	31.5	68.5
2000	1339.52	52.2	47.8	1588.65	34.7	65.3
2001	1638.60	52.4	47.6	1890.26	30.5	69.5
2002	1890.36	55.0	45.0	2205.32	30.7	69.3
2003	2171.53	54.6	45.4	2465.00	30.1	69.9
2004	2639.65	54.9	45.1	2848.69	27.7	72.3
2005	3164.93	52.3	47.7	3393.03	25.9	74.1

Notes:
1. Central and local revenues are calculated before taking account of inter-governmental transfers.
2. Revenues do not include domestic and foreign borrowing.
3. National expenditures before 2000 do not include expenditures for repayment of principal and interest on domestic and foreign debt, and the expenditures on basic construction projects funded by domestic and foreign borrowing. Since 2000 these data do include expenditures for interest payments on domestic and foreign debt.
Sources: *China Statistical Yearbook, 2006*.

Central government's tightened discipline and control on local governments (2003–present).

To ensure the implementation of the newly proposed "scientific perception on development" and to pursue the target of a "socialist harmonious society", the central government has reinforced its *macro-economic control* over local industrial and development projects, especially those projects involving the use of large acreage of land.[6] Nevertheless, the local governments' incentives for promoting a high rate of GDP growth remain strong. To a large extent, the institutions and policy practices which lay the foundation for such incentives have remained untouched.

Decentralization has deeply affected China's urbanization, urban development and governance. The goal in this paper is to investigate the impact of China's decentralization and the changing central-local government relations on urbanization. After this introduction, Section 2 discusses the trends of China's urbanization. Section 3 analyzes how decentralization has affected the spatial expansion and the development of China's urban places. Section 4 studies the causes of such fast expansion. Section 5 intends to investigate the impact of decentralization on rural-urban migration and explain why urban population growth has lagged behind urban spatial expansion. Section 6 analyzes why local governments try to control in-migration. The final section provides concluding remarks and policy suggestions.

2. The Trend of Urbanization

The national population census data revealed that the share of urban population rose from about 18 percent of the total population to 36 percent between the 1964 and 2000 census.[7] The pace of urbanization was slow during 1964–90, with an increase of less than 8 percentage points over the 26 years. By comparison, urbanization accelerated during 1990–2000, as urban population increased from over 26 percent of the total population to just over 36 percent, an increase of nearly 10 percentage points. Furthermore, the One-Percent Population Survey in 2005 reported that urban population increased to 43 percent of the total (see Table 2).

---

[6] The current wave of macro-economic control ("*hongguan jinji tiaokong*" or simply "*hongquan tiaokong*") was initiated in March 2004, after the very high growth rates in investment in the first quarter of 2004 and in 2003 were observed. The central government has adopted contractionary policies to cool down over heated investments, of which many were made at the local level. The administrative measures focus on the tightened bank credits, and more restrictive administrative control over the conversion of agricultural land into industrial and urban use.

[7] Five censuses have been conducted in China: 1953, 1964, 1982, 1990 and 2000. Between censuses, one-percent population surveys were conducted in 1987, 1995 and 2005.

Table 2. Total Population and the Percent Urban as Reported by the Population Census and Survey Data

	1953	1964	1982	1990	2000	2005
Total population (million)	582.6	694.58	1,008.18	1,133.68	1,265.83	1,306.28
Urban %	13.26	18.30	20.60	26.23	36.09	42.99
Average increase in percent urban	—	0.46	0.13	0.70	0.99	1.38

Source: *China Statistical Yearbook, 2006*. The 2005 data were collected from the 2005 one-percent population survey, all the other were from the five population censuses.

It is true that the increased rural-urban mobility has contributed to the faster pace of urbanization. However, we should notice that the urbanization data as reported by census are subject to several qualifications.

2.1. *Qualifications to Urbanization Data: Definitional Changes*

One major issue is how to count the non-registered migrants called "floating population" living in urban places. The 1990 census defined that those non-registered migrants who had stayed at the urban residence for *one year or longer* by the reference date of the census as urban. In the 2000 census this required period of residence was shortened to *six months or longer*. Therefore, rural migrants who had stayed at the urban residence for six months or longer but less than one year were counted as urban by the 2000 census definition, but would have been counted as rural by the 1990 census definition. In addition, the 1990 census used the county as the boundary of migration; that is, only those moves across the county boundary could be regarded as migration. The 2000 census used township/town as the boundary of migration.[8]

[8] Some definitional changes regarding urban places were also made. For more details regarding changes made in the 2000 Census, see NBSC (1999) and Duan & Sun (2006). For a brief description of the evolution of definitional changes regarding urban places in the past five censuses, see Zhou and Yu (2002).

In general, the 2000 census had a looser definition of urban population than the 1990 census. Zhou and Yu (2002) estimated by extrapolation that if the old definition had applied, then the level of urbanization in 2000 would have been 31.14%, or 4.17% points lower that the officially reported figure. The point here is not to argue that the new definition adopted by the 2000 census is an inappropriate measurement of the level of urbanization, but rather to emphasize that such definitional changes tend to overstate *the pace of urbanization* during 1990–2000.

2.2. *About "Floating Population" in Urban Places*

Since the mid-1980s, the scale and the significance of rural-urban mobility have increased, and so has the consequent increase of floating population as a component of urban population. For instance, the 2005 population survey reported a floating population of 147.35 million persons, accounting for about 11 percent of the country's total population. Over three quarters of the floating population are rural-urban migrants, implying that in 2005, over 110 million floating population of rural origin were included in 561.57 million urban population. This is equivalent to nearly 20 percent of the total urban population. Nevertheless, the same data source revealed that nearly half of the total migrants had left home for only three years or less, about 70 percent of the migrants had left home for five years or less (NBSC, 2006), indicating that most migrants stay only temporarily in urban destinations.

Although temporary migration is quite common in developing countries, it is more predominant in China due to the special institutional constraints on migrants' permanent stay in cities. For most migrants, migration is more an event in a certain stage of life cycle than a lifelong one. It is apparent that enumeration of all rural migrants as urban tends to over-estimate the size of urban population or the level of urbanization.

In the reform era, peasants are allowed to move to towns and cities to seek jobs, and as noted above, once they have stayed at an urban place for one year (1990 census) or six months (2000 census), they are counted as urban. As compared with the situation of the planned era, when long-term rural-urban mobility was generally prohibited, peasants are enjoying more opportunities to migrate. Nonetheless, the past migration-restricting policies have been replaced by "migrant policies" aiming at discriminating against non-registered migrants to protect the "urban privilege" of local registered residents. Urban entitlement to formal employment, social services and welfare programs is largely based on urban household registration. Rural migrants are generally not entitled to these services, because they cannot change their place of registration, no matter how long they have lived in an urban place. This segmentation between the registered households and non-registered "floating" households in cities is in fact a mirror image of the profound rural-urban divide in the country.[9]

We can also estimate the size of floating population by studying the difference between the urban population and "non-agricultural households." According to the 2005 survey data, urban population accounted for about 43 percent of the total population, while "non-agricultural households" accounted for about 32 percent of the total. Assuming that all non-agricultural households were living in urban areas, then the difference of the two, 11 percent of the 1,306.28 million total population, or about 143 million, would be migrants living at urban places but with agricultural household registration status.

2.3. *Peasants Turning into Urban Residents Through Land Acquisition*

Spatial expansion of urban areas often involves the acquisition of farmland from the affected rural collectives and households by the government. Most affected peasants get non-agricultural (or urban) household registration status after their farmland has been acquired.

---

[9] Some social phenomenon observed only in China is rooted in this unique institutional arrangement. For instance, due to difficult access to social services in cities, such as schooling of their children, most peasant workers came to cities alone or with only their spouses, leaving their children to live with their grandparents at home villages. This has led to an immense number of rural children waiting at home villages ("*liushou ertong*"). Since tens of millions of peasant workers go back to their home village to reunion with their family members during the Chinese New Year season, every year there is a "spring wave of transportation" ("*chunyun chao*") which causes over-crowding of transportation facilities.

Nevertheless, it is quite common that their entitlement to urban employment and social services is not upgraded to the same level of their urban household counterparts. For instance, in Shanghai those peasants affected by land acquisition are covered by a specially designed social insurance program, the so-called "social insurance for residents in towns" ("*zhenbao*"), which carries a substantially lower level of benefits as compared with the social insurance programs for urban workers and staff ("*chengbao*"). Although many of these peasant households were counted as urban after land acquisition, their transformation to urban residents has not been completed. They are more like the bats swinging between the urban birds and the rural beasts.

The very aggressive spatial expansion of urban places has something to do with China's local government's autonomy, incentives and land institutions.

3. Decentralization and Spatial Expansion of Urban Places

Decentralization empowers local governments with a higher degree of autonomy in urban planning and construction; acquiring land for urban infrastructure, industrial and real estate development projects; and making local industrial policies. Their local government counterparts in many other countries do not have the same level of power. This level of discretion has not been eliminated or weakened by the 1994 tax-sharing reform which aimed at re-centralizing fiscal revenues. Since Deng Xiaoping's speech during his tour to Southern provinces of China in 1992, the enthusiasm of local governments to promote growth had been greatly revived.

As shown in Table 3, the total volume of urban investments increased rapidly in the past decade. China's total investment in fixed assets almost quadrupled from just over 2 trillion to nearly 7.7 trillion. In addition, both urban investments and investments in urban real estate development accounted for larger shares in the total investment. During 2000–05, they grew at the high rate of 22–26 percent per annum.

In the early years of the reform, the limited investments in urban areas were largely allocated to industrial projects. In early 1990s, however,

Table 3. Total Investment in Fixed Assets, and the Share of Urban Investment and Urban Real Estate Development

Year	Total (Y Billion)	Urban (%)	Real Estate Dev. (%)
1995	2001.9	78.1	15.7
1996	2291.4	76.7	14.0
1997	2494.1	77.0	12.7
1998	2840.6	79.2	12.7
1999	2985.5	79.5	13.7
2000	3291.8	79.7	15.1
2001	3721.4	80.6	17.0
2002	4350.0	81.6	17.9
2003	5556.7	82.4	18.3
2004	7047.7	83.8	18.7
2005	7680.7	84.3	17.2
Average annual growth 1995–2000	10.5	10.9	9.6
Ibid. 2000–05 (%)	21.9	23.4	26.1

Source: *China Statistical Yearbook, 2006*.

some new practices of local governments, for example, Dalian City's successful experience in the development of urban infrastructure, from grass fields to big public squares, and Shanghai's experience in leasing out land for fees, have altered the landscape of urban investment. The investment extended from industrial projects to the development of urban infrastructure and real estate, and the sources of financing extended from fiscal appropriations and bank loans to land leasing fees and investments from outside the city (both domestic and foreign). The fast growth of investment in urban places has led to a fast expansion of urban space over this period, as reported in Table 4.

The spatial expansion of the three provincial level municipalities (Beijing, Tianjin and Shanghai) and the capital cities of the 26 provinces are shown, in descending order by their growth rate. We can see that the top 8 cities (with growth rate higher than 8 percent per annum) are

Table 4. The Spatial Expansion of Chinese Cities, 1991–2005

City	Macro Region	Developed Areas (sq km) 1991	2005	Growth 1991–2005 (%)	Average Annual Growth Rate (%)
Urban total		13792	24529	77.8	4.2
Chengdu	W	85	396	365.9	11.6
Hangzhou	E	72	314	336.1	11.1
Guangzhou	E	182	735	303.8	10.5
Nanjing	E	131	513	291.6	10.2
Fuzhou	E	51	170	233.3	9.0
Shanghai	E	254	820	222.8	8.7
Hefei	M	72	225	212.5	8.5
Beijing	E	397	1182	197.7	8.1
Urumqi	W	65	176	170.8	7.4
Haikou	E	29	77	165.5	7.2
Yinchuan	W	39	95	143.6	6.6
Nanning	W	70	170	142.9	6.5
Jinan	E	105	238	126.7	6.0
Zhengzhou	M	117	262	123.9	5.9
Changchun	M	114	231	102.6	5.2
Kunming	W	98	193	96.9	5.0
Hohhot	W	73	143	95.9	4.9
Shijiazhuang	E	85	166	95.3	4.9
Harbin	M	156	302	93.6	4.8
Nanchang	M	65	109	67.7	3.8
Shenyang	E	16	310	66.7	3.7
Xi'an	W	11	231	63.8	3.6
Tianjin	E	336	530	57.7	3.3
Guiyang	W	85	129	51.8	3.0
Lanzhou	W	107	161	50.5	3.0
Changsha	M	101	148	46.5	2.8
Xining	W	52	64	23.1	1.5
Taiyuan	M	168	197	17.3	1.1
Wuhan	M	191	220	15.2	1.0

Source: *China Urban Statistical Yearbook 1992 and 2006*.

predominantly located in coastal provinces, and the bottom 10 cities (with growth rates lower than 4 percent per annum) are predominantly cities in the middle and western regions.[10]

The large investment in urban areas has greatly improved the infrastructure of China's cities. Nevertheless, the marginal returns to such investments are inevitably diminishing. It is important for the Chinese cities to make the investment more efficient.

4. An Analysis on the Causes of Fast Expansion of China's Cities

The fast expansion of China's cities can be attributed to, in addition to the high degree of autonomy of the urban local government in promoting growth/urban development and fiscal decentralization, the city's jurisdiction over counties ("*shi guan xian*"), and their land policies.

The special administrative system in China, the so-called "city jurisdiction over counties" grants the cities jurisdictional power over the surrounding counties. This system made the spatial expansion of cities administratively more convenient. The urban local governments all have strong incentives to pursue rapid economic growth, and the conversion of low-productivity agricultural land into more productive urban or industrial use is readily available to promote growth and generate more revenue.

China's special arrangements concerning the ownership of land helps the urban local governments turn their expansion aspirations into action plans. Under the present land institution in China, all urban land is owned by the state (in fact, it is at the disposal of the various levels of governments), and all rural land is owned by the rural collectives. In the case of land-using development projects, only the government has the authority to acquire land from rural collectives and convert the agricultural land into

[10] In terms of geographic location and level of socio-economic development, China's provinces can be divided into three macro regions. The eastern region consist of Beijing, Tianjin, Shanghai, Hebei, Liaoning, Jiangsu, Zhejiang, Fujian, Shandong, Guangdong, Guangxi and Hainan. The middle region consists of Shanxi, Inner-Mongolia, Jilin, Heilongjiang, Anhui, Jiangxi, Henan, Hubei and Hunan. The western region consists of Chongqing, Sichuan, Guizhou, Yunnan, Tibet, Shaanxi, Gansu, Ningxia and Xinjiang. In the strategic development of the western region, Inner-Mongolia and Guangxi were re-classified into the western region, so that the relevant favorable policies can be applied to them.

urban use. The rural collectives and peasant households are compensated based on the value of agricultural yields of the land, the cost of resettlement and compensation for the buildings and crops on the land, rather than according to the productivity of the future non-agriculture use of the land.[11] This (inadequate) financial compensation is often supplemented by job placement for the affected peasants, and upgrading their household registration status from agricultural to non-agricultural. However, the further development of the market economy made such non-financial measures difficult to sustain. For example, the state or collective enterprises employing the affected peasants may go bankrupt, or these peasants may be laid off due to financial difficulties of their employers.

In spite of all these compensation problems and the resistance from the affected peasants, the local governments continue to acquire land from peasants. Obviously, such an arrangement for land administration and policy implies that the local governments can acquire farmland at the much lower costs than the prices at which they lease out to investors/developers.

In fact, the under-pricing of agricultural land inevitably leads to inefficient and even wasteful use of the scarce land resources in China. Studies find in newly developed areas of cities too many redundant industrial parks, public squares, etc,[12] which are made at the price of creating about 35 million landless peasants (Chen, 2005).

Since 2003, the central authority has called for a "scientific perception of development" and the social target of building a harmonious society. In order to achieve these targets, the Center has strengthened macro-economic controls over local investments, especially over those land-using projects. More restrictive measures have been taken to protect farmland, to evaluate and control the local investment projects, to reduce the number and the size of industrial parks, and to curb the over investment and over expansion of urban places. These macro-economic control measures so far have failed to achieve their targets well, since

[11] For more details, see to the "Land Administration Law of the Peoples Republic of China," second revision approved by the 11th meeting of Standing Committee of the National People's Congress in August 28, 2004. This law is available at the website "xinhuanet.com."

[12] For the criticism on the over expansion of urban places made by Academician Lu Dadao, see the report on the *Southern Weekend* (Zhang 2007).

the institutions which provide local governments with strong incentives to promote growth and expansion have remained in place. Of these institutions, the most important ones are the land ownership and the evaluation of local government's performance. A thorough solution to the problem of over-expansion of urban places must include elimination of such incentives for over expansion.

5. Decentralization and Its Impact on Rural-Urban Migration and Urban Growth

It is surprising to see that urban expansion has not led to a faster growth of urban population. In fact, the population living in cities, especially big cities, has grown much slower than the spatial expansion of cities. For instance, during 2000–05, the size of urban developed areas (or urban built-up area)[13] in the 31 provinces grew by nearly 45 percent, whereas urban population (including non-registered long-term migrants) grew by only 22.5%. As a consequence, the urban population density, defined as urban population divided by urban developed areas, decreased by more than one-seventh over the same period (see Table 5).

Table 5. Growth in Developed Areas, Urban Population and Urban Density in the Three Macro Regions, 2000–05

	Growth During 2000–05 (%)		
Macro Region	Developed Area	Urban Population	Urban Density
National total	44.9	22.5	–15.5
Eastern region	63.7	19.0	–27.3
Middle region	23.4	19.0	–3.6
Western region	37.7	21.7	–11.6

Notes: Calculated from urban developed areas and urban population in 2000 and 2005.
Source: *China Statistical Yearbook 2001 and 2006*.

[13] In China, the countryside is included in the administrative boundary of a city. The developed area or built-up area of a city (*chengshi jiancheng qu*) is used to denote the area with developed urban infrastructure.

From the perspectives of development economics, the eastern region may be assumed reasonably to have the highest urban population growth rate, since its faster growth and prosperity would absorb the largest number of peasant migrants from all over the country.

Nevertheless, China's experience in the past five years did not follow this assumption, as urban permanent population (including the long-term migrants) grew slower in the eastern region than in either the middle or the western regions. Together with the much faster expansion of the developed areas in the region, the density of urban population in the eastern region decreased the most (well over a quarter) compared with the slight decrease in the middle region (less than 4 percent) and the western region (over one-ninth). In addition, as mentioned earlier, long-term rural migrants are already included in the permanent urban population, even though their household registration remains at their rural origin. In contrast to the experiences in most developing countries where rural-urban migration is the most powerful force driving urbanization, China's empirical data reveal that in recent years, in spite of the enormous size of the *stock* of floating population in cities, the *flow* of rural-urban migration can explain only a tiny component of urban growth.

The 2005 survey reported that between the 2000 census and the 2005 survey, urban population increased by 104.73 million. Of this increment, the increase in floating population accounted for only 2.96 million or less than 3 percent (Cui, 2006). Taking into account the fact that natural growth of urban population can explain less than 15 million of this increment,[14] we can conclude that the spatial expansion of urban places, including the re-classification of rural places as urban, is the more predominant explanation of this increase.

The old strategy of urban development was to contain the development of large cities and favor the development of small cities. This has been replaced by the new strategy to emphasize promoting urbanization and coordinating the development of large, medium-sized and small

[14] The 2005 population survey found that the overall population growth rate was about 0.6%. Since urban fertility has been much lower than rural fertility, natural growth rate of urban population is much lower than rural. Even if we apply the natural growth rate of 0.6% per annum to urban population, the natural growth of urban population would have been about 3 percent of urban population.

cities.[15] However, the practice of urban local governments to restrict in-migrants' employment and access to social services has remained in place. Such administrative measures are more common in mega cities such as Beijing and Shanghai than in smaller cities. The World Bank (2004) reported that in China the population in urban agglomeration of more than one million increased from 13 percent of the total population in 1980 to only 14 percent in 2000, while the population in the largest city as percent of urban population fell from 6 to only 3 percent.

6. Causes for Urban Local Governments to Control In-migration

The profound rural-urban divide is rooted in China's institutional arrangement and policy practice, such as local government's strong incentives to pursue a high growth rate in per-capita GDP, and local governments' primary responsibility to finance social security and social welfare programs.

Since the early 1990s, per-capita GDP growth has served as the most important indicator to evaluate the local government's performance. Assuming a production function with constant returns to scale, it is easy to show that per-capita output is a function increasing with per-worker capital endowment, or capital-labor ratio. Therefore, it is economically rational for an urban local government to try to attract more investments from outside (including FDI) to increase the numerator of capital-labor ratio, while in the mean time restraining the in-flow of migration to prevent the denominator from increasing. Unfortunately, it is also easy to prove that the solutions to maximize local per-capita GDP will not maximize the per-capita GDP for the country as a whole, since any migration from less productive areas (industries) to more

[15] In 1980, the State Council issued a document with the summary of the meeting of national urban planning. The document agrees with the strategy proposed by the meeting to "control the size of large cities, to appropriately develop the medium-sized cities and to actively develop the small cities," and asked localities and ministries to follow this strategy. But in the later practice, due to the difficulties in utilizing the positive effects of agglomeration and economy of scale, and the lack of growth potential in small cities, this strategy was not well implemented. In the later documents, such as the 10th and 11th five-year plans for economic and social development, the new strategy emphasized the coordinated development between the large, medium-sized cities and small cities.

productive areas (industries) always increases the country's total output, as the marginal gain (approximately the per-capital GDP at the place of destination) of such migration will surpass its marginal cost (approximately the per-capital GDP at the place of origin).

In addition to pursuing a high per-capita GDP growth rate, the decentralized financing of social services, social security and welfare programs provides local government with another incentive to contain rural-urban migration. When the social security and welfare programs were restructured in the 1990s, the basic principle of "locality management" (*shudi guangli*) was adopted. "Locality" in most cases means prefecture-level cities (prefectures) or county-level cities (counties). Given the substantial income disparities across and within provinces, the conventional wisdom underlying the original design of these highly decentralized social security and welfare programs is understandable. Nevertheless, it may not have been expected that these programs would become a barrier to spatial and social mobility of laborers. This is largely due to the fact that the social insurance programs for urban workers and staff are heavily subsidized by the urban local government, and are too expensive for laborers working in the small private enterprises, especially those low-wage peasant workers, to participate.[16] Some other social services, to which only registered urban households are entitled, include public schooling beyond 9-year compulsory education, better opportunities for university education, and access to urban income maintenance programs (*dibao*).

Since 2003, to pursue the "scientific perception on development," and to build a harmonious society, the Center has encouraged cities to

[16] The major social insurance programs in urban areas consist of the public pension program and the social health insurance program for urban workers and staff. These programs are designed to have two components, the social pooling account and the individual saving account. The former is not portable when workers move across localities. As the benefits of public pension programs tend to be generous for retirees, the contribution rate is very high by any international standard. The employer enterprises are required to contribute 20 percent of the total payroll to the public pension program alone, and employees are required to contribute 8 percent of their wage rate. In spite of the high contribution rate, the public pension program suffers from huge deficits and is subsidized by the central and local governments. For instance, in 2007, the government subsidies to the urban public pension program amounted to over Y100 billion. It is projected that such subsidies will continue to grow in the future due to the increasing dependency ratio; that is, the ratio of retirees to the working employees.

be more open to peasant workers, and required urban local governments to provide peasant workers with social services, for instance, the schooling of their children, and allowing them to get urban household registration once they have a stable job and housing in the urban place.[17] Nevertheless, to ensure a more effective implementation of these new initiatives, it is imperative to change the above-mentioned migration-affecting institutions and policies.

7. Concluding Remarks and Policy Suggestions

Decentralization and local autonomy can play a positive role in promoting growth and spatial expansion of urban areas in China. They also can restrain rural-urban migration, and hence make spatial expansion less efficient and productive.

Since the time of the Asian Financial Crisis in 1997, the sluggish domestic demand has become, for the first time, an important issue of macro-economic management in China. The transition from a supply-driven economy to demand-driven economy has drawn more attention to the impact of policies which restrain migration and the consequent under-urbanization. Under-urbanization, in turn, has led to problems such as an abnormally large rural-urban disparity, the poverty of rural households and hence the sluggish domestic consumption demand; and the under-development of the service sector. As a result of weak domestic consumption demand, the country's growth has relied more on investments and exports, leading to an imbalance between consumption and investment, and between the domestic and external sectors.

By the end of 2005, agriculture still accounted for nearly 45 percent of China's total employment, but only 12.5% of GDP. Urban per-capita household income was over threefold that of rural households. These statistics point out why it is now less controversial to argue that policy measures should be taken to accelerate rural-urban migration and urbanization. In order to achieve this goal, further reform initiatives should be taken to induce changes in the incentives and behavior of urban local governments.

[17] For more details, see the resolution of the Third Plenary Session of the 16th Central Committee of the CCP, "Several Issues on the Perfection of the System of Socialist Market Economy" and "The Outline of the 11th Five-Year Plan for Economic and Social Development." Both documents are available at the website of People's Daily.

A first step would be to reduce the weight given to the growth in local per-capita GDP as an indicator of the local government performance. This is because it provides the local government officials with a strong incentive to curb in-migration or prevent peasant workers from being registered at their urban place of residence.

The present land administration and ownership arrangements provide urban local governments with strong incentives to convert agricultural land to non-agricultural use in what might be an inefficient or wasteful way. This arrangement allows local government to pursue higher per-capita local GDP or fiscal revenues through simply leasing out the land to investors or developers. The direction of the needed reform is to mandate a more complete financial compensation for the land acquired. "Complete financial compensation" here means the fair market prices that reflect the scarcity of the land in the location. This would reduce the profit of the local governments in land trading. Furthermore, once the conversion of agricultural land into non-agricultural use is based on the market price, then the direct involvement of local governments in the land-using commercial development projects would become unnecessary. The government, however, should protect the farmland resources by planning and administering the size, geographic distribution and pace of the conversion of agricultural land into non-agricultural use.[18]

The locality pooling of social security programs serves as another incentive for the urban local governments to control in-migration and in-migrants' access to these programs. Therefore, the basic level of social security programs financing should be upgraded to national pooling, so that in-migration would not cause an extra financial burden

---

[18] In fact, the government's control over the land use is quite common in many other countries, such as in the United States, Canada, Japan and Korea. In China, the legislation about the state control over the land use was first introduced in the 1998 amended "land Administration Law," and was re-confirmed in the 2004 amended Law. The Law mandates that governments of various levels make the land-use plans, which should specify the use of land by three categories, namely, the agricultural land, land for construction use (*jianshe yongdi*) and un-used land. The lower level government's land-use plan should be consistent with that of the higher level government. In particular, the amount of land for construction use specified in the local government's land use plan cannot exceed the quota assigned by the higher level government's plan, and the amount of agricultural land specified in the local government's land use plan cannot be smaller than the amount assigned by the higher level government's plan.

to local governments. The public pension program, for example, should have a national pooling at the first pillar, and differentials in income level and preference can be accommodated in the second and third pillars.[19]

Moreover, the concept of urban entitlement or urban privilege should be phased out. This might be done gradually in order to ensure that such change is smooth and financially sustainable. Finally, the day should come when China includes in her constitution the right to free migration. Without this, it would be impossible to achieve a unified market economy and harmonious society.

References

Bahl, R and C Wallich (1992). Intergovernmental fiscal relations in China. World Bank Policy Research Papers, WPS 863, the World Bank.

Chen X (2004) [in Chinese]. Preface. In *China's Urbanization: Peasants, Land and Urban Development*, P Lou (ed.) Beijing: China Economic Press.

Cui H (2006) [in Chinese]. Migrants and floating population continued to increase in our country. In *China Population Statistics Yearbook, 2006*, NBSC, Department of Population and Employment Statistics. Beijing: China Statistics Press.

Deng X (2001) [in Chinese]. Emancipate our thinking, seeking truth from the fact and unite as one looking to the future. In *Selections from Deng Xiaoping, Vol. 2*. Beijing: People Press.

Duan C and Y Sun (2006) [in Chinese]. The historical change in the definition of China's floating population. In *Population Research*, Vol. 4, pp. 70–76.

Hong Y and Y Cao (1996) [in Chinese]. The Function of Local Governments during the Period of Economic System Transition. Beijing: *Economic Research,* Vol. 5.

NBSC (2001) [in Chinese]. *China Statistical Yearbook, 2001*. Beijing: China Statistics Press.

[19] The pension system can consist of three components or pillars. The first pillar is the compulsory state-run public pension which offers basic coverage focusing on subsistence needs. The second pillar is the voluntary private pension, usually defined-contribution accounts/plans funded by individuals. The third pillar is the personal savings plans, insurance, etc. China's current pension system for urban workers and staff is somewhat similar to the above-mentioned three-pillar system, except for that (1) the first pillar is financed and administered at the locality level, rather than at the national level, and; (2) the second pillar is operated by the local governments, rather than the private pension funds or other specialized fund management firms.

——— (2002) [in Chinese]. *China Urban Statistical Yearbook, 2002*. Beijing: China Statistics Press.

——— (2006a) [in Chinese]. *China Statistical Yearbook, 2006*. Beijing: China Statistics Press.

——— (2006b) [in Chinese]. *China Urban Statistical Yearbook, 2006*. Beijing: China Statistics Press.

——— (1999) [in Chinese]. "Rules about Statistical Classification of Urban and Rural Places," NBSC Document No. [1999] 114, available at the website of the NBSC.

Qian Y and B R Weingast (1997). Federalism as a Commitment to Perserving Market Incentives. In *Journal of Economic Perspectives*, 11(4), pp. 83–92.

Qin Y and F Cong (2007) [in Chinese]. The household registration system creating 20 million rural "home alone" children, to whom the central leadership paying great attention. In Beijing: *Banyue Tan*.

Wong, C (ed.) (1995). Financing local government in the People's Republic of China. Asian Development Bank: Report prepared for the Ministry of Finance under TA 2118-PRC: Study of Sub-provincial Fiscal Relations.

Wong, C, C Heady, and W T Woo (1995). *Fiscal Management and Economic Reform in the People's Republic of China*. Published by Oxford University Press for Asian Development Bank.

World Bank (2004). *World Development Indicators, 2004*. Copyrighted material of the World Bank.

Zhang L (2007) [in Chinese]. The leading expert submitting reports several times to the State Council, expressing concerns over "Great leap forward" in urbanization. In Guangzhou: *Southern Weekend*.

Zhou Y and H Yu (2002) [in Chinese]. A proposal to re-estimate statistics on China's urbanization based on the 2000 Census data. In *Statistical Research*. Beijing, Vol. 4, pp. 44–47.

Chapter V

Fiscal Federalism in India — Trends and Reform

M. GOVINDA RAO

National Institute of Public Finance and Policy,
New Delhi, India

Fiscal arrangements in India's quasi-federal system need to be restructured to meet the challenges of transition from plan to market. The liberalization and opening up of the economy has led to a sharp increase in regional inequalities, and has made transparent many of the inefficiencies in the current system. This paper addresses some of the issues of reform in fiscal arrangements in the changed context.

The analysis brings out some important shortcomings in the fiscal assignment and inter-governmental transfer system. It shows that the transfer system has failed to achieve its objectives due to a lack of coordination among a multiplicity of agencies and to improper design. This paper also analyzes the progress in achieving sub-state decentralization after 1992 when Constitutional amendments recognized the third level of government in rural and urban areas. The analysis shows that the attempt to decentralize the fiscal system below the State level has not been very successful. Based on this research, we explore, reform options in both policies and institutions, that might make the fiscal system more responsive to the changing environment.

1. Introduction

Trends in the design and implementation aspects of fiscal arrangements in India have been heavily influenced by four factors. First, India is the most populated federation and in the world. There are specific problems that come with decentralization in such a large country, so there is much to learn from the India experience. Second, India is implementing market-based reforms in a multilevel framework that involves many difficult issues of co-ordination and sequencing. Third, Indian experience shows how apparently contradictory features like developmental planning, market development and fiscal decentralization can be combined. Finally, India's experience with asymmetrical federalism — of accommodating diverse social, religious, linguistic and ethnic groups, protecting the interest of minorities and catering to the needs of people in atypical regions — can provide useful lessons for designing intergovernmental systems.

The adoption of market oriented reforms since 1991 has redefined the role of the State and this has necessitated a re-examination of fiscal arrangements between different levels of government. In fact, there have been opposing forces at work. While on the one hand, the transition from central planning and market-based resource allocation has enhanced the role of sub-national governments in delivering social and physical infrastructure, the trend of increasing regional inequalities has necessitated a greater central role (Rao *et al.*, 1998). Although after several years, India has been able to bring down the fiscal deficit considerably, off budget liabilities continue to be a problem and more importantly, the infrastructure deficit and its wide inter-State differences pose serious challenges.

There are other important factors which make the analysis of decentralization in Indian federalism interesting: One is the statutory recognition of the third tier of government subsequent to the 73rd and 74th Constitutional amendment in 1992. The introduction of the third tier of fiscal authority (local government) has met with varying degrees of success in delivering public services in different States. Another is that there are important political issues to be factored into India's progress toward fiscal decentralization. The institutional environment for the delivery of services has significantly changed with the advent of a coalition of parties in power at the Central level and with the emergence of regional parties in the States as partners in Central coalitions.

This paper is organized in five sections. Section 2 gives a brief account of the evolution and structure of Indian federalism. Tax and expenditure assignments and their implications for vertical and horizontal fiscal imbalances are examined in Section 3. Fiscal imbalances in Indian federalism are analysed in Section 4. The design of general purpose and specific purpose transfers from the Center to the States are analyzed in Section 5. The salient features of inter-governmental transfer systems in India are summarized in the concluding section.

2. Evolution of Indian Federalism

India represents a classical federation with Constitutional demarcation of functions and finances between the Union[1] and the States. The billion people in the federation are spread over 28 States and 7 Centrally administered territories (two of which have their own elected governments). Separate legislative, executive and judicial arms of government are constituted at both the Central and State levels. The upper house or *Rajya Sabha* in the Parliament is the Council of States, for which members are elected in an Electoral College from each of the States. The seventh schedule to the Constitution specifies the legislative domains of the Central and State governments in terms of Union, State and Concurrent lists. More specifically to the point of inter-governmental fiscal relations, the Constitution requires the President of India to appoint a Finance Commission every five years (or earlier) to review the finances of the Center and the States and recommend devolution of taxes and grants in aid for the ensuing five years.

The fiscal relationships in India evolved as two-tier federalism until the 73rd and 74th Constitutional amendments in 1992 statutorily specified the roles and finances of governmental units below the State level. The history of centralized governance under colonial rule played an important role in the adoption of a federal constitution with strong unitary features in India. The Constitution that was eventually adopted closely followed the Government of India Act, 1935, with pronounced "Quasi-federal" features. The shift was probably because (i) once the Muslim majority areas opted out of India to form Pakistan, a major reason for a decentralized federal structure had vanished and (ii) a strong Center was found desirable to safeguard against

[1] The terms "Union" and "Center" are used interchangeably to denote federal government.

fissiparous tendencies within some of the constituent units (Chelliah, 1991).

The centralization inherent in the constitutional assignments was accentuated by the adoption of a planned economic development strategy. The centralized planning strategy required the Planning Commission to allocate resources according to the envisaged priorities. The Central government issued industrial licenses, allocated credit by controlling financial institutions, and rationed the scarce foreign exchange available to conform to the central priorities. It also introduced a host of measures to control and regulate the private sector in order to ensure that those who were given the license to produce and import did not exercise their oligopoly powers. This automatically centralized economic as well as administrative powers (Chelliah, 1991).

Recent economic and political events, however, have paved the way for a greater degree of decentralization. In the economic sphere, the transition to market oriented liberalization and to a more open economic environment necessitated a greater degree of fiscal decentralization. The failure of the centralized arrangement to provide efficient levels of public services is an added reason. On the political front, the end to single party rule, the emergence of coalition parties in power at the Center and the increasing importance of regional parties in the political affairs of the country have provided a favorable environment for decentralized governance.

2.1. *Sub-State Decentralization*

The Indian federation remained a two-tier structure until 1992. Local government units functioned both in urban and rural areas as agencies of the State governments. In rural areas, historically, Panchayat Raj Institutions (PRIs) in villages provided basic community services and dispensed justice. After independence, based on the report of a committee appointed to review the functioning of these local agencies by the Government of India (India, 1957), most State governments introduced the third level of government in rural areas. In many of the States, a three-tier structure of local government was evolved with Panchayats established at the village, Taluk (block) and District levels. In urban areas, evolution of the third layer of government was natural in the context of rapid urbanization. The State governments instituted municipal corporations, municipalities and notified area committees and devolved to them some revenue bases and expenditure powers to provide urban services.

However, the framework was not adequate and the system was not congenial for the development of local self-government in most of the States. The oligopolistic power structure in rural areas did not provide the elected leaders a representative character. The socially disadvantaged groups and poorer sections of society did not effectively participate in the decentralization process. There was no mechanism to prevent the State governments from superseding the duly elected local governments nor was there any mechanism forcing them to hold regular local elections. The fiscal powers of the local governments did not generate adequate revenues and they had to perennially depend upon the State government grants. Consequently, the third level did not really function as a unit of self-government and it could hardly provide the services corresponding to the varying needs and preferences of different localities. The effectiveness of these institutions varied from State to State depending upon the initiative taken by them.

The statutory recognition of rural local governments came with the 73rd Constitutional amendment in 1992. With this, each of the State governments was required to pass a legislation appointing Panchayat Raj institutions. It was stipulated that election to these Panchayats was to be held within the stipulated period. If the elected governments at local levels were suspended, elections should be held within the six months. Local governments were assigned 29 functions to implement concurrently with the States. The sources of finance were also set out. Each State government was required to appoint a State Finance Commission to recommend tax devolution and grants to the local governments.

The evolution of urban local governments was along similar lines. Each State legislated separate Municipal Acts assigning the civic functions and sources of revenue. In general, the assignment of revenues was inadequate. Though all municipal bodies could levy property taxes, the revenue productivity of the tax was low. Most of the States were allowed to levy "Octroi", a tax on the entry of goods into a local area for consumption, use or sale. In general, the standards of services provided by the municipal bodies were poor and the State governments had to create a number of independent agencies such as housing boards, water supply authorities, and various improvement trusts to ensure minimum services.

The Indian experience shows that the major driving force behind decentralization below the State level was the central government, i.e., the process was top-down rather than bottom-up. Many States did not find it necessary or desirable to decentralize until the Constitution was amended. Of course, there are cases of some States, such as Karnataka, Kerala and West Bengal, that took a proactive approach to decentralization. However, such initiatives were exceptions rather than a rule.

2.2. *The System*

The Constitution demarcates revenue and expenditure powers of the Union and State governments and the later have to share powers with local governments as indicated in separate schedules for the urban and rural areas. The institutional structure of the governance system is shown in Fig. 1. The Constitution also requires the President to appoint a Finance Commission every five years or earlier to review the finances of Center and States and recommend devolution of taxes and grants-in aid to the States for the ensuing five years. In addition, the Planning Commission also gives assistance to the States based on a formula determined by the National Development

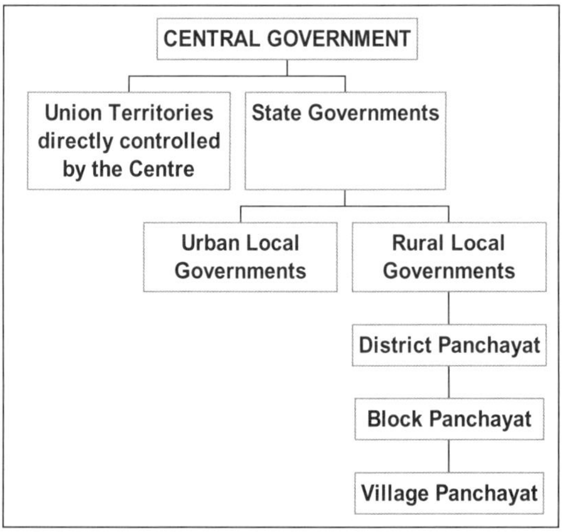

Fig. 1. Organization of Multilevel Fiscal System in India

Council[2] and different central ministries give specific purpose transfers to States. The result is that the system of inter-governmental transfers is quite fragmented.

Below the States, there are over a quarter million local governments. Of this, about 3000 are in urban areas. The urban local governments consist of municipal corporations in large cities, municipalities in smaller cities and towns and notified area committees in smaller towns. Rural local governments are at three levels-district, Taluk (block) and village. Each State government has devolved powers to levy certain taxes and fees to village panchayats and urban local bodies. The States have also instituted a system of sharing of States' revenues and giving grants to urban and rural local bodies. Each State government is required to appoint a State Finance Commission to review the finances of the local bodies and assign tax shares and make grants. In addition, the local governments are entrusted with the task of implementing several central schemes.

3. The Assignment Question

3.1. *Tax and Expenditure Assignments in India*

The tax and expenditure powers of the Central and the State governments are specified in the seventh schedule to the Constitution. The functions required for maintaining macro-economic stability, international relations and activities having significant scale economies have been assigned exclusively to the Center or must be carried out concurrently with the States. The functions which have a State-wide benefit zone are assigned to the States. Most broad-based and progressive taxes have been assigned to the Center. The Center also has residual tax powers. A number of tax handles have been assigned to the States as well, but from the viewpoint of revenue productivity, only the sales tax is important. The States can borrow from the Central government. They have the powers to borrow from the market as well, but if a State is indebted to the Central government, the borrowing must be approved by the Center.

Tax powers are assigned on the basis of the principle of separation, exclusively either to the Center or to the States. Exclusivity is not so

[2] This is called the "Gadgil" formula after the name of the Deputy Chairman of the Planning Commission (Prof. D R Gadgil) who introduced the formula for the first time in 1969.

easily defined and a number of anomalous situations have emerged. Thus, the Center can levy taxes on production (excise duty) but the tax on the sale of goods can be levied by the States. Similarly, taxes on agricultural incomes and wealth are in States' domain, whereas those on non-agricultural incomes and wealth are a Central prerogative. The States find taxing agricultural incomes politically infeasible and administratively difficult. This has provided a way to evade the income tax levied by the Center.

The Constitution recognizes that the States' tax powers are inadequate to meet their expenditure needs and therefore, provides for the sharing of revenues from central taxes. Prior to the enactment of the Constitution (Eightieth Amendment) Act 2000, taxes on incomes other than non-agricultural incomes and union excise duty were shared with the States. Considering the potential adverse incentives of sharing of taxes from individual sources for the Central government, based on the recommendations of the Tenth Finance Commission, the Constitution was amended to include proceeds from all central taxes in the divisible pool. In addition to tax devolution, the Constitution provides for making grants in aid to the States (Article 275). Both tax devolution and grants in aid must be determined by the Finance Commission, an independent body appointed by the President every five years (Article 280).

The shares of Central and State governments in revenues and expenditures are summarized in Tables 1 and 2.[3] The States, on an average, raise about 39 percent of revenues and incur 57 percent of expenditures. However, the States' autonomy in implementing expenditures is less than what is suggested by these figures. This is because about 15 percent of total expenditures is incurred on specific purpose transfer schemes with matching requirements, known as "centrally sponsored schemes." In fact, States' expenditures on these schemes increased from 7 percent of the total in 1985–86 to about 20 percent in 2000–01.

The pattern of expenditures shown in Table 2 indicates that the Central government plays a major role in defence and in the provision of large physical infrastructure facilities. On the other hand, the States have a high share of total government expenditures on internal security, law

[3] The data pertain to the period prior to the Constitutional amendment and hence, refer to tax on personal income and union excise duty as shared taxes. After 2000–01, revenue from all central taxes is kept in the divisible pool.

Table 1. Tax Assignment in India 2003–04

Sr. No	Tax	Percent of GDP	Percent of Total Revenue	Percent of Total Revenue
I	Central taxes	—	—	—
I.1	Personal income tax	1.49	9.9	16.3
I.2	Corporation income tax	2.29	15.2	25.0
I.3	Central excise duties	3.27	21.8	35.7
I.4	Customs duty	1.75	11.7	19.1
I.5	Other taxes	0.36	2.4	3.9
	Total — Central taxes (Gross)	9.18	61.0	100.0
	Total — Central taxes (Net)	6.75	45.0	—
	Total central revenues (Gross)	—	—	—
	Total — Central	—	—	—
II	State taxes	—	—	—
II.1	Tax and land and agricultural	0.16	1.1	2.8
II.2	Incomes	0.55	3.7	9.6
II.3	Stamp duties and registration fees	3.55	23.6	60.4
II.4	Sales tax	0.74	4.9	12.5
II.5	State excise duties	0.53	3.5	9.1
II.6	Taxes on transport	0.23	1.5	3.9
II.7	Electricity duty	0.03	0.2	0.5
II.8	Entertainment tax	0.32	2.2	5.5
	Total taxes	14.97	100.0	

* Revised Estimates. ** Netted for the interest paid to the Central government.
Source: Public Finance Statistics, Ministry of Finance, Government of India, 1993.

and order, and social services, and economic services like agriculture, animal husbandry, forestry, fisheries, irrigation and power and public works. The States' share in expenditure on administrative services is about 48 percent; on social services they spend about 83 percent and on economic services their share is 57 percent. Their role in providing social services like education, public health and family is close to 90 percent.

Table 2. Share of State Governments in Total Expenditures*

Expenditure Item	1985–86			1990–91			1999–00			2002–03 (RE)			% of Total Exp
	Current	Capital	Total	Current	Capital	Total	Current	Capital	Total	Current	Capital	Total	
A. Interest payment	34.6	0.0	34.6	35.5	0.0	35.5	41.1	0.0	41.1	46.2	0.0	46.2	22.7
B. Defence	0.0	0.0	0.0	0.0	0.0	0.0	0.0	0.0	0.0	0.0	0.0	0.0	8.0
C. Administrative service	85.2	0.8	78.0	76.4	1.8	73.4	64.2	13.3	62.5	48.8	29.8	48.4	29.0
D. Soc. and com. services	94.8	67.0	92.7	78.9	74.1	78.7	83.8	73.4	83.2	82.5	84.4	82.7	20.0
i. Education	84.8	79.5	84.7	84.5	61.7	83.9	89.4	90.9	89.4	87.6	59.9	87.0	10.8
ii. Medical and health	92.5	94.8	92.8	90.3	95.3	90.7	88.3	95.5	89.2	87.2	97.8	88.8	4.2
iii. Family welfare	93.4	90.4	93.1	92.2	100.0	92.7	80.2	100.0	80.4	78.9	100.0	79.1	0.6
iv. Others	98.1	40.7	88.2	61.1	64.0	61.4	59.6	49.3	58.2	64.6	79.2	66.7	4.4
E. Eco. Services, of which	78.1	46.3	62.9	50.2	53.1	51.1	59.5	68.5	62.0	51.9	72.3	57.4	23.2
i. Agriculture etc.,	99.9	52.1	96.7	77.8	94.8	78.6	65.1	91.0	67.0	57.5	109.4	61.2	6.6
ii. Industry and minerals	36.7	9.8	18.1	40.7	44.1	41.9	14.0	42.7	16.2	20.4	41.6	22.1	2.4
iii. Power, irrig. flood control	94.7	65.4	73.9	86.2	62.9	69.1	88.8	83.0	86.0	89.9	84.2	87.4	6.1
iv. Tpt. and communication	68.3	68.3	68.3	70.4	32.1	47.3	55.7	60.6	57.9	39.7	74.6	52.6	4.4
v. Others	24.9	18	23.9	16.6	51.3	19.7	79.2	36.6	59.8	27.0	36.8	30.5	3.8
F. Others	80.0	14.7	33.2	57.2	0.0	57.2	55.1	0.0	55.1	100.0	47.6	58.3	5.2
G. Loans and Advances	0.0	51.7	51.7	0.0	51.1	51.1	0.0	79.5	79.5	0.0	97.9	97.9	2.0
H. Total @	55.2	43	52.1	55.0	44.5	52.9	56.4	56.7	56.5	56.4	63.7	57.4	100.0

* Revised estimates. ** Includes food and fertilizer subsidies. @ Excludes appropriation for reduction and avoidance of debt.
Source: Public Finance Statistics, Ministry of Finance, Government of India.

3.2. *Assignment Between State and Local Governments*

With the constitutional amendments in 1992, roles and responsibilities of rural and urban local governments have been specified. Accordingly, in separate schedules, a list of 29 functions to rural local bodies and another list of 18 functions to urban local bodies have been clarified. However, the revenue and expenditure assignments in the lists are concurrent with the States' responsibilities and the actual assignment of specific revenue sources and expenditure depends on the extent to which the State is willing to devolve. However, the extent of devolution of powers and functions to local governments shows wide variation among the States.

In addition to the transfers recommended by the State Finance Commissions, the local governments receive funds for the implementation of various central schemes. The most important is for poverty alleviation, but there are also other schemes for social and community services in which the local governments have a comparative advantage in implementation. Even apart from conditional grants, local governments have very little flexibility in the use of funds (Rao *et al.*, 2003). After deductions of charges for electricity and other facilities by State government, very little is left in the general purpose transfers. In general, there are few funds available to execute developmental schemes.

4. Fiscal Decentralization in India

4.1. *Revenue and Expenditure Shares of Three Levels*

An examination of the shares of different levels of government in raising revenue and incurring expenditures provides insights into the workings of fiscal federalism in India. Unfortunately, data that would enable a comprehensive analysis of local government finances has not been available and therefore, much of the past discussion on their role is based on qualitative judgements. However, the analysis based on the information compiled from the Report of Eleventh and Twelfth Finance Commissions shows that both in terms of revenue raising and spending, local governments have a very limited role. In this sense, there is very little decentralization below the State level in India.

4.2. *Asymmetry Between Expenditure and Revenue Decentralization*

Another salient feature of fiscal federalism in India is that decentralization is more focused on the expenditure side of the budget than on the revenue side. Thus, the Central government could exercise control over the use of one-third of the revenues, but its share in raising revenues is two-thirds. In contrast, State and local governments raised only about one-third of revenues but the revenue accrual to them was about two-thirds. Each of the three levels directly made about one-third of the expenditures. Urban local bodies incurred 28 percent of total expenditures and the share of rural local bodies was less than 4 percent. Even within the urban local governments, the expenditures were mainly in Andhra Pradesh and Maharashtra.

The States raise 35 percent of total government revenues, which finances 51 percent of their expenditures. The expenditure share of the State governments net of grants to local governments is 35 percent. In social services, particularly in the education and health sectors, the expenditure share of the States is more than 80 percent. In economic services, it is about 50 percent. The States depend on central transfers to finance about 37 percent of their expenditures.

The imbalance in revenues and expenditures decentralization is particularly significant at the local government level. In total local governments raise about 0.6% of GDP or 2 percent of total revenues. Rural local governments raise only about 0.05% of GDP from own sources, but receive 1.3% of GDP as transfers. Thus, over one quarter million local governments in rural India account for less than 4 percent of total expenditures. Thus despite constitutional recognition, local governments in India depend on higher level governments for their resources. As State governments themselves are faced with several resource constraints, the revenue accruals to the local bodies are not adequate to enable the provision of required standards of public services.

5. Fiscal Imbalances: Trends and Issues

5.1. *Vertical Fiscal Imbalance in India*

The consequence of Constitutional assignments, as well as developments over the years, is a high degree of fiscal centralization and vertical fiscal imbalance. This is described in Table 3. Over 55 percent of States' total expenditures are financed by transfers from the Center and loans. The relative shares of the Central and State governments in revenues and expenditures presented in Table 3, also bring out the trends in fiscal centralization over the years since 1970–71. The proportion of States' current expenditures financed from own revenues declined from 59 percent in 1995–96 to 49 percent in 2000–01 but increased thereafter to 56 percent in 2005–06. The States' share in total expenditures increased from 52 percent in 1990–91 to 58 percent in 2005–06. However, this does not signify an increase in decentralization for, the spending financed by specific purpose transfer on which the

Table 3. Trends in Vertical Fiscal Imbalance

Year	Percent of States' Own Current Revenues Total Current Rev.	Percent of States' Current Expenditure to Total Current Exp.	Percent of States' Own Current Revenues to States' Current Exp.	Percent of States' Expenditure* to Total Expenditure*
1955–56	41.2	59.0	68.9	61.7
1960–61	36.6	59.9	63.9	56.8
1965–66	32.6	55.6	63.5	53.3
1970–71	35.5	60.2	60.6	53.9
1975–76	33.5	55.1	70.4	47.6
1980–81	35.6	59.6	60.1	56.0
1985–86	35.5	56.0	57.7	52.6
1990–91	35.2	54.6	53.1	51.7
1995–96	39.2	57.0	58.6	55.8
1999–00	38.6	56.4	49.8	56.0
2000–01	37.8	56.0	48.6	56.1
2001–02	40.2	56.9	50.0	56.3
2002–03	38.28	54.31	56.01	55.14
2003–04	37.54	56.27	53.83	57.65
2004–05	38.10	56.28	60.05	56.64
2005–06 (RE)	37.07	56.59	56.07	58.10

* Current + capital expenditures. RE: Revised estimates

Source: Public Finance Statistics, Ministry of Finance, Government of India (relevant years).

States' have little manoeuvrability have shown a sharp increase in recent years.

5.2. *Horizontal Fiscal Imbalance*

An important feature of Indian fiscal federalism is the wide inter-State differences in revenue capacity and consequently, per capita expenditures. There are 17 relatively more homogenous general category States, but even these have wide differences in size, revenue raising capacities, efforts, expenditure levels and fiscal dependence on the Center. In addition, in terms of economic characteristics the 11 mountainous States of the north and the Northeast differ markedly from the rest and therefore are considered "special category" States. Of the 28, three States have been created recently by bifurcating the three large States.[4]

The differences in per capita revenues and expenditures among the States shown in Table 5 bring out several important features. First, there are wide inter-State variations in revenues in both per capita terms and as a percent of Gross State Domestic Product (GSDP). Second, these variations indicate differences both in revenue capacity and in revenue effort. Third, the tax-GSDP ratios in the special category States are lower than in the general category States, even when their per capita GSDP is higher. This is partly because, in these States there is not much production activity and government administration is the major determinant of the GSDP. Fourth, although the revenue bases in the special category States are low, their average per capita current expenditure are higher than not only the all-State average but also higher than the average of high income States.[5] Fifth, in the case of general category States, the fiscal dependence on the Center is not only high but also varies inversely with per capita income. It is seen that per capita expenditures in high income States was higher than the all-State average by 44 percent and that of the low income States is lower by 36 percent. Nevertheless, there has been significant equalization;

---

[4] The three new States are Jharkhand (carved out of Bihar), Chattisgarh (carved out of Madhya Pradesh) and Uttarachal (carved out of Uttar pradesh). While the first two States have continued as general category States, the last is considered to be a special category State.

[5] Of course, the higher than average per capita expenditures in special category States cannot be entirely attributed to their inherent cost disability. This may also be due to poor fiscal management.

while the per capita revenues from own sources in low income States were about 29 percent of those in high income States, per capita expenditure in the former was close to 63 percent.

The inter-State disparities among the general category States are not only high, but have shown an increasing trend. In 1980–81, the per capita SDP in the richest State, Punjab (Rs 2674) was about 2.9 times that of the poorest, Bihar (Rs 919). In 2006–07, this difference increased to 4.8 times with per capita SDPs of Haryana, the highest income State at Rs. 48214 and Bihar at Rs. 10286 (see Table 4). It is also seen that per capita income levels have tended to diverge sharply after market based reforms were initiated. (Rao *et al.*, 1999). With economic liberalization, the States with better access to factor and product markets and better transport infrastructure and connectivity were able to take greater advantage of the opportunities as compared to those with poor transport infrastructure and low levels of market development.

As inter-State differences in the ability to raise revenues increased over the years, and as federal transfers did not entirely offset the fiscal disabilities of the poorer States, the coefficient of variation in expenditures also increased over the time period (Rao, 1998). A detailed analysis of the pattern of regional development in India shows that the poorer states are the ones with abundant natural resources including minerals and often, while the Center exploits these resources, the States hardly receive the compensation for the opportunity cost borne by them.

Inability to offset the fiscal disabilities has resulted in high inter-State disparities in developmental expenditures. There is a very high correlation between per capita development expenditures and per capita incomes of the States and this cannot be explained by differences in own revenues raised. The inequalities in per capita expenditures too have shown an increasing trend. Thus inability to place the poorer States on a level playing field in regard to infrastructure provision combined with poor development of market institutions in these States has contributed to growing inter-State inequalities in levels of living.

6. Inter-governmental Transfers

6.1. *Economic Rationale for Transfers*

Inter-governmental transfers have been employed to fulfil a variety of objectives and the design of the transfer scheme depends on the purpose

Table 4. Selected Fiscal Indicators of States

	Per capita GSDP	Per capita Development Expenditure	Per capita Own Revenues	Per capita Transfers	Percent of Own Tax to GSDP
Non-Special Cat. States					
Andhra Pradesh	32533.0	4977.2	3788.0	1768.1	9.6
Bihar	10286.0	2105.3	530.9	1952.9	4.8
Chhatisgarh	26125.1	4439.6	2974.4	2279.7	9.0
Goa	95663.5	15460.0	9446.7	2886.7	8.3
Gujarat	44332.5	4558.4	4056.2	1432.1	7.5
Haryana	48213.8	5717.8	5736.0	1008.9	9.3
Jharkhand	23591.2	3992.0	1542.9	1888.3	4.5
Karnataka	36037.8	5173.7	4567.3	1733.4	11.7
Kerala	39742.1	4243.7	3841.6	1773.4	9.0
Madhya Pradesh	18984.1	2872.0	1863.2	1841.9	8.0
Maharashtra	46307.9	4587.2	4235.6	1383.3	8.2
Orissa	25997.6	2649.9	1945.3	2568.5	5.7
Punjab	43436.1	4885.9	4362.7	1612.2	8.5
Rajasthan	22210.8	3201.1	2301.3	1735.7	8.1
Tamil Nadu	37635.2	4698.3	4729.4	1454.0	11.4
Uttar Pradesh	16308.2	2368.9	1607.7	1631.9	8.1
West Bengal	30739.3	2419.5	1598.7	1550.0	4.8
Average: Non. Spl. Cat States	28867.0	3606.4	2790.6	1691.0	8.3

(*Continued*)

Table 4. *(Continued)*

	Per capita GSDP	Per capita Development Expenditure	Per capita Own Revenues	Per capita Transfers	Percent of Own Tax to GSDP
Special Cat. States					
Arunachal Pradesh	27747.5	16941.7	2316.7	17625.0	2.1
Assam	21947.7	4579.9	1793.1	3749.5	5.6
Himachal Pradesh	43535.4	7541.5	3690.8	6996.9	5.4
Jammu & Kashmir	26334.2	8067.3	2279.1	8611.8	6.6
Manipur	27992.3	9821.7	1195.7	11795.7	1.7
Meghalaya	28342.6	7399.5	1772.5	8102.9	3.8
Mizoram	27820.5	16250.0	1820.0	18100.0	2.3
Nagaland	27740.1	9209.1	918.2	11545.5	1.9
Sikkim	34820.6	22764.5	4488.1	21177.5	6.4
Tripura	29500.1	6600.0	1247.1	8108.8	3.5
Uttarakhand	30956.0	6426.9	3203.2	4154.8	8.2
Average: Special Cat. States	27189.0	6729.8	2197.1	6375.8	5.6
Average: All States	28762.5	1962.0	1421.2	1023.9	8.1

Note: GSDP — Gross State Domestic Product.
Source: 1. Reserve Bank of India Bulletin, December 2000.
2. Public Finance Statistics, Ministry of Finance, Government of India, 1994–95.

for which it is given. In the international practice, and in India, federal transfers are designed for (i) closing the vertical fiscal gap, (ii) equalization, and (iii) spillovers and merit good reasons.

(i) *Closing the fiscal gap:* An important reason for giving transfers is to compensate the sub-national governments for a shortfall between expenditure responsibilities and revenue raising powers. In most countries, decentralization is more developed on the expenditure side of the budget than on the revenue side. This is because the Center has a comparative advantage in raising revenues and the States, in spending. The resulting vertical fiscal imbalance must be offset through a system of Central transfers to States.

(ii) *Equalization:* The imbalance between revenue capacity and expenditure need varies across States depending upon the size of their tax base, the size and the composition of population and other factors affecting the need and cost of providing public services. Arguments for transfers are made on the grounds of offsetting fiscal disabilities arising from low revenue capacity and high unit cost of providing public services.

The argument for equalization on horizontal equity grounds was advanced initially by Buchanan (1950) and later developed by Boadway and Flatters (1982). Taking comprehensive income as the index of well-being, it is argued that the federal income tax as presently structured cannot ensure horizontal equity for, its base does not take into account the redistributive effect of States' fiscal operations. States' fiscal operations cannot be neutral in distribution except in the unlikely case of benefit taxes. When the States' quasi-public services are financed by resource rents or source-based taxes as against residence-based taxes, the net fiscal benefits (NFBs) will systematically vary. The residents in the resource rich (high income) regions will have higher NFBs and their higher public consumption will not be included in determining the tax base of the Central government.

Boadway and Flatters define horizontal equity in two alternative ways. According to the broad view, the fiscal system should be equitable nation-wide vis-à-vis the actions of all governments. Two persons equally well off before Central and State actions must also be so afterwards. To fulfil this concept of horizontal equity, it is necessary to give transfers so that each province is enabled to provide the same level of public services at a given tax rate (as in a unitary State). In contrast, the narrow view of horizontal equity takes the level of real incomes attained by the individuals after a State's budgetary operation as the starting point and the Central fiscal action will be directed to ensure horizontal equity after the State's fiscal system has been established. The Central budget need not offset the inequalities introduced by the operation of the State budgets *per se*, but takes the income distribution effects of the States' fiscal operations as a given datum.

(iii) ***Transfers to correct spillovers:*** When there is no perfect "mapping", the provision of public services by sub-Central governments may spill over the jurisdictions and such externalities result in the non-optimal provision of public services. A Pigovian subsidy is required to "set the prices right." To be cost-effective, specific purpose transfers made to the States to ensure optimal provision of public services require matching contributions from them.

6.2. *The Design of Inter-governmental Transfers*

General-purpose transfers are given to offset fiscal disabilities. Thus, the objective of these transfers is to offset the fiscal disadvantages arising from lower revenue capacity and higher unit cost of providing public services. This is achieved by unconditional grants equivalent to the "need-revenue" gap (Bradbury *et al.*, 1984). The "need-revenue" gap measures the difference between what a State ought to spend to provide specified levels of public services and the revenue it can raise at a standard level of tax effort.

Specific purpose transfers on the other hand, are intended to compensate the spillovers or are given for merit good reasons or for reasons of "categorical equity." The transfer system, therefore, should be specific purpose and open-ended with matching ratios varying with the size of spillovers. As the responsiveness of the States to a given matching rate could vary with their level of its incomes, equalizing matching ratios are also recommended (Feldstein, 1975).

Thus, in an ideal system, there should be an optimal combination of general and specific purpose transfers. General-purpose transfers would *enable* all the States to provide a given normative standard of public services at a given tax effort. The specific purpose transfers would *ensure* a given standard of outlay on the aided services.

6.3. *Inter-governmental Transfers in India*

A notable feature of transfer system in India is the existence of multiple channels. The Constitution provides for the appointment of the Finance Commission by the President of India every five years to make an assessment of the fiscal resources and needs of the Center and individual States. Based on these, the Commission is required to recommend the shares of personal income tax and union excise duty, and grants-in-aid, to the States. However, with development planning gaining emphasis, the scope of the Finance Commissions was restricted to cover the States' non-plan requirements in the current account. The Planning Commission became a major dispenser of funds to the States by way of both grants and loans. In addition to these two channels, various Central ministries give specific purpose transfers with or without matching requirements.

The trends in the relative shares of the three channels of Central transfers[6] to States since the fourth five-year plan, as shown in Table 5, bring out some interesting features. First, the share of statutory transfers in the total declined from 65 percent during the fourth plan (1969–74) to a little over 60 percent during the seventh plan. Although it increased to 65 percent in 1997–98, declined subsequently to less than 62 percent in 2000–01. Second, the proportion of formula-based transfers given by the Finance Commission and the Planning Commission has declined and that of discretionary transfers has increased in recent years. Third, within the Finance Commission, the proportion of tax devolution is overwhelming though in recent years, this has tended to decline.

6.3.1. *Finance Commission Transfers*

Under Article 280 of the Constitution, the President of India appoints the Finance Commission every five years or earlier as deemed necessary.

[6] There is a considerable amount of confusion in the term "transfers." In Indian fiscal literature, Central loans to States are also characterized as transfers. Such transactions involve transfers only to the extent of any interest subsidy or write off of loans. Sometimes, on the recommendation of the Finance Commissions, the loans to States are rescheduled, the rate of interest reduced and even a portion of the loan itself is written off. Here, we have taken only tax devolution and grants as transfers. Transfers arising from interest subsidy guarantees and loan write off are not taken account of.

Table 5. Composition of Central Transfers to States Rs. Billion

	Finance Commission Transfers			Plan Grants				
Plan Periods/Years	Tax Devolution	Grants	Total	State Plan Scheme	Central Scheme	Total	Other Grants	Total
Fourth Plan	54.4	10.3	64.6	12.9	11.6	24.4	11.1	100.0
Fifth Plan (1974–79)	50.2	17.1	67.3	17.7	11.7	29.4	3.3	100.0
Sixth Plan (1980–85)	57.0	5.1	62.1	17.7	16.6	34.3	3.6	100.0
Seventh Plan (1985–90)	54.2	6.9	61.0	17.0	18.1	35.1	3.9	100.0
Annual Plan (1990–91)	52.2	10.5	62.7	17.4	16.8	34.2	3.1	100.0
Eighth Plan (1992–97)	55.6	6.2	61.8	20.4	15.4	35.8	2.5	100.0
Ninth Plan (1997–2001)	58.7	6.0	64.7	20.0	10.6	27.1	4.9	100.0
2002–03	55.4	8.3	63.7	19.4	10.4	29.7	6.6	100.0
2003–04	51.7	6.9	58.7	21.5	14.7	36.3	5.0	100.0

Note: Figures in parenthesis are percentages to total transfers.
Source: State Finances — A Study of Budgets (various years), Reserve Bank of India Bulletin.

The Commission is required to make recommendations on the following:

1) The distribution between the Union and the States of the net proceeds of shareable taxes and the allocation between the States of the States' share of divisible taxes;
2) The principles that should govern the distribution of grants to the States, and the amounts to be paid to the States in need of assistance;
3) The measures needed to augment the Consolidated Fund of a State to supplement the resources of Panchayats (rural local governments) in the State, on the basis of recommendations made by the State Finance Commissions;
4) The measures needed to augment the Consolidated Fund of a State to supplement the resources of municipalities, on the basis of a recommendations by the State Finance commissions;
5) Any other matter referred to the Commission in the interest of sound finance.

Under (e), the 11th Finance Commission was required to (i) review the finances of the Union and the States and suggest ways and means to restructure the public finances to restore budgetary balance and maintain macroeconomic stability; (ii) assess the debt position of States as on 31st March 1999, and suggest corrective measures to ensure sustainability of central and State finances and (iii) review the prevailing scheme of Calamity Relief Fund and make appropriate recommendations thereon. Later, at the stage of finalization of the Report an additional term of reference was given to the Commission. The Commission was asked to draw up a monitor-able fiscal reform programme to reduce revenue and fiscal deficits and to recommend the manner in which grants to States to cover assessed deficit in the non-plan revenues account may be linked to the progress of implementing the programme. The basic approach followed by the Commissions in dealing with substantive issues of recommending tax devolution and grants are discussed below.

Although the Constitution does not place any restriction on the scope of the Finance Commission, it has come to be restricted to meeting the non-plan current expenditure requirements of the States. The approach of the Finance Commissions to transfers consists of (i) assessment of overall budgetary requirements of the Center and States to determine the volume of resources that can be transferred during the period of their recommendation; (ii) forecasting States' own current revenues and non-plan current expenditures; (iii) determining the States' share in Central tax revenues and distributing this share among the States; (iv) filling the post-devolution projected gaps between non-plan current expenditures and revenues with the grants-in-aid. This has come to be known as the "gap-filling" approach.

Prior to the Constitutional amendment in which devolution of certain central taxes was replaced by general tax sharing, the Finance Commissions were required to recommend the transfer of additional excise duties in respect of sales taxes on sugar, textiles and tobacco. In respect of these three groups of articles, the States had voluntarily surrendered their right to levy sales taxes and the Center has been levying additional excise duties, which was passed back to States on the basis of origin as recommended by the Commission. With the substitution of general tax sharing for sharing of individual taxes, separate assignment of additional excise duties was discontinued. The Twelfth Finance Commission recommended the distribution of 30.5% of net proceeds of Central taxes consisting of 29 percent for general tax sharing and 1.5% in lieu of additional excise duties. The entire 30.5% is to be distributed according to a uniform formula given in Table 6.

Table 6. Criteria and Relative Weights for Tax Devolution

Criterion	Weight (Percent)
1. Population	25
2. Income (Distance method)*	50
3. Area	10
5. Tax effort**	7.5
6. Fiscal discipline***	7.5

Note: *The distance method is given by: $(Y_h - Y_i)P_i/\Sigma(Y_h - Y_i)P_i$ where, Y_i and Y_h represent per capita SDP of the *i*th and the highest income State respectively and P_i is the population of the *i*th State.

** Tax Effort (η) is estimated as $(\eta) = (T_i / Y_i) /(0.5\, l/Y_i)$ where, T_i is the per capita tax revenue collected by the *i*th State and Y_i is the per capita State domestic product of the *i*th State.

*** estimated as the improvement in the ratio of own revenue of a State to its revenue expenditures divided by a similar ratio for all States averaged for the period 1966–99 over 1991–1993.

An important feature of tax devolution recommended by the Finance Commissions is that, while the criteria adopted for distribution are different from the principles of grants-in-aid, nowhere is it made clear that the economic objectives of the two instruments are different (Rao and Sen, 1996, Ch. 6). Tax devolution is recommended mainly on the basis of general economic indicators (see Table 6) and grants are given to offset the residuary fiscal disadvantages of the States as quantified by the Commissions. Further, assigning weights to contradictory factors like "backwardness" and "contribution" in the same formula has rendered the achievement of the overall objective of offsetting revenue and cost disabilities difficult.

Over the years, attempts have been made to improve degree of equalization in the transfer scheme by assigning larger weights to per capita SDP either in the "inverse" or "distance" form by the successive Commissions. Yet, population has continued to receive the largest implicit and explicit weight. Equally important is the unreliability of tax effort and index of fiscal discipline. In a tax system which is predominantly origin based, there can be significant inter-State tax exportation and the tax effort indicator ignores this phenomenon. Besides, there are a number of other factors in addition to per capita SDP that determine the taxable capacity of a State. The changes in the ratios of own revenues to revenue expenditures relative to all-State average and their changes over time can occur due to factors totally extraneous to States own efforts at fiscal discipline. Equalization has been further blunted by the terms of reference, which require the Commissions to use the 1971 population figures in the transfer formula. The purpose of this is to penalize the States with higher population growth rates. The important questions are first, whether, the federal transfer mechanism should be employed as an instrument of population policy and second, even if it is, why should those States with high population growth be penalized.

The "gap-filling" approach outlined above has been subjected to criticism. First, none of the Finance Commissions have assessed the overall resource position and requirements of the Center on any objective basis. Second, the transfers made by the Finance Commissions were not designed specifically to offset fiscal disadvantages of the States arising from lower revenue raising capacity and the higher unit cost of public services. While tax devolution is determined on the basis of general economic indicators, grants are given on the basis of projected post-devolution budgetary gaps. Third, the design of the grants has serious disincentive effects on fiscal management of the States.

There has been considerable concern by the Finance Commissions about following the "gap-filling" approach. This was the reason for modifying the terms of reference of the Ninth Finance Commission to follow a "normative approach". However, the Commission did not fully make use of the estimate of fiscal capacities and needs of the States in formulating its recommendations. The Tenth Finance Commission, simply abandoned the approach. The 11th Finance Commission in the additional terms of reference given to it just before the finalization of its recommendations was asked to "... draw a monitorable fiscal reforms programme aimed at reduction of revenue deficit of the state and recommended the manner in which the grants to the States to cover the assessed deficit in their non-plan revenue account may be linked to progress in implementing the programme."

The 11th Commission worked out a scheme by pooling 15 percent of revenue deficit grants and adding an equal amount to create an incentive fund to be allocated among the States based on fulfilment targets of growth of tax and non-tax revenues and expenditures on salaries, interest payments and subsidies set in the fiscal restructuring plan detailed by the Commission. It gave equal weight to monitorable measures on the revenue and expenditure sides and specified weights to each of the monitor-able measures. The incentive fund was allocated to the States according to their population shares. A State would receive the full amount if it fulfilled the targets and the amount would vary depending on the degree of achievement of monitor-able targets. If a State did not get the full amount during the first four years, the residual would continue to be available in subsequent years, but if by the fifth year the targets are not achieved, the funds would lapse. To implement this scheme a monitoring agency should be set up by the Government of India consisting of representatives of the Planning Commission, Finance Ministry and State governments.

There are a number of problems with the proposed scheme. Some of them have been pointed out in the Note of Dissent presented by one of the Members of the Commission (Government of India, 2000, pp. 9–13). There are concerns both with the monitorable measures and implementation mechanism. The measures can vary not only due to factors within the States' control but also because of factors beyond their control. There are also problems of fiscal autonomy of the States when its actions are supervised by a monitoring agency. Finally, while the scheme tries to monitor the fiscal performance of the States, there is no mechanism to monitor the performance of the Center. Not surprisingly, after a detailed analysis, the Twelfth Finance Commission recommended the discontinuation of the scheme. Instead, it tried to incentivise the fiscal performance of the states by designing the debt restructuring scheme. The States passing the fiscal responsibility legislation and presenting the medium term expenditure framework agreeing to phase out the revenue deficits and compress fiscal deficits to 3 percent of their gross State Domestic Product (GSDP) were given the benefit of debt rescheduling at a lower interest rate (7.5%) and the progress in reduction in revenue deficits was linked to write off of the debt repayable to the central government by an equal magnitude.

It is important to note that the focus of the Twelfth Finance Commission's fiscal restructuring plan was macroeconomic stability even if it meant sacrificing development in fiscally disadvantaged States. The reference is to the uniform targets given to the States to eliminate their revenue deficits and reduce fiscal deficits to three percent of GSDP. Given the low levels of expenditures on social and physical infrastructure in poorer States, achieving the fiscal restructuring targets further entailed compressing their productive expenditures. Thanks to the acceleration in the growth of the economy to over 8 percent since 2003–04, and very high buoyancy of Central revenue collections and consequently, buoyant central transfers, the States have been able to make the necessary corrections as per the fiscal restructuring plan.

6.3.2. *Plan Transfers*

The assistance given by the Planning Commission comprises both grants and loans. In earlier years, both the volume and the loan-grant component was project based, but since 1969 the assistance has been allocated on the basis of a formula (Gadgil formula).[7] At present, 30 percent of the funds is kept apart for the special category States and distributed among them on the basis of plan projects formulated by

[7] The formula and its modifications from time to time are evolved on the basis of consensus the National Development Council (NDC). The NDC is constituted by the cabinet ministers at the Center, chief ministers of the States and the members of the Planning Commission and is chaired by the Prime Minister.

Table 7. Formula for Distributing State Plan Assistance

Variable	Weight
Population (1971)	60.0
Per capita SDP, of which,	25.0
(i) Deviation from the average to the States below average per capita SDP	20.0
(ii) "Distance" from the highest per capita SDP for all the general category States.	5.0
Fiscal Performance, of which,	7.5
(i) Tax effort	2.5
(ii) Fiscal management	2.5
(iii) National objectives	2.5
(iv) Special problems	7.5
Total	100.0

Note: 1. The formula is applied to general category States. They receive 70 percent of the total plan assistance of which, 30 percent is given as grants and the remaining, loans.
2. The Special category States receive 30 percent of total plan assistance and 90 percent of the assistance is given as grants and the remaining 10 percent as loans and the distribution among them is based on approved plans.

them. For these States, 90 percent of the assistance given by way of grants and the remainder as loans. The 70 percent of the funds available to the major States is distributed with a 60 percent weight assigned to population, 25 percent to per capita SDP, 7.5% to fiscal management and the remaining 7.5% to special problems of these States (see Table 7). For the major States, 30 percent of the resources is given by way of grants and the remainder as loans. Thus, plan transfers and their grant-loan components, are determined independently of the required plan investments, their sectoral composition, the resources available to the States or their fiscal performances.

6.3.3. *Assistance to the Central Sector and Centrally Sponsored Schemes*

This is the third component of the transfer system and is given for specified purposes with or without matching provisions. Grants for the

Central sector schemes are given to the States to execute Central projects and are entirely funded by the Center. Centrally sponsored schemes, on the other hand, are shared cost programs falling within the States' ambit with required matching ratios that are uniform across the States but which vary with the projects. There were 262 such schemes in 1985, and more have been added in subsequent years. These transfers have attracted the sharpest criticism due to their discretionary nature and conditionality attached to them. They accounted for about 60 percent of the total plan assistance and about 20 percent of total current transfers were given to these schemes in 2000–01 (see Table 5).

6.3.4. *Financing infrastructure at the State level: Loans*

Borrowing is an important source of financing infrastructure at the State level. Until 1987–88, government savings at the State level did contribute to financing capital expenditures. Since then, however, with increasing dissavings at the State level, borrowing is used not only to finance capital expenditures, but also a significant part of current expenditures of the States. In 1998–99 for example, only about one-half of the States' borrowing was used to finance capital expenditure.

The States' liabilities presently consist of loans from the Central government, market borrowings, share of small savings collections, and provident funds, deposit accounts etc. The Central loans constitute 60 percent of the States' indebtedness. These loans are given mainly for financing the plans under the Gadgil formula. As already mentioned, the States receive 70 percent of plan assistance in the form of loans. Other Central loans consist of ways and means advances and a share of small savings collections.[8]

The States can borrow from the market. However, if a State is indebted to the Center, it must have central permission before borrowing. As all the States are indebted to the Center, the Ministry of Finance, Planning Commission and the Reserve Bank of India determine market borrowing of the States. In determining the volume of market borrowings, the volume of repayments, the plan investments decided upon and the volume of indebtedness of each of the States

[8] Small savings consist of post office savings in national saving certificates. The Center advances two-thirds of net collection of small savings to the states on the basis of origin.

are taken into account. In 1998–99, market borrowings constituted 22 percent of States' indebtedness.

Subscription to State government loans constitutes a part of the Statutory Liquidity Ratio (SLR). Commercial banks are required to maintain 35 percent of the resources available for investment in stipulated assets, which includes state government borrowings. Thus, the investible resources of the banking system are partly pre-empted for government consumption and investment. The interest rates on government bonds were significantly below the market rates. However, financial sector reforms initiated since 1991 have gradually aligned the interest rates on government bonds with market rates.

6.3.5. *Shortcomings of Inter-governmental Transfers Summarized*

The design and implementation of inter-governmental transfer schemes in India suffer from a number of shortcomings. First, multiple agencies with overlapping jurisdictions have blurred the overall objectives of transfers. Second, accommodating different interests has unduly complicated the transfer formula. Third, the design of the transfer system is not well targeted to achieve equalization or to ensure the provision of minimum service levels in the States. Fourth, the present system has introduced disincentive effects on the fiscal management in the States. While there is certainly a role for specific purpose transfers in Indian federation, the design and implementation of the centrally sponsored schemes has not served the purpose. It has tended to multiply State level bureaucracy and distort the choices made by States in unintended ways.

6.4. *Equalizing Effect of Inter-governmental Transfers*

Analysis of inter-governmental transfers shows some inter-State redistribution. The level of per capita transfers varies inversely with the level of per capita State domestic product. The cross-section income elasticity of aggregate transfers in 1998–99 was –0.194 (see Table 8). The progressivism in the transfer system was entirely due to the redistribution achieved in Finance Commission transfers.

The elasticity of Finance Commission transfers with respect to GSDP in 1997–98 was –0.26. In contrast, grants for State Plan schemes and centrally sponsored schemes were not significantly related to per capita GSP. These transfers did not achieve significant equalization. Thus, by

Table 8. Equalization in Fiscal Transfer System in India 1998–99

State	Finance Commission	Planning Commission: State Plan Schemes	Planning Commission: Centrally Sponsored	Planning Commission: Total	Total Current Transfers
1. Major States					
Intercept	8.383	5.859	−2.819	3.848	8.124
T value	8.943	3.527	−0.760	2.011	9.180
Coefficient	−0.260	−0.171	0.736	0.115	−0.194
T value	−2.638	−0.978	1.891	0.573	−2.087
R 2	0.349	0.068	0.216	0.025	0.251

Note: Estimated by employing the functional form: Ln G = a + b Ln Y + e, where G denotes different types of per capita transfers, Y represent per capita NSDP, a and b represent parameter estimates and e is the error term.

and large, the transfer system may be considered equitable. Nevertheless, it should be noted that the absolute value of elasticity is low, suggesting that although the transfer system on the whole has an equalizing impact, it is designed only to offset a small part of the shortfall between fiscal capacity and cost disabilities.

7. Fiscal Transfers from the State to local Governments

Each State is required to appoint a State Finance Commission (SFC) every five years. These Commissions are mandated to make recommendations on the transfers to urban and rural local bodies. They also are required to do the same on the assignment of tax revenues to local bodies, sharing of tax revenues between the States and the local governments and their distribution among individual local bodies, and the grants to be made to them.

The experience with State Finance commissions has not been a great success. Some States are yet to constitute a SFC even after a decade of giving constitutional recognition to local bodies. In some States, SFCs are yet to submit reports and in many where it has been submitted, the State governments have not accepted the recommendations. As regards revenue raising powers, very little has been done in terms of giving revenue raising powers. The volume of transfers made is inadequate mainly because the States themselves have been facing a severe financial crunch and there is a general reluctance to pass on functions as well as funds. The distribution is not done in any scientific manner. Often, particularly in the case of village panchayats, the distribution is done on a lump sum basis irrespective of capacity or need. In fact, after deducting the cost of electricity at source by the State government, very little is available for actual spending by the local bodies. In many States, the rural local bodies hardly collect any revenues from the sources assigned to them. The only major tax that resides with the rural local bodies is the property tax, but its administration and enforcement is so poor that very little revenue is actually collected. Of course, these generalizations are simplistic and there are States where local bodies play more active roles than that has been portrayed here, but that is an exception rather than a rule. (Joshi, 2006; Rao and Rao, 2008; Singh and Sharma, 2007).

8. Federal Fiscal Arrangements in India: Major Issues

The preceding analysis brings out the important features of federal fiscal arrangements in India. The analysis highlights a number of shortcomings, which are due not merely to Constitutional arrangements, but also to conventions, methods and existing institutional rules. These shortcomings have been shaped by the developmental strategy and by economic liberalization would appear to call for a review of the arrangements. Therefore, in re-orienting the federal fiscal arrangements to complement the needs of a market economy, reforms are needed in both policies and institutions.

The analysis of the federal fiscal system should begin with an examination of assignments. As in most other federations, the system of assignments has resulted in a significant degree of vertical fiscal imbalance. The wide differences in per capita incomes among the States have also caused severe horizontal fiscal imbalances. The transfer system should offset the fiscal imbalances. In particular, the transfer system should be designed to offset fiscal disabilities arising from the shortfall between revenue capacity and cost disabilities. These transfers should be general-purpose transfers — to enable all the States to provide a given level of public service at a given tax-price. In addition to these general-purpose transfers, specific purpose transfers are needed to ensure certain minimum standards of specified services, which are in the nature of merit goods.

It must be admitted that the inter-governmental transfer system in India has, over the years, achieved some measure of equalization in the levels of public services across the States. Equally notable is the attempt to reduce discretion in the allocation of transfers by the increasing resort to formula-based distribution. Of course, the formulae used to distribute transfers have left a lot of room for improvement in terms of both equity and incentives. It is therefore necessary to re-design the transfer system to improve accountability, incentives and equity. In a more liberalized environment, inter-State inequality in the standards of public services is likely to increase. The general-purpose transfers should, therefore, be better targeted. Similarly, the centrally sponsored schemes must be designed to ensure minimum outlay on specified services throughout the federation. The States may be allowed to choose from among a number of priority schemes instead of fixing conditionality for each scheme. Further consolidation of the large number of centrally sponsored schemes could improve the flexibility to the States and reduce resource distortions.

Reforms are needed in the institutional mechanism as well. First, overlapping in the functions of different institutions should be avoided. The Finance Commission can assess and recommend transfers to cover the entire current needs of the States, and the Planning Commission can assess the requirements of physical infrastructures and give the required loans. The working of the Finance Commission and the methodology adopted by it too should be changed so that disincentive to fiscal management is avoided. The appointment of professionals to the Finance Commission, strengthening of its research capacity, a permanent secretariat undertaking continuous research and imparting a greater degree of transparency to the functioning of the Commission are some of the other reforms urgently called for.

Notwithstanding the weaknesses, it must be noted that the system of inter-governmental fiscal arrangements in India has served well for over 50 years. It has achieved a significant equalization over the years, instituted a workable system of resolving the outstanding issues between the Center and the States and among the States inter se, and adjusted to the changing requirements and thus has contributed to achieving a degree of cohesiveness in a large and diverse country. No doubt, the analysis brings out several areas of reform; what is however important, it is eminently possible to reform the system.

References

Boadway, R W and F Flatters (1982). *Equalisation in a Federal State: An Economic Analysis*, Economic Council of Canada, Ottawa: Canadian Government Publishing Center.

Bradbury, K L, H F Ladd, M Perrault, A Reschovsky, and J Yinger (1984). State aid to offset fiscal disparities among counties, *National Tax Journal*, 37, pp. 151–170.

Buchanan, J M (1950). Federalism and fiscal equity. *American Economic Review*, 40(4) (September), pp. 421–432.

Chelliah, R J (1991). *Towards a Decentralised Polity*, Fourth L. K. Jha Memorial Lecture, Fiscal Research Foundation, New Delhi.

Feldstein, M S (1975). Wealth neutrality and local choice in public education. *American Economic Review*, 65, pp. 75–89.

India (1972). Report of the Committee on Taxation of Agricultural Wealth and Income, Ministry of Finance, Government of India.

India (2000). Report of the Eleventh Finance Commission on Additional Term of Reference, Ministry of Finance, New Delhi.

Joshi, R (2006). The Working of State Finance Commissions. INRM Policy Brief No. 9, Asian Development Bank, New Delhi.

Rao, M G (1998). Inter-governmental Transfers in a Planned Economy. In R M Bird, and F Vaillancourt, (eds.). *Fiscal Decentralisation in Developing Countries*, Cambridge University Press, Cambridge.

Rao, M G, H K Amar Nath, and B P Vani (2003). Rural Fiscal Decentralisation in Karnataka, Report Prepared for the World Bank. National Institute of Public Finance and Policy (Processed).

Rao, M G and A Das-Gupta (1995). Inter-governmental transfers and poverty alleviation. *Environment and Policy C: Government and Policy*, 24 (Fall), pp. 99–114.

Rao, M G and U A V Rao (2008). Expanding the resource base of Panchayats. *Economic and Political Weekly,* Vol. XLIII No. 4 (January 26), pp. 54–61.

Rao, M G and T K Sen (1996). *Fiscal Federalism in India — Theory and Practice*, Macmillan India, New Delhi.

Rao, M G, R T Shand, and K P Kalirajan (1999). Convergence of incomes in Indian States: A divergent view, *Economic and Political Weekly*, Vol. XXXIV, No. 13, (March 27), pp. 769–778.

Rao, M G and N Singh (1999). How to Think About Local Government Reform in India, Paper presented at the conference on second-generation Indian economic reforms, Madras School of Economics, Chennai, December 8–10.

Rao, M G and N Singh (2000). The Political Economy of Center-State Fiscal Transfers in India. Paper presented at the Columbia University — World Bank Conference on Institutional Elements of Tax Design and Reform, February 18–19.

Singh, S and P Sharma (2007). *Decentralization: Institutions and Politics in* Rural India, Oxford University Press, New Delhi.

Chapter VI

Administrative Reform in Taiwan — An Uneasy and Unfinished Political Task

JAY N. SHIH

National Cheng Chi University, Taiwan

Since 1990 Taiwan has followed the democracy footsteps of the western nations in advocating a more transparent system of governance. During the past decade, the government reform work has been through several administrations formed by the Kuomintang (KMT) and the Democratic Progressive Party (DPP), including two presidents and several premiers of the Executive Yuan. Exactly how did the ideas and execution of Taiwan's central government reform evolve? Are there distinctions regarding the point of view among administrations? Even more importantly, what specific changes have actually taken place? This article uses Taiwan as a case study to explain the content of such a reform, to describe the points of view of the deliberations and to analyze the political development during the course of the reform.

1. Administrative Reform Under Regimes of the KMT

The Taiwanese government's reform program has developed over time. During the administration of KMT's Lee Teng-Hui, the premier of the Executive Yuan Lien Chan pushed for an Administrative Innovation Program in 1992 and 1995 respectively. The *Government Reinvention*

Program was introduced in 1998 when Hsiao Wan-Chang was the premier of the Executive Yuan. In 2000, after Chen Shui-Bien of the DPP became president, the *Government Reform Program* was offered.

Besides these more visible reform initiatives, other important reform plans were in play during this period. For instance, the reorganization plan of the Executive Yuan had always been in progress as a special project. Different versions of draft plans were completed in 1988, 1994, and 1998 respectively, but were never been submitted to the Legislative Yuan for legislation amendments. During this same period the constitution of the Republic of China (ROC) was amended, with the annulling of the Taiwan Province government being particularly important.

The objectives of the KMT reform program changed between the first and the second proposals (see Table 1). The overall objective at the *Administrative Innovation Program* phase was reduce corruption and to establish a more capable government, with an emphasis on integrity, efficiency, and convenience.

The overall objective of the "Government Reorganization Program" phase was to introduce a business entrepreneurial spirit to establish an innovative, flexible, and responsive government in order to enhance the competitiveness of the nation. This second phase was in fact an integration of several separate reform measures that had been previously introduced, including the previous Administrative Innovative Program, administrative reorganization program, a total service quality enhancement program, e-government program, single-window public service program, and various finance improvement programs.

If reform visions or objectives are to be more than rhetoric (March & Olsen, 1983), then the objectives must reflect the longer run goals of the reform group. The first step of the administrative reform under the KMT regime anticipated the switch to a spirit of businesslike government that would emphasize the competitiveness of the nation and a more aggressive and open operating attitude by the government. One of the major components of phase two would be to push for privatizing government-owned enterprises and for outsourcing many public services. Phase one of the reform program would set the stage for this shift by emphasizing more transparency and by emphasizing more traditional public service values.

Table 1. The Outline of Several Administrative Reform Programs in Taiwan

Time	Strategic Goals	Major Objections	Major Enacted Programs
Administrative Innovation Program (1992–1998)	Establish uncorrupted government	Uncorrupt	• Anti-corruption action. • Identifying specific job with strict inspection. • Strictly enforce the financial closure report. • Setting up central uncorrupted conference by the Executive Yuan. • Establishing transparent administrative regulation procedures.
		Efficiency	• Trim and streamline 5% of the established manpower in 3-year period. • Reduce budget deficits. • Promote the participation of public construction by the private sectors. • Promoting government business going private. • Review the establishments of funds not in business operation.

(Continued)

Table 1. (*Continued*)

Time	Strategic Goals	Major Objections	Major Enacted Programs
		Convenience	• Promote employee suggestion system. • Promote outsourcing. • Selecting areas for enacting the public services quality program. • Promoting service automation. • Setting up administrative reform mailboxes. • Public services attitude training. • A transparent in government procurement public bidding.
Government Reinvention Program (1998–2000)	Introduce Business management spirit, to establish an innovative, flexible, responsive government in order to enhance national competitiveness.	Reorganization	• Planning for Executive Yuan's organizational adjustments. • Establishing datum law for government agencies. • Simplify administrative layers.
		Public employees and public service quality	• Review of loosening and tightening of the law and regulations. • Promoting E-government. • Promoting establishing anti-corruption organization. • Improve service quality.

(*Continued*)

Table 1. ***(Continued)***

Time	Strategic Goals	Major Objections	Major Enacted Programs
		Review of regulations	• Promoting participation of public affairs by the private sectors. • Amending the laws and regulations that are not convenient or improperly restricting the market competition.
Government Reorganization (2001–)	A vital government with global competitiveness.	Administrative organization	• Reorganization of the Executive Yuan. • Promoting quasi non-ministerial administrative organizations. • Promoting thorough review of government functions.
		Public personnel system.	
		Congress reform	
		Inter-governmental relations	
		Quality service	

Reinventing Government (Osbrone & Gabler, 1992) that had influenced the reform of the United State's federal government and the thoughts of new public management (e.g., Hood, 1991; Kettl, 2000; Peters, 2001) had become popular with Taiwan's academic circle. Moreover, the book *The Competitive Advantage of Nations* by Michael Porter (1990) and the International Institutions' country ratings had become important references for the Taiwanese government. Secondly, the new premier of the Executive Yuan brought an international economic trade background. The new minister of the Research, Development and Evaluation Commission (RDEC), who is in charge of formulating the reform program, was a former business school professor. This set of backgrounds was greatly different from those of the former premier and reform team. These new views about public management were accepted, and the concept of transforming to a business management orientation became the core target for the government reform.

In fact, the program actually executed under the KMT amounted to little more than fine-tuning and slight improvements. In other words, there was not much connecting between the intended objectives and the actual changes in Taiwan government operations. The first result was more cosmetic than a fundamental change in the focus of government.

2. Administrative Reform Under Regimes of the DPP

In May 2000, the DPP replaced the KMT as the ruling party for the first time in history. Early in their tenure, an incident took place that severely harmed the image of competency that the party had tried to create. While the entire nation watched on national TV, four people trapped in a flood, waited for hours for a rescue team to come to their aid. The impact was considered of great magnitude by the party, and an administrative reform became a high priority and continuing task.

In February 2001, the Executive Yuan held a politically high profile National Administrative Reform Conference, with the themes of administrative re-organization, administrative culture, public opinions and policy making, relationship between central and local government, and policy marketing. However, these themes and the recommended programs for implementation still largely followed the same thinking of the KMT regime. Although some new items were added, a carefully designed reform program did not emerge. The original bureaucratic system remained in place.

According to many DPP observers, there were at least three reasons for the bumpy ride to the DPP office in the initial period. The first is the lack of experience in running the central government. The second is that the number of seats of the DPP in the Legislative Yuan is less than half, and the third is the lack of mutual trust and tension between the new administration and bureaucrats. The weak record of administrative success was magnified by a sudden downturn in the Taiwan economy.

A combination of weak economic condition and inefficient government operations brought President Chen Shui-Bien under pressure. He responded by inviting all political parties, business and academic circles to an *Economic Development Consulting Conference* in August 2001. This conference recommended that the government to continue the administrative reform and form a government reform committee for the purpose of changing the government's role and administrative model. It called for the changes in the styles of decision-making, budget allocation, and public personnel management.

Accepting these recommendations, President Chen immediately began planning a government reform. In October 2001, the *Government Reform Committee* was established at the President's office with President himself as the head of the committee. This was obviously a different approach from the KMT's which left the responsibility for the administrative reform to the Executive Yuan. The total of 29 members consisted of some cabinet members including the Premier of Executive Yuan and Examination Yuan, academic professors with different specialties[1] including this author, and a few chairmen of the corporations.

After a comprehensive discussion, the committee summarized the overall objective of the government reform with the phrase, "the vita government with global competitiveness." The committee also offered ideas to promote the reform: customer orientation, flexible innovation, partnership, political responsibility, and uncorrupted administration. In order for the new administration to truly possess vitality and competitiveness, the committee set up five task forces to handle five different

---

[1] The academic disciplines included Politics, Public Administration, Public Policy, Laws, Business Management and Sociology.

reform directions: downsizing the executive departments, developing a professional and efficient personnel system, rebuilding the relationship between central and local government, reforming the legislative branch, and promoting innovative public service mechanism. Every subgroup had a designated convener, and every subgroup would hire academic professionals to participate in the task of consultation and subject analysis.

The key differences between this reform plan and the previous plans are summarized below:

- As a first step, the academic professionals and the political advisors prepared and analyzed major themes and agendas for the reform.
- The reform is focused on the whole government system rather than on the Executive branch only. The reform placed emphasis on reorganization including, rebuilding the relationship between central and local governments, human resource management policy, enhancing service quality and reviewing laws and regulations.

The reform taskforce for the administrative organization and the congress have completed their proposals. The personnel subgroup has made a partial report and the other two subgroups are still in progress. After the Chief of the Staff of the presidential office became the premier of the Executive Yuan, he quickly submitted the reorganization bill to the Legislative Yuan. He also established a new *Organizational Reform Promoting Committee* in the Executive Yuan and served as the head of the committee. The new minister without portfolio, Professor Yeh Chun-Jung, served the chief executive of this specialized organization with only a small staff. His background specialization is constitutions and administrative law, and he is also the member of the Government Reform Committee. The members of the committee include a few cabinet members and two members of the Government Reform Committee.

From the very start, this new organization did not receive the full attention of the bureaucratic system. The latter was more focused on how to proceed with the organizational adjustment under the Executive Yuan. However, Mr. Yeh's idea was obviously different as he hoped to review the growing role of the government first, and then to discuss how to reorganize the internal design of the departments.

This approach to public management is closely aligned with the corporate management model. To demand that each department analyze each of its roles and functions suggests that there is a capability to eliminate some regulations, public services and policies. Then, the government must go a step further to analyze whether or not it would be feasible to hand over those roles or functions to the private sector (outsourcing), transfer them to the local government (localization), or set up quasi government organizations to handle these. This is a new administrative reform model for Taiwan. The committee would need to establish reviewing criteria and standard operation procedure for each one of the four approaches in question.

3. Executive Yuan's Reorganization Plans Under the DPP

Since the KMT regime, the emphasis of administrative reform has been on reorganization of the Executive Yuan. The question that continues to arise is whether the 30 *plus* cabinet ministries leads to an inefficiency of the government operations. But change is very difficult once a government department is set up (Kaufman, 1976). Efficiency arguments for government organization usually do not stand well against political interests (Moe, 1989). The KMT regime did develop three different versions of government reorganization, but none was sent to Congress for review, suggesting the highly political nature of such reform.

In the initial stages of the DPP administration, the task for government reorganization continued, and a proposal was soon made. The Executive Yuan, under the request by the President Chen Shui-Bien, discussed the proposed new reorganization program and submitted the bill to Congress with hopes that a new Executive Yuan organizational framework could soon be implemented.

The bill called for the reduction in the number of cabinet ministries (by approximately one-third). This is less of a reduction than was proposed by the taskforce. The bill pointed out five critical problems with the present design of the organization of the Taiwan Executive Yuan's. First, there were too many government organizations to control, which caused coordination costs to increase, generated a complicated decision making process, and led to an increase in numbers of public employees. Second, there was a weak policy integration mechanism which meant that the Executive Yuan could not effectively play the role of policy integration and leadership. Third, there was an insufficient correspondence between the core functions of government and its organization, and the policy arms that were promoting internationalization and major social safety net programs, etc. Fourth, independent regulatory organizations were treated as part of the cabinet team, which led to more politicization and less professional independence. Last, there was a lack of clarity about the role of the cabinet-ranked committees, which had been given a large quantity of execution tasks, and no longer were limited to planning and coordination.

The design principles for the Executive Yuan reorganization program that followed from this identification of problems included several items. First is the organizational strategy. The formation of new ministries would be limited to cases where there was a major long-term development policy initiative in play. Second is scale simplification. The Executive Yuan organization would be less than 15 ministries in order to meet the span of control requirements and to reduce the coordination costs. Third is strengthening the capability for policy integration. The Office of the Executive Yuan must have sufficient policy units and policy advisors to carry out planning, coordination, and evaluation, and to make budget resource allocations. Last is the flexibility approach. All ministries would be granted the authority to adjust their own internal organizational structure. These new tools enable the ministry to respond rapidly to changes in the environment.

The biggest difference between this reorganization bill and earlier efforts is the emphasis on involving political leaders in the process of policy coordination and integration. This seems reasonable because Taiwan's president is elected by popular vote. In fact, the whole system is more similar to the US presidential government than to a cabinet government. The proposed new system was radical enough that it found a considerable opposition from various political fronts. Moreover, the DPP did not have a majority in congress, so the outlook for congressional approval was not bright. Up to now, the Legislative Yuan has not yet approved the bill.

The proposed new reform plan was also controversial at the bureaucratic level. The new thinking was that in order for the government to deliver public services or even regulations more efficiently, a business management culture would have to be adopted. The type of organization promoted imitated Britain's Quangos (Flinders & Smith, 1999; Thiel, 2001; OECD, 2002) and the Japanese government's independent administrative organizations. This innovation received positive responses from the old bureaucratic organizations. The major reason was the self-interest of bureaucrats. The previous administrations had planned to privatize or outsource many government organizations or reorganize them as a government-sponsored non-profit foundation, which meant that some lifetime bureaucratic employees would face a significant change in their workplace arrangement.

Finally, changes in the Taiwan Provincial Government were also made. Since the Government of the ROC transferred to Taiwan in 1949, the ruling operation was based on the constitution and the structure that was established when the KMT was ruling the Mainland. Hence, the government was still in 4 levels, the Central Government, Provincial Government and two Central Government Direct Controlled Municipal governments, with County/City governments and Township/County Offices as the lowest level. The jurisdiction of Taiwan Provincial Government was almost the same as the Central Government and it was effectively leading and influencing county and city governments.

Prior to 1994, the Premier of the Executive Yuan appointed the Governor of Taiwan Provincial Government. Thereafter, the governor was elected through direct voting, and the number of votes received by the governor were not much less than that received by the national President. A subtle political divide began to emerge and political representation became problematic. President Lee Teng-Huei of the ruling KMT joined hands with the DPP in amending the constitution to suspend the election of the provincial governor and to eliminate most of the functions and services of the Taiwan Provincial Government. By 1998, the Taiwan Provincial Government had become more an executive agent of the central government than an autonomous body. Both the KMT and the DPP claimed that such a government organization change would promote the efficiency of government operation, because much duplication and bureaucratic cost would be removed. Critics argued that avoiding the popular support for the Provincial Governor played a vital role.

Many reformers believed that all the functions of Taiwan Provincial Government should be transferred to the county and city governments. If this reform was accepted, the relationship between the central and the local governments would be maintained and local government would have some autonomy. What actually happened was that the Central Government absorbed almost all the functions of the Taiwan Provincial Government, plus the manpower and budget for tens of thousand public servants. There are a number of reasons why the decentralization option was not adopted. The county and city governments were reluctant to assume these responsibilities because of their poor financial condition. Moreover, the huge bureaucracy of the provincial government was reluctant to work under the county/city governments. The arguments were that the relocation costs would weigh heavily on family life and that the working conditions in the county/city government would be far less than what they were with the provincial government. The central government was sympathetic to these arguments in its final decision. However, since the reorganization was not accompanied by a significant layoff, of public employees, the costs savings were less than had been envisioned.

4. Administrative Reform and Government Competitiveness in the Past Decade

To what extent have these various reforms moved government toward its goals of efficiency, transparency, reduced corruption, public-private partnership and national competitiveness?

Competitiveness might be taken as the prime standard of assessment, since this was the original driving force behind the government reforms of both the KMT and DPP. According to the rating data for national competitiveness frequently cited by the government, Taiwan has been ranked at the front among Asian countries. For example, World Economic Forum (WEF) rating data in 2003 placed Taiwan in fifth place among countries around the world and as high as No. 3 in 2002. In the Institute of Management Development (IMD) rankings, Taiwan was about 20th in most years, and behind only Singapore and Hong Kong among Asian countries. The ranking in 2003 was the 6th among the more populated countries.[2]

However, the reality is that this strong national competitiveness is mostly due to non-governmental factors. In the WEF rating, the competitiveness of Taiwan is due to an excellent technological environment, while the macro-economic environment is not outstanding and the performance of public institutions is not a recommendable item. The rating data indicate that Taiwan is about average in terms of government operation indicators like judicial independence, syndicate crime, industrial

[2] See World Competitiveness Yearbook 2003, http://www01.imd.ch/wcy/criteria/(2003/5/30). http://www.imd.ch/research/publications/wcy/index.cfm

property rights, corruption and bribery in public utilities, corruption and bribery in tax collection, corruption and bribery in international trade the bureaucratic red tape and the efficiency in judicial system.

IMD rating results indicated that the performance of government efficiency in Taiwan is poorer than economic performance, business efficiency and infrastructure. More specifically, the transparency of government policy, corruption and bribery, the adaptation of economic policy to environmental change, effective execution of policies, the level of consensus over the policy direction, customs management and the advantages of the legal system toward economic competitiveness are all graded relatively low and there exists a large gap with the best performing countries (see Table 2). When compared with the same indicators for 1997, there is no significant change in the ratings. The 2002 IMD report commented that in order to lift up the global ranking in national overall competitiveness, Taiwan might concentrate on 20 indicators requiring improvement, 8 of which are in the governmental efficiency category.

One might conclude from these international ratings that government efficiency and transparency do not make a strong contribution to the overall competitiveness of the country.

The data in Table 3 show that the number of government employees (per 1000 population) has dropped in the past 10 years. However, the reduction is largely due to the privatization of public enterprises. Public employees who deliver core public services have remained at about the same level. The government expenditure share of GDP has fallen over the past decade.

The Corruption Perception Index released by Transparency International indicates that Taiwan's ranking has not changed significantly over the decade. For example, in 2006 Taiwan ranked 34th among 163 countries evaluated, compared to 29th among 54 countries ten years ago. People continue to perceive a problem of corruption.

In some areas of governance there have been significant improvements. E-Government is the one most successful innovations. An international ranking of website services of the worldwide governments conducted by Brown University of USA, rated Taiwan as best.[3] In this regard, the government's active provision of on-line application services

---

[3] See http://www.brown.edu/Departments/Taubman_Center/researchprogram.html for the related information.

Table 2. IMD Rating of Performance in Government Efficiency of Taiwan

	2002 Ranking	2002 Taiwan Level	2002 Best Level	1997 Taiwan Level
Policy transparency	26	4.92	8.11	4.65
Public services free of political influence	17	4.55	6.96	—
Bureaucratic system free of impairment to economic activities	16	4.29	7.46	3.95
Reduced corruption and bribery	26	4.58	9.47	4.40
New legislation favorable to business competition	15	6.08	8.17	3.05
Economic policy adaptive to environment change promptly	27	4.63	8.58	4.92
Capable of executing government decision effectively	29	4.45	8.81	—
Political parties' understanding over the economic challenge the countries faces	26	4.63	8.17	—
Consensus in policy directions	35	4.39	9.04	—
Legal system favorable to economic competitiveness	28	5.00	8.50	5.11
Legislation meets needs in economic competitiveness	—	—	—	3.05
Customs facilitating rapid customs clearance	24	6.58	8.91	5.18
Political system able to adjust effectively to economic challenge	—	—	—	4.50
Administration power sharing free from interference of central government	—	—	—	4.35

Source: Both ranking and raw scores of each item are excerpted from *IMD World Competitiveness Yearbook 1998 & 2003*. The International Institute for Management Development issues the annual report.

Table 3. Several Statistics of the Public Sector in Taiwan

	Net Public Expenditures (NT$ billion)	Net Public Expenditures as % of GDP	Number of Public Employees (per 1000 population)	CPI Ranking
1980	345	25.3	635074 (35.7)	—
1990	1167	27.6	800571 (39.3)	—
1993	1859	32.1	834599 (39.8)	—
1994	1914	30.0	825564 (39.1)	—
1995	2075	29.8	822368 (38.6)	25
1996	2006	26.5	823541 (38.4)	29
1997	2067	25.0	825731 (38.1)	31
1998	2204	24.6	801201 (36.6)	29
1999	2218	23.4	795218 (36.1)	28
2000	3141*	21.1	778050 (35.0)	28
2001	2271	23.0	571667 (25.6)	27
2002	2145	20.8	580645 (25.9)	29
2003	2206	21.0	554010 (24.6)	30
2004	2239	20.2	549715 (24.3)	35
2005	2309	20.2	505648 (22.3)	32
2006	2252	19.0	496861 (21.8)	34

Source:

1. Public expenditures are compiled from the FY2008 Budget Request Book of the Central Government. FY2000 is 1.5 years.
2. Number of public employees is compiled from The Civil Servants Yearbook (annually); the column does not include public teachers after 2001.
3. CPI represents Corruption Perception Index provided by the Transparency International.

is a very significant improvement. It offers a government digital information system for citizen enquiries and, e-documentation of government internal communication and documents. The focus is on public services that are heavily used by people and business, for example household administration, land administration, tax affairs, motor vehicle monitoring services and business affairs, "More Internets, Less Road Net" has become a slogan of e-government. The achievements of e-government are arguably linked with the prosperity of the technology industry in both information manufacturing and R&D, which has indeed provided faster and more easily used services and information to those who make use of the services. However, e-government is not equivalent to e-democracy, because Taiwan's e-governance is still not provided on the broad basis necessary for it to reach a majority of the population.

In parallel with e-government, the government of Taiwan has established a transparent network purchasing system, allowing qualified domestic and foreign individuals and firms, to participate in the competition. This is the antithesis of the "Back Door" approach to winning business opportunity with bribery, that was not so unusual in earlier times.

These improvements in access to government services have led to positive changes in the service attitude of public employees. A " Citizen Services White Paper" includes assessments of more than 100 key citizen service items, including consular affairs, national tax, commerce, communication, medical services and environment protection. The procedures used for delivery, public opinions and utilization of social resources are incorporated in an Assessment in Service Quality Award of the Executive Yuan. Finally the network is used actively to provide a convenient, fast, quality and single window services. This service orientation has become a more and more common service mode of the government. In general, the service attitude and quality has been significantly improved. Particularly the urban area governments have been under pressure to improve services.

5. Conclusion

Since 1990, the Taiwanese Government and the political leadership have been calling for administrative reform and government restructuring. There are major differences between the KMT and the DPP in terms of the strategy to be followed for administrative reform, but there are also points of agreement such as the overarching goal of adopting the new public management applied in many OECD countries. The DPP has been more aggressive in moving in this direction, and has presented a more complete program. It involves review of the role of government functions, and more actively seeking the participation of profit and non-profit organizations in public affairs. In the power sharing with locals and communities, a "partnership" concept has been developed to link the central government, private sector, communities and local government. In the past 10 years, both political parties have asserted that Taiwan must be able to meet the challenge of globalization, and that government reform should be targeted as part of this objective.

Government reform has been emphasized over the past decade but without great success. The OECD countries have been successful in addressing at such issues as controlling the size of government, reducing deficits, enhancing management ability, and gaining public confidence, but Taiwan have mimicked them with little success.

How can this result be interpreted? We might analyze the Taiwan case with the theories of change management. Professor John P. Kotter (1996) of Harvard has pointed out that a successful change management in business organizations must follow eight steps: establishing a sense of urgency, establishing a leadership team, developing a vision and strategy, communicating the change vision, empowering employees for action, generating short-term results, consolidating gains for further advancement and anchoring new approaches in the culture. The government of Taiwan has not scored well on these criteria for success.

The major problem has been the failure to capture widespread support for the program. When the responsible team fails to win the full support from other political leaders in the government, and more importantly, win the general support from the public and the media the reform agenda is very likely be turned down. (Cobb & Ross, 1997). In the meantime, the parties leading the reform will lose full control of the so-called "problem ownership." Have the advocates for reform adequately prepared, their case for why reform is necessary? Has the bureaucracy been convinced that their long-term interests would be compromised if the current style of government were not changed? Are the reformers capable of providing a convincing crisis statement?

In the KMT era, the content of reform was generally a response of the bureaucratic system to an instruction of the premier of the Executive Yuan. The government then quickly proposed a reform plan to be incorporated in the address made by the premier of the Executive Yuan. Obviously, there will not be a representative public voice if the plan visions, goals and contents are drafted by the very bureaucratic system that is going to be reformed.

In the DPP era, the elite from the academies and the business sectors drafted the government reforms. However, there was poor communication, and little two-way dialogue with the officials in the government. As a result, many government employees failed to understand the reform plan. Therefore, the resistance and opposition from the bureaucratic system were even stronger than in the KMT era.

The contents of the DPP government reform program are not so different from those of the KMT government, mainly in the areas of the internal management, inter-governmental relationships and government reorganization. These changes would bring more visible and immediate benefit to the business community than to the general public. The general public is more concerned with public service delivery, which affects their daily life, and the opportunity of participation in public decision-making. The team directing the government reform effort in Taiwan was weak in demonstrating how the administrative reform would benefit the people. Absent grassroots support from taxpayers, the government reform landed at a point with more opposition than support.

Secondly, though the objection of bureaucracy and the general public was predictable, it might be turned around, This, however, would require committed leadership. In the KMT era, though a promoting organization was established, it included heavy representation from the bureaucratic system, but did not include significant involvement and commitment from political leaders. Leadership became a problem.

The Government Reform Committee headed by President Chen Shui-Bien led the government reform of the DPP Administration. The Executive Yuan had a newly-established unit for promoting the reforms. Therefore, a commitment from the political leadership of the government seemed to be in place. This is similar to the situation in UK and New Zealand. Yet, both the dual leadership design of the government system in Taiwan, and the autonomous operation of ministries, has generated negative interference. So, while the two Chief Executives in the administrative system maintained their support, the members of the other political teams were less passionate, and would not actively participate in the government reform by exercising their influence over their subordinate bureaucratic system. There was a passive resistance to the program.

Thirdly, creating positive short-term results of reform would have been an important milestone to change the negative attitude of the bureaucracy towards the reform and to raise the public awareness and acceptance. Reforms in many countries have set short and medium term performance targets to try and insure acceptability of a reform package.[4]

[4] For example, Hong Kong Government has set out a number of targets for her reform program, see Lam (2003).

Such short-term gains were not seen in the government reform plan of either the KMT or the DPP. The approach seems to have been, "just do it". The implementation of government reform programs, with no clear and feasible performance indicators, could not produce the necessary short-term results, no matter how attractive the vision of change or how complete the reform plan. The accumulated effect is that after 10 years of effort, the size of the government remains about the same.

References

Cobb, R W and M H Ross (eds.) (1997). *Cultural strategies of agenda denial: avoidance, attack, and redefinition*. Lawrence, Kan.: University Press of Kansas.

Flinders, M V and M J Smith (1999). Quangos, accountability and reform: The politics of quasi-government. Basingstoke, Hampshire [England]: Macmillan.

Hood, C (1991). A public management for all seasons? *Public Administration*, 69, 3–19.

Kaufman, H (1976). *Are government organizations immortal?* Washington, D.C: Brookings Institution.

Kettl, D F (2000). *The global public management revolution*. Washington, D.C: Brookings Institution.

Kotter, J P (1996). Leading change. Boston, Mass.: Harvard Business School Press.

Kotter, J P and D S Cohen (2002). The heart of change: Real-life stories of how people change their organizations. Boston, Mass.: Harvard Business School Press.

Lam, J T M (2003). Enhanced productivity program in Hong Kong. *Public Performance & Management Review*, 27(1), pp. 53–70.

March, J G and J P Olsen (1983). Organizing political life: What administrative reorganization tells us about government. *American Political Science Review*, 77, pp. 281–296.

March, J G, and J P Olsen (1989). *Rediscovering institutions: The organizational basis of politics*. New York: Basic.

Moe, T (1989). The Politics of Bureaucratic Structure. In *Can the Government Govern?* J. E. Chubb and P. E. Peterson (eds.), Washington, D.C: Brookings Institution.

OECD (2002). *Distributed public service: Agencies, authorities and other government bodies*. Paris: OECD.

Osborne, D and G Ted (1992). Reinventing government: How the entrepreneurial spirit is transforming the public sector. New York: Plume.

Peters, B G (2001). *The future of governing*. (2nd ed.) Lawrence, Kan.: University Press of Kansas.

Porter, M E (1990). The competitive advantage of nations. New York: Free Press.
Rochefort, D A and R W Cobb (eds.) (1994). *The politics of problem definition: Shaping the policy agenda.* Lawrence, Kan.: University Press of Kansas.
Thiel, S van (2001). *Quangos: Trends, causes and consequences.* Aldershot, Hampshire [England]: Burlington.

Chapter VII

Decentralization in the Philippines After Ten Years — What Have We Learned?[1]

BENJAMIN E. DIOKNO[2]

University of the Philippines

1. Introduction

When Corazon Aquino took power and established a revolutionary government in 1986, she promised a wide-ranging package of public sector reforms including the devolution of political and administrative authority to local governments. That promise was kept with the passage of the Local Government Act of 1991 that resulted in the devolution of both political authority and administrative authority over many services, including many aspects of health care, agricultural extension, social welfare, and financial management.

The 1991 decentralization act significantly upgraded the assigned responsibilities and taxing powers of local governments in the Philippines. But more important, it changed the inter-governmental grant system

[1] Paper presented at the Asian Development Conference, 2003 on the theme: Development and Decentralization in Asia, International Conference Hall, Kitakyushu City, Fukuoka Prefecture, Japan, November 10 and 11, 2003. I thank the workshop participants, in particular Professor Shinji Asanuma, for their comments. The financial support from the Philippine Center for Economic Development is gratefully acknowledged. Possible errors or misinterpretations are entirely mine.

[2] Philippine National Bank Professor of Economics, School of Economics of the University of the Philippines, Diliman, Quezon City, Philippines (e-mail: benjamin.diokno@up.edu.ph).

by increasing the amount of financial transfers going to local governments, by making the grants system more rule-based, and by making its fund release automatic. These features have significantly improved the capability of local governments to provide essential public services and to improve budget planning and implementation. But the local governments' gain has been offset to some extent by a potentially large cost in the form of growing fiscal imbalance and macro-economic instability.

This analysis in this paper is focused on whether, after more than ten years, the present political, administrative and fiscal arrangement has resulted in better governance (specifically, more efficient and more equitable service delivery), improved fiscal balance and macro-economic stability. It will also discuss the effect of politics and weak institutions on the design, legislation, and actual implementation of the Local Government Code of 1991. Finally, some views are offered on the policy framework needed to push forward decentralization in the Philippines.

2. Local Government Structure

Before the "people power" revolution of 1986, the government structure in the Philippines was highly centralized. One may argue that such a setup was a necessary arrangement for the totalitarian regime, with the national government selectively delegating powers to its layers of local government.

The 1987 Constitution, ratified about a year and a half after the Aquino revolutionary government was installed, provides for a unitary form of government with a multi-tiered structure. The Philippines is a presidential republic with a bicameral legislature, consisting of the Senate with 24 members and the House of Representatives with 240 members. At the highest level is the central government operating through some 24 departments and other offices under the Office of the President. The country is divided into 15 administrative regions with most departments maintaining regional offices. In addition, there are two autonomous regions: the Autonomous Region of Muslim Mindanao (ARMM) and the Cordillera Autonomous Region (CAR).

The second tier is the local government units (LGUs). These consist of three layers: provinces, cities and municipalities, and barangays. The 79 provinces are each fully subdivided into municipalities and component cities, which are further subdivided into barangays. The barangay, the smallest political unit, has existed as a neighborhood unit of local

Table 1. Philippines: Changing Political Subdivisions

	1981	1991	2003[b]
Provinces	75	76	79
Cities[a]	60	66	115
Municipalities	1,497	1,540	1,497
Barangays	n.a.	n.a.	41,959

Source: Philippine Yearbook 1981, National Statistics Coordination Board.
Notes:
[a] Including cities in Metropolitan Manila.
[b] As of June 30, 2003.

government since the colonial Spanish regime. As of June 30, 2003, there were 79 provinces, 115 cities, 1,497 municipalities, and 41,959 barangays.[3] The changes in this number of political subdivisions over the past two decades are shown in Table 1. As will be discussed below, the unusually high conversion rate from a municipality to a city in recent years is a rational response to the incentive structure embedded in the inter-governmental grant system as provided for in the Local Government Code of 1991. Each level of local government unit is headed by an elected chief executive (provincial governor, city or municipal mayor, and barangay captain) and has a legislative body (including an elected vice-governor or vice mayor and council members). All elected officials have a three-year term of office and are subject to a three-term limit. Each level of local government is autonomous. However, in areas like budgeting and legislation, higher-level government (say, a province) exercises some considerable degree of supervision over lower level governments (say, component cities and municipalities).

The 1987 Constitution explicitly recognized local governments units as important components of the overall government structure. Article II, Section 25 provides that the "State shall ensure the autonomy of local governments" while Article 10, Section 6 provides that: "Local government units shall have a just share, as determined by law, in the national taxes which shall be automatically released to them." The latter has provided the inter-governmental grant system a solid legal basis for revenue sharing.

[3] These numbers fluctuate over time as new local government units are created while others are converted from lower level local government units to higher level ones, say from a barangay to a municipality or a municipality to a city.

3. Inter-governmental Transfer System

The inter-governmental transfer system under the Local Government Code of 1991, called *Internal Revenue Allotment* (or *IRA*), is formula-based and mandatory. The vertical share, i.e., the entitlement of the local government sector, is very transparent. To defray the cost of devolved expenditures, Section 284 of the Code provides for 40 percent of central government revenues collected three years before the year of the distribution to be transferred back to local government units as internal revenue allotment. The IRA is divided among the individual local government units through a two-stage process. The first stage is to distribute the total IRA into four distributable pools by level of local government (province, city, municipality and barangays); the second stage is to allocate the distributable pool available to each level of local government according to a formula based on population, land area, equal sharing.

Specifically, at the first stage, the IRA is divided among the different levels of local government as follows: provinces and cities receive 23 percent each, municipalities receive 34 percent and barangays receive 20 percent. At the second stage, the IRA share of each tier of government is then divided among the individual local government units on the basis of population (50 percent), land area (25 percent) and equal sharing (25 percent). In contrast, under the previous IRA formulation, the total amount was divided: 27 percent to provinces, 22 percent to cities, 41 percent to municipalities and 10 percent to barangays. The IRA share of each level of local governments was then distributed among each local government unit according to the following factors and weights: population (70 percent), land area (20 percent) and equal sharing (10 percent).

As a result of the new formula, there was a sharp increase in the financial grants received by local governments, with the barangays as the biggest beneficiaries, followed by cities. The provinces, on the other hand, were the biggest losers considering that they absorbed almost half of the total cost of devolved functions but saw their allocation share drop from 50 to 27 percent.

The IRA is in the nature of an unconditional block grant, thus giving local governments wide discretion in its utilization. The only condition for the use of the IRA is that each local government unit must earmark in the annual budgets an amount of no less than 20 percent for local development projects that are embodied or contained in the local development plans.[4]

The Local Government Code of 1991 provides that the individual shares in IRA of each local government unit shall be automatically released, directly to the provincial, city, municipal or barangays treasurer, on a quarterly basis but not beyond five days after the end of each quarter. However, the Central Government may adjust the IRA share of local governments in the event that an unmanageable public sector deficit is incurred by the National Government.

4. Assignment of Expenditure Responsibility

Prior to the enactment of the Local Government Code of 1991, the expenditure responsibilities of local governments were limited to the regulation of business activities in their jurisdictions and the operation of services and facilities such as garbage collection, public cemeteries, public markets and slaughterhouses. The Code of 1991 mandated the transfer from national government agencies to LGUs the principal responsibility for the delivery of basic services and the operation of facilities in the following areas:

- agricultural extension and research;
- industrial research and development;
- social forestry, pollution control and protection of the environment;
- health services, including hospitals and other tertiary health services;
- social welfare services;
- construction and maintenance of local infrastructure facilities, waterworks, sewerage and communal irrigation; and
- land use planning.

This devolution in responsibility for delivering services is significant in magnitude, both in terms of the new expenditure assignments and the personnel transferred to the local governments (see Table 2).

---

[4] In practice, this condition is treated rather loosely so that many "soft" facilities improvement projects (e.g. beautification of the plaza) and capacity-building programs (e.g. study tours of local officials) are considered as part of the menu of development projects.

Table 2. Philippines: Costs and Personnel of Devolved Functions Estimates as of March 1993

National Government Agencies	Estimated Devolved Budget (in million pesos)	1992 Agency Budget (in million pesos)	Share of Devolved Budget in Total 1992 Agency Budget (percent)	Number of Devolved Personnel	Number of Personnel Before Devolution[a]	Share of Devolved Personnel to Total Number of Personnel Before Devolution[a]
Agrarian reform	9.4	1,842.4	0.51	—	—	—
Agriculture	1,055.6	5,210	20.3	17,673	29,638	59.6
Budget & Management	172.8	465.4	37.1	1,650	3,532	46.7
Envir. & Nat. Resources	167.7	1,941.8	8.6	895	21,320	4.2
Health	3,851.1	9,991.4	38.5	45,896	74,896	61.3
Pub. W. & Highways	1,096.3	27,109.3	4.0	—	—	—
Soc. Welf. & Develop.	966.4	1,320.7	65.6	4,144	6,932	59.8
Tourism	2.8	207.7	1.4	—	—	—
Transp. & Communic.	0.1	7,563.9	0.0	—	—	—
Ph. Game fowl Comm.	8.7	15.3	56.9	25	191	13.1

[a] Only for departments with devolved personnel.
Source: Government authorities.

The staffing complement of four government agencies were significantly changed: Department of Agriculture, Department of Budget and Management, Department of Health, and Department of Social Welfare and Development. For a more detailed listing of expenditure responsibilities by level of local governments (see Table A.1).

5. Revenue Assignment

Under the current tax structure, most major taxes are assigned exclusively to the national government. These are the individual and corporate income taxes, value added tax, excise taxes on alcoholic beverages, tobacco products and petroleum products, and customs duties. Under the Local Government Code of 1991, LGUs are allowed to collect real property taxes, local business tax and specified other taxes. A more detailed list of taxing powers by level of government is shown in Table A.2. The base for each of these taxes is defined by national government legislation that also imposes limits on tax rates.

The Local Government Code of 1991 expanded the tax base of local government units to include products, activities and sectors that previously were outside the reach of local taxation. It also raised the maximum rates at which most local taxes may be levied. On the other hand, because it reduced the assessment levels for real property taxation, the Code has effectively narrowed the base for real property taxation.

6. Local Government Borrowing

Even before the enactment of the Local Government Code of 1991, provinces, cities and municipalities were allowed to borrow from government financial institutions such as the Philippine National Bank (PNB), the Development Bank of the Philippines (DBP), and the Government Service Insurance System (GSIS). However, local governments have borrowed very little to finance capital projects, because of (a) operational and managerial problems, (b) inadequate information and a conservative fiscal attitude of local officials, and (c) unrealistic loan standards.[5]

[5] These criticisms are longstanding. See L. Kenneth Hubbell, "Local Government Credit Financing", in Roy Bahl and Barbara Miller (eds.), *Local Government Finance in the Third World: A Case Study of the Philippines*, Praeger, 1983.

The Local Government Code of 1991 significantly expanded the borrowing powers of LGUs. An LGU may do any of the following:

Contract loans, credits, and other forms of indebtedness with any government or domestic private banks and other lending institutions to finance the construction, installation, improvement, expansion, operation or maintenance of public facilities, infrastructure facilities, housing projects, the acquisition of real property, and the implementation of other capital investment projects.

Issue bonds, debentures, securities, collaterals, notes, and other obligations to finance self-liquidating, income-producing development or livelihood projects, subject to the rules and regulations of the Central Bank and the Securities and Exchange Commission.

Avail of loans from funds secured by the National Government for the purpose of financing the construction, installation, improvement, expansion, operation or maintenance of public markets and facilities, infrastructure facilities, or housing projects, the acquisition of real property, and the implementation on other capital investment projects.

Enter into contract with any duly pre-qualified individual contractor, for the financing, construction, operation, and maintenance of any financially viable infrastructure facilities, under the build-operate-and-transfer (BOT) agreement, subject to applicable provisions of Republic Act 6957 authorizing the financing, construction, operation, and maintenance of infrastructure projects by the private sector.

Despite this broader scope for credit financing, local governments have continued to borrow very little to finance their capital projects. In practice, their borrowing sources have been limited to government financial institutions and the Municipal Development Fund (MDF).[6] In the late 1990s, a few LGUs successfully issued bonds.

---

[6] The MDF is a facility for relending to LGUs the proceeds of various loans and grants that the National Government has obtained from foreign governments and multilateral lending institutions.

7. Local Government Budgeting and Financial Mechanism

The Local Government Code of 1991 paved the way for a truly decentralized local government budgeting and financial mechanism. One significant move was to transfer the direct control and supervision of local budget officers to the local chief executives. During the early months of the Aquino government, the local budget officers were placed under the direct control and supervision of the Department of Budget and Management, an arrangement that continued until the Code was passed. This "nationalization" of local budget officers was clearly political since there were no strong economic or efficiency arguments for the move.

Before the Code was passed, the budgets of provinces and cities, including all local governments in Metropolitan Manila, were subject to review by the Department of Budget and Management (DBM), through their regional offices. This arrangement was a major source of irritant between the National Government and local governments since the Commission on Audit would not allow disbursements from the local budgets unless there was prior review and approval by the DBM. Before the approval of the Code in 1991, this stringent requirement was relaxed through an Executive Order mandating that the local, provincial and city budgets approved by the Council and the local chief executive were deemed approved even though they were subject to post-review by DBM.

Under the Local Government Code of 1991, the budgets of provinces, highly urbanized cities, independent component cities, and municipalities within the Metropolitan Manila Authority (MMA) remain subject to review by DBM. The provincial board (Sangguniang Panlalawigan) reviews the budgets of component cities and municipalities. Such review is limited to ensuring that local governments comply with limitations prescribed under the Code such as the proportion of the budget that may be spent on personal services[7] and on debt service, and the

[7] The Code limits the total appropriations, whether annual or supplemental, for personal services of an LGU for one fiscal year to not more 45 percent in the case of first to third class provinces, cities and municipalities, and 55 percent in case of fourth and lower class provinces, cities and municipalities. The appropriations for salaries, wages, representation and transportation allowances and officials and employees of public utilities and local economic enterprises are not included in the annual budget and in the computation of the maximum amount for personal services.

requirement that 5 percent of the estimated revenue from regular sources shall be set aside as annual lump sum appropriation for unforeseen expenditures in case of natural calamities. If within ninety (90) days from receipt of copies of the appropriations ordinances, the Sangguniang Panlalawigan takes no action thereon, the budget shall be deemed to have been reviewed and approved.

Local government units are required to submit financial reports to the Commission on Audit (COA). The financial transactions of LGUs are subject to audit by the Commission on Audit (COA). Such audit is designed to ensure that all financial transactions entered into by the local spending units are in accordance with existing budgeting, accounting and auditing rules and regulations.

8. Outcomes After Ten Years

8.1. *The IRA Has Grown Impressively, But at the Expense of Overall Fiscal Stability*

By any standards, the growth of the internal revenue allotment to local governments has been impressive — in absolute peso value, as a percent of total expenditures and as a percent of GDP (see Chart 1). The policy questions raised in various quarters are: Are these the desired results,

	IRA in percent of GDP	IRA as percent of Total Budget
2003	3.17	18.63
2002	3.21	17.69
2001	2.98	16.41
2000	2.80	15.38
1999	3.22	16.33
1998	2.72	13.81
1997	2.92	14.46

Chart 1. Devolution in Serious: IRA Has Grown Impressively.

and to what extent have local governments spent the grant in ways that are consistent with national priorities?

What is not generally known is that the size of the IRA as provided for in the Local Government Code of 1991 turned out to be much higher than what was deemed reasonable and fiscally responsible by the Aquino administration. The original proposal by the Executive Department was an unconditional grant equivalent to 20 percent of national internal revenue taxes plus a 5 percent conditional grant to be distributed on the basis of indicators of tax effort. The actual outcome — 40 percent of national internal revenue taxes — was the result of political grandstanding by the Speaker of the House and Senate President at that time (see Box 1).

Box 1. Political Grandstanding Resulted in a Higher than Desirable IRA

The original IRA proposal by the Executive Department was an unconditional grant of 20 percent of national internal revenue taxes plus a 5 percent conditional grant to be distributed on the basis of indicators of tax effort. The proposed new grant system was formula-based, automatically released and therefore predictable and not subject to political bargaining. It could be seen as superior to the existing system that had the following characteristics: a lower value (*a maximum of* 20 percent of national internal revenue taxes), and it was subject to political bargaining.

The outcome — 40 percent of national internal revenue taxes — was the result of political grandstanding by two political personalities — the Speaker of the House and Senate President at that time. Both were candidates for the Presidency during the 1992 national elections. The Speaker proposed to raise, and the House approved, the Executive Department's proposal from 25 to 35 percent during the house deliberation of the proposed Local Government Code. Not to be outdone, the Senate President proposed to increase, and the Senate approved, the House- approved IRA share of 35 to 45 percent of national internal revenue taxes. Because a presidential veto of the emerging Local Government Code was thought to be politically costly, the Executive Department during the Conference Committee deliberation, agreed to a 40 percent IRA share but subject to a phased implementation: 30 percent during the first year of the Code was effective (1992), 35 percent for the second year (1993), and 40 percent for the third year (1994) and thereafter. The rest is history.

One of the common arguments against rapid decentralization (which presumably involves a larger transfer of resources to lower level governments) is the risk of central fiscal deficits and macro-economic instability. The Philippine experience shows why countries which face chronic fiscal deficits should go slow in the decentralization process. There are three major reasons for the emerging fiscal crisis: first, the large and growing inter-governmental grant or IRA; second, the falling tax effort; and third, the large and rising debt service.

During recent years, the various measures of fiscal imbalance — the national government deficit, the consolidated public sector deficit and the public sector borrowing requirement — all point to a sharp deterioration in the country's fiscal health (see Table 3).

As percent of GDP, the national government deficit (excluding the cost of restructuring the defunct Central Bank) ballooned from 3.2% in 1999, peaked at 5.5% in 2002, before it started to improve slightly to 4.9% in 2004. The primary budget balance has been insignificant: it was in the negative territory in 1999 (–0.2% of GDP) and 2002 (–0.6%) and did not reached even 1 percent during the period under review. A more accurate measure of public sector fiscal performance is the consolidated public sector deficit (CPSD), which is the combined deficits/surpluses of the national government, government-owned and controlled corporations, and other public sector entities.[8] The CPSD deteriorated sharply from 3.2% of GDP in 1999 to 6.6% in 2003. The associated public sector borrowing requirement rose from 4.4% of GDP in 1999 to 7.3% in 2003, the highest in Philippine history.

Another major contributor to the ballooning fiscal deficit is falling revenue effort, the outcome of a much emasculated 1996/97 Tax Reform Program. The tax reform program was certainly a victim of bad timing, having been enacted by Congress just before the May 1998 national elections. Not surprisingly, upon arrival, it was a weak tax program.

---

[8] Also included in the CPSD are funds allocated to the Central Bank Board of Liquidators (CB-BOL) or the sinking fund that pays for the debts incurred by the old Central Bank. The 13 monitored corporations are the Philippine National Oil Company, Metropolitan Waterworks and Sewerage System, National Irrigation Authority, National Development Corporation, Light Railway Transit Authority, Local Water Utilities Administration, National Electrification Authority, National Housing Authority, Philippine National Railways, Philippine Ports Authority, National Food Authority, and Philippine Economic Zone Authority.

Table 3. Consolidated Public Sector Financial Position, 1998–2004 (in billion pesos)

Particulars	1998	1999	2000	2001	2002	2003	2004
Public Sector Borrowing Requirement	**(111.3)**	**(138.0)**	**(174.6)**	**(189.8)**	**(268.3)**	**(275.0)**	**(286.1)**
1. National Government	(50.0)	(111.7)	(134.2)	(147.0)	(210.7)	(199.9)	(187.1)
2. CB Restructuring	(26.4)	(20.5)	(19.1)	(23.5)	(15.1)	(15.7)	(17.5)
3. Monitored non-financial gov. corporations (MNFGCs)	(38.0)	(4.6)	(19.2)	(24.5)	(46.4)	(65.3)	(90.7)
4. Oil Price Stabilization Fund	0.7	1.9	0.3	0.8	0.0	0.0	0.0
5. Adjustments of net lending and equity to GOCCs	0.9	3.0	4.2	4.4	3.9	5.8	9.2
6. Other adjustments	1.5	(6.1)	(6.6)	0.0	0.0	0.0	0.0
Other Public Sector	**28.1**	**41.8**	**25.5**	**20.5**	**49.5**	**53.3**	**49.4**
1. Government Financial Institutions (GFIs)	5.4	3.3	2.8	3.9	5.4	4.9	5.2
2. Bangko Sentral ng Pilipinas (BSP)	3.2	(3.9)	0.0	(0.1)	1.2	6.9	3.3
3. SSS/GSIS	17.8	36.4	15.4	15.6	25.6	17.6	24.4
4. Local Government Units (LGUs)	2.0	7.5	6.6	1.2	18.9	21.0	15.5
5. Timing adjustments of interest payments to BSP	(0.3)	(2.3)	0.5	(0.2)	(1.6)	0.7	3.9
6. Other adjustments	0.0	0.8	0.1	0.1	0.0	2.2	(2.8)
Consolidated Public Sector Surplus/Deficit	(83.2)	(96.2)	(149.1)	(169.3)	(218.8)	(221.7)	(236.7)

(*Continued*)

Table 3. (*Continued*)

Particulars	1998	1999	2000	2001	2002	2003	2004
Public Sector Borrowing Requirement	(4.2)	(4.6)	(5.2)	(5.2)	(6.8)	(6.4)	(5.9)
1. National Government	(1.9)	(3.8)	(4.0)	(4.0)	(5.3)	(4.7)	(3.9)
2. CB Restructuring	(1.0)	(0.7)	(0.6)	(0.6)	(0.4)	(0.4)	(0.4)
3. Monitored non-financial gov. corpor. (MNFGCs)	(1.4)	(0.2)	(0.6)	(0.7)	(1.2)	(1.5)	(1.9)
4. Oil Price Stabilization Fund	0.0	0.1	0.0	0.0	0.0	0.0	0.0
5. Adjustments of net lending and equity to GOCCs	0.0	0.1	0.1	0.1	0.1	0.1	0.2
6. Other adjustments	0.1	(0.2)	(0.2)	0.0	0.0	0.0	0.0
Other Public Sector	**1.1**	**1.4**	**0.8**	**0.6**	**1.3**	**1.2**	**1.0**
1. Government Financial Institutions (GFIs)	**0.2**	**0.1**	**0.1**	**0.1**	**0.1**	**0.1**	**0.1**
2. Bangko Sentral ng Pilipinas (BSP)	**0.1**	**(0.1)**	**0.0**	**(0.0)**	**0.0**	**0.2**	**0.1**
3. SSS/GSIS	**0.7**	**1.2**	**0.5**	**0.4**	**0.6**	**0.4**	**0.5**
4. Local Government Units (LGUs)	**0.1**	**0.3**	**0.2**	**0.0**	**0.5**	**0.5**	**0.3**
5. Timing adjustments of interest payments to BSP	**(0.0)**	**(0.1)**	**0.0**	**(0.0)**	**(0.0)**	**0.0**	**0.1**
6. Other adjustments	**0.0**	**0.0**	**0.0**	**0.0**	**0.0**	**0.1**	**(0.1)**
Consolidated Public Sector Surplus/Deficit	**(3.1)**	**(3.2)**	**(4.4)**	**(4.7)**	**(5.5)**	**(5.2)**	**(4.9)**

This experience and the IRA episode suggest an important policy lesson: real reforms are best done right after an election when the President or the Chief Executive has a new mandate. They should never be done when the campaign is underway.

With respect to this instability threat inherent in the central budget, a politically strong leader in the Philippines is not totally helpless in that he or she can withhold part of the IRA in the event of a fiscal crisis. The President could mitigate the threat of a runaway deficit by invoking the following rules in the Local Government Code of 1991:

- In the event that an unmanageable public sector deficit is incurred by the National Government, the Secretary of Finance, the Secretary of Interior and Local Government, and the Secretary of Budget and Management shall submit to the President a joint recommendation that will institute necessary adjustments in the IRA of LGUs;
- Upon receipt of the joint recommendation of the Secretary of Finance, the Secretary of the Interior and Local Government, and the Secretary of Budget and Management and subject to consultation with the presiding officers of both Houses of Congress and the presidents of the leagues of LGUs, the President shall authorize the necessary adjustments of the total IRA to be distributed among LGUs for the given year, provided that in no case shall the adjusted amount be less than 30 percent of the national internal revenue tax collections of the third year preceding the fiscal year during which the reduction is to be made.
- Adjustments to the IRA share of LGUs shall be made only after effecting a corresponding reduction of the National Government expenditures including cash and non-cash budgetary aids to government-owned and -controlled corporations, government financial institutions, the Oil Price Stabilization Fund, and the Central Bank.

In the face of the worsening fiscal deficit, the question that might be raised is: why didn't the Government invoke these fiscal rules, which could have cut the deficit by P35.2 billion or 0.8% of GDP in 2003? Clearly, while the IRA rules provide an escape clause in the event of unmanageable public sector deficit, it requires a strong political will to accept publicly that the government's finances have become unmanageable during one's watch — especially if one is facing a Presidential election.

This is not the first time that a public admission of a fiscal crisis was avoided. In December 1997, then President Fidel Ramos, through administrative fiat, attempted to withhold the amount equivalent to 10 percent of the IRA without going through the process described above. (To do so would have been to publicly admit that the public sector deficit has become unmanageable). The Philippine Supreme Court later rejected his unilateral act as: "bereft of any legal or constitutional bases" (see Box 2).

Box 2. Balance of Power: The President cannot unilaterally withhold a portion of IRA — Supreme Court

On June 19, 2000, the Supreme Court in its decision stated: "The Constitution vests the President with the power of supervision, not control, over local government units (LGUs). Such power enables him to see to it that LGUs and their officials execute their tasks in accordance with law. While he may issue advisories and seek their cooperation in solving economic difficulties, he cannot prevent them from performing their tasks and using available resources to achieve their goals. He may not withhold or alter any authority or power given them by the law. Thus, the withholding of a portion of internal revenue allotments legally due them cannot be directed by administrative fiat.

The facts: On December 27, 1997, the President of the Philippines issued Administrative Order 372 entitled: Adoption of Economy Measures in Government for FY 1998. *Section 4 of the Act provides: "Pending the assessment and evaluation by the Development Budget Coordination Committee of the emerging fiscal situation, the amount equivalent to 10 percent of the internal revenue allotment to local governments shall be withheld."* Note that there was no admission that "an unmanageable public sector deficit is incurred" and there was no prior consultation with the concerned parties as required by law. On November 17, 1998, the National President of the League of Provinces of the Philippines and Chairman of the League of Local Governments petitioned the Supreme Court to enjoin the Executive Secretary and the Secretary of Budget and Management from implementing Section 4 of the Order which withholds a portion of their internal revenue allotments.

Issue raised: Whether or not the President committed grave abuse of discretion in ordering the withholding of 10 percent of the LGU's IRA?

Supreme Court decision: "Section 4 ... has no color of validity at all. The latter provision effectively encroaches on the fiscal autonomy of local governments."

The important policy question then is whether the existing fiscal rules on IRA are unreasonably hard to comply with so that no President, weak or strong, would be willing to publicly admit that a fiscal crisis has developed during his/her administration.

8.2. *Many Municipalities are Converting to Cities*

From 1981 to 1991, or ten years before the passage of the Local Government Code, only 6 new cities were created. In contrast, within 10 years after the Code was passed, 49 new cities were created (see Table 1). What explains this unusually high rate of conversion from municipalities to cities? One could argue that this is a rational response to the new, higher IRA share of cities. The losers from this conversion are the old cities that have to settle for a lower IRA. The big winners are the newly converted cities. The old municipalities benefit too, because fewer municipalities would be included in the sharing pool for them.

8.3. *Many Devolved Hospitals are Being Nationalized*

Among the devolved national agencies, the Department of Health (DOH) has experienced the most severe adjustment pains. This is not surprising. The original Decentralization Plan of the Executive Department involved the devolution of basic education rather than basic health services. Again as a sign of weakness of the Executive Department, the then Education Secretary lobbied with Congress so that his Department was removed from among the list of agencies to be devolved.[9] When Congress agreed to the request, the DOH was promptly substituted for the Department of Education. Adding uncertainty to this abrupt substitution was the failure of the DOH to clarify its policy on devolution until long after the passage of the Local Government Code. As of 1998, the DOH had yet to restructure itself in order to complement the devolved system and help LGUs implement public health programs and services.[10]

---

[9] Under a strong republic, the President might have fired the Secretary of Education, Culture and Sports for going against the President and the Executive Department's proposal.

[10] "Inter-LGU" Cooperation: The Key Issues of a Devolved Health Care System, *PIDS Development Research News*, 16(6), November–December 1998.

The lack of clarity on the DOH policy on devolution has encouraged politicians to attempt to influence the way curative health care will be delivered. In this respect, district representatives and provincial governors are natural political enemies: the latter prefer a centralized health services delivery as of December 2003, some 72 devolved hospitals had been re-nationalized. The fiscal implications are clear: the move towards re-centralization will add to the National Government's future budgets and its deficits. On the other hand, some local governments would benefit immensely because they would be relieved of the costs of providing basic health care to their constituents. Specially favored are local governments where these formerly devolved health facilities are located, mostly in urban centers. If so, there may be some efficiency gains as a result of scale economies in the provision of health services and the greater catchment area. From the equity standpoint, on the other hand, the re-centralization of health facilities is effectively a lump-sum transfer from the national treasury to favored local communities.

8.4. *Has the Delivery of Devolved Services Improved?*

This question is difficult to answer in the absence of a systematic performance monitoring system. There are a number of initiatives for measuring the performance of local governments. These efforts have been carried out with donor funding on a pilot basis on a small sample of local governments. More than 10 years after the enactment of the Local Government Code of 1991, no nation-wide effort to assess the performance of local governments is operative.

At best, one may conclude that while there is no significant body of evidence to show that large technical or economic efficiency gains from decentralization have been achieved, neither is there evidence that decentralization has resulted in a deterioration of public services. Human Development Indicators that are calculated by provinces suggest no deterioration of social services after the decentralization of 1992.[11] It has also been observed that local governments' social services expenditures (SSE) grew dramatically following the devolution law, growing at an average annual rate of 41 percent from 1991 to 1996. In the year

[11] United Nations Development Program, *Philippine Human Development Report*, 2000, www.undp.org.

immediately after the Asian crisis, SSE increased by 12.5% compared with total spending increasing by only 7.9%.[12]

8.5. *Has the National Government Become Leaner After Devolution?*

A large share of total domestic taxes has been given up by the national government so that local governments can deliver their assigned public services. Ideally, the foregone resources should be partly offset by lower budgets at the central level and leaner staff for the devolved agencies. Here the numbers are mixed. A comparison of the budget shares of the devolved agencies (as a percent of expenditures excluding interest payments) before and after devolution shows a significant decline in budget allocation for these agencies. The Department of Agriculture has shown the sharpest decline in budget share, though the decrease may be slightly exaggerated since there remains a huge lump-sum fund in the national budget for Agricultural Modernization. On the other hand, the Department of Social Welfare and Development has shown the least adjustment in terms of budget share. (see Table 4)

Another way of evaluating the success or failure of the National Government in streamlining the bureaucracy of the devolved agencies after the 1991 decentralization act is by looking at the changes in their respective work force. One agency that has gone against the trend is the Department of Environment and Natural Resources, with its work force expanding rather than contracting ten years after the decentralization process started. One plausible explanation is that its mandate has been expanded because of the Clean Air Act.

The Department of Budget and Management has been the most successful in streamlining it its central office staff. After returning some 1,650 local budget officers to their respective local governments, DBM has progressively reduced its central office staff by 31 percent. On the other hand, the three largest devolved departments — Health, Agriculture, and Social Welfare — have yet to pursue a more aggressive streamlining program (see Table 5). The Local Government Code of 1991 authorizes the abolition of the regional offices of these three Departments. This is one program that may have large benefits in the long term.

[12] Benjamin Diokno, "Local Governments' Expenditures for Social Services Delivery," in Asian Development Bank and World Bank, *The New Social Policy Agenda in Asia: Proceedings of the Manila Social Forum*, August 2000, pp. 115,116.

Table 4. Budget Shares of Devolved Departments Before and After Devolution

National Government Departments[a]	1987	1988	1989	1990	1991	87–91	1999	2000	2001	2002	2003[b]	2004[b]
	Actual										Program	Proposed
	As Percent of Total Expenditures											
Agriculture	2.83	2.60	2.74	2.73	3.12	**2.80**	3.37	0.67	0.71	0.84	0.60	0.52
Budget and Management	0.21	0.27	0.26	0.49	0.24	**0.30**	0.10	0.09	0.12	0.07	0.08	0.07
Envir. & Nat. Resources	1.75	2.10	2.67	2.58	2.40	**2.30**	1.24	1.22	1.31	1.18	1.12	1.00
Health	4.59	5.83	5.15	5.01	4.94	**5.10**	2.58	2.20	2.01	1.99	1.87	1.74
Social Welfare and Development	0.46	0.52	0.64	0.51	0.78	**0.58**	0.40	0.43	0.34	0.33	0.40	0.39
	Levels in Million Pesos											
Agriculture	2349	2349	3213	4009	5369	—	16302	3407	3796	4963	3315	3107
Budget and Management	178	246	309	725	416	—	471	459	623	437	421	416
Envir. & Nat. Resources	1454	1894	3126	3798	4125	—	6015	6182	7017	6988	6218	5982
Health	3811	5255	6038	7364	8510	—	12502	11167	10749	11770	10387	10376
Social Welfare and Development	332	465	751	754	1344	—	1958	2203	1812	1950	2242	2326
Memo items:												
Total expenditures	119907	136067	171978	218096	247136	—	590161	648974	710756	777882	786062	869009
Interest payments	36905	45866	54714	71113	74922	—	106290	140894	174834	185861	230697	271531
Total expend. excl interest payments	83002	90201	117264	146983	172214	—	483871	508080	535922	592021	555365	597478

[a] For departments with devolved personnel only.

[b] Based on the budget of expenditures and sources of financing FY 2004.

Table 5. Philippines: Changes in the Size of the Central Government Bureaucracy Little Gain After 10 Years of Decentralization

National Government Departments[a]	Number of Personnel (1993) Before Devolution	Devolved Personnel	Net of Devolved Personnel	Total Permanent Positions 2003	% Change
Agriculture	29,638	17,673	11,965	11,908	–0.48
Budget and Management	3,532	1,650	1,882	1,298	–31.03
Envir. & Nat. Resources	21,320	895	20,425	22,154	8.47
Health	74,896	45,896	29,000	28,890	–0.38
Social Welfare and Develop.	6,932	4,144	2,788	2,720	–2.44

[a] Only for departments with devolved personnel.

9. The Challenges Ahead

The devolution process that began in 1992 was massive. Ten years after devolution, the results have been mixed. There are some improvements. First, local governments have assumed greater spending responsibilities as they have received more resources from the National Government. Second, fragmentary evidence suggest that some local governments have become more innovative in the delivery of local public services. Third, because the inter-governmental grants are large, predictable and transparent, local governments have gained better control over their finances.

But the new grant system also has some drawbacks. First, local governments have become more dependent on the National Government for their financing needs. The grant system has, by and large, been substitutive rather than stimulative of own source revenues. Rather than provide incentives for local governments to collect more local taxes to complement the IRA in order to finance new or improved programs and projects, many local authorities have become less willing to collect their own taxes. Second, the large IRA has now become a drag on the national budget. As trade taxes decline as a share of total tax revenues, a bigger proportion of total national taxes will be distributed to local governments in the form of IRA. With rising outlays for debt servicing and a weakening tax-to-GDP ratio, the National Government may find it increasingly difficult to fund this entitlement of local governments and finance central government expenditure responsibilities.

The immediate challenge to the Republic is clear: how to get back on the path of fiscal sustainability and macro-economic stability. Three concrete measures might be suggested. None would require legislation, but all would require strong political will.

- First, reduce the IRA shares of local governments from 40 percent of internal revenue tax collections to 30 percent for a three year period, by explicitly recognizing that the current and prospective public sector deficit has become unmanageable.
- Second, cut administrative overhead expenses by streamlining the organizational structure of the devolved departments with a focus on Agriculture, Health, Environment and Natural Resources and Social Welfare and Development. This is consistent with the implementation of Section 5 of Executive Order 503 that mandates national government agencies affected by devolution to adopt new organizational structures and operating systems that are responsive to decentralization imperatives.
- Third, develop and implement a strong performance evaluation mechanism for LGUs. The National Economic and Development Authority (NEDA) or the Department of Budget and Management (DBM) should undertake this activity rather than the Department of Interior and Local Government (DILG). A mandate should be placed on the National Statistical Coordination Board to systematically collect and publish local fiscal statistics.

The existing system of inter-governmental transfers can stand some improvement. Specifically, it should have an unconditional grant component (similar to the present system) and a specific grant component. The distribution formula would consider minimum basic needs and tax effort. The latter should be administered by a professional group of academics, businessmen and senior career officials, reporting directly to the Office of the President, but whose term of office should exceed that of the appointing authority. The best way to push forward decentralization in the Philippines is by implementing the program as mandated in the Local Government Code of 1991, no matter how politically costly such a move may be for an incumbent President.

Table A.1. Philippines: Assignment of Responsibilities

Provinces	Cities	Municipalities	Barangays
a. Agricultural extension and on-site research services and facilities through: 1. Prevention and control of plant and animal pests and diseases; 2. Establishment and maintenance of dairy farms, livestock markets, animal breeding stations, and artificial insemination centers; 3. Assistance in the organization of farmers' and fishermen's cooperatives and other collective organizations, and 4. Transfer of appropriate technology.	All services and facilities provided by the municipality and the province, and in addition thereto, the following: a. Adequate communication and transportation facilities; and b. Support services and facilities for education, police and fire protection.	a. Agriculture and fishery extension and on-site research through: 1. Dispersal of livelihood and poultry, fingerlings, and other seeding materials for agriculture; 2. Establishment and maintenance of seed farms for palay, corn and vegetables; medicinal plant gardens, seedling nurseries for fruit trees, coconuts, and other trees or crops, and demonstration farms; 3. Enforcement of standards for quality control of copra and improvement and development of local distribution channels, preferably through cooperatives; 4. Maintenance and operation of inter-barangay irrigation system;	a. Agricultural support services through a distribution system for agricultural and fishery produce collection and buying stations; b. Health and social welfare services, through maintenance of barangay health and daycare centers; c. Services and facilities related to general hygiene and sanitation, beautification, and solid waste collection;

(*Continued*)

Table A.1. (*Continued*)

Provinces	Cities	Municipalities	Barangays
b. Industrial research and development services, as well as transfer of appropriate technology. c. Pursuant to national policies and subject to supervision, control, and review of the Department of Environment and Natural Resources, enforcement of forestry laws limited to community-based forestry, projects, pollution control law, small-scale mining law, and other laws on the protection of the environment; and mini-hydro-electric projects for local purposes;		5. Implementation of water and soil resource utilization and conservation projects, and 6. Enforcement of fishery laws in municipal waters, including conservations and mangroves. b. In accordance with national policies and subject to supervision, control and review of the Department of Environment and Natural Resources, implementation of community-based forestry projects through: 1. Integrated social forestry programs and similar projects; 2. Management and control of communal forests with an area not exceeding fifty (50) square kilometers; and	d. Administration and maintenance of the Katarungang Pambarangay; e. Maintenance of barangay roads and bridges and water supply system; f. Infrastructure facilities such as multi-purpose hall, multipurpose pavement, plaza, sports center, and other similar facilities; g. Information and reading center; and h. Satellite public market, where viable.

(*Continued*)

Table A.1. (*Continued*)

Provinces	Cities	Municipalities	Barangays
d. Subject to the provision of Rule XXIII on local health boards, health services which include hospitals and other tertiary health services; e. Social welfare services which include programs and projects on rebel returnees and evacuees, relief operations, and population development services; f. Construction and maintenance of parks and public assembly areas, and other similar facilities;		3. Establishment of tree parks, greenbelts, and similar forest development projects. c. Subject to the provisions of Rule XXIII on local health boards and in accordance with the standards and criteria of the Department of Health, provision of health services thru: 1. Implementation of programs and projects on primary health care, maternal and child care, and communicable and non-communicable disease control services;	

(*Continued*)

Table A.1. (*Continued*)

Provinces	Cities	Municipalities	Barangays
g. Construction and maintenance of infra-structure facilities funded by the province to serve the needs of the residents, including but not limited to: 1. Provincial roads and bridges, 2. Inter-municipal waterworks, drainage and sewerage, flood control, and irrigation systems; 3. Reclamation projects; and 4. Other similar facilities.		2. Access to secondary and tertiary health services; and 3. Purchase of medicines, medical supplies, and equipment needed to carry out the devolved health services. d. Provision of social welfare services through: 1. Programs and projects for the welfare of the youth and children, family and community, women, the elderly, and the disabled; 2. Community-based rehabilitation programs for vagrants, beggars, street children, scavengers, juvenile delinquents, and victims of drug abuse; 3. Livelihood and pro-poor projects; 4. Nutrition services; and 5. Family planning services	

(*Continued*)

Table A.1. (*Continued*)

Provinces	Cities	Municipalities	Barangays
h. Planning and implementation of the programs and projects for low-cost housing and other mass dwellings, except those funded by the Social Security System, Government Service Insurance System, and the Home Development Mutual Fund. National funds for these programs and projects shall be equitably allocated to the regions in proportion to the ratio of the homeless to the population; i. Provision for investment support services, including access to credit financing;		e. Provision of information services through investment and job placement information systems, tax and marketing information systems, and maintenance of public library; f. Provision of solid waste disposal or environmental management systems and services or facilities related to general hygiene and sanitation; g. Construction and maintenance of infra-structure facilities funded by the municipality to serve the needs of the residents including but not limited to: 1. Municipal roads and bridges; 2. School buildings and other facilities for public elementary and secondary schools;	

(*Continued*)

Table A.1. (*Continued*)

Provinces	Cities	Municipalities	Barangays
j. Upgrading and modernization of tax information and collection services through the use of computer hardware and software and other means; k. Provision of inter-municipal telecommunication services, subject to national policy guidelines and standards; and l. Planning and implementation of tourism development and promotion programs.		3. Clinics, health centers, and other health facilities necessary to carry out health services; 4. Communal irrigation, small water impounding projects, and other similar projects; 5. Fish ports; 6. Artesian wells, spring development, rainwater collectors, and water supply systems; 7. Seawalls, dikes, drainage and sewerage, and flood control; 8. Traffic signals and road signs; and 9. Other similar facilities. h. Construction, maintenance and operation of municipal public markets, slaughterhouses and other economic enterprises;	

(*Continued*)

Table A.1. (*Continued*)

Provinces	Cities	Municipalities	Barangays
		i. Construction, maintenance, and operation of municipal cemeteries; j. Construction, maintenance and operation of tourism facilities and other tourist attractions, including acquisition of equipment, regulation and supervision of business concessions, and security services for such facilities; and k. Provision of sites for police and fire stations and substations and municipal jail.	

Table A.2. Philippines: Taxing and Other Revenue-Raising Power of Local Governments

Provinces	Cities	Municipalities	Barangays
1. Tax on transfer of real property ownership — tax on the sale, donation, barter, or on any other mode of transferring ownership or title of real property 2. Tax on business of printing and publication 3. Franchise tax 4. Tax on sand, gravel, and other quarry resource 5. Professional tax 6. Amusement tax	1. Taxes, fees, charges and impositions that the province and the municipality may impose. The rates the city may levy may exceed the maximum rates allowed for the province or the municipality by not more than fifty percent (50%) except the rates of professional and amusement taxes.	1. Tax on business, such as: a. Manufactures, assemblers, repackers, professors, brewers, distillers, rectifiers, and compounders of liquors, distilled spirits, and wines or manufacturers of any article of commerce of whatever kind or nature; b. Wholesalers, distributors, or dealers in any article of commerce of whatever kind or nature; c. On exporters, and or manufacturers, millers, producers, wholesalers, distributors dealers or retailers of essential commodities; d. On retailers; e. On contractors and other independent contractors; f. On banks and other financial institutions;	1. Taxes on stores or retailers with fixed business establishments with gross sales or receipts of the preceding calendar year of P50,000 or less in the case of a barangay within a city, and P30,000 or less in case of a barangay within a municipality; 2. Service fees or charges for services rendered in connection with the regulation or the use of barangay-owned properties or service facilities such as palay, copra or tobacco dryers; 3. Fees for the issuance of barangay clearance for any business or activity located or conducted within the territorial jurisdiction of the barangay;

(*Continued*)

Table A.2. (*Continued*)

Provinces	Cities	Municipalities	Barangays
7. Annual fixed tax for every delivery truck or van of manufacturers or producers, wholesalers of, dealers or retailers in, certain products.	2. Percentage tax on any business not otherwise specified under (a) to (g) of the tax on business authorized for municipalities.	g. On peddlers engaged in the sale of any merchandise or article of commerce; h. On any business, not otherwise specified in the preceding paragraphs which the sanggunian concerned may deem proper to tax. 2. Fees and charges on businesses and occupations; 3. Fees are scaling and licensing of weights and measures; 4. Fishery rentals, fees and charges.	4. Other fees and charges on; a. Commercial breeding of cocks; b. Cockfights and cockpits; c. Places of recreation which charge admission fees; d. Billboards, signboards, neon signs, and outdoor advertisements; e. Advertisements by means of vehicles, balloons, kites, etc.

Source: Republic of the Philippines Rules and Regulations Implementing the Local Government Code of 1991.

References

Asanuma, S, R Mahi, and R Simanjuntak, Decentralization: The Philippines Experience, October 2003, mimeo.

Bahl, R and B Miller (eds.) (1983). *Local government finance in the third world: A case study of the Philippines*. Praeger.

Department of Budget and Management, *Budget of Expenditures and Sources of Financing*, various issues.

House of Representatives, Republic of the Philippines, Joint Committee Report No. 1093 (Submitted by the Committees on Local Government, Appropriation and Ways and Means), June 6, 1990.

Inter-LGU Cooperation: The Key Issues of a Devolved Health Care System, *PIDS Development Research News*, 16(6), November–December 1968.

National Statistical Coordination Board, www.nscb.gov.ph.

Republic of the Philippines, *Rules and Regulations Implementing the Local Government Code of 1991,* February 6, 1992.

Supreme Court of the Philippines, *G.R. No. 132988*, July 19, 2000.

United Nations Development Program, *Philippine Human Development Report 2000*, www.undp.org

Chapter VIII

Thailand's Decentralization: Progress and Prospects

CHARAS SUWANMALA[1]

Chulalongkorn University

and

DANA WEIST[2]

The World Bank

1. Introduction

Thailand is a unitary government, that prior to its recent efforts to decentralize, was characterized as a highly centralized fiscal system that granted limited autonomy to local governments in terms of functions, area, staffing, funding and decision making. The extent of its centralization is shown by the fact that, in 2001, the central government spent over 85 percent of total general expenditures and collected 90 percent of general tax revenues.[3] The central government also appoints many chief local officials, determines local salaries and approves local budgets.

Over the past 15 years, various means of decentralizing authority and responsibility to Thai local governments have been discussed. It was

---

[1] Professor and Dean, Faculty of Political Science, Chulalongkorn University, National Decentralization Committee.

[2] Lead Public Sector Specialist, the World Bank. This paper reflects the views of the author and not the World Bank.

[3] International Monetary Fund, *Government Finance Statistics Yearbook*, 2002.

broadly recognized that local government capacity would need to be strengthened if the central government were to lessen its role in the inter-governmental fiscal system. Most Thai local governments have weak capacity in financial management, planning and service delivery, and generally lack adequate resources to deliver services effectively or to provide needed investment (Webster, 2002). While many proposals had been put forth, the Government's decentralization agenda did not gain momentum until the 1997 Constitution was passed.

The intent to decentralize governance was made clear in the 1997 constitution. Since that time, the Royal Thai government has launched a number of decentralization measures. The result has been some progress on decentralization, but there also have been delays in implementation. Some counter-decentralization movements also have emerged. The latest Constitution of 2007, which was promulgated after the political crisis in 2006, not only reaffirms support for decentralization policy but also mandates a number of measures that would strengthen local authorities and democratic representation at the community level. Still, decentralization in Thailand is in the early stages.

This paper reviews the progress that has been achieved in Thailand's decentralization. The next sections review the existing inter-governmental fiscal system and the major decentralization issues; how functional responsibility might be realigned between the central government and local governments and among local governments themselves; whether there are opportunities for enhancing the revenue mobilization of local governments; what changes are needed in the inter-governmental transfer system; and how local accountability might be promoted. The paper concludes with a discussion of the prospects for improving the process of decentralization.

2. Global Experience with Decentralization

Decentralization is a global phenomenon, and this trend is increasingly important in Asia. Thailand's 8th Plan and new Constitution strongly emphasize decentralization. Decentralization is a policy choice, and can be seen as either a good choice or not. International experience shows that if it is designed well, it can move decision making closer to the Thai people, enhance the efficiency and responsiveness of service delivery, improve economic growth, and offer a potential tool for fighting poverty. However, decentralization design is complicated, since it spans political, fiscal, and administrative policies and institutions.

By clearly defining what level of government is responsible for providing and financing various services — and by delegating appropriate authority, responsibility and resources — local services may be provided more effectively and local accountability may be enhanced. The success of decentralization will depend on the extent to which political and economic institutions promote local accountability and responsible fiscal policies. Because these institutions are nascent in Thailand, significant risks may arise. For example, without a strong system of local accountability, devolving more resources to local governments can lead to misused or wasted funds. Similarly, without an appropriate balance between expenditures and revenues, public service levels may deteriorate in a decentralized context. Finally, unless local governments pursue responsible fiscal policies, macro-economic instability may arise in the form of higher overall fiscal deficits or central government "bailouts" of weak local governments (Rodden, Litvack and Eskelund, 2003). The key challenges are to balance responsibilities with resources, accountability and capacity, and create incentives for the implementation of decentralization to match formal decentralization arrangements.

A review of the decentralization experience in other countries has shown that its success or failure often depends on whether a coherent decentralization strategy has been developed, and whether adequate mechanisms exist for developing, monitoring and implementing that strategy. A decentralization strategy should include various components, which fit together in a systematic way. These components include: (i) a clear division of responsibilities (who does what in spending and taxing); (ii) adequate financing; and (iii) a clear system of accountability (who is accountable to whom). Monitoring and implementing that strategy requires clearly defined legal and regulatory frameworks; mechanisms for coordination and for resolving conflicts; accurate, timely and comprehensive information on the decentralization process; and programs to build local government capacity.

Reducing the role of the central government will require significant changes in existing Thai institutions, processes and culture as well as mechanisms for establishing trust among levels of government. The

Ministries of Public Health and Education have been de-concentrating service delivery to local entities: Local Education Authorities and Provincial Hospitals. In the future these may be transferred to local governments. Changes in the inter-governmental transfer system are needed to promote greater predictability and offset fiscal disparities across local governments. Effective decentralization is impossible without the broader reforms in financial and human resource management now underway as part of the Government's public sector reform.

3. Evolution of the Decentralization Agenda

Decentralization had been on the policy agenda for more than a hundred years, beginning with the monarch king regime (King Rama the Fifth) and has been passed on to a number of democratic and military-dictator governments. During the last four decades two popular movements for democracy were the October Fourteen 1973 and the May Five 1992 ones and contributed significantly to the recent national agenda for decentralization.

Strengthening local governments was identified as a policy priority in the Government's 7th National Economic and Social Development Plan (1991–1996) and Eighth Plan (1997–2001). The 7th Plan emphasized developing local infrastructure facilities, providing credit to expand and improve local services and assisting local authorities in mobilizing capital for formulating development projects. The 8th Plan emphasized strengthening the management and budgetary capability of local institutions and supporting decentralization. In support of the 8th Plan objectives, the Department of Local Administration within the Ministry of Interior has worked to enhance local capabilities in three areas: (i) local administrative systems like staff regulations, accounting systems, etc., (ii) developing tax and property maps to enhance local revenue collections, and increasing local tax rates, and (iii) training local personnel. These attempts, similar to a number of previous ones, however, did not have significant impacts on decentralization.

The need for greater local revenue generation had been recognized but the proposed reforms were not successful. In 1993, for example, the Ministry of Finance identified a series of reforms that would significantly improve local revenues, and they were approved by the Cabinet in 1994. These nine measures — ranging from changes in tax

Box 1. Nine Measures to Increase Municipal Revenues

- Decrease the government fee for collecting additional taxes from 5 to 3 percent.
- Improve allocation rules for VAT and specific business tax.
- Allow municipalities to levy an additional 10 percent tax on tobacco and cigarettes.
- Return fishing duties, bird nest duty and log concessionaire charges to municipalities.
- Return mineral and petroleum concessionaire charges to municipalities.
- Transfer real estate transfer tax and fees to municipalities.
- Create a "property tax" by combining the land and buildings and land improvement taxes.
- Double the fees on vehicles and eliminate the reduced rate for older cars.
- Revise the inter-governmental transfer system to enhance the capacity of municipal administrations.

administration to increased shared tax revenues and the institution of new taxes on owner-occupied property and tobacco — were estimated to increase local revenues by as much as 80 percent (see Box 1). Implementation of these reforms was impeded by the need to amend 40 related laws, obtain Cabinet approval, and assure inter-ministerial coordination.

In January 1997, a Fiscal Master Plan for local governments was drafted by the Fiscal Policy Office of the Ministry of Finance and approved by the Cabinet. It identified 17 measures to enhance local revenues, clarify expenditure responsibility, reform the inter-governmental transfer system, establish systems for monitoring and evaluating local fiscal systems, promote new methods of mobilizing capital for local investment, and develop local capacity. The Master Plan set a framework for many proposed reforms for decentralization, but was never implemented because the government regime changed. The 1997 Constitution strongly supported decentralization and specified principles of local autonomy. The objectives envisioned included increasing the share of local government expenditures, assigning more revenue sources to local governments, revising the system of inter-governmental transfers to provide grants in a more transparent and predictable way, and devising mechanisms for local accountability.

A National Commission on Public Sector Reform was established as an outgrowth of the Constitution, and it included a Decentralization Subcommittee. This Subcommittee is composed of three working groups with the following responsibilities: (i) Local Administrative Organizations, (ii) Improving the Fiscal Status of Local Governments, and (iii) Local Civil Service Administration. A working principle of the Decentralization Subcommittee is that no level of local government should be made worse off as a result of reforms brought about by the decentralization process. Draft legislation was prepared by each of the working groups to define central-versus-local responsibilities, reform local budgeting and expenditure management, assign adequate local revenues, and reform the inter-governmental grant system. This legislation — including provisions of the 1997 Constitution, the National Decentralization Act and eight laws — establishes the framework for decentralization and a new system of inter-governmental fiscal relations (see Box 2).

The National Decentralization Act became effective on 18 November 1999. This Act defines the roles and responsibilities of the National Decentralization Committee (NDC) (see Box 3). The NDC is responsible for defining many of the policy parameters necessary to implement the decentralization legal framework, and to monitor the

Box 2. Decentralization Legal Framework

1. 1997 Constitution of the Kingdom of Thailand, Sections 289 and 290
2. 1999 National Decentralization Act, Sections 16–19
3. 1997 Provincial Administrative Organization Act (and 1999 amendments)
4. Tambon Administrative Organization Act
5. Municipality Act
6. Upgrade status of Sub-Municipalities to Full Municipalities
7. Change the status of BMA
8. Change the status of Pattaya City
9. Prepare master plans and procedures for administrative power
10. Establish a centralized personnel body of permanent officials of local administrative organizations

Box 3. Roles of the National Decentralization Committee

The National Decentralization Committee (NDC) is responsible for:

- Producing a Decentralization Plan for submission to the Cabinet and Parliamentary approval that:
    - defines the relationships and functional responsibilities between the central and local governments, as well as among local governments, including the allocation of functions, subsidies and central government budget
    - defines local revenue sources and identifies means to improve local tax and revenue mobilization
    - outlines the stages and means to transfer functions from the central government to local governments
    - recommends means to coordinate the transfer of public officials from the central government, local governments, and state enterprises relative to new assignments of functions and resources
- Proposing criteria or parameters for allocating resources among different levels of government including subsidies and central budget
- Proposing legislation, decrees, regulations, administrative guidelines and rules to implement the decentralization plan in a timely manner
- Proposing a system to achieve transparency and public participation at the local level in terms of government functions
- Monitoring progress in implementing the Decentralization Plan

decentralization outcomes.[4] It is composed of 36 members, including the Deputy Prime Minister (Chair), the Ministers of Interior and Finance; Permanent Secretaries of the Ministries of Interior, Finance, Education, and Health; Secretaries General of the Office of the Council of State, the Office of the Civil Service Commission, the NESDB, the Bureau of the Budget and Department of Local Administration; twelve representatives of local government, and twelve senior experts. While the Constitution envisioned an autonomous agency with sufficient authority, status and funds, the NDC was established in the executive branch, under the auspices of the Prime Minister's Office.

[4] The NDC must review the functions and revenue authority of local governments every five years and consider whether local autonomy should be increased.

Local governments in Thailand are statutory bodies of the national government and exist in five forms: (i) Provincial Administrative Organizations (PAO), (ii) Municipalities, (iii) Bangkok Municipal Administration — a special form of province/municipality with greater local autonomy, (iv) Pattaya City — a special form of municipality, and (v) Tambon Administrative Organizations (TAOs). Each entity is independent and has equal legal status (see Box 4).

Box 4. Structure of Thai Local Governments

- *Provincial Administrative Organizations* (PAOs), act on behalf of the national government, and support local administration by constructing and maintaining local roads, providing water, and other limited services to residents in rural areas. PAOs were established in 1955 to accelerate the development of local administrations in the rural areas outside of sanitary districts and municipalities. The creation of TAOs in 1994 substantially diminished PAO responsibilities. At present there are 75 PAOs, corresponding to the number of provinces. PAOs are subdivided into provincial districts and are administered by centrally appointed officials, either as provincial representatives of line ministries or senior officers in the Ministry of Interior. In early 1999, legislation was approved to enhance PAOs' role in planning, investment, and service provision in each province, as well as coordinating functions delegated to lower-level governments. This legislation also specifies that PAOs will receive a larger portion of existing revenues already shared with TAOs and other local authorities, including 5 percent of the VAT funds assigned to local governments.
- *Municipalities* are the most well-established form of local government, and generally occupy urbanized areas in 149 cities, as well as 983 former sanitary districts. Municipalities are classified into three categories — city (*nakorn*), town (*muang*) and township (*tambon*) — depending on their size and community characteristics. Their category defines their responsibilities. Municipal councils and executive committees are elected and authorized to undertake most functions. The mayor is appointed by the provincial governor based on the party receiving the most votes in the election. Municipalities are absorbing newly decentralized responsibilities reasonably well. Despite significant growth

(*Continued*)

Box 4. (*Continued*)

pressures, new municipalities are rarely created nor expanded through annexation. As a result, the majority of urbanized activities — about 80 percent — is occurring outside of municipal boundaries, which impedes the achievement of decentralization objectives, diminishes the efficiency and quality of services delivered, and hinders local management and planning.

- *Tambon Administrative Organizations* (TAOs) were established in 1994 to serve areas outside of municipalities and sanitary districts. They were designed to provide basic services and facilities, predominantly in rural village areas. By 1999, there were over 6,700 TAOs. They are governed by a council assembly (elected) and a council executive (generally appointed). TAOs have some authority to exercise discretion over the planning and use of funds. Most TAOs are too small and fragmented to be efficient, viable or accountable units of local government — in terms of meeting their responsibilities for infrastructure, environment, human resource development and health care; in raising revenues; and in effectively supporting participatory governance. Many are too small to even support a primary school. The numerous TAOs within ecological regions (e.g., watersheds and river basins, airsheds, etc.) impede coordinated environmental or natural resources planning and management. Proposals have suggested that many of the TAOs should be consolidated so that only 1,000 to 1,500 TAOs exist with each having a critical mass of population, area and resources.
- *Special Administrative Organizations* (SAOs) have been proposed based on the successful model of the Bangkok Metropolitan Administration (BMA), which was established in 1972. BMA operates as a unitary government extending across the geographical equivalent of a province. At present, the Governor of BMA is the only directly elected local government official in Thailand. The Thai Government has agreed to establish other equivalent local governments known as SAOs. These SAOs would be established in areas with high economic and social development with a geographic boundary coterminous with the province or some part thereof. Proposals for transforming Phuket and Pattaya City into a SAO (encompassing the entire provincial area) are under consideration, and other possibilities include Songkhla, Nakorn Ratchasima, Chachoengsao, Chonburi and Rayong.

4. The Inter-governmental Framework

4.1. *Assignment of Expenditure Functions*

The Decentralization plan, adopted in 2000, provides strategic guidelines, scope, direction, and process of decentralization. It targets the following six areas of services for devolution to local authorities:

1, Local infrastructures and utilities (87 activities including local roads and waterways, water supply, public markets, urban planning and construction).
2. Social welfare (103 activities including employment and income promotion, social welfare for the disadvantaged, athletics and recreation, fundamental education, primary health care, housing, and community renovation).
3. Public safety (17 activities including popular participation, civil rights and liberty, law and order, and disaster prevention and restoration).
4. Local economic development (19 activities including local development planning, investment, trading, industry, and tourism promotion).
5. Natural resource and environmental management (17 activities including forestry, land, and water preservation and management, pollution control, and environmental promotion).
6. Cultural promotion (2 activities including preservation and promotion of local heritage and cultures).

The decentralization action plan, adopted in 2002 following the strategic plan, mandated that 245 activities, presently in the charge of 57 central departments, 15 ministries, and one independent public agency — must be devolved to local authorities. The activities were subsequently classified into two groups, "compulsory" and "non-compulsory". Local authorities must carry out the compulsory activities at prescribed minimum standards but can have discretion over the non-compulsory ones. It is also implied that the national government should provide necessary support to enable local governments to carry out those obligatory functions.

The devolution, according to the strategic plan, should progress during 2000–2010. Services that are most plausibly and feasibly provided by local units will be devolved within the first four years (2001–04), while the rest will be gradually transferred.[5]

[5] Details of the devolution planning were to be further articulated in the operation plan.

In practice the functional devolution over the 2000–2008 period did not proceed so smoothly. Only 17 of 83 services proposed for devolution were actually devolved by 2002. Only 40 of the 110 proposed were devolved by 2003. Moreover, it was determined that local governments were not prepared to take on responsibility for a large number of services that had originally been proposed for devolution.

4.1.1. *Educational Decentralization*

Education is one of the most difficult areas for decentralization. Devolution has moved forward, but with stops and starts during the past eight years. One problem was that the Ministry of Education preferred to de-concentrate service responsibility to educational area boards rather than to local authorities, though it subsequently agreed to devolve many public schools to local authorities (see Box 5).

Box 5. Local Education Authorities

The establishment of Local Education Authorities (LEAs) was mandated in the National Education Act, passed in 1999. Over 200 LEAs will be created and given authority over curricula, personnel and finance, with significant citizen participation in governance. The boundaries of LEAs will be determined based on demographic and geographic factors with the objective of promoting efficiency and quality of education. Staff from the Ministry of Education would be expected to be re-deployed to LEAs. The Act also specifies that the education financing system will be changed significantly by providing block grants to LEAs and to schools, based on a standard per capita grant plus additional per capita grants based on poverty and other equity concern, including provision for disadvantaged and handicapped students. Schools within a particular LEA would be funded on the same basis. LEAs and schools would be empowered to raise additional funds and to determine their use.

The Decentralization Action Plan specifies that Ministry of Education functions are to be devolved to local governments once they have met "readiness" criteria. However, there is no time frame for decentralizing responsibility from LEAs to local governments, and to date, teachers have been unwilling to leave their posts as employees of the Ministry of Education for positions with local governments, without clear career paths and comparable wages and benefits.

Table 1. Number of Public Schools Proposed for Devolution by Local Authorities

PAOs	23
Metro municipalities	11
City municipalities	27
Town municipalities	156
TAOs	1,253
Totals	1,490

Progress on this issue was made by a Cabinet resolution on September 29, 2005 to adopt a criteria for assessing the capacity of local authorities to adopt transferred public schools, In 2005, 338 local authorities were certified as having the necessary capability and proposed to adopt 1,490 schools from the Ministry of Education (see Table 1).

The progress of devolving public schools was subsequently suspended for one year because of the political turmoil before it started up again in 2006, (Wuthisan Thanchai, 2005).[6]

Further progress in this area was initiated by the Ministry of Interior on May 17, 2006, when the Regulation on Local Authority's School Budgeting and Financing of 2006 was adopted. The regulation set up an autonomous system for local school financial management, which allowed school principals to do their own budgeting, procurement, financing, accounting and reporting in a comparable fashion to the ministerial public schools. The regulation also ensured that school management would be free from local political intervention.

The latest update on educational devolution in 2007 shows that 69 public schools had been transferred to 55 local authorities, 29 PAOs, 16 Municipalities, and 10 TAOs. In addition, 859 teachers voluntarily worked under local government settings. Another 254 teachers preferred to stay in the Ministry of Education Budget. In total, 67.96 million Baht in teachers' salaries and benefits were transferred to local authorities.[7] The prospect for devolution of education is positive. A 2004 survey of will ingness to adopt transferred public schools from the government covered

[6] Wuthisan Thanchai (2005). Educational Strategies of Local Authorities, *Journal of Prajadhipok*, year 3, September-December 2005; pp. 44–55.

[7] (Official working document of the Division of Local Personnel Administration, Department of Local Administration Promotion, as of November 2007.)

4,640 local authorities. The results of the survey revealed that 34.78% of local authorities are willing to adopt transferred schools, or otherwise to establish new schools in their localities (see Table 2). The willingness to accept transferred schools differed according to the size of the local government. The larger and the more urbanized local governments were more positive than their smaller and rural counterparts. The latter preferred to support public schools in their areas with specific activities, such as school building and utility maintenance activities, providing teaching equipment, teachers' training, cultural and athletic events. At present, 27.78% of local authorities are providing formal education (see Table 3).

Table 2. Willingness of Local Authorities to Adopt Transferred Schools

Willingness and Plan to Adopt Transferred Schools of Local Authorities	Number	Percentage
1. Have a plan to adopt transferred schools or to have new schools established	1,614	34.78
2. Have no plan to adopt transferred schools or to have new schools established	3,026	65.22
Totals	4,640	100.0

Source: College of Local Government Development (2006), *Directions of PAOs' Educational Provision*, Local Forum Vol. 3, KPI, Bangkok; p. 147.

Table 3. Experience of Local Authorities in Providing Educational Services

	Have Been Providing Educational Services	Never Provide Educational Services	Totals	%
Municipalities	273	536	809	16.78
TAOs	1,066	2,883	3,949	81.93
PAOs	—	62	62	1.29
Totals	1,339	3,481	4,820	—
Percentage	27.78	72.22	100.0	100.0

Source: College of Local Government Development (2006), *Directions of PAOs' Educational Provision*, Local Forum Vol. 3, KPI, Bangkok; p. 141.

In addition, a 2004 service quality assessment in education revealed that students in local government schools have significantly higher achievement scores in thinking, analyzing, synthesizing, and gaining knowledge and skills than do those in the Ministry of Education's schools (Chuachan Chongsathityoo, 2006).[8] These findings could have positive impacts on the next steps of educational decentralization in Thailand.

4.1.2. *Health Service Devolution*

The plans for decentralization of the health function had been prepared in detail and implementation planning was underway by 1999–2000. However, this program was suspended after 2001, when the government led by Thai Rak Party introduced the national health assurance, the so-called "Thirty-Baht for Episode," by centralizing the health purchasing unit. Because decentralization was excluded from the national health scheme, no significant health services were devolved to local authorities during 2001–06. Nevertheless, local authorities still had room to provide some health services to their residents in addition to those provided under the national health scheme.

A significant step toward decentralization in public health was made in 2007. Under the administration of Prime Minister Gen. Surayudht Chullanonda, the Ministry of Public Health, the National Health Insurance Office, and the National Decentralization Commission jointly pushed for the devolution of community hospitals and health care centers to local authorities. In April 2007, 35 health care centers in 16 provinces were approved by the National Decentralization Committee to be transferred to 30 TAOs (see Table 4). Twenty-two units had been completely transferred in 2007, the remainder were in progress. The transferred health care centers were expected to be better off financially and managerially, because they would have funding support from multiple sources: TAOs, the National Health Insurance Office, and the communities. In the meantime, the Ministry of Public Health will continue to provide technical and managerial support.

The devolution of health care services represents a kind of turning point for the decentralization initiative in Thailand. It marks the first

[8] Chuachan Chongsathityoo (2006) in College of Local Government Development (2006), *Directions of PAOs' Educational Provision*, Local Forum Vol 3, KPI, Bangkok, p. 141.

Table 4. Devolution of Health Centers to TAOs in 2007–08

Regions	Provinces	TAOs	Health Centers
North	4	8	10
Northeastern	4	4	5
Central	11	14	15
South	4	4	5
Totals	23	30	35

Source: *Local Government News,* Year 2, Vol. 40, March 1–15, 2008, p. 4.

time that the central ministries and departments on one hand, and local authorities on the other, have jointly pushed to devolve fundamental services and achieved a positive outcome. One reason is that the Ministry of Public Health proposed a number of flexible forms of devolution, including individual health care centers, community hospitals, and a network of health care facilities. This allowed local authorities to adjust according to their circumstances. This initiative opened new space for functional devolution in the future.

4.1.3. *Social Welfare Services*

Local authorities, especially TAOs, have increasingly been charged with providing a wide range of social services to local residents as described in Box 6. (Sakon Waranyuwathana, 2008).[9] Still, more than 60 percent of social services at the local level are either directly delivered by central government agencies or directly funded from the central government budget. Most of the social services are delivered by community organizations, by passing the local governments. This indicates a centralizing mode of delivering social services.

4.1.4. *The Overall Picture*

The Decentralization Action Plan did not "cost out" the functions to be decentralized, nor did it compare these costs to the targets for decentralizing revenues. Estimates by the World Bank (2003)

[9] Sakon Waranyuwathana (2008), *Driving Social Welfare Services at TAO Level Through Fiscal Decentralization*, Final report submitted to UNCEF and NESDB.

Box 6. Social Service Activities

1. Education includes pre-school services, meals, scholarships, school activities, teaching and learning equipment, teacher training and curriculum development.
2. Public health includes health promotion for aging, handicaps and disadvantages, infectious decease prevention, medical materials and equipment, community health education and promotion activities.
3. Social welfare include living allowances for aging persons, HIV victims, disadvantage children, and poor families.
4. Community infrastructure development includes roads and bridges, pathways, lighting.
5. Community strengthening includes law and order, drug fighting, economic development and income promotion.
6. Cultural services include cultural and religious activities.

indicated that if all of the functional decentralization targets of the Decentralization Action Plan were met by 2006, it would cost an amount equivalent to about 10 percent of the central government's budget. The World Bank (2003) reported a target of 35 percent of central government revenues being transferred to local governments by 2006.

A significant portion of local expenditures (ranging from 40 to 70 percent) have been centrally mandated. The largest category of these mandated expenditures is personnel expenses (representing, on average, 30 percent of local budgets). Previously, local authorities were required to hire a defined number of personnel, and to pay salaries, wages, and benefits at centrally-determined levels. These unfunded mandates resulted in over-staffing and overspending. Moreover, the organizational structure, staffing levels and staff appointments of local governments have been controlled by central agencies (e.g., the Municipal Personnel Commission and DOLA), thereby limiting the flexibility of local governments to manage their own personnel. A separate Local Government Civil Service Commission, as proposed by the Working Group on Local Civil Service Administration, is under discussion. Over time, local personnel management authority has been delegated to local governments. Local governments are now given discretion to re-design their organization and staffing structure (numbers and positions). The salary standard remains centrally controlled, hence a major part of the mandate remains.

At present, local expenditure assignments are not sufficiently clear. Greater clarity would be achieved by identifying specific expenditure assignments that are compulsory rather than voluntary, as well as the specific duties to be performed at each level of local government. Clarity in expenditure assignment is necessary to eliminate overlapping functions between the central and local governments, and as a foundation for negotiating what duties and skills are required by local governments vs. line ministries. For those local services most appropriately provided by local governments (e.g., local roads, solid waste collection, etc.) the central government's role should be limited to establishing policies, regulating outcomes, and facilitating local provision (especially through building local capacity through training and other means).

4.2. *Local Revenues*

Local revenue includes locally collected taxes and non-tax revenues, in addition to centrally-collected taxes for local governments, shared taxes (mandated in the Decentralization Act of 1999), and general and specific grants.[10] Local governments rely substantially on revenues and grants from the central Government and raise less than 15 percent of total revenues (see Table 5). Heavy reliance on central taxes, shared taxes and grants reduces local government discretion and accountability to voters.

Inter-governmental revenue assignment was a prime strategy of decentralization during the first five years (2001–2006). The change brought on by the Decentralization Act of 1999 was that the share of local revenues was mandated to be no less than 20 percent in 2001 and 35 percent in 2006. An intention behind this mandate was to force the national government to devolve functions along with revenues to local governments. However, the government failed to follow the legal mandate, and there was no political power to force the government to comply with the law. As shown in Table 5, in 2006 share of local revenue to the national government's was only 25.17%. On the other hand, the government, in 2006,

[10] Centrally collected taxes and shared taxes are virtually the same. These terms are used to treat resource flows to local governments differently in order to meet the target decentralization benchmarks.

Table 5. Local Government Revenues: 1999 and 2008

	FY99 Preliminary	FY04 Estimate	FY08 Estimate
Locally Collected Taxes			
Land and building tax	7,707.2	11,880.1	17,164.8
Land development tax	752.0	953.2	1,274.9
Signboard tax	818.7	1,121.1	1,640.6
Slaughter and swallow nest duties	68.2	61.1	89.0
Bird nest tax	0.00	100.0	202.19
Tobacco/petroleum tax (1)	0.00	1,863.7	2,404.9
Total Locally Collected Taxes	9,346.1	15,979.2	22,776.4
Locally Collected Non-Tax Revenue			
Fees and fines	1,222.0	2,798.2	3,819.3
Revenue from property	4,493.2	1,344.6	1,972.5
Revenue from infrastructure services	242.1	522.2	811.1
Miscellaneous	2,213.4	2,043.8	2,832.0
Total Locally Collected Non-Tax Rev.	8,170.7	6,708.8	9,434.9
Revenue from tax admin. Improvement	—	2,318.8	3,011.8
Total Locally Collected Revenues	17,516.8	25,006.8	35,223.1

(*Continued*)

Table 5. *(Continued)*

	FY99 Preliminary	FY04 Estimate	FY08 Estimate
Centrally Collected Taxes for Local Gov.			
VAT	14,085.6	26,405.5	42,385.8
Specific tax	2,145.4	1,790.0	4,000.0
Liquor tax	3,895.7	6,991.2	9,250.0
Excise tax	8,463.0	16,564.1	20,681.6
Vehicle tax	9,965.5	14,093.8	22,510.7
Property registration duties	2,688.6	14,891.7	26,952.3
Gambling tax	142.6	120.0	145.0
Royalties for Minerals	260.7	650.0	1,064.0
Royalties for Petroleum	301.2	950.0	1,522.0
Other	783.3	167.0	165.0
Total Centrally Collected Taxes for LGs	42,731.6	82,623.30	128,676.4
Shared Taxes	—	41,100.0	65,000.0
Grants	37,499.3	91,438.0	147,840.0
Total Local Revenue	97,747.7	241,947.6	376,740.0
Total Government Revenue	708,826.0	1,063,600.0	1,495,000.0
Sub-national revenues and grants as a share of total government revenue	13.8%	22.75%	25.2%

Source: The Office of National Decentralization Committee, Official working documents, March 2008.

proposed to amend the Decentralization Act of 1999 by reducing or removing the stipulated share of local government revenues. It is generally expected, however, that the proportion of local revenues to that of the national government will be maintained at 25 percent unless there is significant progress on education and health decentralization.

Inter-governmental transfers contribute the largest proportion of local government revenues. Most transfers flow from national to local levels. A small amount of transfers flow from the provincial level, the Governor's budget, and the provincial administrative organization (PAO) budget, to its lower tier, sub-district (Tambon) councils.[11] There are two parts of inter-governmental transfers, revenue sharing, and grants.

4.2.1. *Revenue Sharing*

Local governments in Thailand share in the revenues from some national government taxes. The vertical share for local governments is fixed by legal mandates, but there is provision for the national government to adjust this share according to macro fiscal policy. The value added tax is the most important shared tax (mandated by the Decentralization Act of 1999), accounting for 18 percent of local government revenues during the past eight years, 2001–2008.

Grants. Grants are the most important source of inter-governmental transfers, accounting for 35–40 percent of local revenues in 2003 (see Table 5). There are two major grants, general and specific. General grants are classified into seven categories, (1) Fiscal equalization (approximately 50 percent of all grants), (2) Tax effort promotion, (3) Good governance promotion, (4) Devolution of compulsory functions, (5) Reimbursements and compensation, (6) Local development, and (7) Education.

Prior to FY01, over 70 percent of the inter-governmental grants (or "subsidies") in Thailand were allocated for specific investment projects. The Ministry of Interior allocated these grants in an *ad hoc* and highly politicized manner. The amounts allocated varied greatly from year to year, and actual allocations were not known until well after the fiscal year began. Hence the basic requirement of a decentralized system, having transparent and stable inter-governmental transfers, was not yet

[11] The entity will be eliminated in the coming year.

well established. Nor did the grants reflect the broader inter-governmental issue of the vertical fiscal imbalance between the central and local governments. Fiscal disparities across local governments have been partially addressed in the current transfer system, but the *ad-hoc* project grants seem to broaden the overall disparities among urban and rural localities.

The Inter-governmental transfer system was in a process of transition during the first four years, 2001–04, and this has limited the predictability of transfers to local governments. During this period, the total amount of grants (the "distributable pool") and the allocation criteria have differed every year. In FY02, for example, good governance and tax effort grants were initiated, but were discontinued in FY03. In FY04, a portion of the general purpose grant was allocated to enhance local revenue mobilization. Specific grants are declining in importance, while general grants are increasing as an incentive to encourage the performance of the mandatory functions specified in the Decentralization Action Plan. The transfer system still relies heavily on transfers that are determined by negotiation, and whether local governments have the capacity to procure specific projects. This system is not easily used to equalize differences in fiscal capacity or expenditure need.

Except for the certainty of receiving at least last year's amount of the shared tax, local governments have little predictability in their yearly transfers of shared tax and grants since there are neither established allocation rules nor formulas. In FY02, delays in establishing the allocation criteria for distributing the grants resulted in these grants not being disbursed until the end of the fiscal year.

Nor do grant allocations equalize fiscal disparities. In FY03, almost two-thirds of grants were budgeted for local governments to perform devolved functions as defined by the Decentralization Act, especially those related to school programs like the school milk and lunch program and the pre-school program. Provinces with more schools and students received a larger proportion of the grant, whereas poorer provinces with fewer schools and students received a smaller proportion of the grant (World Bank, 2003).

The NDC determines the amount of shared taxes and grants, as well as the allocation among local governments. The Department of Local Government Promotion (DLGP, formerly the Department of Local Administration) in the Ministry of Interior distributes the grants to local governments.

4.3. *Administrative Decentralization*

The Local Civil Service System has been reformed in many respects during the past ten years. The previous local civil service systems, centrally controlled by the DOLA, did not allow local authorities to manage their own staffs. The new law on local civil service system adopted in 1999 (The Local Civil Service Act of 1999) gives the power of local personnel management back to local authorities. Since 2004, central control over local administrative and staffing structures had been deregulated, and local governments were given more flexibility to structure their own administrative apparatus and staffing to suit the diverse needs of individual localities.

The Central government had a policy to devolve central civil service to local governments along with functional and fiscal devolution. In 2004, the Cabinet adopted a plan for transferring personnel to local governments, proposed by the Office of the Civil Service Commission (OCSC). About 3,100 positions from the Public Works Department (PWD), the Office of Accelerated Rural Development (ARD), and the Ministry of Interior were transferred to local governments during 2001–03. An additional 1,359 were transferred after 2003, along with the devolution of education and health services during 2004–08.

The OCSC has established a Public Sector Personnel Development and Deployment Center (PSDC) to serve as a training center and clearinghouse for central government officials that would be transferred to local governments. At present, central officials who are transferred to local government organizations are eligible for the same compensation and benefits as central government officials.

Local governments often have inexperienced staff, that include many new undergraduate students from regional colleges and universities. A profile of the education background of staff is shown in Table 6. Elected officials, who usually come from less educated backgrounds, also lack experience and understanding about local government management. In 2003 the Department of Local Government Promotion, in collaboration with a number of regional universities, initiated academic study programs and training services for local elected and civil service officials. The academic and training service facilities had the capacity to cover 30,000 local staff per year during FY 2003–07.

Local personnel administration in general, and specifically that in small rural areas, has been suffering from a remarkably high turnover

Table 6. Educational Background of Local Government Personnel

	Number	Percent
Below secondary school	86,560	30.84
Obtained the secondary school certification	49,769	17.73
Obtained the primary vocational school certification	23,326	8.31
Obtained the higher vocational school certification	28,895	10.30
Obtained undergraduate degrees	68,007	4.23
Studying in undergraduate programs	14,989	5.34
Obtained graduate degrees	4,611	1.64
Studying in graduate programs	4,437	1.58
Obtained Ph.D. degrees	41	0.01
Total	280,635	100.00

rate of staff. This is due the fact that the local administrations are usually unstable, high risk, subject to a high degree of political patronage, and have little chance to "grow up" professionally in such small organizations. The transfer of personnel among localities has been discouraged and in many cases has not been possible since 2004. On the bright side, a number of initiatives in local personnel management have emerged during the past four years. These include a bonus system, a wide-range of training and education opportunities, and the establishment of comparable benefits to that of the central civil service. These improvements should have positive impacts on local personnel management in the near future.

It should be noted that there remain some central mandates concerning local personnel management that have deterred them from assuming decentralized responsibilities. Among those is a control on the percentage of local personnel expenditures at no more than 40 percent of the total annual budget.

4.4. *Local Accountability*

Local governments in Thailand were insignificant in the fiscal structure and much less accountable than the national government agencies before the turn toward decentralization in 1997. Has the decentralization progress during the past 10 years contributed to an improvement of local government accountability? The answers are both yes and no.

The positive impacts of decentralization on public accountability have been revealed by a number of studies. Sakon Waranyuwathana (2008) argued that local governments' accountability had increased in step with the public services they provided to their residents. This is especially true in the case of social services.

Local accountability also has been improved with increased public participation, the so-called "deliberative democracy" at the community level. A number of studies, such as Charas Suwanmala (2003), Office of the National Health System Reform (2005), and Thawinwadee Bureekul (2006), have tracked the emergence of civic participation in local administration, and the resulting increase in accountability. There have been new policy initiatives in this direction by a number of local governments and governmental departments. The Department of Local Authority Promotion (DLAP), and the Institution of Community Strengthening Promotion, among others, have adopted **the "community development planning through participatory process**" as a key strategy for promoting civic participations and building partnerships between local authorities, community organizations (NGOs), and regional and central government agencies who are working at the community level. The practice was institutionalized in the 2007 constitution and with the passage of the Community Council Act of 2007.

A survey on governance and accountability in 2007 reveals that public trusts in local government institutions, local authorities and city councils had gradually increased from 63.9 to 70.5 during the past years (2002–04) as illustrated in Table 7. It is noticeable that trust in the national civil service is slightly higher trust than in local institutions.

On the other hand, there have been two prominent negative impacts of decentralization on public accountability during the past ten years. The first, corruption at the local level, has grown with the increasing amount of local spending. Research and civic monitoring on corruption at the local level reveals increasing corruption in local procurements. In some cases, the prices of procured goods was 20 to 40 percent above market prices (Nipon Poaponsakorn, Duanden Nokomboreerak and Suwanna Tulayawansinpong, 2001).[12] The number of complaints about

[12] Nipon Poaponsakorn, Duanden Nokomboreerak and Suwanna Tulayawansinpong, "Corruptions in Public Sector: Case Studies and Economic Strategies in Countering Corruptions", in Office of Civil Service (2001), *Corruption in Thailand*, A research report Bangkok, 2001, http://pixiart.com/forum/view.php?frm=1&id=144>, among others.

Table 7. Public Trust in Government Institutions 2002–04 (In Percent)

		2002	2003	2004
Trust in national civil service officers	Yes	62.5	71.1	76.7
	No	28.1	23.2	17.1
	No comment	8.7	4.9	6.2
Trust in local authorities	Yes	63.9	71.4	70.5
	No	31.2	25.2	25.2
	No comment	4.9	3.5	4.5
Trust in city councils	Yes	55.9	67.4	70.5
	No	33.6	25.0	22.8
	No comment	10.5	7.5	6.8

Source: Adapted from Table 3.4 p. 46: Gordon Brown, Thawinwadee Bureekul, eds. (2007), *Monitoring the Pulse of the Nation: Indicators of Democratization and Good Governance in Thailand 2005–2007*, Research and Development Office, King Projadhipok's Institute, September 2007.

local corruption has multiplied so rapidly that the Counter Corruption Commission (CCC) could not handle them. In response, the Provincial Counter Corruption Commission (PCCC) has been established according to the 2007 constitution to bring legal measures against cases of corruption at the local level. It is expected that the PCCC can speed up the anti-corruption campaign and help promote transparency at the local government level.

The second negative impact is the growth in the political patronage system due to decentralization during the past six years. The patronage relationship between local residents and their local elites had existed in most rural Thai areas for many decades. This hierarchical patronage impeded the democratization process, as it generated fear and risk circumstances among the local poor and the dependent population, which in turn prevented them from exercising their vote and discouraged participation.

Viengrat Nethipo (2007)[13] argued that the decentralization process, especially the huge amounts of financial resources devolved to local governments during the past ten years, has significantly strengthened

[13] Viengrat Nethipo (2007), "Master of the Provinces: the Influential networks of Ubon Ratchathani", research paper submitted to the Faculty of Political Science, Chulalongkorn University.

the existing political networks at the local level. National political parties, Thai Rak Thai Party in Ubon Ratchathani province for example, secured its political networks at the local level by supporting the party's political cadres in local elections. It allowed them to enjoy benefits from holding local posts, while securing the party networks for the upcoming national election. The distribution of political benefits to political networks became much easier when the amount of resources and political posts increased.

5. Monitoring the Status of Decentralization

In 2002, the Office of the National Decentralization Committee (ONDC) established a commission on decentralization monitoring, involving participation by colleges and universities. Regional centers for monitoring decentralization were set up in those colleges and universities, to conduct annual surveys on the progress of decentralization in their respective regions. Annual reports of the monitoring since 2003 have indicated the progress of decentralization.[14] The reports address the progress of local decentralization during the fiscal year and cover eight key areas:

1. Functional devolutions to local units.
2. Human resources transfers.
3. Streamlining laws and regulations for decentralization.
4. Findings on decentralization assessment.
5. Civic education on decentralization policy.
6. Major findings and policy recommendations of special studies concerning local government structure, including a study on restructuring Bangkok Metropolitan Administration, a study on the status of the sub-district and village heads in newly established municipalities, and a study on building capability of the Office of Local Decentralization Committee by the World Bank.
7. Problems and obstacles for the decentralization process in the 2003 fiscal years. Review of new Sub-committees under the Local Decentralization Committee, their functions and key performance outputs.
8. New decrees issued by the Local Decentralization Committee concerning revenue sharing and grant allocation.

---

[14] Office of the Local Decentralization Committee, *The 2002 Annual Report of the Local Decentralization Committee* (Kurusapa Printing Office, Bangkok), 2003.

The 2006 report contended that during FY 2005, 73.88% of targeted services (181 out of 245) had been devolved to local authorities, and that 56 percent of rules and regulations (32 out of 57) had been amended.[15]

Another monitoring measure was the best practice award system, where the ONDC in collaboration with DLAP established two principle best practice awards, namely the local good governance award and the local tax effort award. Annual reports of the awards indicated that the number of qualifying localities as well as the average scores in best practices on good governance and tax effort has continually increased.

The NESDB, and later on DLAP, have been attempting to develop an information system for monitoring decentralization. Progress in the design of this system had been steady since 2001, but implementation has not gone forward because of insufficient enforcement and incentive measures, and because there is a lack of coordination among respective central departments and local authorities.

5.1. *Decentralization and Local Performance Indicators*

The DLAP has developed a series of performance indicators to monitor local service performance and management since 2004. These indicators incorporate general management aspects of local government, i.e., the quality of human resources, the policy and planning effectiveness, the efficiency of revenue collection, the transparency and sustainability of financial practices, among others. In addition, a list of local basic services as well as its minimum standards of service delivery was also established and advocated in 2005. It is expected that the issuance of performance indicators will stimulate improvements in local performance. However, DLAP still needs to develop appropriate measures for implementation.

6. Enhancing the Success of Thailand's Decentralization

6.1. *Strengthen Decentralization Strategy*

Thailand has many elements of a strategy in place, including the principles enshrined in the Constitution, the Decentralization Act and

---

[15] Office of the Local Decentralization Committee, *The 2005 Annual Report of the Local Decentralization Committee* (Kurusapa Printing Office, Bangkok), 2006.

various action plans. What is missing at present is a general framework that encompasses all features of decentralization — linking expenditure responsibility with revenue authority, determining grant formulae, developing uniform financial accounts, strengthening capacity in line with devolving responsibility, and monitoring outcomes. A key part of this strategy should be the transition plan necessary to meet the Constitutionally mandated targets for the future. The Central Government must have a clear strategy for how this will be done, and local governments must have certainty about the phasing in of their new responsibilities and resources. In addition, mechanisms for better co-ordination among the various agencies involved and resolving conflicts among levels of government, should be defined more clearly.

6.2. *Integrate Decentralization with Broader Public Sector Reforms*

The Government has embarked on an ambitious public sector reform that will fundamentally redefine the role and operation of government agencies. This reform has profound implications for decentralization — especially in redefining the role of the central government, changing the ways in which financial and human resources are managed, and transferring civil servants to local administrations. Yet public sector reform and decentralization policies are not integrated, as noted above in the discussion of the conflict between the Restructuring Act and the Decentralization Action Plan.

Nor has there been significant sectoral reform. Some ministries, e.g., Education and Public Health, are testing deconcentrated service delivery models. For example, Local Education Authorities were established to deliver local education services in conformity with the National Education Act — yet these Authorities are not necessarily coterminus with local government boundaries, and may not make decisions that reflect local preferences. The Ministry of Public Health is supporting the establishment of Provincial Health Authorities (or Boards) that would be responsible and accountable for improving health indicators by purchasing and/or providing the right mix of health inputs and outputs that raise health outcomes. While this proposal would allow for reallocation of costly or unnecessary hospital care to cost-effective preventive and promotive services, as well as specific targeting of vulnerable populations (the poor, hill tribes, risk populations, etc.), it does not take into account the broader responsibilities and authorities of Provincial Administrative Organizations.

6.3. *Manage Fiscal Risks*

As noted earlier, Thailand has decentralized revenues before working out the cost of devolved responsibilities. Reconciling expenditure decentralization with revenue decentralization is perhaps the greatest challenge facing the Government. This potential fiscal risk of inter-governmental finance had been minimized in the past five years because the government delayed revenue and expenditure decentralization.

Still, financial practices of local authorities have both implicit and explicit risks due to a number of malpractices, political corruption and rent seeking, increasing amounts of off-budget spending, unfunded liabilities, lack of sufficient revenues to cover skyrocketing costs of local public services, unskilled personnel, and lack of a sufficient internal control system and external post-audit. These problems are classic and widespread, at both the national and local government level. The establishment of Provincial Counter Corruption Commissions (PCCCs) in every province, as mandated by the 2007 constitution to speed up legal proceedings of corruption cases at the local level, might alleviate some of the local fiscal risk.

6.4. *Reconsider the Structure of Local Governments*

Success with this policy in Thailand will involve fiscal decentralization to over 8,000 local administrations, many of which cannot adequately deliver or finance services. Few countries have tried this approach. Yet, broader discussions of the appropriate structure of local government (e.g., whether an intermediate tier of government is necessary to oversee service delivery and financing, or whether there are too many local government units to be viable) do not appear to be taking place. The Government might consider an asymmetric approach to decentralization, whereby the larger places with stronger capacity decentralize sooner than the smaller, weaker places. A parliamentary sub-committee on local government has commissioned DLGP to study the optimal size and structure of LGs.

6.5. *Build Local Capacity*

Many government agencies, donors, academic institutions, and non-government organizations are assisting local governments in building their capacity through training and technical assistance. However, these efforts are often *ad hoc* and uncoordinated. To build local capacity, a coherent national training program for local governments should be developed and implemented. Central government agencies whose functions are to be devolved are potential sources of knowledge and training for building the technical skills of local governments. Overcoming the disincentives associated with transferring central personnel to local governments will also be needed to build local capacity.

References

Action Plan on Determining Process of Decentralization to Local Government Organization. Office of the Decentralization to Local Government Organization Committee (National Decentralization Committee), February 2002.

Archer, R W (1995). An outline and a bibliography on local government property tax reform in Thailand. *The Journal of Property Tax Assessment and Administration*, 1, pp. 5–28.

Brown, G and B Thawinwadee (eds.) (2007). *Monitoring the Pulse of the Nation: Indicators of Democratization and Good Governance in Thailand 2005–2007*, Research and Development Office, King Projadhipok's Institute, 2007.

Bureekul, T (2006). Participation of Civil Society in Democratization in Thailand: Community Development. In *Eyes on Democracy: National and Local Issues*, N Rathamarit (ed.), King Projadhipok's Institute, Bankok, pp. 73–102.

Charas, S (2002). Fiscal Decentralization in Thailand. World Bank Workshop on Inter-governmental Fiscal Relations in East Asia (Bali, January 2002).

Charas, S (2003–04). *A Bibliography of Local Government Initiatives in Thailand*, Thailand Research Fund, Bangkok, Thailand (Published in Thai).

Charas, S (2006). Policy Recommendations on the Promotion of Local Government Initiatives in Thailand. Thai Research Fund, Public Policy Document No. 14.

College of Local Government Development (2006), *Directions of PAOs' Educational Provision*, Local Forum Vol. 3, KPI, Bangkok.

Interview with Weerachai Chomsakorn, Office of Local Decentralization Committee, (March 2008), concerning inter-governmental fiscal transfers.

GOLD Network Centre, Suggested Local Government Autonomy Strategies of Decentralization/Devolution Fiscal Decentralization in Problem Areas and Regional Strategies Southeast Asia (2003–2010).

Nelson, M H (2001). Thailand: Problems with Decentralization? International Conference: "Building Institutional Capacity in Asia." Jakarta.

Office of Local Decentralization Committee (2003). *The 2002 Annual Report of the Local Decentralization Committee* (Kurusapa Printing Office, Bangkok).

Office of the Local Decentralization Committee (2006). *The 2005 Annual Report of the Local Decentralization Committee* (Kurusapa Printing Office, Bangkok).

Poaponsakorn, N D N and S Tulayawansinpong (2001). Corruptions in Public Sector: Case Studies and Economic Strategies in Countering Corruptions, in Office of Civil Service (2001), *Corruption in Thailand*, A TDRI research report Bangkok, 2001.

Regional Urban Development Fund: RUDF (2006). *Innovation on Urban Development Credits*, Office of Social Development Fund, the Saving Bank, Bangkok.

Research Triangle Institute and Land Institute Foundation (1991). Property Tax Reform in Thailand, prepared for Royal Thai Government Fiscal Policy Office and the U.S. Agency for International Development.

Rodden, Jonathan, Jennie Litvack and Gunnar Eskelund, Decentralization and the Challenge of Hard Budget Constraints (MIT Press, 2003).

Sakon, W. (2008). *Driving TAOs' Social Welfare Services Through Fiscal Decentralization*, Final report submitted to UNCEF and NESDB.

The National Public Health Reform Office (2005). *Healthy communities*. Sam Dee Printing Equipment Ltd., Bangkok.

Webster, D (2002). Implementing Decentralization in Thailand: The Road Forward. Capacity Building Project. ONDC and the World Bank.

Weerasak, K (2007). Local Government Networking Initiatives, Thailand Research Fund, Bangkok, Published in Thai.

Wegelin, E (2002). Thailand: Decentralization Capacity Assessment. Findings and Recommendations. ONDC and the World Bank.

World Bank Assessment Mission (1997). Report of Assessment Mission: Urban Development Under the 8th and 9th Plans, Prepared for the National Economic and Social Development Board of the Royal Thai Government.

World Bank (1999c). Thailand Economic Monitor, various issues, World Bank Thailand Office.

World Bank (2000). Thailand: Public Finance in Transition.

World Bank (2003). Thailand Country Development Partnership for Governance Monitoring Report.

Wuthisan, T (2005). Educational Strategies of Local Authorities. *Journal of Prajadhipok*, Year 3, September–December 2005; pp. 44–55.

Viengrat, N (2007). Master of the Provinces: The Influential networks of Ubon Ratchathani. Research paper submitted to the Faculty of Political Science, Chulalongkorn University. http://pixiart.com/forum/view.php?frm=1&id=144.

Chapter IX

Political and Administrative Decentralization in Vietnam

NGUYEN KHAC HUNG

Dai Nam University, Hanoi, Vietnam

1. Introduction

The purpose of this paper is to examine the transformation of the role and function of the local authorities in Vietnam. We do this in a context of public administration reform (PAR). The current situation as regards political and administrative decentralization in Vietnam is described in this paper. We also summarize the debate about matters related to the process, including arguments that have been put forward about how to improve local governance to provide better public services and how to enhance grassroots democracy. The paper concludes with a commentary about the need for a deeper examination of decentralization issues.

2. Overview of the Local Authorities in Vietnam

Local authorities or governments are usually defined as political units or instrumentalities constituted by law. Their peculiar or unique characteristics can include their subordinate status to the central government, their control over local affairs and their power to tax (Cahill and Friedman, 1964, quoted by C. Sosmena, Jr., 1991, p. 1). Local authorities have defined boundaries, and the authority to carry out public activities in a particular area. They operate under the national government in a unitary system and under the central and state levels in a federal system.

Local authorities are characterized by the following elements: (i) territory, (ii) population, (iii) work organizations; (iv) separate legal identity; (v) independence from other local units; (vi) government powers and functions; and (vii) power to raise revenue. All these elements interact in practice, and are influenced by historical, cultural and development level factors. The result is that local government takes on a different importance in different countries.

Vietnam has a land area of approximately 326,000 square kilometers, with a coastal zone of more than 300 km and land borders of 3,700 km. The country has had a history of more than 4,000 years, full of wars against different aggressors for the national independence and development. Because Vietnam is a multi-cultural, multi-ethnic nation, it can be seen as an interesting case study of the evolution of the role of local government organization. Throughout history, the system of local authorities has been continuously transforming itself to meet the demands of the different development periods, to serve the wars for the country reunification, and to help deal with the post-war construction.

The country is currently divided into four levels of administration: the central government, the provincial government, and the district and the communal levels. According to the Constitution of the Socialist Republic of Vietnam (SRV), there are three levels of local authorities: namely, the provincial/central city, the district, and the communal levels. The number of provincial administrative units is 64, of which there are 59 provinces and 5 cities under the direct authority of the central government (Hanoi, Ho Chi Minh City, Hai Phong, Da Nang, and Can Tho). They are sub-divided into 639 districts, among which there are 490 rural districts and 110 urban districts and equivalents such as towns and cities belonging to provinces. There are approximately 10,600 communes and wards, which are the grassroots level of administration.

It is recognized in Vietnam that the local administrations play a crucial role in the functioning of the State administration system. The national government can communicate with citizens through the system of local authorities, which have the more direct links with the local population and institutions. The perception is that good local governance is an effective stimulus to ensure the successful implementation of national development policies set forth by the Communist Party

(CPV) and the State of Vietnam. Thus, in the current public administration reform (PAR) efforts, the Government of Vietnam (GOV) has paid special attention to reform initiatives at both the local level and the central level. Le Tu Duyen and Pham Van Diem (1998, p. 116) argued: "*The focal point of the public administration reform at the local level emphasizes the enhancing of the local democracy and the promotion of decentralization in order to build "a State from the people, by the people and for the people"*.

There are two main types of state organs at each of the levels of local authority; i.e., the People's Council, an elected and deliberative organ, and the People's Committee, an executive body. As stipulated in the 1994 amended Law on Organization of People's Council and People's Committee, the People's Council is a state organ that operates in the locality. It is meant to reflect the will of the people and is elected by the people through universal suffrage. It is jointly responsible to the people in the locality and to the state organs at higher levels. The term of office for the People's Council is five years. The People's Committee is an executive arm of the People's Council and is elected by the People's Council at the local level. In other words, the People's Committee is a state administrative body in the locality. The People's Committee has the same term of office as the People's Council, i.e., five years. The People's Committee is in charge of implementing the Constitution, laws and regulatory documents issued by state organs at higher levels, as well as resolutions or decisions approved by the People's Council.

The organizational structure and the operations of the local administrative system are stipulated in the 1992 amended Constitution of the SRV and the 1994 amended Law on Organization of the People's Council and the People's Committee. To carry out its duties and obligations, the People's Council is assisted by several committees that deal with specific areas. The People's Committee, on the other hand, is supported by a number of professional and specialized departments. As the People's Committee is elected by the People's Council at the same level and the election result is then ratified by the head of the government agency at the immediate higher level, these departments function in a system of "double subordination". The term implies that the local operating department is responsible to the People's Committee horizontally, and to the immediate upper level specialized department vertically. Ultimately, all are responsible to their respective central ministry. Le Tu Duyen and Pham Van Diem (1998, *op. cit.*, p. 118) write: "This double subordination constitutes one of the general principles applied to the State management system which combines territorial management on the one hand (local administration) and sectoral management on the other (line ministry)."

Local authorities of all levels are responsible for conducting debates, taking decisions and setting out necessary measures to ensure strict implementation of resolutions and decisions of the state organs at higher levels. This should be done by taking into account the specific conditions of the locality and living standards of the local people. The key sectors with which the local authorities deal includes the following:

— economic development
— culture and education
— social life and security
— technology and environment
— religion and minority affairs
— law enforcement, and
— development and improvement of the local authority capacity.

3. Decentralization in Theory and Practice

3.1. *Central-local Relationships and Issues of Decentralization*

There are two major forms of decentralization: (i) functional decentralization, i.e. the State gives some of its functions, especially the ones for public services, to a public institution which does not carry out a state management function; (ii) territorial decentralization in which the State gives some power to territorial communities.

Five types of decentralization are found in developed and developing countries:

- Decentralization: the State holds the power which is not concentrated at the center, but places officials at the local level to carry out its tasks
- Delegation: an agency or official authorises a unit or subordinate to use some power, on its behalf to carry out some specific tasks
- Devolution: giving power to autonomous units to carry out the functions

- Deregulation: to reduce cumbersome rules and regulations, and to make new and easily applicable rules and regulations for the public to follow.
- Privatization: apart from the notion of shifting the ownership from the State to the private sector, this includes placing ownership in the hands of the State while the tasks are carried out by other sectors to make the State free to focus on macro level issues. There are many types of privatization practices (see Chart 1).

In Vietnam, as argued by M. Turner (1999, p. 1), "the technical impossibility of total centralization, and the political pressure for decentralization, entail a situation in which all systems of government involve a combination of both centralized and decentralized authority". However, finding a combination of central control and local autonomy that satisfies regime requirements and popular demands is a persistent dilemma for Vietnam. This is especially problematic because of the present strong advocacy of decentralization in the world (as argued by strong supporters such as the World Bank (1993, 1998), and UNDP (1992, 2000).

Under central planning, at least four features of local administration can be identified. *First*, local administrative units are demarcated according to production-related factors such as land area, the population

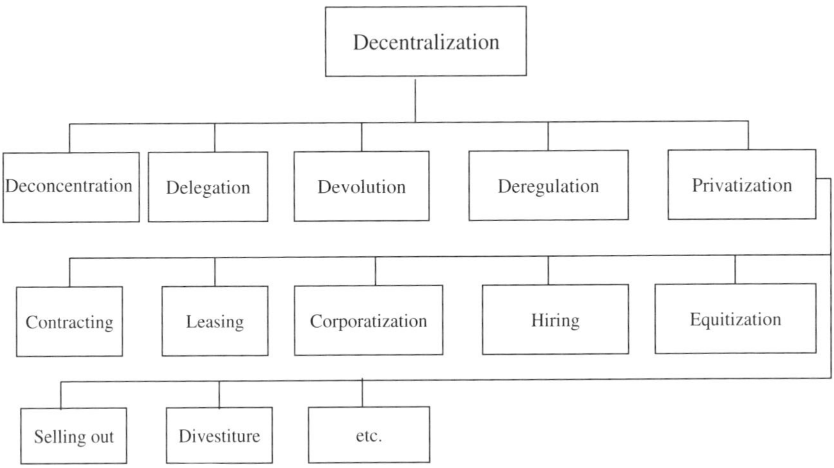

Chart 1. Types of Decentralization

density and economies of scale, rather than historical and cultural factors. *Second*, each administrative level functions both as an administrative agency and as an economic manager (the paternalistic mechanism). Government agencies at all levels are entitled to own and run industrial and agricultural production enterprises of various sizes. *Third*, party committees and mass organizations play an important role in mobilizing the local population to implement party and government policies. *Fourth*, the administrative structure is based on the principle of "management along the territorial lines" (Vasavakul, T. 1999, pp. 169–170). All of these features bring a situation in which activities of all administrative levels are duplicates of those of a nation-state in miniature, since local administrative agencies are allowed to issue administrative orders as if they were independent administrative levels (Nguyen Huu Duc, 1996). Although the term "administrative hierarchies" is used, in reality the situation of most localities was "self-administration".

This situation was combined with the powerlessness of the state under central planning as the political power of the State mainly rested upon its ability to claim property rights, control economic resources, allocate their use and attain output targets. Central-local government relations were focused on resource allocation, resource extraction, management of State assets and fulfilment of production targets. Vasavakul (1999, *op. cit.* pp. 170–172) argued:

> "In the state bureaucracy, politics tended to be vertically confined, and was characterized by a tug of war between State planners and ministerial officials, between ministerial officials and managers of production units, and between managers and workers. In the industrial sector, the issues dealt with were the allocation of investment capital, quota for production material, production targets and workers' wages and social benefits. In the agricultural sector, the issues under contention included the long-term mechanization of agriculture, investment funds, procurement quotas, agricultural prices and agricultural taxes".

The rise of a new, market-oriented economy and the long war gave birth to new patterns in Vietnamese politics. With diminishing resources coming from the center, and the loosening of administrative control over production activities, the vertical administrative and economic ties disintegrated. The transition allowed local authorities to consolidate their economic and political powers because their role as investors and managers and their ability to accumulate resources independent from central supervision was enhanced. During the transition, local officials became involved in law-making and law implementation in their territory. This process in turn allowed many of them to mobilize and allocate resources to their advantage (*ibid.*, p. 172).

With the fragmentation of power (see Fig. 1), a number of problems arose. Because there was no clear delegation of power to the provinces

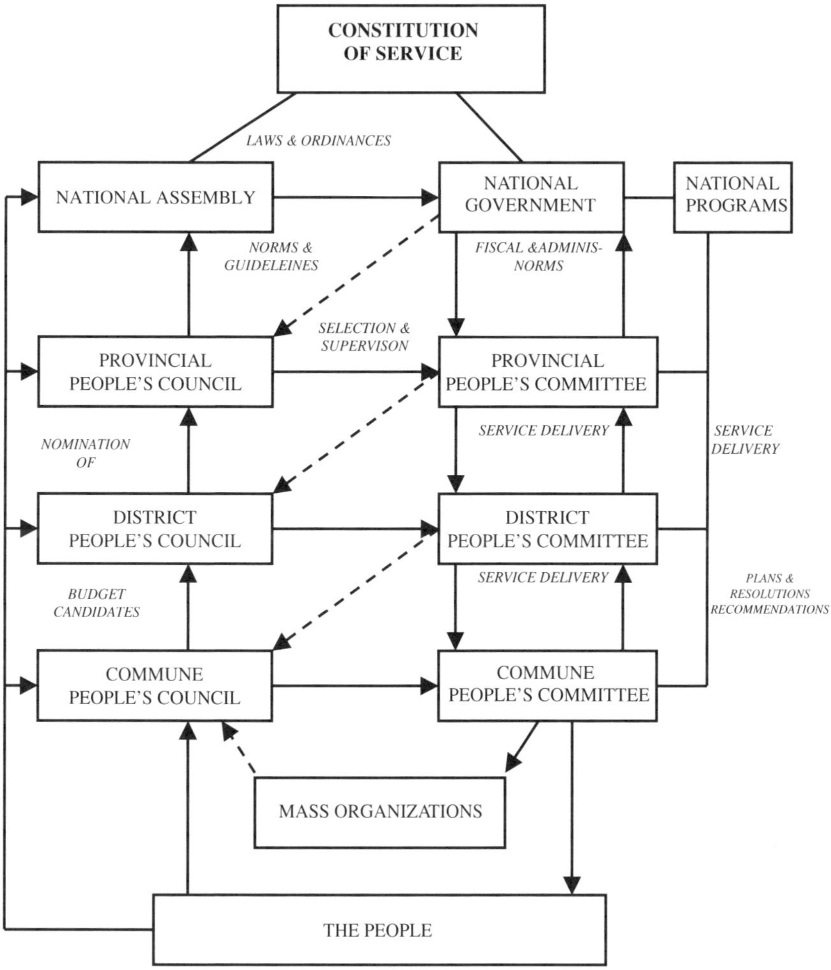

Source: WB (1996, p. 45), quoted by Vasavakul, 1999.

Fig. 1. Administrative Organization of Rural Services Delivery in Vietnam

in the area of managing natural resources, local authorities freely exploited the resources. As a result, the central government was faced with the problem of accessing and protecting natural resources and the environment. Local authorities imported and exported freely, with revenue going to the local budget. They sometimes issued regulations contradictory to those of central government, leading to a weakening of the management power of the latter. In addition, many decisions issued by the central government were not elaborated by local authorities in the form of guidelines, and as a result could not be implemented at the local level.[1]

Faced with this growing ambiguity about administrative boundary and power, reforms were launched both to the administrative state in general and the local administrative state in particular. With the Seventh Party Congress in 1991 and the promulgation of the 1992 Constitution, the central government moved in earnest to redefine central- local-government relations. The delay stemmed mainly from the fact that the leadership focused more on economic reform than on political reform. Furthermore, it is argued (Fforde and de Vylder, 1996, *op. cit.*) that in the late 1980s, the central government was too weak financially to attempt recentralization. In the 1990s, however, it had regained strength and was in position to assert its authority in the relationships. Particularly, since the launching of the PAR in January 1995, the reforms of central-local government relationships have been under way with the rethinking of the basic issues: separation of state administrative management and economic management functions, the rule of law, and types of authorities and power relationships within the administrative State.

According to the new thinking, the new State would be an administrative state, which is not only an instrument of the majority, but is "also a public power with universal characteristics capable of representing public and national interests. State power was based on the ability of state agencies and state cadres to exercise power" (Vasavakul, 1999, *op. cit.*, p. 176). The local authorities would be vertically linked with the central government and their exercise of power would have to be carried out with due recognition of that vertical link. The rule of law was used as a means to create a vertical link with the local agencies. However, the reform policy did not eliminate the old model of power relationships, and the administrative state continued to be diversified (see Fig. 2).

[1] Nguyen Ky, Interview, November 2001 (*op. cit.*).

CITY PEOPLE'S COUNCIL

CITY PEOPLE'S COMMITTEE

General Administration Organizations	
1	Dep. for Planning & Investment
2	City Inspection
3	Dep. of Organization & Personnel
4	Dep. for Finance & Pricing
5	Dep. for Justice
6	Dep. for Science & Technology
7	Dep. for Land Adm. & Housing
8	Chief Architect Office
9	Adm. Office of city PC
Committees	
10	Comm. of religion affairs
11	Comm. for overseas Vietnamese
12	Population and family planning
13	Comm. for Children protection
14	Standing Comm. of Rewarding
15	Comm. for dealing with Chinese

Economic Management Organizations	
16	Dep. of Industries
17	DARD
18	Dep. Transport & Communication
19	Dep. of Construction
20	Dep. of Trade
21	Dep. of Tourism
Service Organizations	
22	Dep. of Health
23	Dep. of Education & Training
24	Dep. of Culture & Information
25	Dep. of Sports
26	Dep. of Labour & social affairs
Other Organizations	
10 temporary agencies	
11 other service organizations under PC	
Office for receiving citizens	
Office of the NA's members	
Office of Standing Committee of People's Council	

Other Agencies	
1	City defence commanding headquarter
2	City Police
3	City Postal Office
4	Taxation Branch
5	Custom Branch
6	Statistic Branch
7	International Relation Dep.
8	Electricity Company
9	Bank systems
10	City Treasury
11	City Social Insurance
12	Dep. for managing State assets in enterprises

Source: HCM City (2001a), quoted by Nguyen Khac Hung, 2002.

Fig. 2. Organizational Structure of HCM Administration

The new thinking is driven by the need to enhance democracy, i.e., that people should participate in or determine the decisions that affect their lives. Decision-making should be located closer to the people, and this requires placing it in the hands of local institutions and officials.

This thinking is in line with the central tenet of decentralization as advocated by institutions like The World Bank (WDR, 1997) through the banner of "bringing the State closer to the people" and UNDP (1999). As argued by Turner (1999, *op. cit.*, p. 4), "decentralization is the conceptual framework that is most frequently employed to address central-local relations".

While analyzing decentralization, Turner and Hulme (1997, p. 153) developed a table of forms of decentralization (see Table 1), in which they drew six forms of decentralization on two bases — territory and function. The organizational structure of HCM City may well illustrate the forms of decentralization that Vietnam has adopted for its local authorities within the 1992 Constitution. It can be argued that from the territorial angle, devolution and decentralization are the two main forms the government of Vietnam has deployed. The 26 departments are the authorities that the central government has delegated to the city level. The twelve other agencies in the box at the bottom are the offices of the central government allocated at the city to fulfil central functions. In

Table 1. Forms of Decentralization

Nature of Delegation	Basis for Delegation	
	Territorial	Functional
Within formal political structures	Devolution (political decentralization, local government, democratic decentralization)	Interest group
Within public administrative or para-statal structures	Decentralization (administrative decentralization, field administration)	Establishment of parastatals and quangos
From State sector to private sector	Privatization of devolved functions (deregulation, contracting out, voucher schemes)	Privatization of national functions (divestiture, deregulation, economic liberalization)

Source: Turner and Hulme (1997, p. 153).

addition, several aspects of production and business functions that used to be undertaken by government agencies have now been transferred to non-State agencies.

However, there has been much confusion about the "right" direction for decentralization in Vietnam. This is indicated in the fact that a distinction is made between decentralization of function (*phan cap*) and decentralization of power (*phan quyen*), whereby the latter is seen as negative, and the former is positive. In reality, there is a tendency for the allocation of tasks (decentralization of function) to become contrary to the desired decentralization of power. This is widely seen as a major unwanted element of the current situation as it amounts to a lack of central power to control, leading to a weaker State rather than stronger one. The reasons may be several.

First, while the roles between the CPV and the government are still not fully distinguished, the notion of the widely used slogan "The party to lead, the State to manage, and the people to be the masters" has not been sufficiently clarified. The 1992 Constitution considers sectoral (*nganh*) and territorial (*lanh tho*) divisions of the State administration as roughly on the same footing of power, leading to difficulties in working out whose authority is relevant in each instance. In addition, Fforde (1997, pp. 5–6) argued: "A … simpler explanation … of the main cause of current problems is that the real costs involved in carrying out the institutional changes required by the market economy are considerable, and so, when the resources (both material and intellectual) available to the party and the State administration remains limited, it inevitably takes time and effort to do so".

Second, the situation is further exacerbated by the fact that even though provincial and city authorities are given a prescribed amount of authority, their departments are still in a double subordination situation. The Law on organization and operation of People's Councils and People's Committees in 1994 states that while the local authority provides the departments with office, finance, staff, and is responsible for the day-to-day management of the departments, the departments must report to their superior line ministries and are subject to guidelines and instructions of the ministries in professional matters. The heads of the departments are appointed by the local authority, but must be approved by the superior ministries and agencies. This double subordination has created a number of delays and conflicts in central-local relations, has compromised local autonomy, and has been one of the reasons for the complaints from the local staff as in the case of PAR in HCM City. The issue of power is, therefore, further analyzed and clarified in the current amendment of the 1992 Constitution and 1994 Law on local authorities. Debate is ongoing about how to eliminate the double subordination and to make improvements to central-local relations.

3.2. *1992 Constitution and 1994 Law on Organization*

Since 1986, Vietnam has been engaged in an overall innovation process (*Doi Moi*) which includes a focus on economic reform. The goal is to enhance the living standards of the people. The transformation from a centrally planned economy towards a market-oriented economy has had a significant impact on the way the government regulates the national economy, as well as on the structure of the state apparatus for governance. This basic shift in thinking about economy and governance led to demand for a new Constitution to replace the 1980 Constitution. After considerable debate on a nation-wide scale, the National Assembly enacted the new Constitution on April 15th, 1992. Based on the Constitution, on July 5th, 1994, the National Assembly (NA) enacted an amended Law on Organization of the People's Council and People's Committee, and a Law on Election of the Members of the People's Council. This is the key legislation governing the role and structure of the system of local authorities in Vietnam.

This period has also witnessed a comprehensive programme for public administration reform (PAR) in Vietnam. Although the official national programme was announced in 1995, a number of activities were undertaken long before. The aim of the PAR programme is to develop "a competent, transparent public administration which properly uses its powers and gradually moves towards modernization, to effectively and efficiently manage State affairs, promote the healthy development in the right direction, better serve the people and develop working habits and life-styles conforming to the rule-of-law in the whole society" (GOV, 2001, Master Plan for PAR).

The PAR program, which has been implemented in almost all sectors and local authorities in the country, has focused on the following key areas:

(1) Reform of administrative institutions, focused on the legal basis and operating procedures;

(2) Reform of organizational structures to remove some ambiguity between State management functions and service delivery. The number of ministries has been reduced to 26 and some decentralization of state administrative power has been realized;
(3) Developing cadres and civil servants. The most significant result of this effort is the Ordinance on Public Employees, which moves towards a more competence-based management in, for example, recruitment, evaluation, and promotion. Some changes in the remuneration scales have been implemented and retraining of the cadres and civil servants has been placed high on the agenda;
(4) Public finance reform comprising a new budget system, establishment of audit systems and some financial autonomy granted to local authorities.

The 1992 Constitution and 1994 law provided the legal status for the People's Council as an organ of State power at the locality, elected by the local population (Article 119 of the Constitution, and Article 1 of the law). The People's Committee was also stipulated as an executive organ of the People's Council and a State administrative organ at the locality (Article 123 of the Constitution, and Article 2 of the law). Unlike the previous set-up, the membership structure of the People's Council and People's Committee became much streamlined, with an average reduction of 25 — 30 percent.

There were now 15–25 members of the People's Council at the communal level, 25–35 at the district level, and 45–75 at the provincial level. The law also stipulated that Hanoi, Ho Chi Minh City and provinces with more than 2.5 million inhabitants each could elect more than 75 members for their People's Council, however, the number should not exceed 85 deputies. The number of members and Vice-Chairs of the People's Committee have considerably decreased. For example, there are now 5–7 members of the People's Committee at the communal level, including a Chairperson and a Vice-Chair (there had been 7–9 members, including a Chairperson and two Vice-Chairs before); 7–9 members at the district level; and 11–13 at the provincial level including a Chairperson and three Vice-Chairs. The Hanoi and Ho Chi Minh City People's Committees formerly included thirteen members, including four Vice-Chairs.

The 1994 Law provided that there would be no secretariat and permanent commission in the People's Council at the communal, ward and township level. However, the Chairperson and Vice-Chair of the People's Council were given the functions, tasks and powers similar to those of the permanent commission.

Although there were no substantial changes in the tasks and powers of the People's Council and People's Committee, attempts were made to differentiate and make clear the tasks and powers of the two bodies. On July 3rd, 1996, the Standing Committee of the NA passed an Ordinance on Specific Tasks and Powers of the People's Council and People's Committee at each level. It should be noted that the ordinance not only clarified the responsibilities of the People's Council and People's Committee at each level, but also provided specific stipulations about the state management responsibilities in different types of local governments (rural area: provinces, rural districts, communes, municipalities; urban area: cities, urban districts, wards, towns; islands–island districts).

In order to ensure democracy and encourage initiatives of the collective People's Committee in dealing with important issues in the life of the locality, Article 49 of the 1994 Law defined issues that had to be discussed collectively and voted by majority at the People's Committee session including:

— Work programme of the People's Committee;
— Socio-economic development plans;
— Budget preparation;
— Measures to carry out resolutions of the People's Council in social and economic spheres; approval of the People's Committee reports before the People's Council;
— Proposals on new establishment, merging or dissolving professional bodies of the People's Committee, and changes in administrative jurisdiction.

In addition, to ensure the dynamics and swift actions in administrative execution, Article 52 of the 1994 law stipulated that the Chairperson of the People's Committee was entrusted with all authority in dealing with the following matters:

— To certify the election results of the members of the immediate lower level People's Committee; to move, or release from office the Chairperson, and the Vice-Chair of the immediate lower level

People's Committee; to certify the release from office and removal of other members of the immediate lower level People's Committee; to appoint, release from office, move, remove, reward, provide disciplinary actions for civil servants and public employees in line with management devolution;

— To suspend the implementation of incorrect documents of the professional bodies of the People's Committee; and incorrect documents of the People's Committee or of the Chairperson of the People's Committee at the lower level;
— To suspend the implementation of incorrect resolutions of the immediate lower level People's Council, and to propose to the People's Council/People's Committee to remove such resolutions;
— To decide matters within the jurisdiction of the People's Council/People's Committee level apart from those that had to be decided by the collective People's Council as provided in Article 49 of the 1994 amended law.

In an attempt to devolve management functions between the central and local levels, among different levels of local authorities, and to define the tasks and power of the People's Council and People's Committee at each level, the Permanent Committee of the National Assembly issued an Ordinance in 1996 on specific tasks and powers of the People's Council and People's Committee at each level. The ordinance also was intended to distinguish the differences in state management functions between rural, urban and island areas. In order to ensure the unity of leadership in the State administration system from the central government to the local level, Article 5 of the Law on Organization of the Government (2000) stipulated that the Prime Minister had the authority to suspend from office, move or remove the Chairperson, Vice-Chair of the People's Committee at the provincial or central city level.

Referring to the lowest level in Vietnam's administrative hierarchy, President Ho Chi Minh once wrote: "the commune level, being closest to the people, is the foundation of our public administration. If the commune level works, then all our work will proceed smoothly." The statement shows the importance of the local level, especially the grassroots level. However, the system of administration had long been centralized. National program planning was heavily dominated by line ministries, while provincial responsibility was limited to "organizing and implementing the programs in their respective localities". The decisions made by the central government and the local level simply followed the guidelines given by the central government. The common attitude from the central government was that "provinces do what we tell them to with the money we allocate to them".

During the transition period, Vietnam is incrementally transferring greater administrative and fiscal responsibilities to the provincial level. Many central level policy statements are strongly in favor of administrative decentralization, the framework for which is laid out in the Master Programme on Public Administration Reform (PAR) approved by the Vietnamese Government in September 2001. Explicit support for the idea of administrative decentralization is given in the PAR framework, as captured in the National Assembly resolution in 2000 to "review and adjust the division of specific responsibilities between the central government and provincial governments; what can be allocated to local government should be decentralized immediately". Most elements of the PAR framework directly or indirectly facilitate administrative decentralization.

Decentralization in Vietnam was also institutionalized through the Grassroots Democracy Resolution promulgated in the Government Decree on May 29th, 1998. The Decree aims to legalize people's direct participation in local decision-making, and to establish transparency and accountability mechanisms at the commune level and upwards for the supervision of public programmes and locally financed projects. In general, it aims to improve "governance" at the local levels. The decree of 1998 was influenced by national assessments that concluded that the "people were hungry for two way flow of information — from the government to them about the nature and timing of public policies and programmes affecting their lives and from them to the government to influence those policies and programmes". Thus the Grassroots Democracy Decree aims to bring more democracy to the communes and make the local population's voice heard better. The decree is centered on four key forms of participation — *people know, people discuss, people execute and people supervise.*

4. Some Current Issues Under Debate

First, the 1992 Constitution reflected a dramatic transformation not only in terms of the socio-economic conditions of the country, but also in the mindset of the people about economy and governance. On questions of the specific form of governance, however, there was a hot debate that took place during the drafting of the Constitution. The contentious questions included how many levels of government should there be, and what levels should have full authority comprising both elected and administrative organs.

In particular, there were arguments for and against the district level being a full level of local government. Those who argued for this proposal took the position that in Vietnam all the power belongs to the people, therefore every level should be a full level of authority. The districts should then have both a People's Council and a People's Committee.

The other side took the position that the role of the district as a full level of authority had considerably decreased since the war. The district would add one more layer of bureaucracy, and so it may take more time for the policies and directions from the central level to come down to the people at the grassroots level. There also is the possibility that more layers of pass-through creates more possibilities for distortion. On the other hand, the individual citizens may easily approach the communal authority which is closest to them, or the provincial authority which is not far away. As such, some would argue, there should be only an administrative organ at the district level (Nguyen Khac Hung, 1998).

These and other arguments led to general provisions in the Constitution, while leaving the 1994 law to define more specific issues on local authorities.

Second, both the Constitution and the law have been in the direction of enhancing the role and powers of the People's Councils in relation to the People's Committees. This follows the Soviet model: "the people exercise their power through the National Assembly and People's Councils at all levels", and "People's Councils are the organ of state power while People's Committees are the executive organs of People's Councils". The authority of People's Committees has also been much strengthened, particularly through the centralization of authority in the administrative system. While the People's Councils have the authority to elect and suspend members of the People's Committees, the Prime Minister has the authority to remove from office the Chairperson and Vice-Chairs of the People's Committee at the provincial level. The Chairperson and Vice-Chairs of the People's Committee at the higher level have the authority to move and remove from office the Chairperson and Vice-Chairs of the People's Committee at the immediate lower level. However, it has been argued that the administrative system must be unified, particularly in the case of the single-party unilateral State of Vietnam, requiring that the head of the higher administrative authority have the power to appoint or dismiss the head of the lower administrative unit. The rationale for this is to avoid possible vested interests in case the local interest is different from the national one. While the practice in the country is not yet in this direction, the issue calls for comprehensive study.

Third, the 1992 Constitution, 1994 law and 1996 ordinance still maintain the practice of equivalent authorities (e.g., province, rural district and commune are equivalent to a city and under the direct control of the central government, urban district and ward). Despite of the fact that there are very different socio-economic features between the rural and urban areas, the organizational structure is parallel. Although the ordinance contains different chapters for each level, the number of tasks and powers has been defined in a uniform way. This shows that a proper study of the specific characteristics of each level of authority, and between rural and urban areas, had not been done before the issuance of the law and the ordinance.

Finally, there is still some blur between the powers and responsibilities of the People's Committee and those of the Chairperson. On the one hand, it is provided that the People's Committee works on a collective basis, and discusses and votes with majority in regard to issues under its jurisdiction. On the other hand, there has been a strengthening of the power and the role of the Chairperson as the head of the administrative organ at the locality. The relationships between the collective People's Committee and the Chairperson have not been clearly defined.

5. Conclusion

This discussion points out that the practice of central-local relationship and political and administrative decentralization in Vietnam has gone through significant changes. Some of these changes have been contentious and provoked a debate among academics and practitioners. Particularly during the *Doi Moi* period, these issues have attracted special attention from the Party and the State of Vietnam. The problems are difficult ones. On the one hand there is an attempt to provide more local autonomy and grassroots democracy to promote local participation in governance. On the other hand, there is a goal of re-centralizing some functions to have better control and supervision over local authorities.

Several new measures have been implemented. Some initial improvements have been made, but there is still a long way to go with the PAR process.

References

Chinh phu (GOV) (2004) Resolution No. 08/2004/NQ-CP of 30 June 2004. Nghi quyet cua Chinh phu ve day manh phan cao quan ly Nha nuoc giua Chinh phu va chinh quyen tinh, thanh pho truc thuoc Trung uong (Government Resolution on Pushing up State Management Decentralization between the Government and the Provincial and Central City Authorities). Hanoi.

Chinh phu (GOV) (2003). No. 79/2003/ND-CP. *Nghi dinh cua Chinh phu: Ban hanh qui che thuc hien dan chu o xa* (Government Decree to Enact the Regulations on Implementation of Democracy at the Communal Level). Hanoi.

Doan Trong Truyen (1996). "Local Administration in Vietnam" in LGC & KAS *Reform of Centralised Administration Structures in Southeast Asia: The Contribution of Local Administration to Economic and Social Development*. Manila: Local Government Development Foundation & Konrad Adenauer Foundation.

Hoc Vien Hanh Chinh Quoc Gia (NAPA) (2001b). Research Topic on *To chuc va hoat dong chinh quyen dia phuong* (Organization and operations of local authorities). Hanoi: NAPA (unpublished).

Nguyen Khac Hung (2002). *The Role of Public Administration Reform in Economic Transition: the Case of Vietnam* (Ph.D. thesis). Manchester: University of Manchester (unpublished).

Nguyen Huu Khien (2003). *Strengthening the Local Autonomy in Vietnam*. Paper of NAPA to the Regional Conference of IIAS: "Share Governance: Combating Poverty and Exclusion" (unpublished).

Sosmeña, GC (1991). *Decentralization and Empowerment*. Manila: Local Government Development Foundation, Inc.

Thaveeporn Vasavakul (2000). Rethinking the Philosophy of Central-local Relations in Post-central Planning Vietnam. In *Central-Local Relations is Asia-Pacific: Convergence or Divergence*, Turner, M. (Ed.). USA: St. Martin's Press, Inc.

The Japan Council of Local Authorities for International Relations (CLAIR), Singapore (1998). *Local Administrative Activities and Its Financial Basis: Report on the ASEAN Regional Local Administration Forum '97*. Singapore.

To Tu Ha *et al.* (1998). *Cai cach hanh chinh dia phuong: ly luan va thuc tien* (Local administration reform: theory and practice). Hanoi: National Political Publishing House.

Tran Mong Lang (2002). *Hien phap Viet Nam tu nam 1946 den nam 2001* (Constitutions of Vietnam from 1946 to 2001). Vietnam: Ho Chi Minh City Publishing House.

UNDP (2001). *Modernising Governance in Vietnam*. (Online). UNDP Office in Hanoi, Vietnam. http://www.undp.org.vn/undp/docs/fact/english/gov.htm.

Chapter X

Managing Indonesia's Rapid Decentralization: Achievements and Challenges

WOLFGANG FENGLER and BERT HOFMAN[1]

The World Bank, Jakarta

Indonesia has embarked upon a radical and rapid decentralization program. Regional autonomy has transformed one of the most centralized countries in the world into one of the more decentralized ones. After the *big bang* decentralization in 2001, Indonesia experienced a second big bang in 2006, when transfers to the regions increased by another 30 percent, followed by a further 15 percent in 2007 (all in real terms).

As a result, provinces and districts are now managing 36 percent of total expenditures and half of public investment in Indonesia. Despite an equalitarian culture in Java, Indonesia is one of the most diverse and unequal countries, which makes decentralization more challenging. Poverty rates in Papua and other eastern Indonesian provinces are as high as in Africa, while Jakarta and several resource-rich regions have per capita incomes several times higher than Mexico.

Indonesia's fiscal transfer system recognizes these inequalities and transfers substantial funds to the poorest and most remote regions.

---

[1] Wolfgang Fengler, Senior Economist, World Bank, Indonesia.
Bert Hofman, Country Director, World Bank, Philippines and former Lead Economist, Indonesia.

We are grateful to the inputs of Bambang Suharnoko, Bastian Zaini, Vishnu Juwono, Daan Pattinasarany and Adrianus Hendrawan.

Today, Indonesia's main development challenge is not to transfer significant additional resources to poor regions, but to make sure that the existing resources are spent effectively. The poorest districts and provinces are among the main beneficiaries of decentralization and the *second big bang*. Their main challenge is to absorb the increasing inflows and many regions have had difficulty in doing so. Many have invested their reserves in Bank Indonesia bills (SBIs), one-month central bank promissory notes. At the end of 2006, districts and provinces held the equivalent of almost 3 percent of GDP in SBIs. While the inter-governmental fiscal framework appears strong and equalizing compared with other countries, much remains to be done to make decentralization work. The administrative and accountability relations are often weak and hampered by a lack of incentives and clarity in assignments between the center and the regions, as well as among central government agencies.

1. Indonesia's *Big Bangs*

Indonesia's 2001 decentralization has transformed the country from having one of the most centralized systems in the world towards one of the most decentralized. Designed in the aftermath of the political turmoil of the fall of Soeharto in 1998, the 1999 decentralization laws were implemented in one major reform in 2001. The country embarked upon a program of fiscal, administrative, and political decentralization all at the same time. Law No. 22/1999 gives broad autonomy to the regions while only a few tasks are explicitly assigned to the center — including defense, security, justice, foreign affairs, fiscal affairs and religion. With this authority came the resources, and lots of them. In the first year of 2001, the regional share of government spending jumped from 17 percent to over 30 percent, and to 36 percent in 2006 (see Table 1).

In 2001, Indonesia received a completely new inter-governmental fiscal system to finance these new expenditure responsibilities. The system moves away from the earmarked grants of the past and instead relies largely on a general grant allocation (DAU, or Dana Alokasi Umum). In addition, for the first time some of Indonesia's abundant natural resource revenues are shared with the regions. Regions also have obtained the right to create new taxes through regional regulations without the approval of the center, as long as these taxes abide by general

Table 1. Sub-national Shares of Government Revenue and Expenditures

	Sub-national Revenue as a Percentage of Total National Revenue	Sub-national Expenditure as a Percentage of Total National Expenditure
Developing countries 1990s	9	14
Transition countries 1990s	17	26
OECD countries 1990s	19	32
Republic of Indonesia 2000	4.7	17.1
Republic of Indonesia 2006	8.5 (2005)	36

Source: World Bank/Government of Indonesia (2007), World Bank (2005) and staff estimates.

principles stated in the law. But in contrast to the jump in spending authority, the regions' own revenues from taxes and levies declined even further from an already low base.

In 2006, Indonesia experienced a "second big bang", when total transfers to the regions increased by almost 50 percent (about 30 percent in real terms), of which the DAU increased by a staggering 64 percent. The increase in transfers was mainly due to a more realistic and substantially higher revenue estimate for the 2006 national budget, on which the DAU is based. The poorest and most remote regions have been the main beneficiaries of this second big bang, many of which have seen a doubling of their transfers. With stronger efforts in own-source revenue collection, Indonesia's regions may soon reach an expenditure share of close to 40 percent, which is much larger than can be expected on the basis of Indonesia's size, income, and other characteristics.[2]

In addition to financial resources, much of the apparatus of government was placed under the control of the regions. Over 2 million civil servants, or almost two thirds of the central government workforce, were transferred to the regions in 2001. Now, out of a civil service of 3.7 million, some 2.8 million are classified as regional — a measure of decentralization that is even more pronounced than that seen in India (see Table 2). Overall, 239 provincial-level offices of the central government, 3,933

[2] Bahl and Tumennasan (2002).

Table 2. Public Sector Employment (million)

	Indonesia 1999	Indonesia 2006	India	China 2004
Public sector	5.4	5.5	21.2	112.1
State enterprises	1.0	1.0	6.5	71.9
General government	4.5	4.5	13.5	40.2
Military & police	0.5	0.8	1.8	2.7
Civil servants*	4.1	3.7	8.2	37.5
Central	3.6	0.9	2.7	n/a
Regional	0.5	2.8	5.5	n/a
Civil servants as share of population	1.9%	1.6%	0.8%	3.0%
Regional civil servants as share of total civil servants	12.2%	75.7%	67.1%	93/55%

* Civilian Civil Servants (including education and health workers).
Source: Buentjen (1999), BKN, China Statistical Yearbook 2006, Indonesia, Coordinating Ministry of Security, World Bank Database on Public Sector Employment.

local-level offices,[3] and more than 16,000 service facilities — schools, hospitals, health centers — were transferred lock, stock and barrel to the regional governments throughout Indonesia in the first months of 2001.

Finally, a new system of governance was put in place at the regional level. The head of the region is no longer accountable to the center, but instead is elected by and accountable to a local parliament. Members of the local parliaments are elected through a party list. Parties in Indonesia remain national parties (they must have offices in at least half the provinces and half the local governments), although some parties have entered the regional parliaments while not entering national parliaments.[4] Now, more than seven years into

[3] This report uses "local government" and "local level" to indicate the second level regions, or *kabupaten* (regencies or districts) and *kota* (cities). "Regions" refers to provinces, districts and cities together. In fact, cities and regencies are sometimes hard to distinguish: more people inhabit urban areas in regencies than in cities.

[4] Hofman, Bert and Kai Kaiser (2003), *Decentralization, Democratic Transition, and Local Governance in Indonesia,* paper presented at the Decentralization Conference, "The Rise of Local Governments", London School of Economics (LSE), 23rd–25th May 2003.

the decentralization program, an assessment of the program can be made.[5]

2. Achievement 1: Indonesia Survived the "Big Bang"

Indonesia's "big bang" decentralization of 2001 went remarkably smoothly. The preparation was ridden with problems, had to meet tight deadlines, and was far from complete by the time regional autonomy took effect. There was no clear implementation plan, the decentralization laws themselves were — and are — far from clear, little dissemination of knowledge to regional governments had taken place, and the core team that was supposed to be in charge of implementation ("Tim Keppres 157" as it became known) never really functioned optimally. Yet, no major incidents in implementation of the radical program occurred: services did not break down, the transfer of the civil service went relatively smoothly, and no fiscal issues arose. In part this success was due to some last minute safeguards that were built into the program. First, the central government banned regions from new borrowing in 2001, except through the center. Law No. 25/1999 allowed the regions to borrow and Government Regulation No. 107/2000 provided affordability limits to borrowing by individual regions. However, these rules could not ensure that aggregate regional borrowing would remain in line with macroeconomic conditions, and the ban therefore prevented regional borrowing that might have derailed the government's stabilization program.

Second, in the 2001 budget the government included a contingency fund of Rp 6 trillion for those regions that would fall short of money.[6] The quick implementation of the new inter-governmental fiscal framework made it virtually impossible to match decentralized expenditures with the needed revenues. Despite transitional elements in the DAU formula, budget shortfalls in some regions were therefore inevitable.

---

[5] A more elaborate evaluation than in this paper can be found in *World Bank 2007, Spending for Development — Making the Most of Indonesia's New Opportunities* (*Public Expenditure Review 2007*), Jakarta 2007 [www.worldbank.org/id]. See also *World Bank 2003, Decentralizing Indonesia*, Jakarta 2003.

[6] Under normal circumstances, such a fund would provide poor incentives for the regions by encouraging overspending in the hope to receive additional central government money.

The contingency came in handy, especially at the provincial level, and about half of it was disbursed in FY2001.[7] The central government also decided to continue to pay former central civil servants through the central payroll system for a transitional period of five months, while deducting the wage bill from the DAU transfers to the regions. This ensured a much smoother transition of personnel than many had anticipated.

Finally, the central government protected its own fiscal health by disbursing transfers to the regions based on *budgeted* amounts rather than actual. During 2001, the rupiah depreciated against the US dollar, which drove up central government revenues, and spending, by a similar amount. But the increase in revenues had to be shared with the regions — at least in principle. The central government's decision to stick with the budgeted amounts for transfers saved the national budget some Rp 9 trillion, or 0.5 percent of GDP. This system of systematic under-budgeting of government revenues and expenditures, and in turn the DAU, lasted until 2005. After a mini macro-economic crisis in August 2005 and stronger pressure from parliament, the Indonesian government was pressed into presenting a more realistic 2006 budget, which resulted in the second "big bang".

3. Achievement 2: People are More Content with Services Now than Before

Testament to the smooth transition is people's perception of the quality of service delivery. The results of two nationwide surveys on service delivery conducted in 2002 and 2006 are encouraging: more than 70 percent of households believe health and education services have improved compared with before decentralization. Households even observed significant improvements in administrative and police services (see Fig. 1).

Households have similar opinions on education and health services in their regions. On average, only 6 percent of households believe that education services and 3 percent of households believe that health services have deteriorated after decentralization. Even in the region surveyed

[7] The contingency may also have distracted attention from the fact that the center decided to disburse the DAU according to budget rather than to actual revenues.

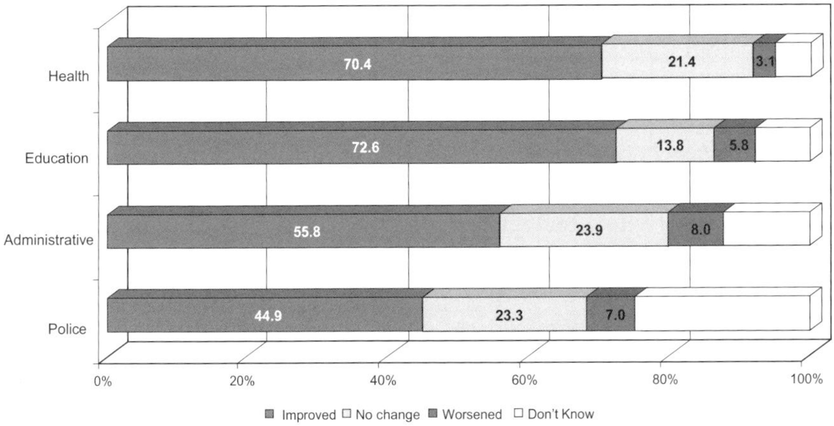

Note: Percent of households that perceives services to be worse/same/better than before decentralization.
Source: Governance and Decentralization Survey 2006. This survey covered 12,861 households in 111 *kabupaten* and 23 *kota*.

Fig. 1. Improved Perception (*Household Perception of Service Quality in Health, Education, Administration and Police*)

that had performed worst according to the GDS survey, only one third believed that services had deteriorated. Overall, satisfaction with services is over 50 percent — with the exception of the police, a centrally administered service, which receives a satisfaction rating of only 35 percent.

However, household perceptions as reflected in the survey results have some issues. In general, the perceptions of service quality seem out of line with results from more objective sources of information, including the Susenas (National Socio-Economic Survey) household surveys and sectoral data. In general, however, Indonesians seem to be rather positive in their perceptions of service delivery.

4. Achievement 3: Fiscal Consolidation Continues

One of the fears in the run-up to the 2001 decentralization was macroeconomic stability. The laws were passed when Indonesia was still in the midst of the Asian crisis, and fiscal consolidation was of paramount importance. However, while the principle of "finance follows function" was stated in the decentralization laws, in practice the new inter-governmental fiscal system was designed without much knowledge on the expenditure responsibilities of regional governments. Notably the 25 percent share of central revenues that was to be shared with the regions through the DAU was chosen rather arbitrarily. Nevertheless, the impact on the central government deficit remained limited and Indonesia has delivered consistently low budget deficits since 2001, resulting in one of the most rapid declines in public debt in any developing country: from 80 percent of GDP in 2000 to below 35 percent by end-2007. There are two reasons that aggregate fiscal deficits remained low. First, the central government was able to cut other spending, most notably the wasteful fuel subsidies that had taken up an increasing share of the budget since the onset of the crisis. Second, sub-national governments encountered unexpected difficulties spending their resources. Unlike many Latin American countries, most regions have been running substantial surpluses, not deficits.

5. Achievement 4: Development Spending Recovered

A further fear in the run-up to decentralization was that local governments would "waste" the money and not pay any attention to the need for development spending. This, combined with the need for fiscal consolidation at the central government level, could have led to a lower-than-desirable level of general government development spending.

In reality, consolidated development spending recovered after 2001, having reached a record low in 2000. At the regional level, the percentage increase from 2000 to 2001 was larger, reflecting the increased responsibilities, but this trend continued in the following years. More detailed data show that within development spending, education saw the largest increase, while transport (including roads) and health expenditures also increased.

6. Achievement 5: Sufficient Funding for Poor Regions

Indonesia has expressed its desire for a significant amount of fiscal equalization among the regions by transferring larger amounts to regions with higher needs. The Preamble to the Constitution speaks of

"Unity in Diversity", while the fiscal decentralization law specifies the broad objective of equalization among regions. Indonesia is one of the most diverse countries in the world and living standards range from developed country standards to entrenched poverty. Population density also varies greatly: Java is one of the most densely populated islands in the world, while Papua is one of the least densely populated. Poverty rates range from less than three percent in the cities of Denpasar (Bali) and Bekasi (West Java) to more than 50 percent in Manokwari (West Papua) and Pancak Jaya (Papua).

When Indonesia decentralized in 2001, the government allocated a large amount of resources to poorer regions in an effort to balance the country's disparities. Although inter-governmental fiscal transfers could be even more equalizing, the poorest and most remote parts of Indonesia have received very substantial transfers since 2001. Remote provinces with high levels of poverty, including Aceh, Papua and Maluku, were also the main beneficiaries of the second big bang in 2006. Due to Indonesia's disparities, the per-capita allocations of fiscal resources vary substantially — and they should. The districts in Papua and West Papua are each managing Rp 5 million (about US$600) per capita annually, more than 10 times the province of Banten in Java, with to only Rp 400,000 per capita (see Fig. 2). Some resource rich regions, particularly in East Kalimantan and Riau, are also benefiting from substantial oil and gas revenues, and are receiving substantially more revenues than their DAU allocation would predict.

Overall, Indonesia's fiscal disparities are much starker than in other decentralized countries, including the US, Germany and Brazil, but they are a reflection of Indonesia's disparities and its underlying diversity.

Despite these achievements, many challenges remain. The rest of this paper highlights some of the key ones. Notably, this paper does not discuss the intricate and central issue of the need for better clarification of functional responsibilities across levels of government. While central for decentralization, the complexity of the issue simply requires more space than available in this paper.

7. Challenge 1: Spending Resources Well

Since decentralization in 2001, regional governments have had difficulty spending their increasing resources. By the end of 2006, provincial and district reserves had increased to almost Rp 100 trillion

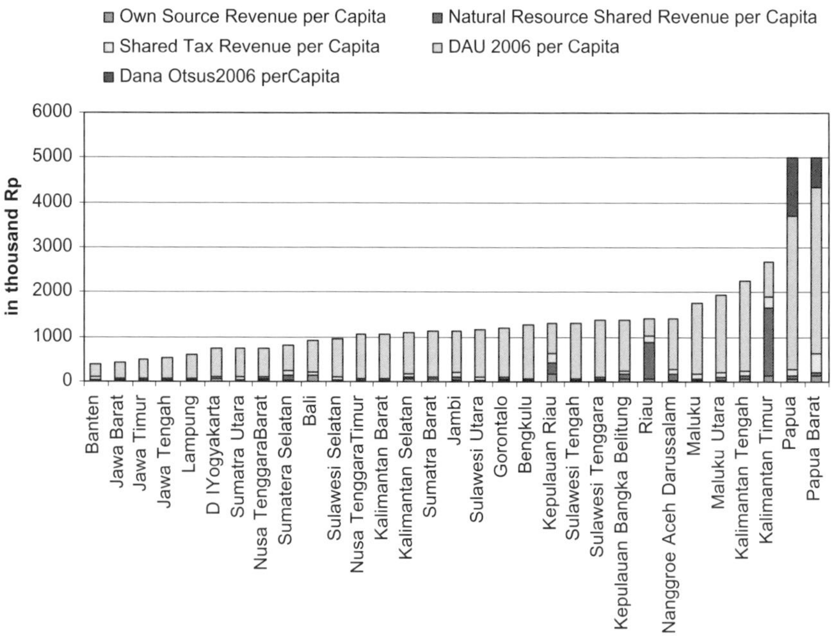

Note: The numbers for consolidated province are aggregates of the local level and the provincial level government within the same province.
Source: SIKD, authors' calculation.

Fig. 2. Poor Regions are Cashing in (*Per Capita Revenues*)

(US$12 billion), or three percent of GDP. Some districts and provinces are doing better than others but particularly the poor and remote districts in Aceh and eastern Indonesia have the largest amounts of money sitting in bank accounts. Even more problematic, the single largest spending item of sub-national governments is on "government apparatus", including buildings for government departments, which increased to 32 percent of regional spending in 2006. This may in part reflect the need of the many *new* district/provincial governments that have been created since decentralization,[8] but it is clearly out of line with international standards of 5–10 percent. By contrast, district spending on infrastructure has only been 15 percent.

[8] See World Bank 2007 and Hofman, Bert, and Kai Kaiser. *What explains the creation of new regions in Indonesia?* Mimeo, World Bank, 2003.

8. Challenge 2: Dependency on Transfers

Before the 2001 decentralization, most resources were transferred from central to regional governments through earmarked grants. The largest of these was the subsidy for autonomous regions grant (SDO, or Subsidi Daerah Otonom) program, which covered most of the civil service salaries and recurrent expenditures of the regions. In addition, Inpres (Instruksi Presiden) grants aimed to finance development spending in the regions. The Inpres grant started its life as a block grant for development spending in the 1980s, but gradually evolved into an array of specific grants for purposes ranging from re-greening to the construction of public markets.[9]

In Indonesia's new inter-governmental fiscal system, central-regional transfers remain the dominant means of financing. The bulk of regional government spending is financed by transfers from the center (see Table 3): over 90 percent of regional revenues comes from the Balancing Fund (Dana Perimbangan), which includes the DAU, shared taxes, natural resource revenue-sharing (SDA, or Sumber Daya Alam), and a special allocation grant channel (DAK, or Dana Alokasi Khusus). In addition, Aceh and Papua receive special autonomy transfers. Local governments have limited own-source revenues (PAD, or Pendapatan Asli Daerah), which comprised only 5.6% of regional revenues in 2004.[10]

High dependence on central grants does not bode well for the governance of that money: international evidence suggests that this high degree of dependence is inversely associated with governance outcomes.[11] Accountability of local governments over spending financed by transfers is not as high as over the same spending financed by taxes. In other words, it is easier to spend other people's money. In addition to this, a high dependency on transfers may cause the typical problem with a soft budget constraint: the regions can argue that the central government does not provide enough money for their tasks. While the center has granted the regions with the right to issue taxes, most of these are highly unproductive in terms of revenues. The cost of administering local taxes and charges consumes over 50 percent of receipts.

---

[9] See Silver, Christopher, Iwan J. Azis, and Larry Schroeder (2001).

[10] By contrast, provinces are financing their expenditures to 55 percent from own-source revenues. See World Bank 2007, Chapter 7.

[11] Refer to de Melo, Luiz and Matias Barenstrein (2001).

Table 3. DAU Dominates

	2001		2002		2003		2004		2005		2006*	
	Rp	%	Rp	%	Rp	%	Rp	%	Rp	%	Rp	%
Shared revenues	22.1	21	23.4	21	26.4	20	26.9	20	36.1	25	36.4	20
General Allocation Fund (DAU)	61.9	59	63.2	56	67.7	52	66.3	50	63.4	45	92.5	52
Special Allocation Fund (DAK)	1.0	1	0.8	1	3.2	2	2.9	2	2.9	2	7.3	4
Total Regional Transfers	**85.1**	**82**	**87.4**	**77**	**97.3**	**75**	**96.1**	**72**	**102.4**	**72**	**136.2**	**76**
Regional Own-Source Revenues	15.3	15	19.4	17	22.2	17	25.9	20	28.9	20	31.7	18
Others	3.9	4	6.1	5	10.4	8	10.7	8	10.8	8	10.6	6
Total Revenues	**104.2**	**100**	**112.9**	**100**	**129.9**	**100**	**132.7**	**100**	**142.1**	**100**	**178.5**	**100**

Consolidated Revenues (Province and *kabupaten/kota*) FY2001–2006, Rp trillion (real, 2001=100) and percent; data in real terms (2001 price = 100); * = planned budget.
Source: World Bank staff calculation based on SIKD MOF.

In addition, many of these local taxes damage the investment climate (World Bank 2007, Chapter 7).

9. Challenge 3: The Investment Climate

Business undoubtedly felt the pinch of decentralization. Although problems of security, political unrest and macro-economic instability probably dominated, the uncertainties created by decentralization certainly did not help to promote a good investment climate. For one thing, businesses had to face new arrangements for obtaining licenses (although investment approval remained central, as described above), which are now under the authority of the regions. A number of local governments even tried to improvise by issuing local licenses before the issuance of the ministerial decree.[12] Starting even before 2001, provinces were given the right to set regional minimum wages and they have shown themselves all too willing to give wage increases far exceeding market trends.[13] Business also became the principal target for the plethora of taxes, levies and fees that were issued by the regions under the new law on regional taxes and levies. In particular, mining suffered because of its large location-specific investment and the popular perception that mining rights had been obtained because of close connections with the previous regime.

The incomplete regulations at the onset of the big bang and the tug-of-war between the center and the regions on issues such as investment approval, land, mining licenses and the like affected the "bankability" of many investments. Inexperience in attracting business and lack of understanding of what it takes to create good business conditions did not help either. And finally, businesses had to face the corruption that flourishes in the regions as it does in the center.

Six years into decentralization, local governments continue to erect obstacles to improving the investment climate. Overall, the investment climate has been improving since 2003 across almost all categories but local corruption, regulations and licensing remain important bottlenecks and more so than at the central level (see Fig. 3).

---

[12] This is the opposite of the legal process. See World Bank, Government of the Netherlands, and LPEM FE-UI (2007). *Monitoring the Investment Climate in Indonesia: A Report from Mid-2006 Survey* for a more elaborate evaluation.

[13] See World Bank (2001b).

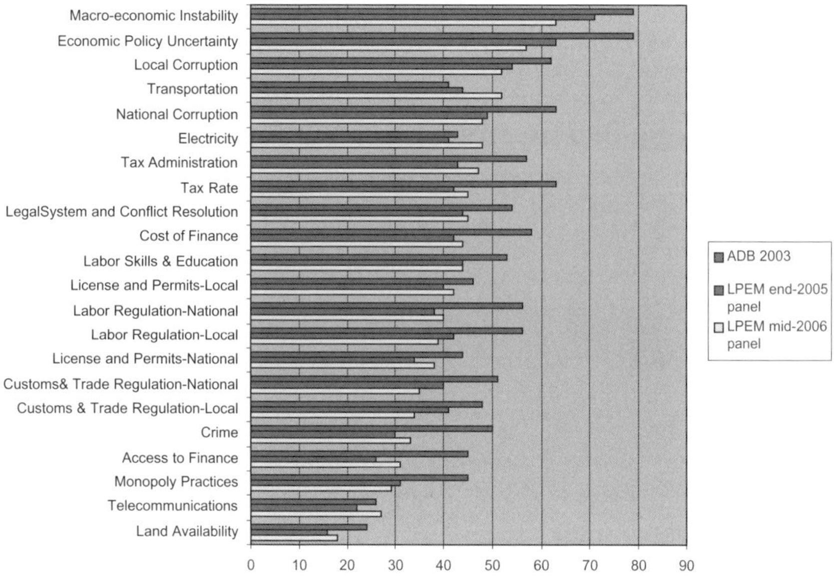

Source: World Bank, Government of Netherlands, and LPEM FE-UI (2007).

Fig. 3. Factors Affecting the Investment Climate

10. Challenge 4: The Center Holding On

The central government continues to spend significant amounts of resources on local government tasks and, in 2006, even at the highest levels since decentralization. For the initial post-decentralization years, continued spending by the center on local responsibilities appears justified, as it was decided that the center would finish already started development projects. However, since 2003, central spending on local functions has been even higher than in the immediate post-decentralization years. It is not just the sectoral departments that are holding on to the past; the national parliament is at fault as well. Notably in education, parliament has repeatedly upped the central allocation to this sector — now largely a local task. This spending is problematic not only from the point of view of the division of responsibility, but also from the perspective of accountability. Specifically, this money does not enter the local government budget — even though large parts are implemented by the local administration on behalf of central government.

If the government decides to devolve more resources to the regions, it has several means of doing so. Instead of increasing the 26 percent share of general revenues that the regions receive through the DAU, it could opt for establishing an additional special allocation grant (DAK) for purposes close to the center's heart but in sectors that the regions administer. In addition, it could give the regions more authority to levy taxes. The choice of instrument depends on the extent of control the government wants to retain. After the center's own decentralized spending, a special allocation grant gives most control and would allow financing of the central government's priorities at the local level. Increasing the revenue share for the DAU at this point in time would further increase the region's resources without much control by the center. With the DAU already making up much of local revenues, this seems less desirable. However, devolving more taxing power to the regions seems an attractive option to reduce the fiscal dependency observed.

11. Challenge 5: Local Governance

The accountability of local governments to their constituents is crucial for the success of regional autonomy but, by necessity, developing new

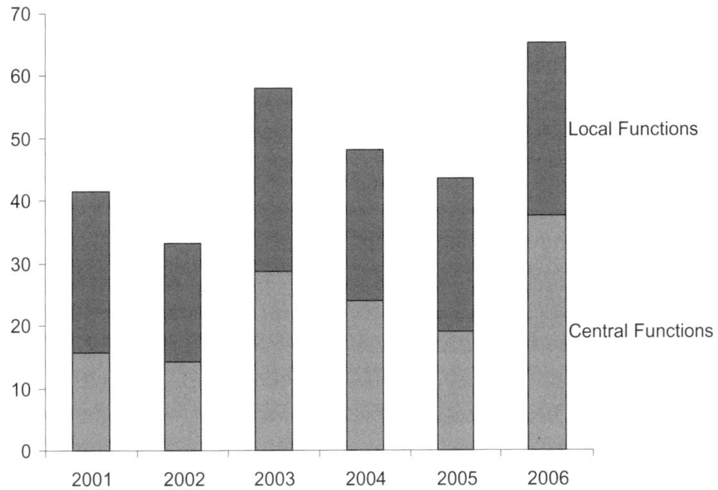

Note: In trillion rupiah, real terms (2001 price = 100).
Source: Central government budgets/WB staff estimates.

Fig. 4. Holding On (*Central Development Spending on Local Tasks*)

Table 4. BPK Audit Findings (Percentage deviations)

	2001 Semester II	2002 Semester I
Central	**13.6**	**16.1***
Routine	20.5	9.8
Development	6.4	15.6
Province	**3.7**	**27.9**
Routine	1.8	8.1
Development	5.1	30.7
District/Cities	**12.7**	**21.8**
Routine	13.8	21.6
Development	11.6	22.0

Source: Chairperson of the BPK welcome speech at the presentation of the audit results for Semester II of Fiscal Year 2002, Jakarta, February 2003.

* Total includes military, which is excluded from the sub-totals.

accountability relationships will take time. Surveys show that citizens believe there is a significant amount of corruption in their regional governments, but central functions such as the police and the courts are seen to be the most corrupt (see Fig. 4). Audits of central and local governments by the State Audit Agency (BPK) suggest that, by and large, abuse of government money is the same at the central and the local level (see Table 4). The level of "deviations" was somewhat higher at the center in 2001 and higher in the regions in 2002. "Deviation" can imply anything ranging from wrong procedures to outright theft. Worrisome is the increasing trend in local government irregularities: over the first semester of 2001, the BPK only found 7 percent of deviations at this level. In particular, the jump in irregularities at the provincial level is of concern. Of equal concern is the apparent lack of follow-up on the audit findings, even though the BPK submits its findings to the regional legislatures.

12. Conclusion

The achievements in Indonesia's decentralization are as real as the challenges going forward are daunting. But addressing these challenges will be no easy feat. The absence of an articulated decentralization *policy*, as contrasted to decentralization laws, is not helping, as the direction of change cannot be simply derived from such documents. Moreover, the political tide within the central government seems to be changing and decentralization is no longer a very popular policy. Finally, there is no obvious champion for the policy and a champion is needed to address the issues identified in this paper.

Part B

The Reform of Local Public Finance

Chapter XI

The Reform of Japanese Local Governments*

SHIN SAITO[†]

Graduate School of Economics, Osaka University

and

HIDEO YUNOUE

Osaka School of International Public Policy, Osaka University

1. Introduction

There are four major problems in Japanese public finance. First, both central and local governments must deal with what they perceive as the lack of tax revenue and with the consequences of how revenues are divided between the two levels. In 2003, the share of tax revenue in the total revenues was 51 percent for central government and 34.4% for local government. In 2005, because of economic recovery, the tax share of local governments increased slightly to 37.4%. Well over one-half of local government revenues are derived from central transfers and borrowing. Second, public borrowing has increased significantly in recent years. The share of borrowing in general revenues of the central government reached 38.5% in 2000 and 41.8% in 2005 (see Table 1). This share was less than 10 percent in 1990, the share of bond revenue have

* This paper was reported at Asian Development Conference on 10–11 November, 2003. We gratefully acknowledge Duvvuri Subbarao for his helpful comments.

† Corresponding author, e-mail:saito@econ.osaka-u.ac.jp

Table 1. Government Revenues (billion yen, %)

	2000 Amount	Share (%)	2005 Amount	Share (%)
Central Gov.	89,770	100.0	82,183	100.0
Taxes	49,895	55.6	44,007	53.5
Bond Revenues	34,598	38.5	34,390	41.8
Others	5,277	5.9	3,786	4.6
Local Gov.	100,275	100.0	92,936	100.0
Local Taxes	35,546	35.4	34,804	37.4
Transfer from Central Gov.	37,690	37.6	32,135	34.6
Bond Revenues	11,116	11.1	10,376	11.2
Others	15,923	15.9	15,621	16.8
Prefectures	52,804	100.0	48,695	100.0
Local Taxes	18,090	34.3	17,137	35.2
Transfer from Central Gov.	15,926	30.2	17,531	36.0
Bond Revenues	4,905	9.3	5,709	11.7
Others	13,883	26.3	8,317	17.1
Cities and Towns	54,415	100.0	50,479	100.0
Local Taxes	17,456	32.1	17,667	35.0
Transfer from Central Gov.	21,764	40.0	14,604	28.9
Bond Revenues	6,268	11.5	4,719	9.3
Others	8,926	16.4	13,489	26.7

Note: Settlement of account for the fiscal years.

rapidly increased in last decade. As the result, the stock of public bond reached about 758 trillion yen at the end of 2005, and this measure is about 151 percent of GDP. The stock of bond was 410 trillion yen (that is 83 percent of GDP) at the end of 1995, Japanese government incur the stock of bond whose amount reaches over a half of GDP in a recent decade. This amount of outstanding debt is the worst in OECD countries, the debt sustainability is suspected in Japan. Debt reduction is required.

The third point is the "incremental-ism" that seems to characterize public spending. As shown in Fig. 1, the expenditure share of the ministries has not changed for many years. The fourth problem is the move toward fiscal decentralization, but with an imperfect assignment of taxing powers.

In *Basic Policies for Economic and Fiscal Management and Structure Reform 2003*, the Japanese Council of Economic Advisers called for

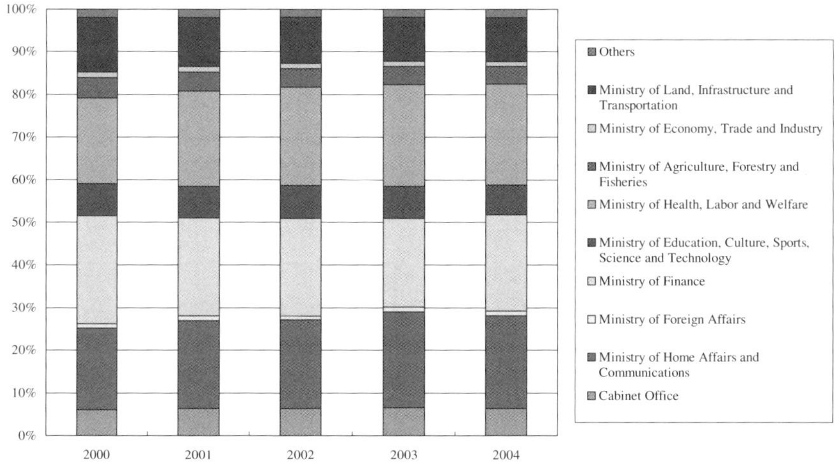

Fig. 1. Expenditure Share of Ministries

execution of a plan called "sanmi-ittai-no-kaikaku" (the trinity reform). These intent of these reforms is to replace specific and general purpose subsidies with local taxes. The goal in this paper is to estimate the possible effects of the Triple Reform of Fiscal Relationships. We mainly analyzing the effects of reforming subsidies and shifting tax revenues. Since, however, Local Allocation Tax grants system (general grants system in Japan) has extremely strong effects on fiscal adjustment; their effects are included into the analyses. We analyze the impacts under four different scenarios. We begin with an explanation of the Japanese Local Public Finance system, and then provide an overview of Triple Reform of Fiscal Relationships. In Section 3, we use a simulation model to estimate the effect of the reform on local government, and we conclude in a final section.

2. Background of Japanese Local Public Finance

2.1. *Fiscal Relationship Between Central and Local Government*

The "reversal pattern" of expenditure and tax revenue between central and local government is very important to understanding Japanese public finance. The reversal pattern was caused by the existence of transfers from central government to local government, which is composed

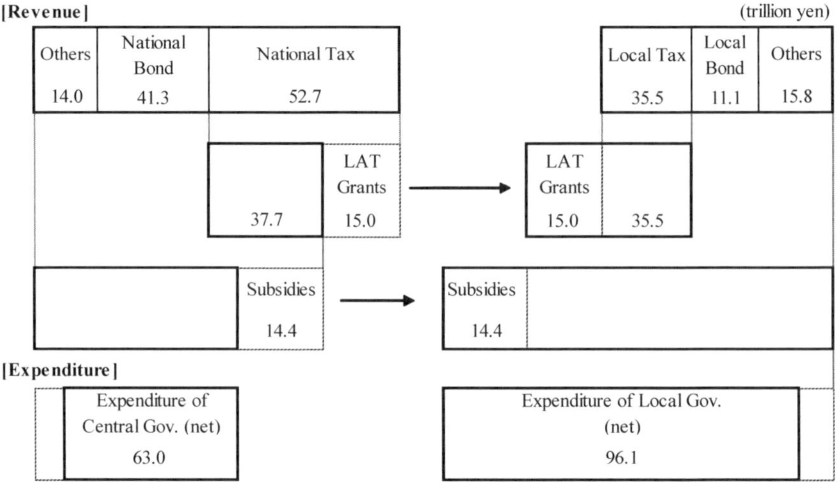

Note: Since the expenditures are net value, the sum of expenditures are not balanced the sum of revenues. This figure mainly represents the general account of governments. Both central and local governments have the special accounts, but these special accounts are omitted because of avoiding the confusion.

Fig. 2. Fiscal Relationships Between Central and Local Government in 2000

of local transfer taxes, subsidies and general grants (Local Allocation Tax Grants, abbreviated as LAT grants).

The fiscal relationship between central and local government is described in Fig. 2. Tax revenue was 88.2 trillion yen in 2000. About 60 percent supported the central government budget and 40 percent was allocated to the local government sector. A share of national government income taxes, corporate taxes, alcohol taxes, consumption taxes and cigarette taxes are the basis of the LAT grants. In addition, the central government distributes subsidies to local governments (about 14.4 trillion yen in 2000). These subsidies are used for education, specific projects, etc.

The data in Table 1 report the details of both central and local revenues. The share of tax revenues of local governments increased from 2000 to 2005 while that of the central government decreased. This is in part due to the effect of the Triple Reform of Fiscal Relationships.

There are two types of local governments in Japan, the prefectures and their component cities, towns and villages. Prefectures and cities depend on the transfers from their upper level governments for

Table 2. Government Expenditure (billion yen, %)

	Gross Amount	Net Amount	Share (%)	GDP Ratio (%)
Central Gov.				
2000	100,726	62,961	39.6	12.5
2001	93,908	57,407	37.4	11.6
2005	93,435	61,220	40.6	12.2
Local Gov.				
2000	97,616	96,070	60.4	19.1
2001	97,432	95,897	62.6	19.4
2005	90,697	89,424	59.4	17.8
Total				
2000		159,031	100.0	31.5
2001		153,304	100.0	31.1
2005		150,644	100.0	29.9

Note: Settlement of account for the fiscal years.

about 30 to 40 percent of their revenues, and on taxes for about 30 percent of their revenues.

After transfers, the net expenditure was about 60 percent by local governments and 40 percent by the central government in 2000.[1] This compares with a ratio of about 40 to 60 in taxes raised. This shows the reversal pattern that characterizes the Japanese inter-governmental fiscal system.

The allocation of LAT grants is formulated by the central government in the following way.[2] LAT grants are the difference between expenditure needs and "standard tax revenues" that are considered exogenous variables for the local authorities.

(Amount of LAT grants) = (standard fiscal needs) – (standard tax revenue)

The first item of the right-hand side represents the amount of standard expenditure. The "standard fiscal needs" is calculated as the product of

[1] See also Table 2. We find the similar results in 2001 and 2005.

[2] Nagamine (1995) and Shirai (2005) also provide the explanation of Japanese local finance systems. Okamoto (2002) provides the comprehensive explanation of the LAT grants system.

"unit cost," "measuring unit" and "correction coefficient."[3] For example, when we consider compulsory education, the wage of teachers is included the "unit cost" and the number of teachers of each local government is the "measuring unit." The "correction coefficient" is adjusted for the economy of scale. The *standard tax revenue* is defined as 75 percent of actual collections for prefectures, cities and towns. Thus the amount of LAT grants is determined by the difference of fiscal needs of the individual authority and the revenue of the authority. All else being the same, a local authority whose *standard fiscal needs* is high will receive more LAT grants. Another local government whose "standard tax revenue" is low will also receive more LAT grants.

LAT grants play a strong distribution role in local public finance in that they recognize high expenditure needs. But there is also a distortive effect on revenue mobilization. For example, consider the case of a local government raising 100 billion yen in additional tax revenue. The LAT grants system incorporates 75 billion yen of this increase into the *standard tax revenues*. Therefore, the additional increase in tax revenues by 100 billion yen causes a reduction of in LAT grants by 75 billion yen, leaving the local government with 25 billion yen because of fiscal adjustment effect of LAT system.[4] The following regression result is derived by cross-section data in 2001, showing the proportional relationship between standard tax revenues and actual tax revenue.

$$\textit{Standard tax revenue} = \underset{(220.28^{***})}{0.762}\ \textit{Tax revenue}, \quad R^2 = 0.9767$$

There is considerable variation in the fiscal condition of local governments in Japan. The Correlations between the gross regional product (GRP) and revenues from the three main sources for local government are

[3] The "standard fiscal needs" is basically calculated by the population and area of each local authority. Honma *et al.* (1986) and Nakai (1987) are earlier empirical works for standard fiscal needs. They found out that the "standard fiscal needs" had a quadric function of population.

[4] This example of revenue changes is formulated as follows:

$$\begin{aligned}
\text{d(Total Revenue)} &= \text{d(Tax Revenue)} + \text{d(LAT grants)}\\
&= \text{d(Tax Revenue)} + \{\text{d(standard fiscal needs)} - \text{d(standard tax revenue)}\}\\
&= \text{d(Tax Revenue)} + \{\text{d(standard fiscal needs)} - \text{d}(0.75 \times \text{(Tax Revenue)})\}\\
&= (+100) + (0 - 0.75 \times 100)\\
&= 100 - 75 = 25
\end{aligned}$$

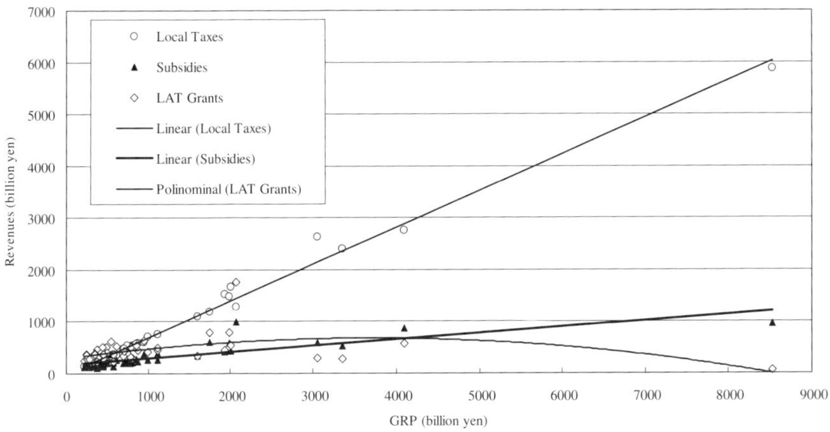

Fig. 3. Scatter Diagram: Sources of Revenues vs. GRP

reported in Fig. 3.[5] Local government tax revenue is almost proportional to GRP. Tokyo has the highest GRP, about 16 percent of the national total. It also raises about 16 percent of total local government taxes. Osaka has a national share of GRP of about 7.7%. Tottori (the lowest) has a share of only 0.44%. Both Osaka and Tottori raise local revenues about commensurate to their GRP shares. We also estimated the tax function by using cross-section data in 2001.[6] The results show the regression coefficient of GRP to be positive and highly significant. The tax revenue raised by local governments is determined by their level of income. On average, a 100 yen higher GRP is associated with a 0.07 higher level of tax revenue.

$$\underset{}{\textit{Tax Revenue}} = \underset{(-0.6436)}{-11797.096} + \underset{(67.96^{***})}{0.0708\,\textit{GRP}}, \quad R^2 = 0.9901.$$

Subsidies received are also positively correlated with GRP (see Fig. 3). The slope of the subsidies function is flatter than that of tax revenues but a strong positive correlation is observed. Hokkaido obtains the highest amount of subsidies. The second highest is Tokyo. The smallest are Kagawa and Tottori. Again we estimate the relationship between

[5] These revenues are summed up with the revenue of prefectures and that of cities, towns and villages. We call this sum of revenues "aggregated local authority" in this paper.

[6] t-values are in the parentheses. ***represents significant at 1 percent, **represents significant at 5 percent and *represents significant at 10 percent.

subsidies received and GRP. The coefficient of GRP is positive and significant at 1 percent level. The dummy variables for Tokyo and Hokkaido are significant and have the expected signs.

$$
\begin{aligned}
\textit{Subsidies} &= \underset{(8.63^{***})}{131{,}783} + \underset{(13.14^{***})}{0.0163}\ \textit{GRP} - \underset{(-4.75^{***})}{561{,}476}\ \textit{Dummy for Tokyo} \\
&\quad + \underset{(7.22^{***})}{523{,}556}\ \textit{Dummy for Hokkaido}, \quad R^2 = 0.8861.
\end{aligned}
$$

By contrast with the tax revenue and the subsidies curves, the shape of LAT grants shown in Fig. 3 is an inverted U-curve with GRP. The approximate curve is derived from a quadric function. This pattern results because Tokyo, which has the highest amount of GRP, receives nearly zero amounts of LAT grants. Hokkaido which has the eighth largest GRP obtains the highest share of LAT grants.

The sum of these three revenue sources makes up the bulk of local government revenue. Tokyo's share is greatest at 9.8%, but this is compared to its GRP share of 16 percent. Tottori's overall revenue share (0.72%) is the lowest among the local governments but its GRP share is only 0.44%. This suggests a significant degree of equalization in the LAT grants. Further evidence is that the coefficient of variation of local taxes is 0.028 and that of subsidies and LAT grants are 0.014 and 0.012, respectively. The coefficient of variation of these three revenues combined is 0.017. This shows that transfers from the central government, not only LAT grants but also subsidies, play a significant role in fiscal adjustment.

2.2. *The Triple Reform*

The *Basic Policies for Economic and Fiscal Management and Structural Reform 2003* was approved by Cabinet and made three points. The first is the promotion of fiscal efficiency. The second is the need for progress with decentralization. These two are closely related because the matching the preferences of citizens with actual expenditure patterns is necessary to achieve fiscal efficiency. The third point is the Triple Reform of Fiscal Relationships.[7]

[7] The report states the phrase "Plan on the Reform of the Three Major Policies" instead of "Triple Reform of Fiscal Relationships" in the English edition.

The goal of The Triple Reform of Fiscal Relationships is to modify the gap of revenues and expenditures between central and local government. To achieve this purpose, the Triple Reform contains three policies. First, the reform intends to reduce specific subsidies by about 4 trillion yen. The second policy is to shift tax sources from central government to local government. The proposed amount of the shift would increase local government revenues by about 3.2 trillion yen, i.e., about 80 percent of the amount of reduction in subsidies.[8] The third policy directive is to review the LAT grants.[9] Note that the first two reforms identify an amount, but the latter remains open.

The subsidy reduction of 4 trillion yen will be phased in gradually over a three year period. In 2004, the first year of reform, the subsidies, mainly for mandatory education, were reduced by about one trillion yen.[10] The corresponding revenue increase from the shift to local taxes was about 0.6 trillion yen in 2004. In 2005, subsidies were reduced by an additional 1.8 trillion yen, and tax revenues increased by an additional 1.1 trillion yen. The LAT grants declined during 2005, so the revenue shortfall became very serious. In 2006, the last year of the reform, the further reduction of subsidies was about 1.8 trillion yen, raising the total amount to 4.6 trillion yen. On the other hand, the total revenue increase from the tax shift raised only 3 trillion yen. By 2006, the local government budgetary position had been weakened by the Triple Reform program.

3. Results of Simulation

In this section we use a simulation model to assess the Trinity Reform. In particular, we attempt to estimate the revenue impacts in each region. The data in most recent years are influenced by the reform, which is still ongoing, hence they are inappropriate to use our simulation. Thus we use cross sectional data from 2001.

---

[8] This ratio, 80 percent, was mentioned in the "Basic Policies for Economic and Fiscal Management and Structural Reform 2003." Note that this is a rough standard or target of the reform. In the "Basic Policy," a conditional statement; "after promoting the efficiency," was appended.

[9] Recently, Ihori *et al.* (2006a, 2006b) evaluate the system of LAT grants and suggest new formulation of standard fiscal needs.

[10] Yuasa and Saito (2004) investigate the welfare changes in the subsidy reform. They focused on the difference between the encouragement subsidy and mandatory subsidy. They concluded that the reform of the encouragement subsidy is desirable.

The values used in the simulation were taken from the *Basic Policies for Economic and Fiscal Management and Structure Reform 2003*. First we assume a 4 trillion yen cut in subsidies. The second assumption is that 80 percent of the cut amount will be re-allocated to "aggregated local authority" which is the combination of prefectures and their component municipals. The third assumption is that the amount to be allocated to each "aggregated local authority" will be proportional to the current tax revenue.[11]

The more difficult problem to deal with is how to estimate the LAT grants. According to the re-allocation formula of tax transfers from the national to local governments, an increase of local taxes by 3.2 trillion yen gives the local government its 75 percent as the corresponding increase of the standard tax revenue. Then, the central government reduces its LAT grants about 2.4 trillion yen. On the other hand, a 4 trillion yen cut of subsidies will result in an increase in standard fiscal needs.[12]

First, we set up CASE-1. We consider the four trillion yen cut of subsidies and the 3.2 trillion yen re-allocation of local taxes. The total amount of the current subsidies is 14.4 trillion yen, and a four trillion yen cut averages about a 28 percent cut[13] for every "aggregated local authority." Also, a 3.2 trillion yen increase in revenue is on average approximately a 9 percent increase. In this case, we assume no change of the LAT grants. This leads to an estimated 2.4 trillion yen increase in standard fiscal needs, instead of the 4 trillion yen. The total amount of revenue changes is reported in Table 3. In the CASE-1 the total revenue decline is about 0.8 trillion yen.

Second, in CASE-2, we assume a 4 trillion yen increase in the standard fiscal needs instead of a 2.4 trillion yen increase in CASE-1. If an increment of the standard fiscal needs is proportional to the existing standard fiscal needs, then the receipt of the LAT grants to almost all "aggregated local authorities" will increase by the same rate,[14] that is,

---

[11] This assumption may not be exactly correct. It is said that the re-allocation of taxes should be the main local tax, which means the local inhabitant tax or the local consumption tax.

[12] As we mentioned above, the standard fiscal needs is defined as the products of the unit-cost, the measuring unit and the correction coefficient. In the case of subsidies reform, the unit-cost will increase proportional to the cut amount of subsidies, if the total constraint of the LAT grants is unbounded.

[13] A major policy question is whether all subsidies will be cut at the same rate.

[14] The "aggregated local authority" of a non-consignation is invariant.

Table 3. Changes of the Revenues in Each Case (trillion yen)

	Cutting Subsidies (A)	Shifting Tax Sources (B)	Standard Fiscal Needs (C)	Standard Fiscal Revenues (D) = (B) × 0.75	LAT Grants (E) = (C) – (D)	Improve the Efficiency (F) = (A) × 0.2	Changes in Total Revenue (G) = (A) + (B) + (E) + (F)
CASE-1	–4.0	+3.2	+2.4	+2.4	0	0	–0.8
CASE-2	–4.0	+3.2	+4.0	+2.4	+1.6	0	+0.8
CASE-3	–4.0	+3.2	+4.0	+2.4	+1.6	+0.8	+1.6
CASE-4	–4.0	+3.2	+2.4	+2.4	0	+0.8	0

by about 1.667 (= 4/2.4) times of the value in CASE-1. When the reform is simulated in CASE-2, the net revenue increase is about 0.8 trillion yen. By comparison with CASE-1, there is an incremental revenue gain of 1.6 trillion yen.

Third, depending on the subsidy-cut, in CASE-3, the "aggregated local authority" is assumed to promote the efficiency of the expenditure proportional to the subsidy-cut. We assume that the efficiency of the expenditure can be made to compensate for about 20 percent of the subsidy-cut. Thus the fiscal surplus could be about 0.8 trillion yen. The increment value in this case is about 1.6 trillion yen.

Finally, we also investigate the effect of LAT grants, we remove the increment value of LAT grants in CASE-4 from CASE-3. In this case, the increment value becomes zero because the amount of subsidy-cut and the amount of efficiency effect are balanced. Thus the net effect of subsidy-cut and shifting tax shows up in this case. In other words, we can see the balancing effect of a 3.2 trillion yen subsidy-cut (4 trillion yen subsidy-cut and 0.8 trillion yen improving the efficiency) and a 3.2 trillion yen shift of tax revenues.

The simulation results for individual local authorities (see Figs. 4 and 5), show the gap in local tax revenues to be widening. The data in

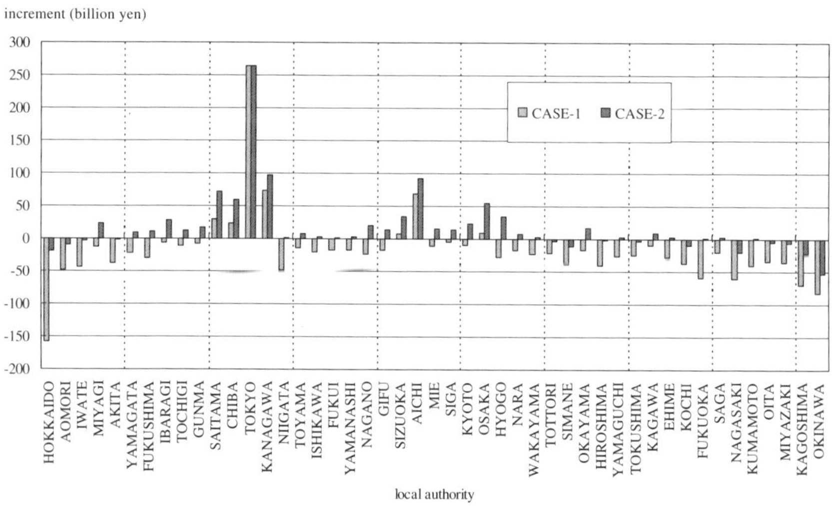

Fig. 4. Simulation Result in CASE 1 and CASE 2:
Amount of Increment (Level)

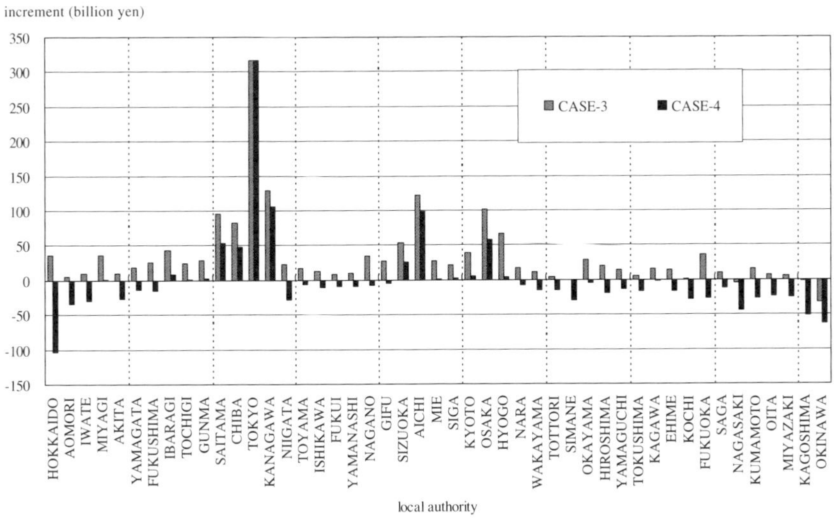

Fig. 5. Simulation Result in CASE 3 and CASE 4: Amount of Increment (Level)

Fig. 4 report the amount of increment in CASE-1 and CASE-2, and Fig. 5 represents the results in CASE-3 and CASE-4. In CASE-1, we have a clear result, for local tax revenue is approximately proportional to the strength of the economy in each area. Local authorities in Tokyo will gain more than any other authorities (Tokyo Problem of revenue concentration). Tokyo will receive over 250 billion yen which is three times higher than the second highest region, Kanagawa. On the other hand, there are the regions whose revenues are decreased. Hokkaido, which receives the highest subsidies, loses revenues in most regions. The amount of loss in Hokkaido is twice as much as Okinawa, the second largest losing region.

In CASE-2, the increment value rises in all regions except Tokyo. This is because Tokyo receives almost zero amounts of LAT grants. Because of the strong fiscal adjustment effect of LAT grants, the reduction in Hokkaido become smaller than CASE-1.

The effect of improving fiscal efficiency is reported in Fig. 5. In the CASE-3, the total amount of increment value is about 1.44 trillion yen. Tokyo still achieves the highest value and almost every region obtains positive income in this case. Only a few local authorities, including Okinawa, face a decrease in revenues in CASE-3.

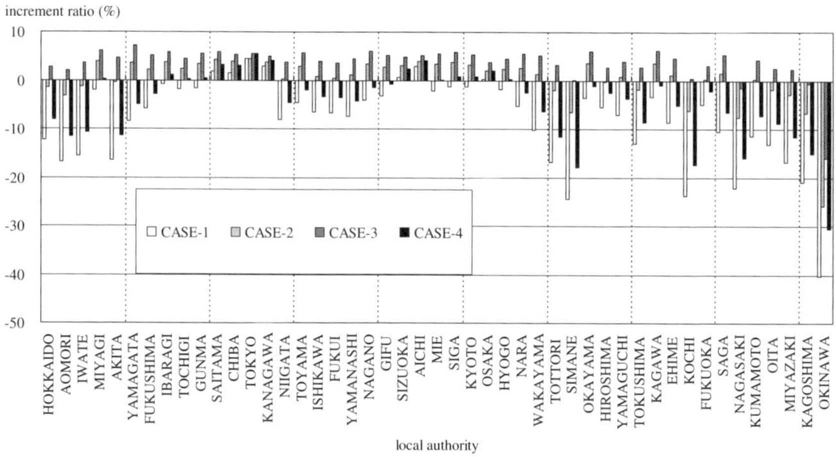

Fig. 6. Increment Ratio to Local Tax Revenue in Each Case

In order to determine the effect of improving fiscal efficiency, we need to remove the LAT grants effect. The result of this simulation is reported as CASE-4 in Fig. 5. The value of Tokyo does not change because it receives nearly zero amounts of LAT grants. Kanagawa and Aichi receive small LAT grants and see only a small change between CASE-3 and CASE-4. Although the total amount of revenues is unchanged, the majority of regions experience a reduction of revenues in CASE-4.

These simulations predict a tighter fiscal constraint in some local authorities. The increment and decrement ratio in each region is reported in Fig. 6. The increment ratio is defined as the quotient of the amount of increment value and relevant tax revenue. Local governments have the possibility of a worsening fiscal position because the decrease in subsidies could exceed the amount of increase from the reallocation of the taxes. This could lead to a widening gap in local government tax revenues that could affect many local authorities other than Tokyo.

4. Conclusion

In this paper, we estimate the effect of the Triple Reform of Fiscal Relationships. This reform covers subsidy reductions, the shifting of tax revenues from national to local government and a review of the impact of the LAT grants system. In this paper, the focus is on the effects of subsidy reductions and tax-shifting on the local governments.

First, the amount of national tax revenue decreases. This result is very clear, because about 3.2 trillion yen is moved from the central tax revenue to local tax revenues. This movement is one small step for Japanese governments, but one great step for decentralization in Japan. Secondly, the tax revenues are unevenly distributed among the local authorities. A few areas, especially Tokyo, could receive significant additional tax revenues. Thirdly, some local authorities will face a more serious fiscal problem than before. Even when we take account the fiscal adjustment effect of LAT grants, our results show that some regions like Okinawa receive less tax revenues than they did before the reform.

Following these simulation results, the reform of local administrative structure is required. Many local authorities may confront the reduction of revenues. On another front, they will get more tax revenue than before. From economic theory, we can show the effect of the change in fiscal resources, decreasing specific grants and increasing tax revenues, on the assumption of freely exercising choice.

Remaining problems are the existing regulations by the central government, and the failure of public management in local authorities. Although the local authorities receive enough tax revenue, some kinds of regulations have possibilities to keep the action of authorities almost same as before, for example the actual number of teachers or police officers in local authority is nearly the same as that of central government decree. The financial matters are discussed on the Triple Reform of Fiscal Relationships. The administrative power of local government is a future issue.

References

Ihori, T, Y Iwamoto, Y Kawanishi, T Doi and K Yamamoto (2006a). Empirical Analysis on the recent trends of standard fiscal needs — Toward the Reform of Local Allocation Tax System, *Keio Economic Society Discussion Paper Series*, No. 06–1 (in Japanese).

Ihori, T, Y Iwamoto, Y Kawanishi, T Doi and K Yamamoto (2006b). "Empirical Analysis on Mandatory Expense in the standard fiscal needs," *Keio Economic Society Discussion Paper Series*, No. 06–4 (in Japanese).

Kaizuka, K, H Masaaki, K Takabayashi, J Nagamine and K Fukuma (1986). The role of LAT grants and its evaluation, part I. *Financial Review*, 2, pp. 6–27 (in Japanese).

Nagamine, J (1995). Japanese local finance and the "Institutionalized" flypaper effect, *Public Finance*, 50(3), pp. 420–441.

Nakai, H (1987). *Numerical analysis of contemporary fiscal burden*. Yuhikaku, Tokyo (in Japanese).

Okamoto, M (2002). *Discussion on Local Public Finance Reform: Future of Local Allocation Tax*. Gyosei, Tokyo (in Japanese).

Shirai, S (2004). Growing problems in the local public finance system of Japan. *Social Science Japan Journal*, 8(2), pp. 213–238.

Yuasa, K and S Saito (2004). Economic Evaluation on *Triple Reform of Fiscal Relationships*, Reported in the 12th Conference of Japanese Institute for Local Finance (in Japanese).

Chapter XII

Local Public Finance in Taiwan: Reform and Trend

CHU-WEI TSENG

National Cheng Chi University

and

HSIEN-FENG LEE

National Taiwan University

1. Introduction

This article assesses the allocation of local government revenues and expenditures, and inter-governmental grants in Taiwan. According to the Law for Allocating Government Revenues and Expenditures, tax revenues are composed of two categories, i.e. national taxes, and metropolitan, county (or city) and village taxes. National taxes accounts for the lion's share of total tax revenues, which was about 80.6% of total tax revenues in 2001. Local governments have met with serious financial shortage. After the revision of the Law for Allocating Government Revenues and Expenditures in January 1999, the autonomous revenue ratio of the local governments, which is the ratio of non-granted revenues to total expenditures in average, increased from 55.73% in 1999 to 64.31% in 2000. However, most of the local governments have depended heavily on inter-governmental grants for a long time. Financial resources of the local governments are composed of the distribution of Centrally-Allotted tax revenues, general grants, project-based grants, and several taxes etc. Local governments do not have strong tax-collecting powers.

In August 2002 the Distribution Guidelines for Centrally-Allotted Tax Revenues was revised, with the objective of reducing deficits of local governments. Furthermore, both the General Rules of Local Tax Law and the Charges and Fees Law went into effect in December 2002, authorizing municipal and county (or city) governments to impose surtaxes on existing national taxes excluding customs duties, commodity tax, and value-added tax. However, the power of taxation of local governments is still restricted. Moreover, the Distribution Guidelines for Centrally-Allotted Tax Revenues could be revised to improve the vertical and horizontal equity in the fiscal decentralization in Taiwan. In addition, the fiscal efforts to increase the revenues of local governments should be encouraged and enhanced in the same time.[1]

In Taiwan the inter-governmental structure is more similar to that in unitary states such as Britain, France and Japan than to that in federal states. There are four levels of governments in Taiwan, the central unit, metropolitan districts, county or city, urban township, county city or village. There are two metropolitan districts, and 23 counties or cities. The central government accounts for more than one half of government revenues. Since the public administration reform of 1999 there are only two categories of taxes: national taxes and local taxes. Local governments depend heavily on grants from the center to finance their expenditure budgets. In 1998, the average ratio of non-grant revenue sources to expenditures of 21 counties and cities was only about 40 percent. In 15 counties, the ratio was less than 50 percent, and in 4 of them was less than 20 percent. Since fiscal capacity is distributed so unevenly, there exists significant competition for intergovernmental transfers among local governments. The distribution of transfers is stipulated in the Law.

Tax revenues have changed in an unstable way since 1990 in Taiwan. The national tax burden ratio, i.e. the ratio of tax revenues to the GDP, shows a decreasing tendency since 1990. In 2005 it was only 13.7%. The overall tax burden still remains relatively low among the nations of the world. The ratio of the governmental expenditures to GDP has been more than that of tax revenues to GDP. Tax revenues can finance only about 60 percent of government expenditures with a chronic fiscal deficit.

The data in Table 2 show an international comparison of the structure of central and local government taxation in 2004. In Taiwan, the central government claimed 48.2% of income, profit and capital gains

---

[1] The authors thank kind comments from Professor Motohiro Sato.

Table 1. Fiscal Indicators in Taiwan (unit: %)

Year	Tax/GDP	Tax/Gov't Net Expenditure	Expenditure/ GDP	Change Rate of Tax	Change Rate of Nominal GDP	Economic Growth Rate
1990	20.1	77.2	27.67	25.1	10.8	5.39
1991	17.4	63.4	29.58	–4.6	10.2	7.55
1992	18.5	62.0	28.83	19.7	12.4	7.49
1993	18.1	59.5	28.25	8.0	10.7	7.01
1994	17.7	61.7	27.57	7.8	10.3	7.11
1995	17.7	64.5	27.27	9.3	9.0	6.42
1996	15.8	65.0	26.53	–2.8	9.1	6.10
1997	15.4	67.7	25.98	6.1	8.9	6.68
1998	15.6	70.1	26.11	9.9	8.7	4.57
1999	14.3	66.1	26.02	–3.0	5.6	5.42
2000	12.9	61.4	24.34	–1.7	57.5	5.86
2001	12.8	55.4	25.00	–1.7	–33.9	–2.18
2002	11.9	55.5	24.23	–2.6	4.4	3.54
2003	11.9	55.3	22.40	2.2	2.2	3.50
2004	12.5	60.4	23.00	10.7	5.2	6.15
2005	13.7	66.3	19.71	13.0	3.2	4.16
2006	13.5	N.A.	N.A.	2.1	3.8	4.89

Source: *Statistical Yearbook of Public Finance*, Ministry of Finance, Taipei.
Note: N.A.: No data.

Table 2. International Comparison of Structure of Central and Local Governments by Taxation, 2004 (unit: %)

	Central Government						Local Government (State and City)					
	Income, Profit, Capital Gains	Social Security	Pay-roll Tax	Property Tax	Commodity, Service Tax	Others	Income, Profit, Capital Gains	Social Security	Pay-roll Tax	Property Tax	Commodity, Service Tax	Others
Germany	41.4	—	—	—	58.6	—	48.3	—	—	5.4	46.3	—
USA	90.1	—	—	2.4	7.5	—	39.4	—	—	2.8	57.8	—
France	33.4	6.2	—	4.5	53.7	2.2	—	—	4.4	51.6	10.5	33.5
Italy	52.9	—	—	7.0	39.5	0.6	7.7	—	—	21.7	26.0	44.6
Japan	55.2	—	—	5.4	37.1	2.3	45.3	—	—	32.4	21.3	1.0
S. Korea	41.3	—	—	4.0	52.9	1.8	13.7	—	1.5	56.4	25.7	2.7
UK	48.7	—	—	9.6	40.1	1.6	—	—	—	99.7	—	0.3
Taiwan	48.2	—	—	2.1	46.4	3.3	—	—	—	90.7	9.3	—

Source: OECD, Revenues Statistics 2005, Paris. Taiwan: Ministry of Finance, Taipei.

tax, 2.1% of property tax, and 46.4% of commodity tax, while local governments took 90.7% of property tax, and 9.3% of commodity tax. The case of Taiwan was more or less similar to those of France, Italy, South Korea, and UK.

In the next section, Taiwan's fiscal revenues and expenditures are described. Then, we review the status of fiscal equalization, the local reallocation tax and other allocation systems. Non-tax fiscal sources of local governments also are described. Finally, we suggest possibilities for improving the local public finances.

2. Fiscal Revenues and Expenditures

The data in Tables 2 to 7 show the net revenues, net expenditures and expenditure structure of all levels of governments in Taiwan from 1980 to 2005, together with international comparisons. From 1993 to 2005 all levels of governments have been in a deficit position, except in FY 1998 and 1999. In 2001 the fiscal deficit was 142.5 billion NT Dollars, and it increased to 246.5 NT Dollars in 2005. Since 1998, the

Table 3. A Contribution of Tax Revenues to Sub-sectors of General Government (2004) (unit: % of total tax revenue)

	Central Government	State Government	Local Government	Social Security Funds
Austria	54.5	8.6	9.4	27.5
Canada	44.9	37.9	8.6	8.6
Germany	30.2	21.7	7.4	40.7
USA	38.5	20.6	14.7	26.3
Finland	54.5	—	20.8	24.7
France	42.4	—	11.1	46.5
Italy	53.1	—	16.6	30.3
Japan	36.7	—	25.6	37.7
S. Korea	61.4	—	17.8	20.7
Netherlands	59.2	—	4.0	36.9
New Zealand	94.5	—	5.5	—
UK	76.5	—	4.8	18.8
Taiwan (2006)	79.7	—	16.3	—

Source: OECD, Revenues Statistics, 2005, Paris; Taiwan, Ministry of Finance, Taipei.

Table 4. Net Revenues of All Levels of Government by Sources in Taiwan (unit: NT$ billion, %)

Fiscal Year	Total (NT$ Billion, %)	Tax Revenue %	Monopoly Revenue %	Surplus of Public Business, utilities %	Fee, Fine %	Public Property %	Others %
1980	340.3 (100)	69.6	7.1	9.7	4.6	4.3	4.7
1985	546.3 (100)	65.1	7.7	14.2	5.1	2.5	5.5
1990	1,097.5 (100)	72.8	4.8	11.1	3.4	3.9	4.0
1995	1,910.0 (100)	75.1	3.9	9.1	5.6	3.3	3.0
2000*	3,140.9 (100)	66.5	2.8	16.5	6.2	4.7	3.3
2001	2,271.2 (100)	63.3	3.0	18.3	6.3	5.7	3.4
2005	2,115.2 (100)	72.4	—	13.3	6.3	5.3	2.8

* In FY2000 the data included one and one half years. 1US$ = 33.988 NT$ on October 29, 2003.

Source: *Taiwan Statistics Data Book 2007*, CEPD, Taipei.

Note: Fiscal year: from July 1 until June 30 next year before 2000, then from January 1 to December 31 after 2000. Debt repayments are excluded.

Table 5. Net Expenditures of All Levels of Government by Use in Taiwan (unit: NT$ billion, %)

Fiscal Year	Total (NT$ Billion, %)	General Administration %	Defense %	Education Science, Culture %	Economic Development %	Social Security %	Obligations %	Others %
1980	340.3	9.4	30.3	15.5	32.0	11.2	0.5	1.0
1985	546.3	11.3	24.8	20.4	25.3	16.2	1.1	0.9
1990	1,097.5	11.5	19.2	20.7	27.5	18.6	1.5	1.0
1995	1,910.0	11.6	14.1	18.7	22.9	21.7	10.2	0.6
2000*	3,140.9	14.9	11.4	20.9	15.1	28.7	8.6	0.4
2001	2,271.2	14.5	10.9	18.9	17.6	30.0	7.6	0.6
2005	2,309.5	14.9	10.8	20.4	20.2	27.4	5.7	0.7

* In FY2000 the data included one and one half years. 1US$ = 33.988NT$ on October 29, 2003.

Source: *Taiwan Statistics Data Book 2007*, CEPD, Taipei.

Note: Fiscal year: from July 1 until June 30 next year before 2000, then from January 1 to December 31 after 2000. Debt repayments are excluded.

Table 6. Expenditures Structure of Governments (unit: NT$ billion, %)

Fiscal Year	Total Amount (NT$ Billion, %)	Central Gov't %	Province, Metropolitan %	County, City %	Villages %
1981	433.2 (100)	55.1	28.3	13.2	3.4
1991	1,275.6 (100)	53.3	28.4	13.3	5.1
1996	1,843.8 (100)	50.6	33.3	15.2	4.0
1999	2,050.0 (100)	57.0	24.8	14.4	3.8
2001	2,271.3 (100)	65.2	10.4	19.0	5.4

Source: Ministry of Finance, Taipei.
Note: Since FY2000 the level of province government was abolished.

budget deficit in Taiwan has been driven by external events: the Asian financial crisis, the cost of earthquake reconstruction, and the world recession.

Fiscal revenues from surpluses of public enterprises and public utilities are shown in Table 4. Due to the increasing erosion of the tax base and the economic slump, total governmental revenues from taxes and monopolies, and surpluses from public enterprises and public utilities have fallen remarkably in recent years. Taxes remain the major source of governmental revenue. (see also Table 4)

According to the Law Governing the Allocation of Government Revenues and Expenditures (LGAGRE), taxes are categorized as (1) national taxes, and (2) metropolitan, county and city taxes etc. National taxes are allocated to the central government. While metropolitan taxes, county and city taxes are allocated to the local governments (special metropolitan districts, counties or cities). The data in Table 6 show the tax shares in Taiwan since January 1999. In addition to independent tax revenues, each of the various levels of governments share some common tax sources, either through grants or shared taxes.

There are 16 statutory tax items in Taiwan. Taxes are categorized as (1) national taxes, and (2) metropolitan, county and city taxes etc. National taxes consist of individual income tax and profit-seeking enterprise income tax, estate and gift tax, customs duties, business tax, commodity tax, tobacco and alcohol tax, securities transactions tax, future transactions tax, and mine concession tax. Following the LGAGRE 10 percent of total revenue from income tax and 40 percent

Table 7. Total Tax Revenue in Taiwan (Unit: NT$ billion, ratio (%))

	1997		1998		1999		2000		2005	
Item	Amount	%	Amount	%	Amount	%	Amount	%	Amount	%
Total revenues	13,672.5	100	1,372.6	100	1,330.0	100	1,354.4	100	1,600.8	100
Taxes	1,309.6	95.8	1,314.0	95.7	1,279.0	96.2	1,296.2	95.7	1,556.6	95.4
Custom duties	111.5	8.2	109.6	8.0	100.8	7.6	105.5	7.8	79.5	7.4
Income tax	371.5	27.2	412.6	30.1	428.7	32.2	449.8	33.2	646.2	38.0
Profit-seeking enterprise income tax	151.7	11.1	193.3	14.1	188.1	14.1	213.2	15.7	311.8	18.6
Personal income tax	219.7	16.1	219.3	16.0	240.5	18.1	236.5	17.5	334.3	19.5
Commodity tax	149.7	10.9	147.1	10.8	147.1	11.1	148.7	11.0	159.2	10.6
Business tax	234.6	17.2	249.8	18.2	237.6	17.9	212.2	15.7	236.9	16.2
Land value tax	45.8	3.4	46.6	3.4	46.2	3.5	53.4	3.9	54.6	4.0
Land value increment tax	141.7	10.4	114.5	8.3	88.0	6.6	79.5	5.9	76.5	3.4
Others	255.0	18.7	233.0	17.0	230.3	17.3	246.8	18.2	347.2	20.9
Monopoly reven.	57.6	4.2	58.6	4.3	50.9	3.8	58.1	4.3	—	—

Source: Ministry of Finance, Taipei.

of business tax revenue (after subtracting the prize money awarded to invoice lottery winners) is allocated to the special district and county. In the case of the estate and gift tax, 50 percent of the total revenue collected by a metropolitan collects will be retained by that districts. In the case of countries/cities, 80 percent of estate and gift duty is retained.

Metropolitan, county and administratively equivalent city taxes consist of land taxes (land value tax, agricultural land tax and land value increment tax), house tax, vehicle license tax, deed tax, stamp tax, and amusement tax. Land value increment tax will be 20 percent of its total revenue allocated by the central government among all counties. However, the total revenues of these local taxes still go to metropolitan government. Since January 2002 tobacco and alcohol taxes have been levied separately and categorized as a national tax. 18 percent of the total revenue from tobacco and alcohol taxes is allocated to the special districts and counties in Taiwan Province based on population, and 2 percent is distributed to two small island counties.

Because social situations have changed, and as the LGAGRE has been revised in the last two decades, the distribution of tax revenues among all levels of government has changed. The central government continues to control the majority of fiscal resources. In the fiscal year 1992, the central government held 53.1%, provincial and metropolitan governments 21.1% and county and city governments 25.8%.

3. Fiscal Equalization and Local Reallocation Tax

Until the beginning of the 1990s local governments were more or less subordinate to the central government in Taiwan. Since then, local autonomy has been stressed as a goal of government policy, and the function of local assemblies has been enhanced. The public administration system also has moved toward local decentralization. Because the central government often delegates public service delivery to non-government organizations (NGO) and local governments the size of local government will be larger than that shown in official statistics.

Local governments have varying capacities to finance their responsibilities. Due to regional disparities in tax revenues, a fiscal equalization program is necessary to provide local services in poor regions. In Taiwan there are three means of fiscal equalization. The first is the Centrally-Allotted Tax Revenues. It is similar to the Local Allocation Tax (tax-sharing grants) and Local Transfer Tax in Japan. The second is general grants-in-aid, and the third is specific-purpose grants, i.e. project grants. (Chu and Lee, 2001; Lin, 1985; Tseng and Lee, 2000; Lee and Chu *et al.*, 2002; Research Committee of Local Allocation Tax, Japan, 1999, 2000).

3.1. *The Centrally-Allotted Tax Revenues*

The data in Table 8 show the revenues dedicated to the Centrally-Allotted Tax. The vertical sharing of central taxes specifies that local governments will receive 10 percent of income tax revenues, 10 percent

Table 8. Tax Sharing in Taiwan (since January 1999) (unit: %)

	Central Government		Local Government		
Tax Item	Central	Allotted	Metropolitan	County	Village
I. *National taxes*					
Income tax	90	10	—	—	—
Estate and gift tax	20(50)	—	(50)	80	80
Custom duties	100	—	—	—	—
Value-added & Non-value added busi. tax	60	40	—	—	—
Commodity tax	90	10	—	—	—
Tobac. & alcohol tax	80	20	—	—	—
Securities transact.tax	100	—	—	—	—
Futures transaction tax	100	—	—	—	—
Mine concession tax	100	—	—	—	—
II. *Local taxes*					
Agricultural land tax	—	—	(100)	—	100
Land value tax	—	—	(100)	50	50
Land val. increm. tax	—	20	(100)	80	—
House tax	—	—	(100)	40	60
Vehicle license tax	—	—	(100)	100	—
Deed tax	—	—	(100)	—	100
Stamp tax	—	—	(100)	—	—
Amusement tax	—	—	(100)	100	—
Special tax	—	—	—	—	—

Source: Ministry of Finance, 1999.
Note: Allotted: Centrally-Allotted Tax Revenues.

of commodity tax revenues, 40 percent of business tax revenues, and 20 percent of land value increment tax revenues. The sharing of the land value increment tax is with the city and county.

3.2. *Grants-in-Aid*

The central government gives general grants and specific grants-in-aid (or project grants) to the local governments. Since 1999 the aim of the general grants is to fill the remaining gap of basic fiscal needs of local governments, after taking account of local revenue sources and shared taxes. The purpose of specific grants is to subsidize specific projects that are thought to be in the national interest, e.g., municipal subway.

Since the revision of the Law Governing Government Revenues and Expenditures, the fiscal autonomy of local governments has improved. The data in Tables 10 and 11 exhibit the change in the ratio of fiscal

Table 9. Comparison Between Prevailing and Proposal Revision of Centrally-Allotted Tax Revenues (CATR)

Item	Prevailing	Proposal Revision
Category	1. General (indicator-distributed): 94% 2. Specific: 6%	1. Indicator-distributed: 90% 2. Balancing purpose: 6% 3. Adjustment purpose: 4%
General CATR	Metropolitan: 43% County, city: 39% Villages, township: 12%	90%: indicator-distributed with the same allocation basis. Village and township are included in county.
Specific CATR	For emergency, disaster purpose	6%; balancing; 4%: adjustment
Allocation indicators	Metropolitan business sales 50%, Population: 20%, Area: 20%, Fiscal ability: 10%, County, city fiscal ability: 85% (= basic needs – basic revenues) contribution ratio of business sales: 15%	With the same basis. Fiscal ability: 75% (= basic needs – basic revenues) Fiscal effort: 25%

Table 10. Fiscal Autonomy Ratio of Local Governments in Taiwan (1997–1999FY) (unit: numbers of authorities)

Ranking	Fiscal Autonomy Indicator A	Fiscal Autonomy Indicator B	Fiscal Autonomy Indicator C
More than 80%	2	1	—
70–79.9%	—	1	—
60–69.9%	6	5	—
50–59.9%	1	1	—
40–49.9%	2	1	—
30–39.9%	3	4	—
20–29%	5	2	1
10–19.9%	3	7	2
0–9.9%	1	1	23

Source: By authors.
Note: Fiscal autonomy indicator A = the ratio of non-grant revenues to total fiscal revenues. Fiscal autonomy indicator B = the ratio of non-grant revenues to total fiscal expenditures. Fiscal autonomy indicator C = (the ratio of per capita non-grant revenues to average per capita total fiscal revenues) × 100%.

Table 11. Change in Fiscal Autonomy Ratio of Local Governments (1999–2000FY) (unit: %)

	1999(1)	2000(2)	Change Ratio (3) = (((2) – (1))/(1)) × 100%
Govt. units	25	25	—
Mean	55.73	64.31	15.39
Standard deviation	15.48	19.12	—
Variance	239.63	365.57	—
Range	74.10	101.49	—
Maximum	94.80	129.22	—
Minimum	20.70	27.74	—

Source: Tseng, M. S. and T. C. Wu (2003), p. 42 and Corrected by authors.
Note: fiscal autonomy ratio = non-grant revenues/total expenditures.

autonomy of local governments before and after the revision of this Law, respectively. In 2000 the average ratio of fiscal autonomy of 25 local governments amounted to 64.31%, which was more than the 55.73% in 1999.

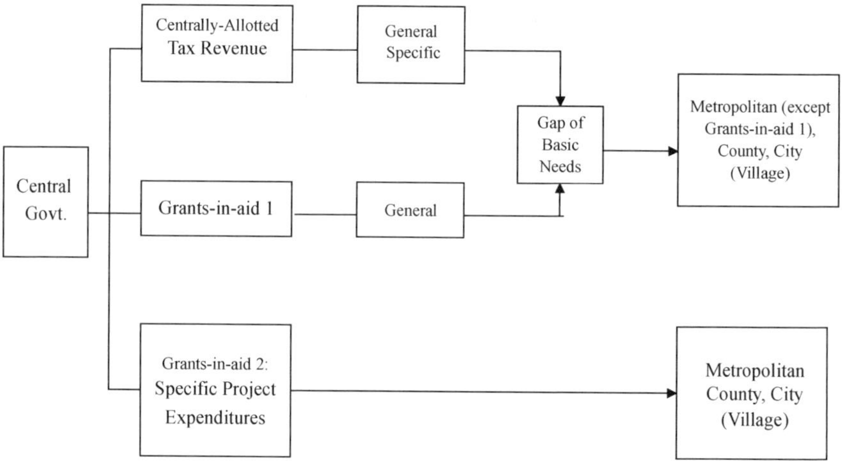

Fig. 1. Inter-governmental Fiscal Relation in Taiwan

The present inter-governmental fiscal system is illustrated in Fig. 1.

We use three indicators to measure the fiscal autonomy of local government:

a. Fiscal autonomy indicator A = the ratio of non-grant revenues to total fiscal revenues
b. Fiscal autonomy indicator B = the ratio of non-grant revenues to total fiscal expenditures
c. Fiscal autonomy indicator C = (the ratio of per capita non-grant revenues to average per capita total fiscal revenues) × 100 percent.

The Ministry of Finance is responsible for the allocation of the Centrally-Allotted Tax Revenues, and in charge of defining the equalization parameters. The overall measurement of horizontal fiscal imbalance among local governments is influenced by both revenue-raising capacity and expenditure needs assessment. (Clark, 1997, pp. 20–21.) To assess the overall revenue-raising capacity of local governments, several steps are required. First, define and quantify revenue-raising capacity. Second, the expenditures needs of each level of government should be justified. (Rye and Searle, 1997, pp. 43–48.) The most important work here is to evaluate the basic unit cost of public services or goods for each local government, and the per capita fiscal needs for each local government. Recently, Tseng and Lee (2000) and Lee and Chu *et al.* (2002), have begun to evaluate the basic fiscal needs and basic unit cost of public services. In fact, the calculations are difficult because there is no adequate bank of local public finance data.

In addition, the central government offers block grants to county and city governments with a distribution among eligible local governments by formula. Since 1999 it has become a very complicated system, because many counties and cities, or interest groups usually compete for the general grants. The Directorate General of Budget, Accounting and Statistics (DGBAS) is in charge of this general grant. Over time, more and more indicators have been integrated into the allocation equation.

There are three categories of general grants: educational establishment, social welfare, and basic social construction. There are several categories of indicators and weights for each category of general grants.

3.3. *Educational Establishment Grants*

In total, there are 6 indicators used for the distribution of educational grants. These indicators (and their weights in the formula) are fiscal ability (20%), population (5%), number of pupils (45%), number of classes (30%), and number of special schools.

3.4. *Social Welfare Grants*

The 5 indicators used in the distribution are: fiscal ability (20%), disabled population (45%), numbers of low income family and children (18%), labor supply of low income family (1%), number of elderly, women, youth, and children (16%) etc.

3.5. *Social Construction Grants*

There are 6 indicators in this category. They are population (30%), area of under urban planning (16%), area not under urban planning (16%), area of motorway (19.5%), completed area of motorway in urban planning areas etc. In every year the DGBAS forecasts the fiscal sources for the general grants, then calculates the allocation amount of each local government. Finally, DGBAS discusses the allocation with local governments for adjustments. The allocation behaves as a zero-sum game. (Tsai and Lin, 1999)

4. Non-Taxation Fiscal Sources of Local Governments

The fiscal autonomy of local governments in Taiwan has been very limited. Most local governments have no incentive to increase their non-taxation sources, which include fines, donations, impact fees, revenues of public business, charges and fees, services of public establishment etc. The data in Table 12 show the level of non-tax revenues of local governments between in 1999 and 2000. Even after the revision the LGAGRE, the ratio of non-tax revenues to total revenues decreased in the second half of 1999 and 2000. Thus, the Law Governing Allocation of Government Revenues and Expenditures to Local Government is in need of revision, so as to provide incentives to enhance the fiscal efforts of local governments. Local governments should take more responsibility in the collection of their own financial sources.

Table 12. Non-tax Revenues of Local Governments in Taiwan (unit: NT$ million, %)

Revenues	1999II, 2000 (1)	(1)/Total Revenues, % (2)	1999 (3)	(3)/Total Revenues, % (4)	Change %: ((2) – (4))/ (4) × 100
Total revenues	791,075	100.00	628,320	100.00	—
Non-tax revenues	296,201	37.44	242,780	38.64	–3.10
Fine	23,980	3.03	15,527	2.47	22.67
Donation	844	0.11	596	0.09	12.48
Impact fee	6	0.00	11	0.00	–54.79
Revenues of public business	20,204	2.53	4,948	0.79	221.41
Charges and fees	36,308	4.59	21,849	3.48	31.99
Others	215,038	27.18	199,848	31.81	–14.54
Public establishments	2,230	0.28	1,296	0.21	36.65

Source: Central office, Executive Yuan.

5. Improvement of Fiscal Ability of Local Governments

There are two approaches to strengthening the fiscal health of local governments. On one hand, the expenditures of local government could be reduced, and on the other hand, revenues could be enhanced.

There are several suggestions to reduce the growth of governmental expenditures.

- To reduce the governmental expenditures and costs, the Law of government procurement has been promulgated in May 1998 and revised later. It can improve transparency and reduce of the costs of public construction and administration.
- Due to the limitation of tax revenues and constraints on the government budget, all levels of governments have been encouraged to do outsourcing and introduce BOT (Build, Operate, Transfer) arrangements. The Taiwan High-Speed Railway Project is the first case of the BOT in Taiwan.
- The share of social welfare benefits in total central governmental expenditures has been the largest since the 1990s in Taiwan. It could crowd out economic development expenditures in the government budget. In addition, it could create a moral hazard situation for local governments and waste limited budget resources.
- The imposition of a ceiling on the growth rate of current government expenditures may help restrain current expenditures and avoid waste by local governments.

There also are some proposals to enhance governmental revenues. Among these, the need to provide incentives for local governments to increase revenues is the most important.

5.1. *Revenues Enhancements and Incentives*

5.1.1. *Halt Erosion of Tax Base*

The erosion of tax base of both central and local government tax revenues has become severe since 1990s. This problem might be addressed by giving local governments more access to the tax base.

The General Rules of Local Tax Laws (hereinafter named as GRLTL) went into effect on December 11 2002. This Law grants powers of taxation to local governments. The GRLTL authorizes each local government to levy special taxes, surtaxes or temporary taxes on certain groups under its jurisdiction. Local taxes are regulated under the Law on Allocation of Government Revenues and Expenditures to Local Government. The specific tax, temporary taxes and surtaxes of municipalities and counties (or cities), and temporary taxes of rural townships (urban townships or county cities) are all regulated under the Law for Local Systems. Municipal and county (or city) governments can increase tax rates but not more than 30 percent of the **premium tax levy** on municipal and county (or city) taxes (excluding Stamp taxes and Land Value Increment Tax). In addition, local governments can impose surtaxes on existing national taxes (excluding Custom Duties, Commodity Tax, VAT and Non-VAT Business Tax). The rates of surtaxes imposed shall not exceed 30 percent of their **premium tax levy**.

5.1.2. *Enlargement of Local Tax Base*

Local governments cannot levy taxes on transactions outside of their jurisdiction, natural resources and mineral products exported from their jurisdiction, the operation of public utility institutions, and generally any items impairing national and local public interest. Lower levels of government can collect local taxes **prior to** national taxes to safeguard their financial resources, whereas rural townships (urban townships or county cities) governments shall collect taxes **prior to** taxes imposed by counties or cities.

5.1.3. *Benefit Charges*

Local governments can draft a bill on the Autonomy Law for Local Taxation and send the bill to the council of assembly for approval. After permission is granted, the government can register the approved bill with the Ministry of Finance and the Directorate General of Budget Accounting and Statistics, Executive Yuan, and then promulgate the Law. Several local governments have tried to design and collect a local surcharge tax for items such as spring water.

In addition, to improve fairness in the distribution of financial burdens, and to utilize public resources more effectively, the Charges and Fees Law was promulgated on December 11, 2002. Finally, a proposed amendment to the Law Governing the Allocation of Government Revenues and Expenditures to Local Government has been submitted. A draft of the amendment to the LGAGRE was submitted to the Cabinet in May 2002, then submitted to the Legislative Yuan (Parliament) for approval. The first hearing passed and the second and third hearings are in process.

Local governments are encouraged and permitted to use tax incentives to attract domestic or foreign investment. Recently, magistrates and mayors of local governments have become more active in this area. In order to improve their fiscal position, local governments might increase fiscal revenues or appeal for more grants from the center. The central government could provide more financial grants to local governments. The data in Table 13 show the proposal revision of the Law Governing Allocation of Government Revenues and Expenditures. First, the financial sources of the Centrally-Allotted Tax Revenues for local governments will increase. The change between the present and proposed versions is shown in Tables 9 and 13. However, the distribution system would become more complicated. The basic concept of fiscal capacity of local governments is already known and accepted. However, a new "balancing factor" and an "adjustment factor" will be added. These are described in Table 13. In addition, the complicated measurement of land prices has been continued. In Taiwan, there are three prices for the same piece of land, i.e., traded price in market, declared value and declared price by local government, respectively. The allocation system for General Grants remains the same, but a Standard Committee of Education in the, Ministry of Education has been founded to reallocate the educational grants.

Hopefully, the fiscal autonomy of local governments could be improved in the future. In order to do a proper evaluation and monitoring of local governments, however, it is necessary to establish a special committee of local public finance to collect panel data and do more research.

The fiscal ability of local governments could be significantly improved according to a simulation made by Lee and Chu (2002). Along with the possible revision of the Law Governing Allocation of Government Revenues and Expenditures, the proposed structure of fiscal relations between central and local governments is illustrated in Fig. 2.

Table 13. A Revision Proposal of the Law Governing Allocation of Government Revenues and Expenditures to Local Government in May 2002

I. Centrally-Allotted Tax Revenues (CATR)		
(I) Financial sources A	A = A1 + A2 + A3	
1. Business tax B	B [1 – administrative fee 1.5% – invoice reward 3%] = A1	
2. Tobacco and alcohol taxes TA	1. Metropolitan, county, and city: TA [1 – administrative fee 1.0% – (1 – processed fee 1.0%) 0.19] = A2 2. In 2 island counties: TA [1 – administrative fee 1.0% – (1 – processed fee 1.0%) 0.80] = A3	
(II) Distribution:	Indicator	Share
1. Metropolitan, county, City	75%: Fiscal ability* = basic fiscal needs — basic fiscal revenues	75% × 90% A
	25%: a. Contribution ratio of business sales	15% × 90% A
	b. Ratio of declared price to market price of a land	4% × 90% A
	c. Ratio of declared value to market price of a land	4% × 90% A
	d. Ratio of charge, fine, and impact fee to its own financial sources#	2% × 90% A
2. Balancing purpose	Payment to the shortage after distribution of CATR	6% A
3. Adjustment amount	For disaster, unexpected damage usage. If it accumulated more than 10% of annual CATR, it will be added into for next years.	4% A
II. General grants		
(I) Financial sources B	B = 10% income tax + 10% commodity tax	Indicator

(Continued)

Table 13. (*Continued*)

(II) Distribution (block grants)		
1. Education grants	Standard Committee of Education, Ministry of Education	(see the context)
2. Social welfare grants		(see the context)
3. Basic social construction grants		
(III) Reward for investment competition of local gov.	General Rules of Local Tax Laws	
III. Project grants (specific grants)		Conditional or unconditional grants

Source: Executive Yuan, May 2002.
Note: The grants and reallocation tax of villages are included in counties.
*Basic fiscal needs = Salaries and wages of officially civic servants + basic administration cost + overtime pay of policemen and fire fighters + Salary of members of local assembly and grants to head of district officer + Insurance grants of teachers and staff in private schools + grants of contributions to official insurance and welfare costs from governments.

Basic fiscal revenues: metropolitan and city: 90% (land value tax + agricultural land tax + land value increment tax + house tax + vehicle license tax + deed tax + stamp tax + amusement tax) + sharing of tobacco and alcohol taxes + sharing of estate and gift tax. County = 90% [county sharing of (land value tax + land value increment tax + house tax + vehicle license tax + stamp tax)] + 80% [sharing of village or township (agricultural land tax + agricultural land tax + house tax + deed tax + amusement tax)] + County-allotted tax revenues + Sharing of estate and gift tax of villages and township.
#Own financial sources = realized revenues–project grants.

6. Conclusions and Prospects

The fiscal autonomy of local governments has been very weak in Taiwan. According to the Law for Allocating Government Revenues and Expenditures, tax revenues are composed of two categories, i.e., national taxes, and metropolitan, county (or city) and village taxes. National

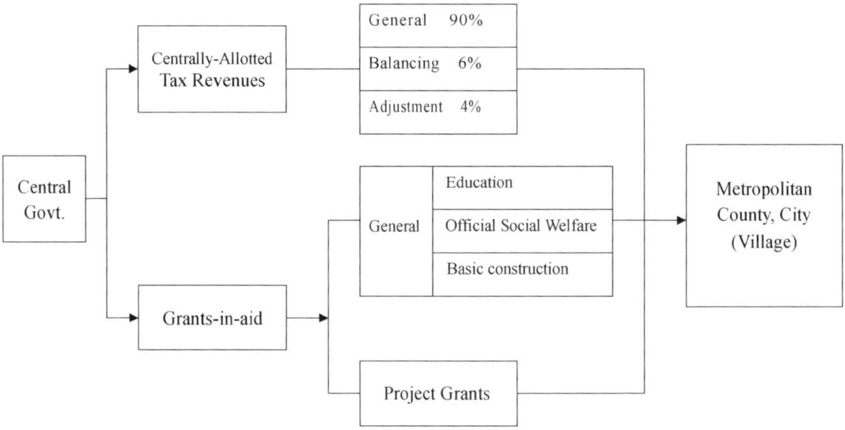

Fig. 2. Proposal Revision of Law Governing Allocation of Government Revenues and Expenditures

taxes accounted for the lion's share of total tax revenues, which was about 80.6% of total tax revenues in 2001. Local governments have faced a serious financial shortage. After the revision of the Law Governing Allocating Government Revenues and Expenditures in January 1999, the autonomous revenue ratio of the local governments (the ratio of non-grant revenues to total expenditures) increased from 55.73% in 1999 to 64.31% in 2000.

Most local governments have been heavily dependent on inter-governmental transfers for a long time. Financial resources of the local governments are composed of the distribution of Centrally-Allotted tax revenues, general grants, project-based grants, and several taxes. Local governments have limited abilities in the area of tax collection and in terms of their power to set tax rates. In August 2002 the Distribution Guidelines for Centrally-Allotted Tax Revenues was revised with the objective of reducing the deficits of local governments. Furthermore, both the General Rules of Local Tax Laws and the Charges and Fees Law went into effect in December 2002, authorizing municipal and county (or city) governments to impose surtaxes on existing national taxes excluding customs duties, commodity tax, and value-added tax. However, the power of taxation of local governments is still restricted. The Distribution Guidelines for Centrally-Allotted Tax Revenues could be revised to improve the vertical and horizontal equity in the decentralization system.

Recently, Taiwan's Centrally-Allotted Tax has followed a reform path similar to that of the Local Allocation Tax in Japan. There is still more work to do to improve the fiscal ability of local governments. Recently, local governments have become more active in using tax incentives to attract domestic or foreign investment. In addition, public expenditure controls have been introduced to reduce the fiscal deficit. The Revision Proposal of the Law Governing Allocation of Government Revenues and Expenditures to Local Government is still under review by the Central Government. Its final adoption will require consensus at all levels of government and of people.

Appendix

Table A.1. Accumulated Debt of Central Government in Taiwan (unit: NT$ billion, %)

Fiscal Year	Amount (NT$ Billion, %)	Ratio of Central Government Expenditures %	Ratio of GDP %
1986	60.1 (100)	14.8	2.2
1991	266.9 (100)	30.5	5.8
1996	1,226.6 (100)	101.9	16.5
2000	2,479.9 (100)	141.8	25.3
2001*	2,735.6 (100)	158.3	28.2
2002	3,031.2 (100)	189.6	31.1

Source: Statistical Yearbook of Public Finance, Ministry of Finance, Taipei.
Note: *The debt of province government was included in this year.

Table A.2. Income Elasticity of Income Tax in Taiwan

Period	In Nominal Prices	At Constant Prices
1964–1980	1.119	1.222
1981–1990	1.052	1.062
1991–2001	0.524	0.369
1981–2001	0.922	0.898
1964–2001	1.005	1.003

Source: K.L. Sun (2003).
Note: The simple regression equation is used to estimate the income elasticity of income tax.

References

Ahmad, E and R Thomas (1997). Types of transfers — a general formulation. In *Financing Decentralized Expenditures: An International Comparison of Grants*, E Ahmad (ed.), Edward Elgar Publishing, pp. 361–381.

Clark, D H (1997). Assessing provincial revenues-raising capacity for transfers. In *Financing Decentralized Expenditures: An International Comparison of Grants*, E Ahmad (ed.), Edward Elgar Publishing, pp. 18–42.

Chu, T M and P Y Lee (2001) [in Chinese]. Assessment of the Centrally-Allotted Tax Revenues in Taiwan. *Public Fiscal Studies*, 33(3), pp. 36–55.

Chu, T M (2003) [in Chinese]. How to increase the revenues and cut the expenditures of local governments? Presented in the Workshop of Local Governments, Taiwan Institute of Economic Research and Ministry of Finance, Taipei, August 7, 2003.

Gandhi, V P (1995). Inter-governmental fiscal relations and economic performance. In *Macroeconomic Management and Fiscal Decentralization*, J Roy (ed.), Washington DC: World Bank, pp. 39–47.

Ishi, H (2001). *The Japanese Tax System*, Oxford University Press.

King, D (1997). Inter-governmental fiscal relations: Concepts and models. In *Inter-governmental Fiscal Relations*, R C Fisher (ed.), Kluwer Academic Publishers, pp. 19–59.

Lee, H F, T M Chu, T C Liu, S M Chiang, W S Hsieh and C I Chau (2002) [in Chinese]. *Improvement in the Distribution Guidelines for Centrally-Allotted Tax Revenues*, Department of Treasury, Ministry of Finance, Taipei.

Lin, C (1985) [in Chinese]. Function and distribution of Centrally-Allotted Tax Revenues. *Socioeconomic Law and Institution Review*, Taipei, 15, pp. 119–155.

Musgrave, R A and P B Musgrave (1989). *Public Finance in Theory and Practice*, 5th ed., McGraw-Hill International editions.

Revision Proposal of the Law Governing Allocation of Governments Revenues and Expenditures, Executive Yuan, Taipei, May 2003.

Research Committee of Local Allocation Tax, Japan (ed.) (1999) [in Japanese]. *Japan's Local Allocation Tax: Correction Coefficients and Basic Fiscal Needs FY1999*, Association of Local Public Finance, Japan.

Research Committee of Local Allocation Tax, Japan (ed.) (2000) [in Japanese]. *Japan's Local Allocation Tax: Unit Costs FY2000*, Association of Local Public Finance, Japan.

Rye, C R and B Searle (1997). Expenditures needs: Institutions and data. In *Financing Decentralized Expenditures: An International Comparison of Grants*, E Ahmad (ed.), Edward Elgar Publishing, pp. 43–69.

Sun, K L (2003) [in Chinese]. Taiwan's tax system in prospect, presented in the Workshop on Globalization and beyond 2008, Foundation of National Prospect, Taipei, October 19, 2003.

Taxation and Tariff Committee, Ministry of Finance (2007), *Guide to Taiwan Taxes 2007*, Taipei.

Tsai, G Y and C T Lin (1999) [in Chinese]. Fiscal game? Zero-sum? Positive sum? Negative sum? On centrally-allotted tax revenues and the law for allocating government revenues and expenditures. *Public Fiscal Studies*, 31(3), pp. 1–11.

Tseng, C W and H F Lee (2000) [in Chinese]. *Basic fiscal needs and revenues in Taiwan*, Council for Economic Planning and Development, Executive Yuan, Taipei.

Tseng, C W (2001) [in Chinese]. *Incentives to Increase in Financial Resources Through the Distribution Guidelines for Centrally-Allotted Tax Revenues*, Research, Development and Evaluation Commission, Executive Yuan, Taipei.

Tseng, M S and T C Wu (2003) [in Chinese]. *Enlarging autonomous financial sources of local governments in Taiwan*, Research, Development and Evaluation Commission, Executive Yuan, Taipei.

Chapter XIII

The Revenue Performance of Malaysian Local Government

AZMI SETAPA *and* ELAYNE YEE SIEW LIN

Malaysian Institute for Economic Research

1. Introduction

High economic growth, especially prior to the economic crisis in 1997, significantly improved living standards in Malaysia. GDP per capita increased by 33 percent between 1995 and 2000. This growth has provided funding for an improved quality of local public services, and it has also generated new roles and responsibilities for the local authorities. The growing population within urban areas, however, has put pressure on these budgets. The question is what wins out: the higher cost of servicing this population and maintaining a clean and healthy environment, or the increased tax base and the growing ability of the local governments to manage their services.

2. Sources of Revenue

Local government expenditures are financed by own source revenues, federal reimbursements, and grants from federal and state governments. Local own sources of revenue can be broken down into tax revenue, non-tax revenue, and capital revenue. The tax revenue is mainly comprised of the assessment tax (property tax) whereas the non-tax revenue is generated through investment income, fees, rents, charges, licenses, and fines. Capital revenue is generated from the sale of land, houses, and other capital assets.

Table 1. Major Sources of Revenue of Selected Local Authorities for 2000 (Percent distribution)

	MPPJ	MPK	MPSA	MPAJ
Assessment tax	65.2	68.9	76.4	72.5
Licenses & Permits	3.8	4.0	1.9	2.9
Services	10.1	4.2	2.5	2.0
Rentals	4.2	5.0	4.8	2.2
Interest & Investment	2.4	3.3	3.6	1.0
Fines	5.6	3.1	3.1	0.4
Grants	3.5	5.2	4.6	12.3
Car Park	–3.7	—	—	—
Sales	0.1	0.7	0.6	0.3
Others	5.1	1.9	2.5	6.4

Source: Malaysian Institute for Economic Research.

The data in Table 1 present the composition of revenues for four selected local governments namely, the Petaling Jaya Town council (MPPJ), Kelang Town Council (MPK), Shah Alam City Council (MPSA) and Ampang Jaya Town Council (MPAJ). The assessment tax is the largest source of revenue in every case whereas the other sources of revenue make only a small contribution.

3. Trends of Revenue and Expenditure

The consolidated fiscal position of local governments is summarized in Table 2. These data show a healthy financial position for local governments, in that there is a surplus on current account. In fact, the surplus in 2001 was equivalent to about 36 percent of current expenditures. Nearly 80 percent of all development expenditures could be financed by this surplus. Compared to local governments in developing countries around the world, this is a strong financial position.

There is now some pressure on this favorable position. While current revenues and expenditures have both grown at about 34 percent over the 1995–2001 period, development expenditures have risen by about twice this rate. The result is that an overall deficit has appeared and some resort to capital financing has been necessary. Funding capital projects with borrowing is not necessarily a bad thing, since capital assets have

Table 2. Local Governments' Consolidated Finance (in RM million)

	1995	1996	1997	1998	1999	2000	2001
Revenue	2,872	3,108	3,242	3,343	3,535	3,410	3,844
	(9.2)	(8.2)	(4.3)	(3.1)	(5.8)	(–3.5)	(12.7)
Own revenue	2,294	2,364	2,509	2,586	2,769	2,815	3,170
State and federal grants	545	721	688	712	721	527	608
Federal reimbursements	33	23	45	45	45	66	66
Current expenditure	2,105	2,140	2,030	2,256	2,573	2,415	2,821
	(20.6)	(1.7)	(–5.1)	(11.2)	(14.0)	(–7.5)	(16.8)
Current surplus/deficit	767	968	1,212	1,087	962	1,098	1,023
Net development expenditure	760	782	824	1,428	1,262	1,225	1,320
	(–5.7)	(2.9)	(5.4)	(73.2)	(–11.6)	(–2.9)	(20.3)
Overall balance	7	186	388	–341	–300	–103	–297
Sources of financing							
Net federal loans	–9	–38	–11	–15	–11	–13	–9
Net state loans	10	–1	–1	–6	–3	—	–1
Change in assets	–8	–147	–376	362	314	314	307

Note: 1. Figures in parentheses are annual percentage changes (–) indicates a build-up in reserves.
Source: Ministry of Finance, Malaysia.

long lives, but this change in fiscal position does suggest the need for finding new sources of revenues to fund operation and maintenance, to cover the service on this debt, and to provide for future capital expansion.

Total revenue of local governments rose by 33.8% between 1995 and 2001 (see Table 2). It is interesting to note that this increase is due primarily to the 38.1% rise in own revenues. State and Federal grants increased by only 11.5% for this period. By 2001, own source revenues accounted for over 80 percent of total local government revenue. This is in contrast with the contribution of state and federal grants which had declined from 18.9% in 1995 to only 15.8% in 2001. It is interesting to note that state and federal grants were highest for the period 1996–1999, which may be attributable to the economic crisis. We may now turn to the financial condition in the four cases that have been selected for this study.

The revenue and expenditure of the MPPJ from 1996–2000 are shown in Table 3. Except for 1997 when the council recorded lower revenues

Table 3. Petaling Jaya Town Council (MPPJ) Revenue and Expenditure (RM million)

	1996	1997	1998	1999	2000
10.1 *Revenue*					
Own revenue					
Tax revenue	60.1	55.4	64.8	83.7	90.8
Non-tax revenue	48.5	50.2	48.9	38.2	43.2
Grants/contributions	5.2	4.7	10.0	5.1	4.9
Total revenue	113.8	110.3	123.7	127.0	138.9
10.2 *Expenditure*					
Operating expenditure	113.6	112.3	100.8	102.4	118.9
Development expenditure	4.8	6.2	5.0	9.1	7.4
Total expenditure	118.4	118.5	105.8	111.5	126.3
10.3 *Balances*					
Own revenue					
Operating expenditure	–5.0	–6.7	12.9	19.5	15.1
Total expenditure	–9.8	–12.9	7.9	10.4	7.7
Total revenue					
Total expenditure	–4.6	–8.2	17.9	15.5	12.6

(the economy was facing a financial meltdown), total revenues have trended up since 1996. The major part of the MPPJ's total revenue has been derived from tax sources while grants and transfers from the state and federal governments have made a negligible contribution to financing. Expenditures have risen dramatically since 1998, and at a faster rate than revenues. This is primarily due to a significant run-up in operating expenditures. The local government maintained a surplus between 1998 and 2000, on both current account and overall. This was primarily due to the robust growth in own source revenues.

The Ampang Jaya Municipal Council (MPAJ) (see Table 4) also presents a picture of fiscal discipline, though the fundamentals are not as strong as that observed in the case of MPPJ. Own source revenue growth was less strong between 1998 and 2000, but expenditure growth was also slowed. As a result, the budgetary position was in balance in 2000 (in contrast to 1996–1997 when there was a budget deficit).

Table 4. Ampang Jaya Municipal Council (MPAJ) Revenue and Expenditure (RM million)

	1996	1997	1998	1999	2000
10.4 *Revenue*					
Own revenue					
Tax revenue	31.7	40	52.9	52.8	56.2
Non-tax revenue	6.0	8.1	6.0	7.2	7.1
Grants/contributions	5.1	7.2	7.4	9.7	8.9
Total revenue	42.8	55.3	66.3	69.7	72.2
10.5 *Expenditure*					
Operating expenditure					
Development expenditure					
Total expenditure	45.4	57.9	63.2	60.7	64.1
10.6 *Balances*					
Own revenue					
Operating expenditure					
Total expenditure					
Total revenue					
Total expenditure	–2.6	–2.6	3.1	9.0	8.1

Table 5. Klang Town Council (MPK) Revenue and Expenditure (RM million)

	1996	1997	1998	1999	2000
10.7 *Revenue*					
Own revenue					
Tax revenue	42.1	43.9	53.1	61.3	68.8
Non-tax revenue	26.9	32.8	33.9	24.9	24.3
Grants/contributions	7.2	7.7	4.9	4.9	5.1
Total revenue	76.9	84.4	91.9	91.1	97.7
10.8 *Expenditure*					
Operating expenditure	73.6	87.7	68.6	75.3	86.6
Development expenditure	20.6	10.6	8.2	4.9	12.7
Total expenditure	94.2	98.3	76.8	80.2	99.3
10.9 *Balances*					
Own revenue					
Operating expenditure	–4.6	–11.0	18.4	10.9	6.5
Total expenditure	–25.2	–21.6	10.2	6.0	–6.2
Total revenue					
Total expenditure	–18.0	–13.9	15.1	10.9	–1.6

The Klang municipal council shows a weaker financial position, and a deficit in three of the five years between 1996 and 2000 (see Table 5). There has been steady revenue growth, but this has been outstripped by increases in spending, especially that for development purposes. Still, the deficit for 2000 was only Rm. 1.6 billion, less than 2 percent of own source revenues.

The Shah Alam City Council (MPSA) (see Table 6) has the largest expenditure budget of the four municipalities, and showed a quite significant deterioration in fiscal balance in 2000. While the match between current account revenues and expenditures was maintained, development spending rose faster than resources available. The deficit in 2000 was equivalent to about 4.3% of own source revenues.

The patterns are roughly similar in these four municipalities. Own source revenue growth is reasonably strong and there is relatively little dependence on grants. Non tax revenue growth has not been as robust as own source revenue growth. For the most part, budget balance has

Table 6. Shah Alam City Council (MPSA) Revenue and Expenditure (RM million)

	1996	1997	1998	1999	2000
10.10 *Revenue*					
Own revenue					
Tax revenue	41.0	75.9	100.2	104.2	113.4
Non-tax revenue	23.4	27.4	27.3	24.7	28.0
Grants/contributions	5.4	3.8	6.4	7.6	6.9
Total revenue	73.8	107.1	133.9	136.5	148.3
10.11 *Expenditure*					
Operating expenditure	50.7	57.6	73.2	81.1	107.3
Development expenditure	16.4	16.8	16.1	15.5	34.9
Total expenditure	67.1	74.4	89.6	96.6	142.2
10.12 *Balances*					
Own revenue					
Operating expenditure	17.7	45.7	54.3	47.8	34.1
Total expenditure	1.3	28.9	38.2	32.3	–0.8
Total revenue					
Total expenditure	6.7	32.7	44.6	39.9	6.1

been maintained on the current fiscal account. To the extent there is a concern in any of these local governments, it is about capital financing to accommodate the increased demands of the urban population.

4. Challenges to Local Authorities

High economic growth and access to better quality education has improved the quality of life of populations across the Asia-Pacific region. This change not only enhances the resource base of local governments, but it puts strong pressure on local authorities to respond to the increased demand for local public services. The problem that is now emerging is that institutional rigidities have kept the resource base from expanding as fast as the demand for services has expanded. This constrains the ability of the local governments to meet the expectations of the local population and to be innovative in service provision.

Table 7. Urban Population Growth (million)

Year	Total Population	Urban Population	Ratio (%)
1980	13.1	4.45	34
1991	17.6	8.80	50
2000	21.3	12.38	60
2010	23.3	16.17	70
2020	24.7	19.76	80

Source: M. of Housing and Local Government.

The emerging fiscal problems of local governments are not all on the revenue side. There also are serious administrative constraints to better local services that must be removed. These include a shortage of skilled personnel, a low level of computerization, a low standard of reporting, weak management and poor monitoring. All of these factors result in a low public confidence in local authorities. In this web of financial constraints there remains little choice except for local government to begin moving toward a better balance between what they spend and the revenues they have available.

The data in Table 7 present the forecast for urban population in Malaysia from 1980 to 2020. The percentage of urban population increased from only 34 percent in 1980 to 60 percent in 2000. It is forecast that this ratio will increase further to 80 percent in 2020. This forecast underlines the urgent need to equip the local authorities with sufficient capabilities to face what almost certainly will be significant public financing challenges.

Urbanization will impose many different kinds of challenges for local governments in Malaysia. Certainly it will require higher expenditure for extension of basic facilities such as housing, roads, and transportation and health care facilities. The costs of serving a larger urban population are multiplied because of deteriorating health, environmental and social conditions. The scarcity of clean water, traffic jams, flooding, and an unsatisfactory environment all must be addressed by local governments as long term problems.

Sustainable development can be enhanced by transparency and participatory governance. The process of policy formulation and implementation has to be moved through consensus-building among various concerned sectors with the aim of improving the overall quality of life of all citizens. This approach can encourage the public to contribute their energy, and perhaps, financial assistance to the local councils. More importantly, transparency and good governance can reduce corruption and increase the willingness of the public to pay taxes. While local governments have seen significant growth in own revenues, this has been outstripped by expenditure growth in recent years. With increasing pressures of urbanization, local government financial resources will be increasingly short. The financing of local government, therefore, becomes a critical issue to be dealt with. New options for financing local government and increasing their revenues need to be forthcoming.

The limited or weak financial position of local government can be illustrated using data for three municipal councils (MPPJ, MPAJ and MPK) and one city council (MPSA) for the period 1996–2000, as presented in Tables 3–6. In all cases, the majority of revenues are from own source tax and non-tax levies with minimal assistance from the federal and/or state government through the provision of grants/transfers. Except for the MPAJ, for which we could not obtain a breakdown of total expenditure, total expenditure is dominated by spending for operating purposes with development expenditure constituting only a small proportion. This clearly is an indication of inflexibility and inability on the part of local government to meet the aspirations of their constituencies.

While grants and transfers are necessary for local authorities to carry out their social and economic development functions, the amounts presently given are far too small to cope with new pressures and challenges. An average grant of between RM5 million and RM7 million is being provided to each of these four city councils for each financial year. This is probably not adequate. Local governments are now facing a changing urban environment and are expected to serve a wider area and an increased population. Maintenance of public cleanliness, a healthy environment and basic amenities will need to be provided, and probably at an increasing rate. Inside and out of local government, there will be enormous changes, stemming from new policies and regulations, including environmental issues, privatization of functions and services, new building and planning procedures, new arrangements for solid waste management, and youth and community care effects.

In our preliminary interviews with representatives of the four selected councils, the challenges listed by them were very similar.

Maintenance of infrastructure is a major challenge. The expenditure requirements to upgrade and maintain roads and drains in these municipalities are very great. Of the four councils, the task appears most daunting for the MPAJ as, according to its president Ahmad Kabit, development in Ampang Jaya was not planned. When MPAJ was established, the areas which came under its jurisdiction were made up of existing housing estates and villages. This, he added, was unlike the gradual and systematically-planned development of areas under the other councils like the Subang Jaya Municipal Council (MPSJ) and the MPSA.

The councils faced another problem of population growth which spilled over into the mushrooming squatter colonies. All of the council representatives interviewed, however, are confident of solving their squatter problems to achieve a zero squatter status by 2005 as more housing projects, including low-cost housing development are in progress. The most common public complaint is about bad roads and drainage problems. Another challenge for these councils is the relocation of hawkers into proper stalls. Interviewees continue to cite problems confronting their municipalities such as lack of land to build facilities like a mini stadium, fields, bus terminals and sports complexes. There also is the problem of lack of burial grounds to cater to all people of the various religious faiths. And the list goes on.

5. Potential Sources of Revenue for the Local Government

It is imperative that local authorities should increase their revenue if they want to be in a position to meet the challenges of today's world of globalization and technological advances. The central government and the local governments should start to look beyond traditional sources of finance to strengthen their financial position. In the next section of this paper, we identify strategies that could lead to revenue enhancements for local government.

5.1. *Re-zoning*

Re-zoning can be a fiscal enhancement strategy if it moves the classification of land from a lower (tax) rate to a higher (tax) rate category.

The implementation of this strategy will require a redefinition of agricultural, residential and commercial land with the hope of moving a significant amount of land to higher rate categories. This technique can be applied to certain residential areas where a large number of houses have been permitted to operate their businesses from within their premises but are still being assessed by the local authority as "residential" status. Within some local authority areas, there are still pockets of agricultural land which are subject to minimal assessment levels. Such pieces of land could be converted to other categories of land use more in-line with the activities of a city or municipal zone. A higher assessment rate may then be charged on such converted lands. Local authorities need to be cautious in applying this technique due to possible negative public reaction and opposition from politicians.

5.2. *Land Pooling/Readjustment Scheme*

The land pooling scheme is a strategy to encourage a population to surrender small plots to the local authorities which, in turn, will combine these lands for the implementation of profitable projects. This technique, or readjustment, is widely used in various countries, and especially prominent in Japan and Korea. Although it is known by different names in different countries — "land consolidation" in Taiwan and Indonesia, "land pooling" in Australia and Nepal, and "land plotting" in Canada — it is essentially the same technique.

5.3. *Request Housing Developers to Allocate Land for Community Use*

This strategy is widely used in Malaysia. It is normal for the authorities in Malaysia to lay down a condition that housing developers allocate a piece of land for local authorities to turn into playing fields, or alternatively, to provide community halls or sports centers in exchange for planning permits and council services. These buildings become the assets of the council, whereupon fees and charges can be collected for the use of the facilities in the buildings. The housing developers may include and transfer this cost onto the house buyers, thereby burdening them.

5.4. *Sale of Municipal Bonds*

For local authorities that have highly profitable projects with stable rates of return, borrowing from the public through the issuance of local authority bonds is a feasible option to address financial shortfalls. Hence, a local authority which needs funds to finance particular projects may raise the capital by such means. However, the legalities and regulatory arrangements related to issuing bonds to the public will need to be sorted out with governments at the state and federal levels. This financing option is elaborated below.

5.5. *Fees*

It is very important to set appropriate levels for charges, permits, licenses and so on. An excessive level of fees will encourage people not to pay or may discourage people from participating in socially beneficial activities. The result could be underconsumption of a social good, and possibly a reduction in the revenue of the local authorities. The first necessary step is to identify the "right" level of fees, perhaps by study and observation of the fees charged in similarly situated jurisdictions. Certainly, a more efficient administration of fees and charges, regular monitoring of compliance rates and facility usage, and strong enforcement are suitable strategies for generating more revenue from fees and charges.

5.6. *Privatization*

Following the national government's encouragement of privatization, beginning in the mid-1980s, activities such as car parks, sport centers, community centers and properties were privatized by the local governments. Another possibility for local governments is the privatization of bigger projects such as property developments, and the construction of roads and bridges. In most cases, local governments will arrange a deferred payment method with contractors to finance the cost of the privatized project. There are cases in Malaysia where local authorities have successfully implemented Build-Operate-Transfer arrangements with the private sector. Under this method, the private sector, which will bear the full cost of construction, will operate and collect revenue from the project for an agreed period of time. After that period, they are required to turn the asset over to the local authorities. This method has gained popularity since the Asian economic crisis in 1997.

5.7. *Share-equity*

Under this revenue mobilization scheme, the local authority engages in joint-ventures with a private company by holding a certain percentage of equity in a company that will be awarded a project for privatization. The problems with this approach are that (a) it may produce an unfair competition and lead to a cost outcome that does not benefit taxpayers, and (b) it may crowd out private sector investment.

5.8. *Taxation and Constitutional Bias*

Constitutionally, the federal government has access to tax bases that are responsive to economic growth and that will enable it to meet the increasing costs of its expenditure responsibilities. The state and local governments, on the other hand, are not similarly endowed with buoyant sources of revenue. Yet, the demand for state and local government expenditures appears to be income elastic in Malaysia. Currently, there are concerns that state governments may face difficulties in financing their expenditures responsibilities under the current constitutional and federal-state fiscal arrangements. Many countries resolve this imbalance in revenue buoyancy by allowing the sub-national governments to share in the revenues collected by higher level governments.

A re-assignment of taxing powers and new arrangements for revenue sharing could lead to enhancement of the financial position of the local authorities. The following would seem likely candidates for such a reform:

- *Taxes on motor vehicles through road licenses and transfers, especially in larger Municipalities and cities.* An annual transfer from the central government or partial re-allocation of the revenue from this source could produce substantial income to local authorities, and would seem to meet the usual tests for a good local tax.
- *Taxes on local products, especially on agricultural produce where there is a monopoly marketing organization.* This has to be carefully

structured and administered as it can create a disincentive to production. On the other hand, it is clear that the marketing activity benefits from the use of local services and local infrastructure.

- *Taxes on entertainment such as hotels, restaurants, cinemas, etc. could be distributed to local authorities.* These are easy to administer, meet the normal equity tests, and tend not to be politically objectionable.
- *Sales taxes could be shared with local authorities.* They are buoyant and can be elastic depending upon the economic activities of the areas.
- *Stamp Duty Grant.* There is a surcharge on the state government stamp duty of one-half percent. The additional income presently is passed on to the village local authorities in the form of stamp duty grants. The local share could be increased.
- *Forest Revenue Grants.* A forest grant is given to the village local authorities. The amount is equal to two percent of the amount of gross revenue realized from forests. This grant is earmarked for forest development activities.
- *Surcharge on vehicle fuel.* This surcharge could be collected through the oil companies on behalf of the local authorities. Depending on the level of the surcharge, this could yield beneficial social effects. To the extent it discourages vehicle use, it reduces congestion and pollution, and to the extent it does not discourage vehicle use, it provides a stronger base for local government financing. It would seem an equitable levy, whether judged on a benefits or an ability to pay basis. The main drawback, however, is that it can be politically contentious and in many countries has been a lightning rod for taxpayer complaint.
- *Taxes on utility bills, notably on electricity, telephone and water.* A surcharge can be added to the bills, with the revenues designated for the local authorities. This surcharge is relatively equitable and easy to administer. The problem is that there would be an increase in prices that taxpayers and voters may object to.

These are some of the taxes available to local authorities either directly or through transfers on a revenue-sharing basis. Local taxation, however, is more than just a matter of raising revenue. There are administrative issues to consider and distortions to avoid. In some cases, a local authority may want to consider getting rid of some types of its local revenue sources which are inequitable, low yielding, and have high collection costs. Ideally, these would be replaced by revenue sources that yield more with lower administrative cost. A local authority may also want to choose the taxes or surcharges that would do the least damage to the economy and the people in its area of jurisdiction (Phang S.N., 1997, pp. 72–82).

6. Improve the System of Revenue Administration

This present revenue administration is weak and is characterized by poor monitoring, delayed revenue collection and substantial revenue delinquency. In administering its revenues, a local authority should aim for more efficient and effective collection, and to have a set of performance standards against which the local authorities can measure their performance (benchmarking). At present, Malaysian local government revenues do not meet these standards. Financial management and reporting still lag far behind best practices. The existing financial system of local authorities needs to be updated in line with international standards.

One way of improving revenue administration is in the area of property taxation. Local authorities should improve and update their registration list of tax-payers. Revaluation of all properties needs to be carried out every five years. This would add buoyancy to the revenue base. An attractive incentive/penalty method should be formulated to encourage more people to pay on time. To supplement an incentive-based revenue collection system, personal contact and persuasion are also important in order to encourage payment. A proper system of enforcement should also be in place to stimulate compliance.

For the other sources of revenue, notably charges and fees, there should be a systematic revision of tariffs, either on an annual or on some other regular basis. A simple indexing with respect to GDP or inflation would insure some buoyancy to the system, though this may bring both administrative difficulties and political resistance.

Collections are an especially important issue for all local authority revenue sources. The local authority must ensure that those who should pay do pay the actual amount and on time, and that the money collected is properly accounted for. Otherwise, improper accounting methods and misappropriation of funds will become a liability to a local authority. At every level, where possible, records should be checked, and cross-checked, while random spot checks should be carried out by senior management personnel.

7. Viability of Bond Financing for Local Government

The issuance of bonds has long been identified as a potential solution to capital financing problems of local governments in Malaysia. However there are economic, constitutional and operational issues and limitations surrounding this proposal.

7.1. *Impact on Monetary and Fiscal Policy*

One major drawback to proposals for local government borrowing is the possible negative impact on the macro-economy. The objective of economic stabilization is always a high priority at the federal level in Malaysia. With respect to monetary policy, the federal government needs to ensure that the volume of money and credit are suitable for a targeted level of prices, interest rates and exchange rates. To many, this suggests that the government should determine/allocate the amount of borrowing for each state in line with national budget objectives. Such an allocation process would require a transparent and unambiguous allocation method.

Under present arrangements, the local governments submit their budget/project proposal to the state governments who, in turn, forward it to the Budget Division of the Ministry of Finance. Bond market financing will require the involvement of two more institutions, the Central Bank and the Securities Commission. A formula allocation of credit, its design and monitoring, therefore, would need to involve at least local governments, state governments, the Ministry of Finance, the Central Bank and the Securities Commission.

7.2. *Constitutional Restrictions on Borrowing*

It is stipulated, under part 5, Section 39 of the Local Government Act 1976 for Peninsular Malaysia, under Section 55 Local Government Ordinance 1961 for the state of Sabah, and in Chapter 117 of the Local Authority Ordinance 1948 for the state of Sarawak, that a local authority/local government may raise loans from the market with the approval of the state government. These Acts appear to open the door for local government borrowing to finance capital projects. Indeed, the state government usually finds it in their interest to support local government efforts to mobilize resources to implement their development plans. The President of the local government is answerable to the State Assembly, hence an appropriate direct line of negotiation is available. However, the state government is itself limited by Article 111 of the Malaysian Constitution. Article 111(2) makes it clear that the state governments cannot give loan guarantees except with the approval of the Federal Government and subject to such conditions as may be specified by it. Therefore, while local authorities might be given the power to borrow, they cannot take advantage of the creditworthiness of the state government.

Article 111 of the Constitution further regulates the borrowing power of the federal and state governments. The federal government can borrow, as provided for under federal law, from domestic as well as from foreign sources. State governments, however, can borrow only from the federal government or from a bank or other financial source approved for that purpose by the federal government. States may not take a loan with a maturity exceeding five years. Prior to the 1976 Constitution Amendment, the state government could only borrow from the federal government or from any approved bank for a period not exceeding 12 months. Thus, the federal government can prescribe the terms and conditions which will apply to all loans raised by the state governments.

The plan for bond financing for local government in Malaysia must be formulated within the present constitutional and regulatory framework. The view here is that it would be unwise to bundle any new bond financing proposals with the more general issue of power allocation among levels of government. A better course might be to develop the capacity of local governments to borrow inside the present practice where the local government is required to submit project proposals to the state.

7.3. *Inadequacy of Financial Reporting and Transparency*

A first enabling step to be taken in developing the capacity of local governments to borrow is an improvement of accounting practices and a rethinking of transparency issues. Local governments do have up-to-date, audited financial statements. However, bond financing will require more detailed information from local authorities than is presently reported. While some weaknesses in the accounting standard of local governments are technical in nature and can be easily rectified, a full information disclosure, as that required by rating agencies, may be more problematic. To enable rating agencies to execute the jobs successfully, they need to be allowed to explore, examine and analyze all information and data related to local government activities. Thus, the transparency issue relating to the adequacy of accounting, auditing and disclosure standards will need to be addressed prior to the implementation of bond financing for the local governments (Fabozzi, F. J., 1997).

The transparency of information is critical for the overall growth of the bond market, and an active secondary market is also highly dependent on the availability of information to all market participants. To address the information deficiency, the Bond Information and Dissemination System (BIDS) was launched in October 1997 by the government to facilitate pricing, trading and revaluation of securities information on Malaysian government Securities (MGS) and private debt securities (PDS). BIDS provides a comprehensive database on the government and PDS market, and stock and facility information on all ringgit-denominated, non-equity linked debt securities as well as their last traded prices and volumes (Bee C.K. and Choy T.C., 2001, pp. 397). In 1999, BNM integrated certain functions of FAST with BIDS to improve the operating efficiency of the BIDS.

7.4. *Bond Market Infrastructure*

The Malaysian capital market, particularly its private debt securities' market, is still young. However, it is developing fast and equipping itself with the necessary institutional and regulatory infrastructure during the process. In time, there will be no market inadequacy in accommodating the issuance of bonds by local governments.

7.4.1. *Benchmark Yield Curve*

There are two types of securities used as a basis for constructing the yield curve in Malaysia. The first is the Malaysian Government

Securities (MGS) and the second is the Khazanah bonds. The advantage of using government securities as the benchmark yield curve is that they are free from default risk. The use of the MGS yield curve is not limited to government or quasi-government bonds. It is also widely used in determining bond prices and yield in other debt markets such as the corporate bond market.

There was a steady decline in the yields of bonds in all tenures, with the yield curves continuing to shift downwards throughout 2000–2001 (see Fig. 1). A case in point is the yield on 10-year MGS. The MGS has declined from around six percent in December 2000 to 4.5% in December 2001. In Malaysia, the MGS has not proven to be a good benchmark because of its irregular issuance. Furthermore, insurance companies and pension funds are legally required to invest in these securities. As their funds grow, their requirement to purchase government securities increases, and unless the rate of new issuance keeps pace, this leads to a greater proportion of these securities being locked up and not traded. Such artificial demand disturbs yields, and discourages independent assessment of other available investment opportunities (Bee C.K. and Choy T.C., 2001, pp. 395).

To overcome the inadequacy and weakness of the MGS as a benchmark yield curve, the government set up Khazanah Nasional Berhad in September 1997 to issue bonds, later known as Khazanah bonds. Khazanah bonds are an Islamic zero coupon bond, guaranteed by the government and issued quarterly by way of competitive

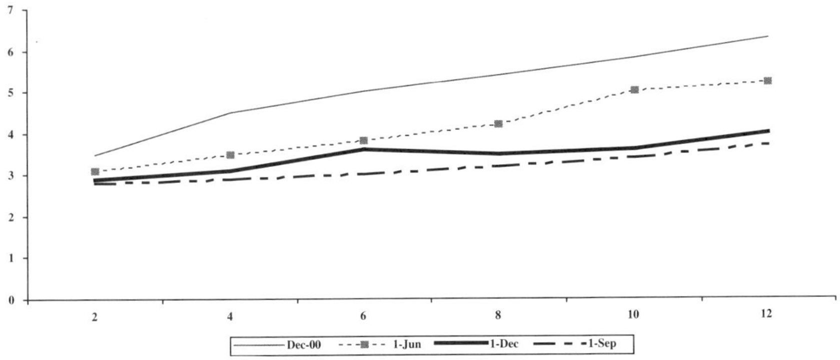

Fig. 1. MGS Yield Curves

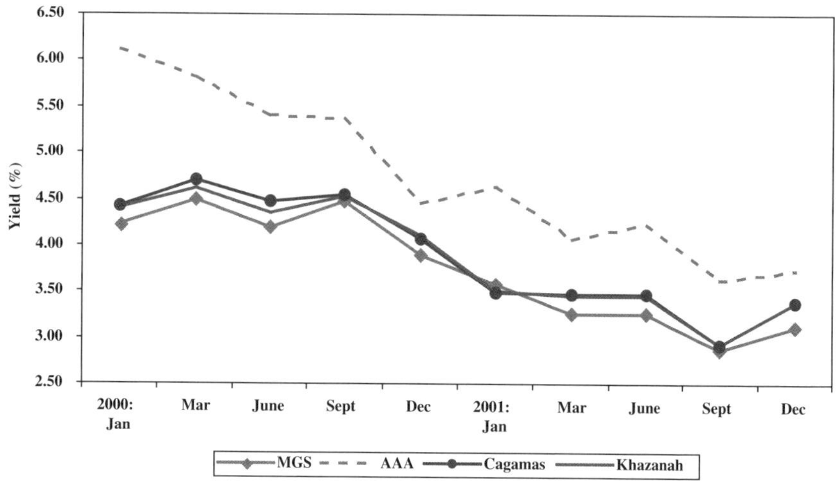

Fig. 2. Indicative Yields of Selected Three-year Bond

tender through principal dealers. Their covering maturity are 3, 5, 7 and 10 years with the issue size ranging from RM1 billion to RM2 billion.

As may be seen in Fig. 2, the three-year MGS fell from 4.02% at end-1999 to 3.07% at end-2000. The same trend was observed for the 10-year MGS which had fallen by 188 basis points during the same period. Yields for other papers such as the three-year Khazanah and Cagamas bonds also trended lower with narrowing yield differentials vis-à-vis the MGS papers. The yield differentials between the three-year Cagamas bonds and three-year MGS in the secondary market were about 6 to 18 points. The narrow spreads enabled Cagamas to continue to play its role in providing low cost funds to financial institutions. The declining yield trend was due to market expectations of further reduction in interest rates, continued ample liquidity in the market and the shift of investments from equities to bonds in an environment of greater volatility in the global stock markets. The yields fell further in September following further interest rate cuts in the United States and the reduction in the three-month BNM Intervention Rate. In December, however, some upward shifting of yields occurred due to the expectations of interest rates bottoming out, in line with the shifting of yield curves in the regional markets, following indications of a US economic recovery.

7.4.2. *Rating Agency*

All issues, offers or invitations that come within the scope of these Guidelines must be graded by a rating agency recognized by the Commission, unless otherwise allowed in writing by the Commission. An indicative rating must have been obtained by the issuer at the time of submission of the declarations and information to the Commission.

There are two credit rating agencies in Malaysia, namely the Rating Agency of Malaysia (RAM) and Malaysia Rating Corporation Berhad (MRCB). These two bodies perform their duties professionally and have gained the confidence of the players in the market. In February 1998, RAM in collaboration with Quant Shop Pty Ltd, an Australian company, constructed a bond index called RAM-Quantshop MGS. This index, which provides up-to-date information on the risk, return and inter-relationships of different MGS maturity terms, is a useful guide for portfolio managers to select securities and to allocate assets across broad markets in order to guide players in the market. Since April 1996, RAM publishes a monthly bond index which has been formulated to measure the overall performance of the corporate bond market in Malaysia.

Requests for ratings are high as corporations, especially those with strong credit ratings, shift to bonds as a cheaper funding option. In 2001, RAM completed 88 new ratings with the proposed gross issue valued at RM27.1 billion. Long-term issues represented 76 percent and 87 percent of the total number and gross issue values, respectively. Meanwhile, the MRCB completed 29 new corporate debt ratings with a total rated value of RM9.5 billion during the same year. The rated issues are generally concentrated in the AA and A categories, as companies with good credit quality take advantage of the relatively easy access to the bond market.

Of the total 192 rating views of existing long-term debt securities conducted by RAM and MARC in 2001, 153 were affirmations/reaffirmations, 14 issues were upgrades while 25 issues were downgrades. As at the end of 2001, the bulk of the long-term bonds were in the AA and A categories (see Fig. 3).

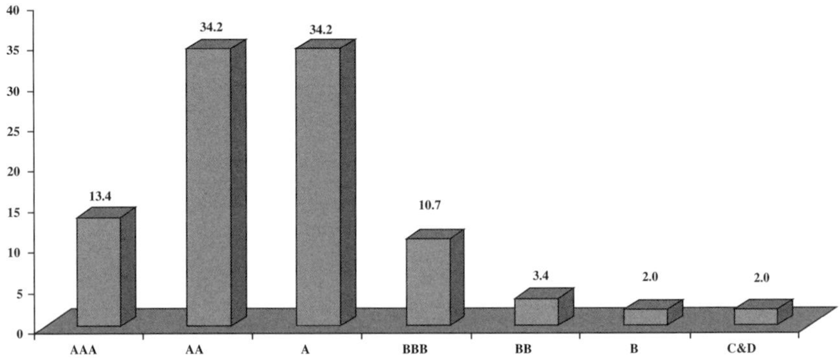

Fig. 3. Rating Distribution of Outstanding PDS as at December 2001

7.4.3. *Regulatory Structure*

There are two bodies responsible for private debt issuance in Malaysia, namely the BNM and Securities Commission (SC). The BNM regulates debt issues by private limited companies while the SC regulates debt issue by public and listed companies. In the case of public issue and listing purposes, the Registrar of Companies (ROC) and Kuala Lumpur Stock Exchange (KLSE) are involved.

The SC was established on 1st March 1993 and is aimed at consolidating and streamlining regulations, regulating and promoting development of the Malaysian capital market. Beginning 1st July 2000, the SC became the sole regulator of fund-raising activities in Malaysia. The ROC is a body under the Ministry of Domestic Trade and Consumer Affairs and has extensive powers under the Company Act 1965, which lays down the statutory requirements and policies on disclosure of information. This act has made it compulsory for a corporation to issue a prospectus before they raise money from the public. This Act further stipulates that the Prospectus must be registered with the ROC and it must contain an undertaking that the corporation will issue to that person a document acknowledging the indebtedness, after the acceptance of any money, deposit or loan.

In the case of local government bonds, the state government and Ministry of Finance will also be involved. The local government must obtain the approval of both the state government and Ministry of Finance before they can proceed with the necessary step of issuing bonds. This is stated Under Section 40, sub-section (4), Local Government

Act 1976 which states that, any such monies may be invested in securities in which trustees are empowered to invest, or in such other manner as authorized by the Minister of Finance. The issue of upper level government involvement, also covered under Section 4(1)(a)(b) of the Trustee Act 1949, states that the trustee may invest any trust funds in any government securities; any securities where the interest payment is guaranteed by Parliament or the federal government; and in fixed interest securities issued with the approval of the Treasury in Malaysia by any public authority established under federal or state law.

8. Conclusion

This study finds that the financial position of governments, particularly of the four local governments under study, is in surplus. However, this good financial outcome has been achieved through careful planning of their expenditure in parallel to their forecasted revenue. A fiscal surplus, however, is not necessarily an indicator of financial health. Because local governments have obeyed a hard budget constraint, and because revenue sources may not have been as buoyant as expenditure demand, there may be significant unmet needs as regards the provision of public services. Moreover, the limited flow of resources to the local authorities may make them passive with respect to opportunities which might appear anytime after the plan has been drafted. In other words, there is lack of flexibility and dynamism in local government expenditure in Malaysia.

This paper argues that bond financing could offer part of the solution to the financing problems of local governments. There are indications that good co-operation between state and local governments could lead to an ironing out of constitutional and legislative problems. The federal government would continue to be responsible for supervision and monitoring of borrowing by local authorities.

This programme, if implemented, will increase the number and volume of quality bonds and will be in line with the government's serious efforts in developing the Malaysian capital market. Furthermore, the opening up of doors to rating agencies, which require greater transparency on information disclosure, will bring another positive impact on the efficiency of services provided by the local governments.

The Malaysian bond market, though growing fast, is still relatively young and under-developed. In order to develop a bond market as a viable financing alternative for corporations seeking long-term funds, it is crucial to address the lack of benchmarks in bond pricing when the supply of new government papers in Malaysia's bond market dwindles. This is because the shortage in Malaysian Government Securities and its captive market can lead to an inefficient pricing of bond issues, which could cause companies to source funds from offshore markets. However, with the introduction of the Khazanah bonds, the benchmark problem has been greatly reduced.

In addition, the future of the Malaysian bond market ought to work towards increasing liquidity in the secondary market, as the lack of liquidity has led to investors demanding a higher liquidity risk premium which increases the funding cost of issuers. Investors are also discouraged from using bank guarantees, as it could mask the overall risk profile of the corporate bond market, as banks are assuming the credit risks of the companies they guarantee. Asset securitization should be promoted to allow companies to increase their liquidity and financing flexibility through the issuance of bonds backed by assets.

Clearly, bond financing is an appropriate option to consider as it could go a long way towards improving and increasing capital project finance by local governments in Malaysia. This new source of funds for infrastructure development would enable local authorities to play a role in the national goal of attaining industrialized status by the year 2020.

References

Bank Negara Malaysia, Annual Report, Various Issues.

Banking and Financial Institution Act, 1989.

Bee, C K, and T C Choy (eds.) (2001). Malaysia Bond Market, in, Government Bond Market Development in Asia, Y-H Kim, Asian Development Bank, Manila.

Cagamas Berhad, Annual Report, Various Years.

Economic Report, Ministry of Finance, Various Issues.

Fabozzi, F J (1997). The Handbook of Fixed Income Securities. New York: Irwin.

Financial Report, Shah Alam City Council, Various Issues.

Financial Report, Petaling Jaya Municipal council, Various Issues.

Financial Report, Ampang Jaya Municipal Council, Various Issues.

Financial Report, Klang Municipal Council, Various Issues.

Government of Malaysia (1971). Report of the Royal Committee to Study the Implication of the Report of Royal Commission of Enquiry to Investigate into the Working of local Authorities in West Malaysia, Government Printer, Kuala Lumpur.

Government of Malaysia (1970). Report of the Royal Commission of Enquiry to Investigate into the Working of Local Authorities in West Malaysia, Government Printer, Kuala Lumpur.

Government of Malaysia, Street, Drainage and Building Act 1974, Government Printer.

Government of Malaysia, Local Government Act, 1976, Laws of Malaysia (Act 171), Government Printer, Kuala Lumpur.

Ministry of Local Government, Sarawak (1983). A Brief History of Local Government in Sarawak, Kuching.

Ministry of Housing and Local Government, Laporan Program/Projek Pembangunan Jabatan Kerajaan Tempatan dan Kedudukan Kewangan bagi bulan September 1995.

Norashikin Abdul Hamid (2000). Guide to the Malaysian Bond Market, Network Press Sdn. Bhd., Kuala Lumpur.

Norris, M W (1980). Restructuring of local government division, *Malaysia Management Review*, 15(1).

Phang S N (1996). Non-Land Based Sources of Municipal Revenues. In *Increasing the Income of Cities: Tapping the Potential of Non-Land-Based Source of Municipal Revenues*, O P Mathur and N V Einsiedel (eds.), New Delhi: Centax Publications.

Phang S N, S Chee and Siti Rohani Yahya (1988). Local Authorities Revenue Equalisation System — A Study of Ten Sample Local Authorities in Peninsular Malaysia. A report submitted to the Ministry of Housing and Local Government, Kuala Lumpur.

Phang S N (1997). Financing Local Government in Malaysia, Universiti Malaya Press, Kuala Lumpur.

Phang S N (1997). Sistem Kerajaan Tempatan di Malaysia, Dewan Bahasa dan Pustaka, Kuala Lumpur.

Securities Commission Act, 1993.

Securities Commission (Amendment) Act, 2000.

Chapter XIV

Local Public Finance in the Philippines — Balancing Autonomy and Accountability

ROSARIO G. MANASAN

Philippine Institute for Development Studies

1. Introduction

Fiscal decentralization started in earnest in the Philippines in 1991 with the passage of the Local Government Code (LGC). After more than 15 years since then, it is an appropriate time to ask how the key features of this landmark legislation have contributed to or detracted from achieving the balance between local autonomy and accountability.

It is clear from the literature on fiscal decentralization that these two goals are not incompatible. In fact, real autonomy, in the sense of sub-national governments being able to link their spending decisions with their revenue/tax decisions, promotes fiscal responsibility. In the context of the ongoing debate in the Philippines, however, local autonomy has been equated by LGUs officials with the independence of LGUs from central government interference. As such, LGU officials have focused on securing even higher levels of block grants in order to address the widely perceived vertical fiscal imbalance. However, closer scrutiny of the problem indicates that greater tax decentralization coupled with a well designed fiscal equalization program would enhance the gains from decentralization while minimizing the risks of macro-instability.

The Local Government Code (Republic Act 7160) of 1991 and the Organic Act for Muslim Mindanao (Republic Act 6734) of 1989[1] jointly define central-local relations in the Philippines. The Organic Act for Muslim Mindanao granted the regional government powers that were previously held by the central government. It provides for the ARMM's expanded share and automatic retention of national internal revenue taxes collected in the region, significant discretion in development planning, and primacy in the delivery of basic services and the utilization and management of natural resources.

The Local Government Code in 1991 was a ground-breaking legislation that gave rise to a major shift in local governance. It consolidated and amended the Local Government Code of 1983, the Local Tax Code (Presidential Decree 231), and the Real Property Tax Code (Presidential Decree 464). The Code includes far-reaching provisions affecting the assignment of functions across different levels of government, the revenue sharing between the central and the local governments, the resource generation/utilization authorities of LGUs and the participation of civil society in various aspects of local governance. In total, these provisions aimed at providing the framework to support increased local autonomy.

2. Expenditure Assignment and Spending Distribution

2.1. *Legal Framework*

Prior to the implementation of the Local Government Code, the functions assigned to LGUs were limited to: the levy and collection of local taxes; the regulation of business activities in their jurisdiction; and the administration of services and facilities such as garbage collection, public cemeteries, public markets and slaughterhouses. The central government had the primary responsibility for agricultural planning and extension, construction and maintenance of local roads and public buildings and operation of high schools, hospitals and basic health facilities. The LGC also transfers to LGUs the principal responsibility for the delivery of basic services and the operation of facilities in the following areas: agricultural extension and research, social forestry, environmental

[1] This Law was subsequently amended in 2001.

management and pollution control, primary health care, hospital care, social welfare services, repair and maintenance of infrastructure facilities, water supply and communal irrigation and land use planning. In general, provinces are assigned functions that involve the inter-municipal provision of services, e.g., operation and maintenance of district and provincial hospitals whose catchment area covers more than one municipality. Municipalities are generally responsible for the delivery of frontline basic services, e.g., primary health care, construction, repair and maintenance of public elementary schools.

This program of devolution is substantial not only in terms of the sheer number of functions that were shifted but even more so in terms of number of personnel transferred (see Table 1) and the corresponding reductions implied in the budgets of affected central government agencies (see Table 2). The central government agencies that were most heavily affected by devolution were the Department of Agriculture

Table 1. Number of Devolved Personnel, 1992

	Number of Personnel Before Devolution	Number of Devolved Personnel	Ratio of Devolved Personnel to Pre-Devolution Personnel (%)
Department of Agriculture	29,638	17,673	59.6
Office of the Secretary	29,234	17,664	60.4
National Meat Inspection Commission	404	9	2.2
Department of Budget and Management	3,532	1,650	46.7
Department of Environment and Natural Resources	21,320	895	4.2
Department of Health	74,896	45,896	61.3
Department of Social Welfare and Development	6,932	4,144	59.8
Other Executive Offices	191	25	13.1
Philippines Gamefowl Commission	191	25	13.1
Total	136,509	70,283	51.5

Source: 1993 National Expenditure Program, Regional Coordination Staff.

Table 2. Agency Budgets and Devolution, 1992 (in million pesos)

	Budget Before Devolution[a]	Devolved Budget[b]	Ratio of Devolved Budget to Pre-Devolution Budget (%)
Department of Agriculture	5,210.0	1,160.7	22.3
Department of Budget and Management	465.4	193.2	41.5
Department of Environment and Natural Resources	1,941.8	87.6	4.5
Department of Health	9,991.4	4,079.6	40.8
Department of Social Welfare and Development	1,320.7	742.7	56.2
Philippine Gamefowl Commission	15.2	0.6	4.1
Total	18,944.5	6,264.4	33.1

[a] Based on the 1992 Expenditure Program.
[b] Based on cost of devolved functions as allocated notionally by DBM to individual LGUs.
Source: 1993 National Expenditure Program.

(DA), Department of Health (DOH) and the Department of Social Welfare and Development (DSWD).

It should be stressed that under Executive Order 507[2] many health programs, like immunization, control of communicable diseases, provision of drugs and medicines to devolved facilities and operation of hospitals in the NCR, continue to be funded by the central government under the budget of the Department of Health (DOH). This implies that the central government budget for these activities was not devolved in the sense of being "disallowed" in the budget of the DOH in the post-devolution period. Similarly, the central government continues up to this day to allocate monies for the school building program (now called the Basic Education Facilities Fund) despite the fact that construction of school buildings is a function that has been devolved to LGUs. This

[2] Executive Order 507 defined the actual implementation of the devolution program mandated under the Local Government Code and which guided DBM as to which programs and activities will be "excluded" or "disallowed" from the budgets of devolved central government agencies post-devolution.

practice has serious implications for how the cost of devolved functions is determined, which is an important first step in gauging the adequacy of the inter-governmental transfers to LGUs.

The Organic Act for Muslim Mindanao transfers to the regional government of the Autonomous Region of Muslim Mindanao (ARMM) all powers, functions and responsibilities heretofore being exercised by the central government except (1) foreign affairs, (2) national defense, (3) postal service, (4) fiscal and monetary policy, (5) administration of justice, (6) quarantine, (7) citizenship, naturalization and immigration, (8) general auditing, civil service and elections, (9) foreign trade, (10) maritime, land and air transportation and communications that affect areas outside the ARMM, and (11) patents, trademarks, trade names and copyrights. Consequently, the regional government is primarily responsible for the implementation of programs and projects on: agriculture; agrarian reform, education; environment and natural resources; health; tourism, trade and industry; social welfare; industrial peace, protection of workers welfare and promotion of employment; promotion of cooperatives; provision of assistance to local government units; and development and regulation of cooperatives.

2.2. *Assessment*

The key features of expenditure assignment that would enhance the likelihood of efficiency gains from fiscal decentralization are: (1) appropriate assignment of expenditure responsibilities across levels of government, and (2) unambiguous and clear assignment of functions.

On the one hand, the assignment of functions to the different levels of government is guided by the decentralization theorem which states that "each public service should be provided by the jurisdiction having control over the minimum geographic area that would internalize the benefits and costs of such provision" (Oates 1972). On the other hand, the lack of clarity in assigning the expenditure responsibility gives rise to disputes among the different levels of governments and tends to blur accountability across levels of local government (McLure and Martinez-Vazquez, 2002).

Consistency with decentralization theorem. The following discussion will focus on the assessment of expenditure assignment under the Local Government Code of 1991. The expenditure assignment under the Organic Act of the ARMM is reviewed in Box 1.

Box 1. Assessment of Expenditure Assignment Under the Organic Act of ARMM

A comparison of RA 6734 and RA 7160 shows that non-ARMM LGUs are treated on an almost equal footing as the regional government of ARMM in terms of expenditure assignment, although the functions and responsibilities assigned to the regional government of ARMM are slightly broader than those given to non-ARMM LGUs. In particular, the regional government of the ARMM is charged with the provision of agrarian reform and education services, the promotion of employment and workers' welfare and the promotion of trade and industry while non-ARMM LGUs are not.

On the other hand, ARMM-LGUs and non-ARMM LGUs are treated asymmetrically in terms of the expenditure responsibilities that are assigned to them. This is so because the regional government of the ARMM has not devolved any of their functions to the LGUs within their jurisdiction even if RA 6734 allows them to do so. Thus, ARMM-LGUs are not responsible for any of the devolved activities that have been transferred to non-ARMM LGUs under the Local Government Code of 1991.

The devolution of expenditure responsibilities to local governments under the LGC has been found to be generally consistent with the decentralization theorem (Loehr and Manasan, 1999). The activities devolved are those that can be provided at lower levels of government. Few of them have benefits that spillover outside the territorial jurisdiction of the LGU except perhaps those related to environmental management. However, the Code permits LGUs to group themselves and consolidate/coordinate their efforts, services and resources for purposes that are commonly beneficial to them (Section 23). Thus, there are many cases when smaller LGUs join together to carry out specific responsibilities (like coastal resource management, solid waste management, water supply development and distribution) when economies of scale and/or externalities make such cooperative undertakings appropriate. This development has contributed to the emergence of metropolitan arrangements in many places around the country (Mercado and Manasan, 1999).

One important exception to the application of the decentralization theorem in the Philippines is education. The primary responsibility for the provision of basic education rests with the central government although the construction and maintenance of school buildings is devolved to LGUs under the Local Government Code.[3]

In contrast, basic education is administered by local governments in many countries. Three arguments are generally offered why primary education should be decentralized: (1) the provision of education services is spread out geographically; (2) smaller schools are generally found to provide higher quality education and (3) direct involvement of parents and the local community in schools is observed to be a beneficial determinant of school quality (Ahmad *et al.*, 1997). On the other hand, the decentralization of education finance tends to lead to large differences in the quality of educational services and many countries take steps to enforce minimum standards of access and quality even as they decentralize the delivery of education services.

Clarity in expenditure assignment. Section 17(b) of the Local Government Code provides an explicit and clear delineation of functions across levels of governments except perhaps in the area of environment and natural resource management.[4] However, Section 17(c) allows central government agencies to continue to implement devolved public works and infrastructure projects and other facilities, programs and services provided these are "*funded by the national government under the annual General Appropriations Act, other special laws, pertinent executive orders, and those wholly or partially funded from foreign sources.*" In line with this, Executive Order 53 mandates national government agencies (NGAs) to retain management control over all foreign-assisted projects and/or nationally funded projects even if the same involve devolved activities. At the same time, the Code and its Implementing Rules and Regulations failed to define the mechanisms through which the central government can direct assistance to LGUs under Section 17(f) which allows the national government or the next higher level of local government unit to "provide or *augment* the basic services and

---

[3] One of the reasons for not devolving education can be traced to the fact that teachers serve on the Board of Election Inspectors. That is, the teachers man the precincts during elections and play an important role in the counting of votes. During debate prior to the enactment of the Local Government Code, concerns were reportedly raised that teachers could overly politicize elections at the local level.

[4] To wit, the Code gives municipalities responsibility for the implementation of community-based forestry and watershed projects but allows the Department of Environment and Natural Resources (DENR) to retain supervision and control over such projects.

facilities assigned to a lower level of local government unit when such services or facilities are not made available or, if made available, are inadequate to meet the requirements of its inhabitants".

Because many of the so-called devolved NGAs are made accountable for the overall outcome in their respective areas, they deem it their responsibility to direct LGU behavior in support of national objectives.[5] Thus, most of them tend to make full use of Section 17(f) of the Code and EO 53 regarding augmentation (Loehr and Manasan, 1999). Gonzalez (1996) goes even further to say that the prevailing regulatory framework effectively permits the existence of a two-track delivery system, where both NGAs and LGUs can initiate devolved activities. In effect, then, Section 17(c) and (f) obfuscate what initially appears to be a clear cut assignment of expenditure responsibilities.

Loehr and Manasan (1999) also point out that Congressmen are enamored by Section 17(f) of the Code as it allows them easy access to pork barrel funds by the simple act of inserting a special provision in the General Appropriations Act which ordains that monies from such augmentation funds can only be released for "projects that are identified by members of Congress." Because of these incentives on the part of both national government agencies and Congress to retain funding and implementation of devolved activities at the center, the budgets of devolved central government agencies grew disproportionately relative to the IRA. In particular, the IRA grew by 15 percent yearly on the average during 1994–1997 while the budget of the Department of Agriculture expanded by 48 percent, that of the Department of Health by 25 percent, and that of the Department of Social Welfare and Development by 22 percent. Capuno *et al.* (2001) estimate that central government agencies (specifically, the DepEd, DOH, DPWH and DILG) spent significant amounts on devolved activities in 1995–1999 (see Table 3).

Still a continuing source of irritant between the central government and LGUs is the propensity of the central government to pass on so-called unfunded mandates to LGUs. The most important of these unfunded mandates are the implementation of the salary standardization law and the provision of additional benefits to health workers

[5] For instance, DOH is accountable for the overall health status of the country in the same way that the DENR is accountable for overall environmental and natural resource management results.

Table 3. Budget Allocations of Selected Central Government Agencies for Devolved Activities, 1995–99 (in billion pesos)

	DepEd	DOH	DILG	DPWH	Total
1995	4.7	0.6	0.2	4.7	10.2
1996	4.2	0.5	0.2	10.6	15.5
1997	4.7	0.4	0.6	10.8	16.5
1998	2.9	0.3	0.2	30.6	34.0
1999	2.8	0.5	0.1	4.0	7.4

Source: Capuno *et al.* (2001), Table 1a, Table 1b, Table 1c, Table 1d and Table 1e.

under the Magna Carta for Health Workers.[6] LGUs are also expected to provide budgetary support (either in the form of additional personnel benefits or outlays for MOOE) to many central government agencies operating at the local level like the police, fire protection bureau, and local courts.

2.3. *Trend and Composition of LGU Expenditures, 1991–2001*

Central-local expenditure distribution. Consistent with the devolution program, total LGU expenditure doubled relative to the GNP and relative to total general government expenditure. Total LGU spending increased from an average of 1.6% of GNP in 1985–1991 to 3.5% of GNP in 1992–2003. Similarly, the share of LGUs in total general government expenditure net of debt service rose from an average of 11 percent in the pre-Code period to an average of 23.1 percent in the post-Code period (see Table 4).

The data in Table 5 document the changing distribution of government spending on various sectors across different levels of government over time. It confirms that many devolved functions continue to be shared by the LGUs with the central government in a significant way. However, in line with the transfer of functions to LGUs mandated under the Local Government Code, the share of local governments in total general government spending (net of debt service)

[6] The salary standardization law mandates increases in the salaries of all government employees. In the Philippines, most government agencies, including local governments, follow a uniform compensation structure.

Table 4. LGU Expenditure Relative to GNP and to General Government Expenditure

	Ratio of LGU Expenditure to GNP (%)	Ratio of LGU Expenditure to General Gov't Expenditure. Net of Debt Service
1985	1.54	12.01
1987	1.44	10.55
1989	1.53	11.10
1991	1.89	12.65
1993	2.72	19.99
1995	3.53	21.84
1997	3.75	21.45
1999	3.67	23.05
2001	3.75	25.73
2003	3.56	26.21
Average		
1985–1991	1.61	11.00
1992–2003	3,493.49	23.10

doubled from 12.6% in 1991 to 25.6% in 2001. In particular, the subnational government share in general government spending registered substantial increases in the areas of housing and community development (from 33 percent in 1991 to 81 percent in 2001), health (from 10 to 56 percent), other economic services (from 57 to 91 percent), water resource development and flood control (from 13 to 49 percent), agriculture (from 3 to 16 percent), power and energy (from 4 to 14 percent), environment and natural resource management (from 0 to 10 percent), and education (from 2 to 8 percent). It is remarkable, however, that the share of LGUs in total general government spending on social welfare and in the labor and employment sector has not changed much (from 11 percent in 1991 to 12 percent in 2001) despite the transfer of about 60 percent of pre-devolution DSWD personnel to LGUs. The same is true of the transportation and communication sector where the share of LGUs has grown only minimally (from 15 to 17 percent) although the Local Government Code calls for the devolution of the construction and maintenance of all local infrastructure facilities and the provision of local telecommunication services to LGUs.

Table 5. Percent Distribution of NG and LGU Expenditures, by Type of Government

Sectors	1991			1995			2001		
	Total	NG	LGU	Total	NG	LGU	Total	NG	LGU
Grand total	100.0	91.0	9.0	100.0	82.0	18.0	100.0	80.2	19.8
Total economic services	100.0	88.5	11.5	100.0	81.5	18.5	100.0	77.1	22.9
Agrarian reform	100.0	100.0	0.0	100.0	100.0	0.0	100.0	100.0	0.0
Agriculture	100.0	96.6	3.4	100.0	86.1	13.9	100.0	84.1	15.9
Natural resources	100.0	100.0	0.0	100.0	94.6	5.4	100.0	89.8	10.2
Industry	100.0	100.0	0.0	100.0	100.0	0.0	100.0	100.0	0.0
Trade	100.0	100.0	0.0	100.0	100.0	0.0	100.0	100.0	0.0
Tourism	100.0	100.0	0.0	100.0	100.0	0.0	100.0	100.0	0.0
Power and energy	100.0	95.6	4.4	100.0	93.0	7.0	100.0	86.4	13.6
Water resource devt./flood control	100.0	86.6	13.4	100.0	82.5	17.5	100.0	51.0	49.0
Transportation and communication	100.0	84.7	15.3	100.0	82.5	17.5	100.0	82.5	17.5
Other economic services	100.0	42.5	57.5	100.0	29.3	70.7	100.0	8.7	91.3
Total social services	100.0	93.2	6.8	100.0	82.2	17.8	100.0	80.6	19.4

(Continued)

Table 5. (*Continued*)

Sectors	1991			1995			2001		
	Total	NG	LGU	Total	NG	LGU	Total	NG	LGU
Education	100.0	97.5	2.5	100.0	92.6	7.4	100.0	91.6	8.4
Health	100.0	90.3	9.7	100.0	51.5	48.5	100.0	44.2	55.8
Soc. Welfare, labor, other soc. serv.	100.0	89.3	10.7	100.0	88.2	11.8	100.0	88.0	12.0
Housing, community development	100.0	67.4	32.6	100.0	46.0	54.0	100.0	19.1	80.9
General public service	100.0	74.2	25.8	100.0	64.8	35.2	100.0	61.2	38.8
Public administration	100.0	60.7	39.3	100.0	49.9	50.1	100.0	42.1	57.9
Peace and order	100.0	99.3	0.7	100.0	98.4	1.6	100.0	98.9	1.1
Others	100.0	75.4	24.6	100.0	0.0	100.0	100.0	19.4	80.6
Defense	100.0	100.0	0.0	100.0	100.0	0.0	100.0	100.0	0.0
Debt service	100.0	99.8	0.2	100.0	97.8	2.2	100.0	98.2	1.8
Total net of debt service	100.0	87.4	12.6	100.0	78.2	21.8	100.0	74.4	25.6

This came about because the central government (through the Department of Public Works and Highways) continues to be heavily involved in the construction and maintenance of various local infrastructures largely because of the inclusion of pork barrel allocations for members of Congress in the DPWH budget. At the same time, spending on the transportation/communication sub-sector of all LGUs in the aggregate remained at pre-Code levels in relative terms. On the one hand, the devolution of local infrastructure was not accompanied by the transfer of personnel from the national government to the LGUs and, therefore, LGUs were not as hard pressed to increase their spending on local infrastructure as they were in the health and social welfare subsectors. On the other hand, as indicated below, this development is linked to the mismatch in the distribution of resources and expenditure responsibilities across levels of local governments.

For instance, the infrastructure spending of cities (which were more favored as a group in terms of the net fiscal transfer) went up in relative terms in the post-Code period largely because they had the fiscal capacity to do so. In contrast, that of provinces and municipalities (which were losers in terms of the net fiscal transfer) declined.

Distribution of LGU spending across levels of local government. In 1991, prior to the implementation of the Local Government Code, provinces contributed 29 percent, municipalities 40.1% and cities 30.9% of total local government expenditure (see Table 6). Under the devolution program, provinces absorbed 47.5%, municipalities 48.1%, cities 4.3% of the total cost of functions devolved to said levels of government (see Table 6). Given the relative importance of the provincial and municipal levels in terms of both pre-Code spending levels and the cost of devolved functions, the dramatic expansion in the share of cities and the corresponding contraction in the share of provinces and municipalities in total LGU expenditure in the post-Code period is unexpected. It is perhaps best explained by the distribution of revenue across levels of local government in the post-Code period. Moreover, this trend appears to have gained in intensity over time.

Note the contraction in the share of provinces and municipalities in spending on the economic services sector. This development is largely driven by the growing share of cities in total LGU spending on the transportation/communication sub-sector in the post-Code period. This dominates the expansion in the share of provinces in total LGU spending

Table 6. Distribution or LGU Expenditures Across Levels of Local Government by Function

	1991				2001			
Sectors	Local	Prov.	Mun.	Cities	Local	Prov.	Mun.	Cities
Grand total	100.0	29.0	40.1	30.9	100.0	23.9	34.8	41.3
Total economic services	100.0	35.4	33.7	30.9	100.0	27.6	30.2	42.2
Agriculture	100.0	46.9	8.2	44.9	100.0	33.5	48.6	17.9
Natural resources	—	—	—	—	100.0	21.4	4.5	74.1
Power and energy	100.0	16.2	16.3	67.5	100.0	4.2	18.3	77.5
Water resource devt. & flood control	100.0	37.0	49.3	13.7	100.0	6.8	64.0	29.2
Transportation and communication	100.0	40.4	31.1	28.5	100.0	24.9	19.4	55.7
Other economic services	100.0	15.2	51.6	33.2	100.0	30.8	37.0	32.2
Total social services	100.0	33.5	24.1	42.4	100.0	27.7	26.8	45.5
Education	100.0	12.9	41.8	45.3	100.0	17.6	18.4	64.0
Health	100.0	19.8	16.7	63.5	100.0	42.3	28.8	28.9
Soc. Welfare, labor, other soc. serv.	100.0	19.2	32.1	48.7	100.0	21.4	44.3	34.3
Housing, community development	100.0	68.9	12.8	18.3	100.0	13.1	26.3	60.6
General public service	100.0	22.4	51.0	26.6	100.0	19.1	45.0	35.8
Public administration	100.0	22.6	51.2	26.2	100.0	19.3	45.3	35.4
Peace and order	100.0	1.6	25.5	72.9	100.0	1.7	19.2	79.0
Others	100.0	30.1	44.9	24.9	100.0	25.0	25.9	49.2
Debt service	100.0	10.1	15.4	74.5	100.0	22.0	18.4	59.6
Total net of debt service	100.0	29.1	40.3	30.5	100.0	23.9	35.2	40.9

on the environment/natural resource management sub-sector and the increase in the share of municipalities in total LGU spending on the agriculture and the water resource development sub-sectors. Similarly, the share of provinces in total LGU spending on the social services sector declined despite the absorption of a large number of personnel in the health sub-sector and increased spending on social welfare and housing/community development. In contrast, the share of both municipalities and cities in expenditure on the social services sector increased.

Distribution of LGU spending by function. With more resources at their disposal, total LGU expenditures rose from an average of 1.6% of GNP in 1985–1991 to 3.6% of GNP in 1993–2001 (see Table 7). The increase in total LGU expenditure was particularly rapid in 1993–1995 but started to taper off in 1996. It is noteworthy that LGU expenditure at all levels of local government (with the exception of cities) declined relative to GNP in 1998 and 1999 following the onset of the Asian financial crisis. It bounced back in 2000 but contracted once again in 2001 due to the adverse impact of fiscal restraints on LGU financing.

The mandated transfer to LGUs of functions previously discharged by national government agencies caused a major shift in the size and composition of LGU budgets. Amongst the major sectors, the social services sector posted the fastest rate of growth in 1991–2001, 10.8% yearly by comparison with a total growth of 8.2%. In contrast, the general public services sector and the economic services sector grew at a slower pace, and the share of the social services sector to total LGU expenditure expanded.

The increase in LGU spending on social services between 1991 and 2001 reflected a tripling of health and education expenditures relative to GNP (see Table 7). These hefty increases in LGU spending on health and social welfare were largely due to the fact that the LGUs had very little discretion but to absorb the cost of devolved health and social welfare personnel, which accounted for more than half of the total cost of all devolved personnel. On the other hand, higher LGU expenditures on education and housing/community development in the post-Code period largely reflect the higher priority that local officials assigned to these sectors in the more decentralized regime. This is because LGUs were not locked into previously set (i.e., pre-devolution) central government expenditure levels in these sectors precisely because LGUs did not have to absorb devolved personnel.

Table 7. Ratio to GNP of Local Government Expenditures (in percent)

All LGUs	1991	1993*	1995	1997	1998	1999	2000	2001
Grand total	1.9	2.7	3.5	3.8	3.7	3.7	3.9	3.8
Total economic services	0.7	0.7	1.0	1.0	0.9	0.9	1.0	0.9
Agrarian reform	0.0	0.0	0.0	0.0	0.0	0.0	0.0	0.0
Agriculture	0.0	0.1	0.1	0.1	0.1	0.1	0.1	0.1
Natural resources	0.0	0.0	0.0	0.0	0.0	0.0	0.0	0.0
Industry	0.0	0.0	0.0	0.0	0.0	0.0	0.0	0.0
Trade	0.0	0.0	0.0	0.0	0.0	0.0	0.0	0.0
Tourism	0.0	0.0	0.0	0.0	0.0	0.0	0.0	0.0
Power and energy	0.0	0.0	0.0	0.0	0.0	0.0	0.0	0.0
Water resource devt. & flood control	0.0	0.0	0.0	0.0	0.0	0.0	0.0	0.0
Transportation and communication	0.5	0.4	0.5	0.5	0.4	0.4	0.5	0.4
Other economic services	0.1	0.2	0.3	0.3	0.3	0.3	0.4	0.4
Total social services	0.3	0.8	0.9	1.0	1.0	1.0	1.0	1.0
Education	0.1	0.2	0.3	0.3	0.3	0.3	0.3	0.3
Health	0.1	0.3	0.4	0.5	0.5	0.4	0.5	0.4
Soc. Welfare, labor, other soc. serv.	0.1	0.1	0.1	0.1	0.1	0.1	0.1	0.1
Housing, community development	0.1	0.2	0.2	0.2	0.2	0.2	0.2	0.2
General public service	0.8	1.1	1.4	1.5	1.5	1.5	1.6	1.5
Public administration	0.8	1.1	1.3	1.5	1.4	1.5	1.6	1.5
Peace and order	0.0	0.0	0.0	0.0	0.0	0.0	0.0	0.0
Others	0.1	0.1	0.2	0.2	0.2	0.2	0.3	0.2
Debt service	0.0	0.0	0.1	0.1	0.1	0.1	0.1	0.1

* Adjusted for DOH & DA advances.

Source: Annex Table 2.

Aggregate LGU spending on the social services sector registered a general upward trend in 1991–2001 when measured relative to GNP and in real per capita terms. However, some stagnation (especially with respect to health expenditures) is evident in 1998–2001 when either of these measures is used (see Tables 7 and 8).

These movements are common across all levels of local government and appear to be related to the fiscal difficulties faced by LGUs during this period.[7] This may be a cause of concern considering that provinces and municipalities are primarily responsible for the delivery of basic health services. It highlights the importance of designing a grant program aimed at ensuring that LGUs provide education and health services that are consistent with minimum standard levels of access and quality.

The transportation/communication sub-sector has borne the brunt of the contraction in the budget share of the economic services sector. With the devolution of agricultural extension and environment/natural resource management, the expenditure share of these sub-sectors rose somewhat between 1991 and 2001. In contrast, the share of the transportation communication sub-sector in total LGU expenditure dipped from 26.9% in 1991 to 10.2% in 2001.

Although aggregate LGU spending on transportation communication was fairly stable at 0.4% of GNP in the post-Code period, this situation conceals variations across the different levels of local government. The expenditures on the transportation/communication sub-sector of provincial and municipal governments (when measured relative to total LGU spending or to GNP) have been on a downtrend since 1997. However, the opposite is true in the case of cities.

These developments appear to be linked to the mismatch in the distribution of resources and expenditure responsibilities across levels of local governments. This is a cause of concern considering the robust and strong association between economic growth and infrastructure spending. Given that the Code assigns primary responsibility for the construction and maintenance of local infrastructure to local governments, this trend also points to the increasing disparity in economic development across levels of local government. It likewise underscores the importance of creating a suitable regulatory framework for encouraging

[7] While the IRA share of LGUs declined relative to GNP in 1998 and then again in 2001, own-source LGU revenue has been on a downtrend since 1998.

Table 8. Per Capita Local Government Expenditures, in 1985 Prices (Including Transfers to NG)

All LGUs	1991	1993*	1995	1997	1998	1999	2000	2001
Grand total	218	311	426	488	466	474	518	502
Total economic services	78	79	118	127	112	119	130	123
Agriculture	2	11	13	14	16	15	15	15
Natural resources	0	1	2	2	1	3	3	3
Power and energy	3	2	3	3	3	3	3	3
Water resource devt. & flood contr.	1	1	1	2	1	1	1	1
Transportation and communication	59	41	58	62	51	56	60	51
Other economic services	13	23	41	44	40	42	46	50
Total social services	34	87	113	131	129	125	133	134
	0	0	0	0	0	0	0	0
Education	8	22	31	39	40	35	38	38
Health	9	40	49	59	59	58	60	57
Soc. welfare, labor, other soc. serv.	6	7	9	11	11	11	12	12
Housing, community development	11	18	25	21	20	21	22	26
General public service	97	127	164	191	186	189	209	204
Public administration	96	124	161	189	184	188	208	202
Peace and order	1	2	2	1	1	2	2	2
Others	8	15	22	26	29	31	35	30
Debt. service	2	3	10	13	10	10	11	11

* Adjusted for DOH & DA advances.

Source: Annex Table 4.

private sector participation in infrastructure (through BOT and joint ventures) at the local level as well as the need for an appropriate grants program for LGU capital investments.

Distribution of LGU expenditure by economic category. In the aggregate, LGU spending on personal services (PS) grew from an average of 0.7% of GNP in 1985–1991 to an average of 1.6% of GNP in 1992–2003 (see Table 9). Because it grew at the same pace as total LGU expenditures, its share in total LGU spending remained fairly stable at 46 percent in the pre-Code period as well as the post-Code period, making it the most important expenditure item according to economic category (see Table 10).

The salary structure applicable to mandatory LGU positions is set by the Compensation and Position Classification Act (CPCA) of 1989. The CPCA in tandem with the Code provisions on mandatory positions restrict LGUs' ability to re-align their outlays for personal services in consonance with their specific needs and circumstances. In some cases, these restrictions impose a heavy fiscal burden on LGUs (particularly in the case of provinces and municipalities), and squeeze the ability of these LGUs' to fund maintenance and capital outlays. In other cases, they make it difficult for low income LGUs to retain personnel, particularly in the health sector.

Although the Local Government Code imposes a ceiling on PS spending of LGUs (45–55 percent of total regular income depending on LGU's income class), many exemptions are allowed in determining compliance with this mandate. Thus, aggregate LGU spending on personal services was, on the average, 53.9% of total LGU regular income in 1992–2003 (see Table 10). The share was highest for municipalities (61.7%) and clearly exceeded the cap on personal services.

Personal services expenditure as recorded in the financial statements of LGUs tends to underestimate the amounts that LGUs actually spend on compensation of personnel because of the practice of charging the salaries and wages of contractual employees hired under so-called "job orders" or "service contracts" against MOOE or CO (for development projects). Some LGUs report that this practice is no longer allowed under the new government accounting system (NGAS) but other sample LGUs report that this practice is still in effect. For instance, a number of the LGUs report that 15–20 percent of their MOOE is actually used to pay for contractual personnel. Still other LGUs charge some

Table 9. Ratio to GNP of Local Government by Object

	Average								
	1985–1991	1992–2003	1991	1993	1995	1997	1999	2001	2003
A. All LGUs									
Grand total	1.6	3.5	1.9	2.7	3.5	3.8	3.7	3.8	3.4
Personal services	0.7	1.6	0.8	1.3	1.6	1.8	1.8	1.7	1.4
Maintenance & other operating expenses	0.6	1.2	0.6	0.9	1.2	1.2	1.3	1.3	1.4
Capital outlays	0.3	0.7	0.4	0.5	0.8	0.7	0.6	0.7	0.6
B. All Provinces									
Grand total	0.5	0.8	0.5	0.7	0.9	0.9	0.8	0.9	0.8
Personal services	0.2	0.4	0.2	0.3	0.4	0.4	0.4	0.4	0.3
Maintenance & other operating expenses	0.2	0.3	0.2	0.3	0.3	0.3	0.3	0.3	0.3
Capital outlays	0.1	0.1	0.1	0.1	0.1	0.2	0.1	0.2	0.1

(Continued)

Table 9. (*Continued*)

	Average								
	1985–1991	1992–2003	1991	1993	1995	1997	1999	2001	2003
C. All Municipalities									
Grand total	0.6	1.3	0.8	1.2	1.3	1.4	1.3	1.3	1.2
Personal services	0.3	0.7	0.4	0.6	0.7	0.8	0.8	0.7	0.6
Maintenance & other operating expenses	0.2	0.4	0.3	0.4	0.4	0.4	0.4	0.4	0.4
Capital outlays	0.1	0.2	0.2	0.2	0.2	0.2	0.1	0.2	0.1
D. All Cities									
Grand total	0.5	1.4	0.6	0.9	1.3	1.5	1.5	1.5	1.4
Personal services	0.3	0.5	0.3	0.3	0.5	0.6	0.6	0.6	0.5
Maintenance & other operating expenses	0.2	0.5	0.2	0.3	0.5	0.5	0.6	0.6	0.6
Capital outlays	0.1	0.3	0.1	0.2	0.4	0.4	0.4	0.4	0.3

Table 10. Percent Distribution of Local Government Expenditures by Type of Expenditure (in percent)

	Average								
	1985–1991	1992–2003	1991	1993**	1995	1997	1999	2001	2003
A. All LGUs									
Grand total	100.0	100.0	100.0	100.0	100.0	100.0	100.0	100.0	100.0
Personal services	46.5	46.4	44.7	46.6	45.3	47.3	48.1	45.5	49.2
Maintenance & other operating expense	37.1	35.2	32.8	34.5	33.4	33.0	34.3	35.5	34.1
Capital outlays	16.4	18.4	22.4	18.9	21.4	19.7	17.5	19.1	16.7
Ratio of PS to reg. income in previous year	63.9	53.9	66.0	72.8	55.4	62.4	57.8	50.4	54.2
B. All Provinces									
Grand total	100.0	100.0	100.0	100.0	100.0	100.0	100.0	100.0	100.0
Personal services	44.2	47.7	41.6	49.9	48.4	48.8	50.8	45.1	42.1
Maintenance & other operating expense	36.9	35.7	35.2	37.3	35.9	33.8	33.9	35.4	42.8
Capital outlays	18.9	16.5	23.3	12.8	15.6	17.4	15.3	19.6	15.1
Ratio of PS to reg. income in previous year	75.5	55.2	75.9	87.1	58.4	67.5	59.1	50.1	41.2

(Continued)

Table 10. (*Continued*)

	Average								
	1985–1991	1992–2003	1991	1993**	1995	1997	1999	2001	2003
C. All Municipalities									
Grand total	100.0	100.0	100.0	100.0	100.0	100.0	100.0	100.0	100.0
Personal services	45.9	55.0	46.1	51.5	52.6	55.7	57.9	55.3	50.8
Maintenance & other operating expense	39.2	32.0	33.3	32.4	31.3	30.8	31.0	31.1	36.9
Capital outlays	14.9	13.0	20.5	16.1	16.1	13.5	11.2	13.6	12.3
Ratio of PS to reg. income in previous year	63.6	61.7	68.4	80.7	62.4	71.8	68.8	57.6	48.4
D. All Cities									
Grand total	100.0	100.0	100.0	100.0	100.0	100.0	100.0	100.0	100.0
Personal services	49.4	37.8	45.8	37.4	35.9	38.4	38.1	37.5	34.2
Maintenance & other operating expense	34.6	37.8	30.0	35.1	33.8	34.5	37.6	39.2	43.7
Capital outlays	16.0	24.4	24.2	27.4	30.3	27.1	24.3	23.4	22.1
Ratio of PS to reg. income in previous year	57.1	45.4	57.1	53.8	45.8	50.5	47.0	43.8	36.1

of their "excess" personal services against the accounts of public enterprises such as public markets.

The share of capital outlays (CO) in aggregate LGU expenditures expanded from an average of 16.4% in 1985–1991 to an average of 18.4% in 1992–2003. This development is largely driven by the dramatic growth in the capital outlays of cities. There is a squeeze not only on MOOE but also on capital outlays in the case of municipalities and provinces in the post-Code period (see Table 10). Nonetheless, because the LGU expenditure pie has grown bigger relative to GNP, aggregate LGU spending on capital outlays increased from an average of 0.3% of GNP in the pre-Code period to an average of 0.7% of GNP in the post-Code period.

3. Revenue Assignment and Distribution

3.1. *Legal Framework*

Tax assignment in the ARMM is described in Box 2.

Box 2. Tax Assignment in ARMM

Under RA 6733, the regional government of the ARMM was authorized to levy all types of taxes with the exception of the income tax and customs duties. In practice, however, the regional government of the ARMM does not touch any of the taxes that the central government levies. Instead, it has chosen to impose a supplementary rate (i.e., a surcharge) on taxes that are typically levied by provincial governments under the Local Government Code like the real property tax, the sand and gravel tax, the amusement tax, the professional tax, and the franchise tax. In this sense, the amended Organic Act of the ARMM (Republic Act 9054) simply formalizes the symmetrical treatment of the ARMM and the LGUs with regards to the limitations on their taxing powers.

The various taxes that are assigned to the different levels of local government are summarized in Table 11. Under the Local Government Code, only provinces and cities are authorized to levy the real property tax but the proceeds from this tax are shared with lower levels of governments (i.e., municipalities and barangays in the case of the province and barangays in the case of the city). In addition, both provinces and

Table 11. Tax Assignment in Cities, Provinces, and Municipalities

Subject	Cities	Prov.	Muni's	Brgy.
On real property transfers	□	□		
On business of printing and publication	□	□		
On franchise				
On sand, gravel and other quarry resources	□	□	[a]	[a]
On amusement places	□	□	[a]	
On professionals	□	□		
On delivery vans and trucks	□	□		
On real property	□	□	[a]	[a]
On idle lands	□	□		
On business	□		□	□
On community tax	□		□	[a]

[a] Shares in proceeds of levy of province.

cities are also allowed to impose a tax on the transfer of real property, on sand, gravel and other quarry resources, on amusement places, on franchises, on professionals, on delivery vans and trucks, and on idle lands.[8] Municipalities and cities (but not provinces) are authorized to levy the community tax and the local business tax (basically a turnover tax that is levied on the gross receipts of businesses/traders).

Section 133 of the LGC lists in some detail the taxes that LGUs are not allowed to touch. The income tax (both individual and corporate), customs duties, the value added tax, and excise taxes on alcoholic beverages, tobacco products and petroleum products are reserved for the central government alone. At the same time, the National Internal Revenue Code does not provide for a central government real property tax nor for a central government community tax (poll tax).

The Local Government Code defines the base of each of these local taxes, and it sets limits (i.e., floors and/or ceilings) on the tax rates that LGUs may impose. In general, the maximum allowable tax rates applicable to cities are higher than those applicable to provinces/municipalities.

[8] Lower level local governments likewise have a share in the proceeds of the sand/gravel tax, amusement tax and the community tax.

Compared to Presidential Decree (PD) 231 and Presidential Decree 464 (which defined the taxing powers of LGUs prior to the enactment of the Code), RA 7160 expanded the tax base of LGUs to include products, activities and sectors (like banks and other financial institutions, and printing/publication) that previously were outside the reach of local taxation. It also increased the maximum allowable rates at which most local taxes may be levied. However, the Code effectively reduced the assessment levels (for purposes of real property taxation) of residential land, all types of buildings and all types of machinery. Also, the Code provided for the exemption of residential buildings with market value below P175,000 from real property taxation. Meanwhile, the Local Government Code has liberalized the LGUs' scope for the collection of user charges.

3.2. *Assessment*

The traditional literature on fiscal federalism (e.g., Shah, 1994; Ter-Minassian, 1997; Bird, 1999) provides three general criteria in assessing the appropriateness of tax assignment: economic efficiency, equity and administrative feasibility. The economic efficiency criterion suggests that each level of government should be assigned taxes that are related to the benefits of its spending responsibility. Thus, user charges for identifiable public services that are provided by sub-national governments and taxes that are levied based on the benefit principle (e.g., motor vehicle taxes and fuel taxes which may be used to finance the construction of local infrastructure) are best assigned to LGUs. To the extent that LGUs have to resort to non-benefit taxation, they should tax bases which have low inter-jurisdictional mobility. Otherwise, non-uniform tax rates levied by different LGUs will distort the geographic allocation of economic resources.

At the same time, it is argued that progressive taxes (i.e., those that are based on ability to pay) should finance the redistributive function of government. Because redistributive functions are generally viewed as central government responsibilities, and progressive taxes are best assigned to the central government, most analysts have taken the view that primary responsibility for redistribution should not rest with local governments. Lastly, the concern for administrative efficiency indicates that the authority to collect particular types of taxes should be given to the level of government that is able to do so with the lowest possible collection and enforcement cost.

On the other hand, the new view on tax assignment (e.g., McLure, 1999; Bird, 1999) emphasizes the need to provide sub-national governments with fiscal autonomy. What is important is (1) for LGUs to have their own source of revenues and (2) for LGUs to have the power to control the amount of revenues they receive at the margin so as to be able to fund the level of services they prefer.[9] In this way, "sub-national governments would have to face the full marginal tax price of the spending decisions for which they are responsible" (Bird, 1999).

Given this background, the Philippine tax assignment appears to largely be consistent with the conventional wisdom. The two most important sources of tax revenue for LGUs, the real property tax and the community tax, are taxes on immobile factors. LGUs are given wide latitude to levy fees and other user charges.

However, the current tax assignment scores low in terms of the autonomy criterion. While the Local Government Code authorizes LGUs to levy a good number of taxes, it also seriously limits their power to set tax rates. First, the Code fixes the tax rate for some types of taxes like the SEF real property tax rate, and the community tax. Second, even for those taxes over which LGUs have some discretion in setting tax rates, the maximum allowable rates appear to be too low. Note that all provinces presently impose the maximum allowable basic real property tax rate. Third, the Code mandates that tax rates can only be adjusted once in 5 years and by no more than 10 percent. This provision is particularly restrictive in the case of taxes (like the professional tax and the tax on delivery vans and trucks) whose rates are specified in nominal peso terms. Clearly, the resulting adjustments will not allow LGUs to maintain the real value of revenues.

The discussion below makes it clear that there is a mismatch between the assignment of taxes and the assignment of expenditure responsibilities to the different levels of local government. The share of provinces and municipalities in total LGU own-source revenue declined in the post-Code period despite their large share in the cost of devolved

[9] It should be noted that while revenue sharing (with the central government) may provide LGUs with adequate own-source revenues, this scheme does not provide fiscal autonomy because subnational governments do not have the power to affect the amount of shared revenues they receive.

functions. Many local tax experts have suggested that future Code amendments should look at giving LGUs greater discretion in setting tax rates by raising the maximum allowable tax rates. Moreover, there is a need to move toward ad valorem (vs. specific) tax rates in order to avoid frequent revisions of local tax ordinances and to keep own-source revenues buoyant.

The tax structure prescribed by the Code for the local business tax calls for different categories of firms to be subject to different rate schedules. This complication tends to increase administrative and compliance costs and further strains the capacity of an already weak local tax administration (Taliercio, 2003).

Tax administration is severely inadequate in many LGUs. This is illustrated dramatically by the collection efficiency for the real property tax (see Table 12). Many of the personnel assigned to the tax division are not well-equipped technically for their tasks. Very few of these units have certified public accountants in their rolls, thereby impairing their audit capability. Also, not many LGUs have computers that will help them improve their revenue performance.

Finally, many LGU officials tend not to fully utilize the tax powers assigned to them. For instance, many provinces and cities have done a general revision of the schedule of market values only once since 1991. This has resulted in declining property tax collections in real

Table 12. Tax Collection Rate of Current Year for Basic Real Property Tax, 1983–1999

	All LGUs	Provinces	Cities
1985	46.85	41.98	53.20
1987	52.77	49.53	56.74
1989	57.98	55.55	60.98
1991	58.92	54.09	65.06
1994	60.65	53.96	66.28
1997	57.40	50.00	62.01
1999	54.08	52.36	54.87
2000	54.60	44.70	57.10
Average			
1989–1991	58.22	54.40	63.11
1992–1999	55.40	49.00	59.70

terms.[10] This development is reportedly due to resistance on the part of either the local chief executive or the local Sanggunian (or both) to increase the tax rates for fear of a backlash from their constituents during election.[11]

3.3. *Trend and Composition of LGU Revenues, 1991–2001*

National/subnational revenue distribution. Tables 13 and 14 confirm that the bulk of the revenue-productive sources remain with the central government even in the post-Code period. Also, many LGUs have not fully utilized their revenue raising powers due to political constraints and to the dis-incentive effect of the IRA distribution formula on local tax effort. Thus, the contribution of LGUs to total revenues of the general government (central government and LGUs combined) remains low — an average of 6.9% in 1992–2003 compared to an average of 4.9%

Table 13. Collection Rates for the Real Property Tax Collection Rate of Current Year for Basic RPT, 1983–1999 (in percent)

	National Government			Local Government		
Levels	Total	Tax	Non-Tax	Total	Tax	Non-Tax
1985	94.1	95.5	84.2	5.9	4.5	15.8
1987	95.5	96.2	92.2	4.5	3.8	7.8
1989	95.2	96.3	90.6	4.8	3.7	9.4
1991	95.4	96.3	91.6	4.6	3.7	8.4
1993	93.6	94.4	88.2	6.4	5.6	11.8
1995	94.1	94.8	90.0	5.9	5.2	10.0
1997	93.5	94.4	87.4	6.5	5.6	12.6
1999	92.7	93.8	83.8	7.3	6.2	16.2
2001	92.8	93.6	87.4	7.2	6.4	12.6
2003	92.0	92.6	88.6	8.0	7.4	11.4
Average						
1985–1991	95.1	96.1	90.9	4.9	3.9	9.1
1992–2003	93.1	94.0	87.4	6.9	6.0	12.6

[10] The Code mandated that LGUs conduct a general revision of market values once every three years, beginning with 1994.

[11] The Sanggunian refers to the local legislative body.

Table 14. General Government Revenues by Level of Local Government as a Percent of GNP

Levels	General Government			National Government			Local Government		
	Total	Tax	Non-Tax	Total	Tax	Non-Tax	Total	Tax	Non-Tax
1985	13.3	11.6	1.7	12.5	11.1	1.4	0.8	0.5	0.3
1987	16.2	13.4	2.8	15.5	12.9	2.6	0.7	0.5	0.2
1989	17.7	14.0	3.6	16.8	13.5	3.3	0.9	0.5	0.3
1991	18.4	15.1	3.4	17.6	14.5	3.1	0.8	0.6	0.3
1993	18.5	16.3	2.3	17.4	15.3	2.0	1.2	0.9	0.3
1995	19.6	16.7	2.9	18.4	15.9	2.6	1.2	0.9	0.3
1997	20.0	17.3	2.7	18.7	16.3	2.4	1.3	1.0	0.3
1999	16.5	14.7	1.8	15.3	13.8	1.5	1.2	0.9	0.3
2001	15.7	13.5	2.2	14.5	12.6	1.9	1.1	0.9	0.3
2003	14.8	12.6	2.2	13.6	11.6	1.9	1.2	0.9	0.2
Average									
1985–1991	16.6	13.6	3.0	15.8	13.1	2.7	0.8	0.5	0.3
1992–2003	16.9	14.7	2.3	15.8	13.8	2.0	1.2	0.9	0.3

in 1985–1991. Moreover, local government revenue effort rose only marginally from an average of 0.8% of GNP in the pre-Code period to an average of 1.2% in the post-Code period.

The assignment of revenues under the Local Government Code has effectively shifted the distribution of own-source revenue from municipalities and provinces in favor of cities. The Code not only allows cities to impose all the taxes that provinces and municipalities are authorized to levy but also gives them a greater discretion in setting the tax rates. Also, the share of the province and the municipality in the proceeds of the real property tax was reduced by the LGC relative to PD 464. A comparison of the shares of the different levels of local government in total LGU own-source revenues (see Table 14) with their share in the cost of devolved functions[12] reveals the inconsistency between tax assignment and expenditure assignment.

Distribution of LGU own-source revenues by type. For all LGUs in the aggregate, taxes accounted for two-thirds of own-source revenue in 1985–1991 and 75 percent in 1992–2003. Real property tax effort for all LGUs in aggregate increased in the post code period (see Table 15), primarily because of the efforts of cities and municipalities.

In cities, all sources of own-source revenues increased in the post-Code period but the improvement in local tax effort (both RPT and other taxes) was dramatic. On the other hand, the expansion in the own-source revenue effort of municipalities was largely driven by increases in their other taxes and in their operating/miscellaneous revenues. These differences in the revenue performance of provinces, cities and municipalities may be explained by differences in their tax bases as well as differences in their taxing powers. Being more urbanized and having economies that are more market-based, the tax base of cities tends to be more buoyant when compared to those of municipalities and provinces.

4. Inter-governmental Transfers

4.1. *Legal Framework*

In the Philippines, central government transfers to sub-national governments are of two types: formula-based block grants (i.e., internal revenue

[12] The share of provinces in the total cost of devolved functions was 47.5%, that of municipalities was 48.1% and that of cities was 4.3%.

Table 15. Revenue Effort of All Local Governments (Ratio to GNP in Percent)

	Average								
	1985–1991	1992–2003	1991	1993	1995	1997	1999	2001	2003
All LGUs									
Total own-source revenue	0.81	1.17	0.84	1.18	1.15	1.30	1.20	1.13	1.18
I. Tax revenues	0.53	0.89	0.56	0.91	0.87	0.96	0.91	0.86	0.93
Real property tax	0.33	0.45	0.34	0.37	0.45	0.50	0.46	0.45	0.47
Others	0.21	0.44	0.21	0.53	0.42	0.46	0.45	0.41	0.46
II. Operating & misc. revenues	0.25	0.28	0.26	0.27	0.28	0.31	0.29	0.27	0.25
III. Capital	0.02	0.01	0.02	0.00	0.00	0.03	0.00	0.01	0.00
Province									
Total own-source revenue	0.16	0.15	0.15	0.16	0.17	0.17	0.15	0.14	0.12
I. Tax revenues	0.08	0.09	0.07	0.11	0.11	0.10	0.11	0.09	0.08
Real property tax	0.07	0.07	0.06	0.08	0.08	0.08	0.07	0.07	0.06
Others	0.02	0.02	0.01	0.03	0.04	0.02	0.03	0.02	0.02
II. Operating & misc. revenues	0.07	0.05	0.08	0.06	0.06	0.06	0.05	0.04	0.04
III. Capital	0.01	0.00	0.00	0.00	0.00	0.02	0.00	0.01	0.00

(Continued)

Table 15. (*Continued*)

	Average								
	1985–1991	1992–2003	1991	1993	1995	1997	1999	2001	2003
Municipalities									
Total own-source revenue	0.30	0.32	0.33	0.57	0.37	0.39	0.31	0.26	0.26
I. Tax revenues	0.20	0.22	0.23	0.45	0.26	0.26	0.20	0.17	0.18
Real property tax	0.12	0.10	0.13	0.15	0.12	0.12	0.09	0.08	0.08
Others	0.08	0.12	0.09	0.30	0.14	0.14	0.11	0.09	0.10
II. Operating & misc. revenues	0.09	0.10	0.10	0.12	0.11	0.12	0.11	0.09	0.09
III. Capital	0.00	0.00	0.00	0.00	0.00	0.00	0.00	0.00	0.00
Cities									
Total own-source revenue	0.35	0.71	0.36	0.44	0.62	0.74	0.74	0.73	0.80
I. Tax revenues	0.25	0.58	0.26	0.35	0.50	0.60	0.61	0.60	0.68
Real property tax	0.14	0.28	0.15	0.15	0.25	0.30	0.30	0.30	0.33
Others	0.11	0.30	0.11	0.20	0.24	0.30	0.31	0.30	0.35
II. Operating & misc. revenues	0.09	0.13	0.09	0.09	0.12	0.14	0.13	0.14	0.12
III. Capital	0.01	0.00	0.01	0.00	0.00	0.00	0.00	0.00	0.00

allotment or IRA) and *ad hoc* categorical grants. In principle, LGUs have almost full discretion in the utilization of their IRA. In contrast, the categorical grants are conditional on their use for specific purposes.

Internal revenue allotment. While LGUs receive a share of central government tax revenues (IRA) on the basis of a formula fixed by law, the ARMM's share is based on the origin principle. Specifically, a share of internal revenue tax collections is transferred as a block grant and, as such, both the regional government of the ARMM and the LGUs enjoy considerable discretion in its utilization.

The IRA is allocated to the different levels of local government and to specific LGUs within each level according to a pre-determined formula that is based on population, land area and equal sharing. Under the Local Government Code, the aggregate IRA of LGUs is set at 40 percent of actual internal revenue tax collections of the central government three years prior to the current year.[13]

Under the Code, the IRA is divided amongst the different levels of local government as follows: 23 percent to provinces, 23 percent to cities, 34 percent to municipalities and 20 percent to barangays.[14] In turn, the IRA share of each tier of local government is then apportioned to individual LGUs on the basis of population (50 percent), land area (25 percent) and equal sharing (25 percent).[15]

Actual collections of internal revenue taxes in the ARMM area are divided as follows: 30 percent to the central government, 35 percent to the regional government and 35 percent to the local governments in the region (distributed according to the derivation principle).[16] The collecting agent (in this case the regional office of the Bureau of Internal Revenue) *automatically* remits to the regional government the latter's share

[13] In comparison, the share of LGUs in national taxes was equal to 20 percent of internal revenue taxes *at the maximum* in the pre-Code regime. The amount of IRA that was actually appropriated in the pre-Code era was 13% of net BIR tax receipts on the average in 1987–1990.

[14] Prior to the implementation of the Code, the inter-tier allocation of the IRA was: 27 percent to provinces, 22 percent to cities, 41 percent to municipalities and 10 percent to barangays.

[15] In the pre-Code period, the intra-tier allocation to individual LGUs was determined as follows: 70 percent on the basis of population, 20 percent based on land area, and 10 percent based on equal sharing.

[16] Prior to the amendement of the organic act of the ARMM in 2001, the share of the central government was 40%, that of the regional government was 30% and that of the province or city was 30%.

together with those of its constituent LGUs. Thus, LGUs in the ARMM are not only entitled to their share under the Local Government Code but also to their share under the organic act of ARMM.

While the Local Government Code provides for the *automatic release* of the IRA, the IRA has been a highly unpredictable source of financing for LGUs since 1998. This is because of the severe fiscal constraints faced by central government (see Table 16). For instance, in 1998, 5 percent of the IRA was not released to LGUs on the basis of a fiscal austerity measure implemented by the DBM.[17] A case questioning the legality of the central government's action in this regard was brought to the Supreme Court which subsequently ruled in favor of LGUs.

In 2000, Congress cut P10 billion from the mandated IRA share of LGUs and set aside this amount under unprogrammed Funds (i.e., appropriations that will only be released when revenues in excess of targets are realized). In that year, DBM also required the submission of LGUs Annual Investment Plan prior to releasing 20 percent of the IRA of individual LGUs. This was an attempt to delay the release of the IRA so as to reduce the central government's fiscal deficit.

In 2001, when the government had to operate on the basis of the previous year's appropriations because of the failure of Congress to enact a new GAA on time, the DBM initially set aside P121.8 billion for the IRA (the full amount including the unprogrammed portion that was appropriated under the 2000 General Appropriation Act (GAA). This

Table 16. Comparison of IRA Appropriations and IRA Obligations (in billion pesos)

	1998	1999	2000	2001
Mandated IRA share	81.0	96.8	121.8	131.8
Appropriations	81.0	96.8	111.8[a]	121.8
Obligations	76.9	95.3	114.3[b]	115.8
Ratio of oblig. to mandated share	94.9	98.5	93.8	87.9

[a] P10 billion was of the P121.8 billion mandated share was put under "unprogrammed funds" by a member of the Senate.
[b] In the course of the budget year, P2.5 billion was transferred from the "unprogrammed fund" to the "programmed" portion of budget.

[17] Initially, 10 percent of the IRA was withheld by the DBM. However, towards the end of the year, the DBM announced that it would release half of this amount.

was P10 billion short of the 40 percent share in internal revenue taxes that is mandated under the Local Government Code. In the end, the DBM actually obligated only P115.8 billion.

Categorical grants. Categorical grants to LGUs may come from various sources: (1) lump sum allocations under the GAA of various years, (2) allocations made by the central government sector agencies from their own budgets, and (3) lump sum and/or line item appropriations for pork barrel funds of legislators.

In the 1998 and 1999 GAA, for instance, there are three major lump sum funds that finance the implementation of devolved activities supportive of major national government programs. These are the Local Government Service Equalization Fund (LGSEF), the Local Government Empowerment Fund (LGEF), and the Municipal Development Fund (MDF).[18] The principal difference amongst these funds stems from (1) the nature of the fund transfers and (2) the agencies that administer them. Both the LGEF and the LGSEF are comprised exclusively of grant funds. In addition, many national government line agencies have also set aside funds in their budget for various matching grant programs aimed at encouraging LGUs to undertake activities that are supportive of national programs and objectives. In contrast, the MDF includes funds for both loans and grants.

The LGSEF was created by Executive Order 48 of 1998 and, consequently, the 1999 and the 2000 GAA earmarked P5 billion (carved out of the aggregate IRA share of LGUs) to support the "funding requirement of programs, projects and activities arising from the full and effective implementation of devolved functions and services of LGUs towards effective governance, decentralization and sustained growth and development." The LGSEF was originally designed to provide equalization grants to LGUs. However, many LGU officials resent the fact that the money for the LGSEF was taken from the IRA — thus, diminishing what they interpret to be theirs as a matter of entitlement. Because of this, the LGSEF was short-lived.

The LGEF provides budget cover for foreign-assisted projects supportive of major national government programs in the 21 priority

[18] The LGSEF was discontinued in 2000 but both the LGEF and MDF are still operational. The LGSEF is discussed here because it is one of the first attempts to address equalization concerns.

provinces, and in "5th and 6th class local governments" as identified under the Social Reform Agenda. The list of projects under the LGEF in the 2002 GAA includes: (1) the Cordillera Highland Agricultural Resource Management Project; (2) Certain Rural Water Supply, Sewerage and Sanitation Projects; and (3) Integrated Community Health Services Projects.

In addition, many sector agencies implement matching grants program out of their own GAA budgets. The Matching Grants Program of the Department of Health for the promotion of family planning is an example. Generally, LGUs have to apply for the grant and, if they qualify, are required to open a special bank account that will be used for the purpose of tracking implementation.

Initially, many LGUs did not encounter difficulties in providing counterpart funding support. This situation has changed because of convergence of a number of these projects in the same LGUs, thus, putting a strain on the absorptive capacity. Moreover, the provinces which are targeted by many of these projects are inherently less capable financially to start with.[19]

In contrast, the MDF is a facility for channeling the proceeds of various loans, assistance and grants that the central government has obtained from foreign governments and multilateral institutions. Official development assistance (ODA) funds intended for LGUs are first appropriated and allotted to the MDF. The MDF then releases the funds in the form of either loans and/or grants to LGUs. The MDF prescribes a loan/equity/grant mix in the financing of varying types of LGU projects depending on the income class of the LGU concerned and the project in question. For instance, LGUs of whatever class are not entitled to grants for revenue generating projects. On the other hand, grants are made available for projects with social and environment objectives with the grant share of lower income LGUs being larger than that of higher income LGUs. For loans, the required equity share of less-well-off LGUs is smaller than that of their better-off LGUs.

One of the issues relating to the operation of the MDF is the need to unbundle grants from loans. It is argued that decisions involving the grant system should be isolated from the credit system. An LGU which

---

[19] Thus, there appears to be some tension between equity and efficiency considerations i.e., to focus on the most needy LGUs and to encourage LGUs to take fuller responsibility for devolved activities.

has access to a grant should not automatically be given access to a loan, and vice versa. This is so because the reasons for providing grants are quite different and independent from the reasons for giving credit. Grants to LGUs are typically justified on grounds of economic efficiency (e.g., existence of externalities) and equity while the decision to grant a loan depends on creditworthiness. Unbundling does not mean that an LGU cannot access both sources of financing at the same time. What is critical, here is the separate and independent evaluation of the grant and the loan application of LGUs.

The present system (by prescribing a loan-equity-grant mix for various types of projects) effectively results in a subsidized credit program even if the credit component is priced at market rates of interest. In turn, such a situation tends to promote continued LGU dependence on subsidized credit while crowding out private capital in the LGU credit market (Llanto *et al.*, 1998). There has been some attempt to move the administration of all central government grant transfers to LGUs to another agency but this proposal was shelved.

Finally, the rationale for the continued involvement of central government agencies in the affairs of LGUs, should be revisited.[20] While this issue appears to have waned given the current fiscal difficulties faced by the government, it is one that is likely to recur in times when the fiscal position of the central government is stronger. On the one hand, there appears to be some justification for matching grants in cases of activities that have significant benefit spillovers across LGU jurisdictions since LGUs would tend to under-provide these services without national government grants. On the other hand, there is a need to evaluate these expenditures in the context of possible turf-maximization behavior on the part of national agency bureaucrats.

4.2. *Size and Composition of Central Government Transfers to LGUs*

With the implementation of the Local Government Code, there has been a remarkable increase in the size of central government transfers to LGUs as well as a palpable shift in their composition. On the one

[20] Note that not all of the budgets of sector agencies that have devolved activities are transferred as grants to LGUs. In many instances, the funds are used for the direct provision of devolved services by the central government agency concerned.

Table 17. IRA and Other Grants as a Portion of National Revenues and National Expenditures

	NG Transfers as Percent of NG Revenue			NG Transfers as Percent of NG Expd.		
	Total	IRA	Other Grant	Total	IRA	Other Grant
1985	6.4	5.3	1.1	5.5	4.6	0.9
1987	4.2	3.6	0.6	3.6	3.0	0.5
1989	5.2	3.6	1.6	5.1	3.5	1.6
1991	6.3	4.8	1.5	5.6	4.3	1.4
1993	12.5	12.3	0.2	11.8	11.5	0.2
1995	14.7	14.5	0.2	14.3	14.1	0.2
1997	15.1	14.9	0.1	14.4	14.3	0.1
1999	20.0	19.9	0.1	16.5	16.4	0.1
2001	19.4	19.3	0.1	15.5	15.3	0.1
Average						
1985–1991	6.4	4.8	1.6	5.5	4.1	1.3
1992–2001	16.5	16.3	0.1	14.5	14.4	0.1

hand, central government transfers to LGUs surged from 6.4% of national government revenues (or 5.5% of national government expenditures) in the pre-Code period to 16.5% of national government revenues (or 14.5% of national government expenditures) in the post-Code period (see Table 17). This development has been a source of increasing pressure on national government expenditures in recent years.

On the other hand, there has been a movement away from *ad hoc* grants in favor of formula-based block grants in the post-Code period. In particular, the share of the IRA in total central government transfers to LGUs rose from 76 percent in 1985–1991 to 99 percent in 1992–2001 while the share of *ad hoc* grants declined from 24 to 1 percent. These developments affirm the thrusts towards increased local autonomy under the Local Government Code.

4.3. *Consistency of Revenue and Expenditure Assignment Across Levels of Local Government*

As is the case in other countries, there is a mismatch between revenue from local taxes and the expenditures needs of various levels of local government in the Philippines. Many types of taxes are either easier to administer at the central level or are deemed to be unsuitable for local sub-national government imposition because their tax bases are geographically mobile. On the other hand, the principle of subsidiarity implies that many functions are best assigned to local governments. In this context, inter-governmental transfers are generally viewed as an instrument that may be used to correct for the imbalance in the tax and expenditure assignment.

Vertical balance in the ARMM. RA 6734 as amended and the Local Government Code, in combination, has resulted in a severe vertical fiscal imbalance in the ARMM, i.e., a mismatch between the expenditure responsibilities that were transferred and the revenues available to the sub-national government. On the one hand, the regional government's share in internal revenue taxes is sufficient only to cover the expenditure responsibilities assigned to it. In particular, the share of the regional government in internal revenue taxes is only equivalent to about 3 percent of the cost of the devolved functions. This occurs largely because the ARMM's share in national taxes is computed on a derivation basis (i.e., where the tax is actually collected). But precisely because the ARMM is a less-developed region, its tax base is lower than the average tax base in the rest of the country. However, the problem also partly stems from the fact that all of the responsibilities devolved by the central government are shifted to the regional government, with none being assigned to the LGUs in the area despite the fact that RA 6734 allows the regional government to devolve their functions to the LGUs.[21]

As a result, the regional government of ARMM is dependent on yearly allocations from the central government's general appropriations to carry out its mandate. The regional government has very little control over the size and the composition of this funding. To wit, the size of this direct funding support is entirely dependent on the central government and the ARMM competes for these resources just like other central government agencies. The allocation of these transfers to various uses is predetermined by the central government as these uses are represented by line items in the General Appropriations Act.

[21] Note, however, that even if one adds the IRA share of ARMM LGUs to the share of the regional government in internal revenue taxes, the sum would still be substantially lower than cost of functions devolved to the ARMM.

As such, the regional government is reduced to an administrative arm of the central government — simply implementing the latter's plans and programs.

It should be pointed out that since 1992 central government transfers to the regional government have grown at a faster pace than would have been the case if one were simply making adjustments for inflation and population growth. In fact, the central government allotment for the ARMM's regular operations is about twice the amount that was previously spent in the region. Some might argue that this was the central government's way of making up for its past negligence of the region's needs.

On the other hand, ARMM LGUs get the resources but not the expenditure responsibilities. LGUs in the ARMM are entitled not only to their IRA share as provided by the Local Government Code but also to their share in internal revenue collections in the ARMM as mandated by the organic act of the autonomous region. Consequently, the aggregate inter-governmental transfer accruing to ARMM LGUs is more than 20 times that of the regional government itself.

Vertical balance under the Local Government Code. The mismatch between the revenue means and the expenditure needs of various levels of government may be measured by comparing the sub-national government's share in general government revenues with its share in general government expenditures (Shah, 1994). The data in Table 18 show that the vertical fiscal imbalance has worsened at all levels of local government with the implementation of the Local Government Code. Thus, the fiscal deficiency for all LGUs in the aggregate grew from 6.1% in the pre-Code period to over 16 percent in the post-Code period. Furthermore, transfers have not been able to fully close the vertical fiscal imbalance. This is true as well for provinces, cities and municipalities.

While the vertical fiscal imbalance (including IRA) was trimmed down to less than 1 percent in 1999–2000, it has risen to over 4 percent in 2001–2003 because of additional unfunded mandates (see Table 18). This resonates with the widespread perception that the LGUs' prevailing share in national taxes is deficient to cover both the cost of devolved functions and the cost of the so-called unfunded mandates. The significant increase in the IRA share of LGUs under the Code has not resolved this problem. These unfunded mandates include the salary increases under the Salary Standardization Law, the additional personnel benefits

Table 18. Indicator of Vertical Imbalance, With and Without the IRA

All LGUs	Ratio of Own-Source Revenue to General Government Revenue %	Ratio of Own-Source Revenue Plus IRA to Gen. Gov't. Revenue %	Ratio of LGU Expenditure to General Gov't. Expenditure Net of Debt Service %	Surplus/ (Deficit)-Without the IRA %	Surplus/ (Deficit)-With the IRA %
1985	5.62	9.88	12.01	–6.39	–2.13
1987	4.36	7.35	10.55	–6.20	–3.21
1989	4.63	7.61	11.10	–6.47	–3.50
1991	4.31	8.20	12.65	–8.33	–4.44
1993	5.81	14.20	19.99	–14.18	–5.79
1995	5.30	15.14	21.85	–16.54	–6.71
1997	5.86	15.89	21.47	–15.61	–5.57
1999	6.36	19.21	23.05	–16.69	–3.84
2001	6.32	18.89	25.73	–19.41	–6.85
2003	6.85	21.21	25.41	–18.56	–4.20
Average					
1985–1991	4.62	8.13	11.30	–6.67	–3.17
1992–2003	6.09	17.85	22.96	–16.87	–5.12

under the Magna Carta for Health Workers, and the additional number of mandatory positions as well as the sectoral representation mandated under the Local Government Code.

In 1996, 1997 and 1998, the salary adjustments under the Salary Standardization Law were so hefty that the increases in the IRA were not able to keep up with the rising cost of devolved functions, unfunded mandates and population growth (see Table 20).[22] However, the analysis also shows that in 1999 and 2000 the natural increase in the IRA arising from the implementation of the Code was sufficient to cover the adjusted costs of devolved functions and unfunded mandates (Manasan, 2001).

The data in Table 19 also show that in the period 1995–1999 the net resource transfer is negative for provinces and municipalities. This implies that the increase in the IRA was not sufficient to finance their adjusted cost of devolved functions and unfunded mandates.[23] However, the opposite is true for all cities combined.

It is easy to see why. Provinces absorbed 37 percent of the total cost of devolved functions, municipalities 38.5%, cities 5.7% and barangays 18.8.[24] Contrast this with the mandated share of LGUs in the IRA (provinces 23 percent, cities 23 percent, municipalities 34 percent and barangays 20 percent) and it becomes immediately clear that there is a mismatch in the resources transferred and the expenditure responsibilities devolved to the different levels of local government.

---

[22] The analysis underlying Table 19 is limited by the fact that only the cost of devolved personnel and facilities and the MOOE associated with them were included in the computation. However, there are other cases where functions were transferred to LGUs without any corresponding devolution of personnel and facilities from the central government. This is prevalent in the environment and natural resource management and public works area. Moreover, the cost used in this estimation refer to the cost of the devolved functions as budgeted by the central government prior to devolution and as such they do not necessarily reflect local preferences.

[23] The net resource transfer for any given year is computed as the difference between the IRA for that year, and the sum of the adjusted cost of devolved functions, the cost of other mandates, and 1992 IRA. Adjustments on the cost side were made to take into account population growth and inflation.

[24] Barangays received P1.5 billion in Barangay Administration Fund under the National Assistance to Local Government Units (NALGU) in 1991. This assistance, which was used to pay for the salaries of barangay officials, was discontinued with the implementation of the Local Government Code and barangays were then expected to pay salaries out of their IRA share.

Table 19. Matching of IRA and LGU Responsibilities, 1995–2000

	Province	Cities	Municipalities	All LGUs
1995				
Aggregate net resource transfer (in billion pesos)[a]	–0.32	2.692	–0.114	2.258
Number of LGUs with negative per capita net resource transfer	48	0	983	
1997				
Aggregate net resource transfer (in billion pesos)[b]	–1.569	1.501	–2.231	–2.299
Number of LGUs with negative per capita net resource transfer	58	12	1,327	
1998				
Aggregate net resource transfer (in billion pesos)[c]	–2.743	0.052	–3.029	–5.72
Number of LGUs with negative per capita net resource transfer	65	35	1,336	
1999				
Aggregate net resource transfer (in billion pesos)[d]	–0.745	2.746	–0.312	1.689
Number of LGUs with negative per capita net resource transfer	50	28	893	
2000				
Aggregate net resource transfer (in billion pesos)[e]	0.115	5.052	1.555	6.722
Number of LGUs with negative per capita net resource transfer	38	11	684	

(Continued)

Table 19. (*Continued*)

	Province	Cities	Municipalities	All LGUs
2001				
Aggregate net resource transfer (in billion pesos)[f]	–0.139	4.692	0.284	4.837
Number of LGUs with negative per capita net resource transfer	45	17	772	
2002				
Aggregate net resource transfer (in billion pesos)[f]	3.548	7.989	8.073	19.61
Number of LGUs with negative per capita net resource transfer	12	18	141	
2003				
Aggregate net resource transfer (in billion pesos)[f]	4.040	8.830	8.811	21.681
Number of LGUs with Negative per capita net resource transfer	12	15	68	

Note: see annex 1 for footnotes.

[a] LGU cost adjusted for inflation, salary standardization increases (1.42), benefits under the Magna Carta for Health Workers, salaries of additional mandatory positions and 3 sectoral representatives and population growth.

[b] LGU cost adjusted for inflation, salary standardization increases (1.79), benefits under the Magna Carta for Health Workers, salaries of additional mandatory positions and 3 sectoral representatives and population growth.

[c] LGU cost adjusted for inflation, salary standardization increases (2.22), benefits under the Magna Carta for Health Workers, salaries of additional mandatory positions and 3 sectoral representatives and population growth.

[d] LGU cost adjusted for inflation, salary standardization increases (2.5), benefits under the Magna Carta for Health Workers, salaries of additional mandatory positions and 3 sectoral representatives and population growth.

[e] LGU cost adjusted for inflation, salary standardization increases (2.5), benefits under the Magna Carta for Health Workers, salaries of additional mandatory positions and 3 sectoral representatives and population growth.

[f] LGU cost adjusted for inflation, salary standardization increases (2.625), benefits under the Magna Carta for Health Workers, salaries of additional mandatory positions and 3 sectoral representatives and population growth.

Source: 1995–1998 results from Manasan (2001), 1999–2000 re-estimated to reflect actual developments in IRA in those years.

This imbalance may be traced to the fact that the IRA distribution formula was decided much earlier (i.e., during the Congressional debate on RA7160) than the actual assignment of functions (including the devolution of personnel) to different levels of local government. However, some observers note that this skewed distribution may reflect the reality that governors are a more common threat to congressmen than are mayors since the latter either represent congressional districts that are coterminous with the boundaries of a single province or are one of many districts within a single province. While mayors pose similar threats to some congressmen, big city mayors are fewer than governors, and most legislators represent districts without highly urbanized cities. Thus, by making provinces responsible for more services than they could pay for with automatic revenue transfers, Congress ensured that governors would remain dependent on legislators who could subsequently offer their services as brokers of additional revenues from the center in a personalized manner (Eaton, 2000).[25]

Horizontal imbalance. In addition to the vertical imbalance across levels of local government, an imbalance also exists across LGUs within each level. Thus, while the increase in the IRA share of some LGUs is not enough to finance the functions devolved to them, others have received resources beyond their requirements. For instance, in 1993, per capita net resource transfer was negative in 37 out the 66 provinces for which data were available.[26] The situation has worsened since then given the enormity of unfunded mandates: Magna Carta for Health Workers, Salary Standardization Law, among others. Thus, in

---

[25] When the Code was being debated in Congress, the attitude of congressmen towards decentralization was ambiguous. On the one hand, many of them felt threatened knowing that true local autonomy would reduce their political clout over their respective constituents (who heretofore were largely dependent on projects identified by the congressmen and funded from pork barrel funds) as local government politicians become more empowered with the higher revenue share and expanded expenditure responsibility with fiscal decentralization. On the other hand, many congressmen maintain fraternal relations with local government politicians as Philippine local politics is very much dominated by a small number of families. Thus, it is not uncommon to find cities (or provinces) where the mayor (or governor) is the congressman's wife (or brother/sister/father/son). Thus, in agreeing to decentralize revenues and expenditures, the congressmen then tried to protect against what they feared most about decentralization.

[26] Per capita net resource transfer in 1993 is defined as per capita 1993 IRA less per capita 1992 IRA less per capita cost of devolved functions adjusted for inflation.

1998, 65 (82 percent) out of 78 provinces, 1,336 (87 percent) out of 1,538 municipalities and 35 (51 percent) out of 69 cities suffered negative net resource transfers (see Table 19). Clearly, there is a need to improve on the IRA distribution formula so that the expenditure needs of the various levels of local government and the different LGUs within each level are taken into account.

4.4. *Impact of Inter-governmental Fiscal Structure on Horizontal Fiscal Balance*

In the literature on fiscal decentralization, inter-governmental transfers are generally expected to perform an equalizing role, i.e., help reduce disparities in revenue capacities across levels of local government and within each level.

The correlation coefficient between per capita IRA of city governments and per capita household income is consistently negative for all years in 1995–2000, suggesting that the IRA distribution formula has had some success in equalizing the fiscal capacities of cities. That is, cities with lower per capita household income tend to receive higher per capita IRA. Nonetheless, the equalizing effect of the IRA in the case of cities is not enough to counteract the large disparities in their tax base. Thus, the sum of per capita own-source revenue of cities and their per capita IRA is found have a positive relationship with per capita household income (see Table 20).

The IRA is found to be counter-equalizing for all years in the case of provinces, but appears to have some equalizing impact on municipalities (aggregated by province) in 1999–2000 but not in 1995–1998. The difference in the sign of the correlation coefficient between per capita IRA and per capita household income may be due to the implementation of the LGSEF which provided additional transfers to 5th and 6th income class municipalities. Note that the LGSEF transfers were treated as part of the IRA in the financial statements of LGUs. When all LGUs are aggregated at the provincial level, per capita IRA is found to be positively related to per capita household income in 1995–1999 (see Table 20). In contrast, in 2000, the correlation coefficient between these two variables is negative indicating that LGUs with lower per capita household income tend to receive higher per capita IRA. However, even in 2000, the equalizing effect of the IRA is not sufficient to compensate for the inherent disparities in the tax base.

Table 20. Simple Correlation Coefficient between the Per Capita Transfer and Per Capita Household Income

	1991	1995	1996	1997	1998	1999	2000
All LGUs Aggregated At Provincial Level							
PC IRA w/PC Household income	–0.08	0.10	0.10	0.21	0.25	0.00	–0.02
PC Grants w/PC Household income	0.38	–0.05	0.12	0.15	–0.12	–0.01	–0.10
PC OSR + PC IRA w/PC Household income	0.31	0.22	0.19	0.35	0.44	0.16	0.14
PC OSR + PC IRA + PC Grants w/PC Household income	0.40	0.22	0.19	0.35	0.44	0.16	0.14
PC OSR w/PC Household income	0.49	0.48	0.44	0.53	0.61	0.59	0.61
Provinces							
PC IRA w/PC Household income	0.12	0.16	0.28	0.33	0.31	0.06	0.05
PC Grants w/PC Household income	0.40	–0.11	0.14	0.04	0.02	–0.02	–0.03
PC OSR + PC IRA w/PC Household income	0.27	0.21	0.35	0.38	0.39	0.13	0.10
PC OSR + PC IRA + PC Grants w/PC Household income	0.38	0.21	0.35	0.38	0.39	0.13	0.10
PC OSR w/PC Household income	0.34	0.34	0.50	0.51	0.48	0.45	0.52

(*Continued*)

Table 20. *(Continued)*

	1991	1995	1996	1997	1998	1999	2000
Cities							
PC IRA w/PC Household income	–0.38	–0.41	–0.38	–0.43	–0.46	–0.57	–0.55
PC Grants w/PC Household income	0.02	–0.09	0.03	0.20	0.12	0.05	0.02
PC LSR + PC IRA w/PC Household income	0.31	0.32	0.49	0.31	0.45	0.30	0.28
PC LSR + PC IRA + PC Grants w/PC Household income	0.28	0.30	0.48	0.31	0.45	0.30	0.28
PC OSR w/PC Household income	0.61	0.81	0.84	0.77	0.80	0.69	0.69
Muncipalities by Provincial Level							
PC IRA w/PC Household income	–0.10	0.02	–0.02	0.09	0.12	–0.08	–0.11
PC Grants w/PC Household income	0.20	–0.11	0.02	0.33	–0.02	0.09	0.01
PC LSR + PC IRA w/PC Household income	0.68	0.29	0.09	0.36	0.43	0.21	0.18
PC LSR + PC IRA + PC Grants w/PC Household income	0.59	0.29	0.09	0.37	0.43	0.21	0.18
PC OSR w/PC Household income	0.81	0.71	0.42	0.72	0.75	0.81	0.83

It is also interesting to note that categorical grants did not always result in greater equalization of fiscal capacity in the period under study. In particular, the categorical grants for cities tend to be counter-equalizing in 1996–2000.

4.5. *Impact of Inter-governmental Fiscal Structure on Revenue Mobilization*

An interesting question to raise, is whether there are incentive effects of inter-governmental transfers for local government revenue mobilization.

Dis-incentive effect of IRA on own source revenue. Earlier studies shows that while inter-governmental transfers had a neutral effect on local revenue performance in 1985 (prior to the Code), it substituted for local tax revenues in all levels of local governments in 1992 and 1993 (Manasan, 1995).

Using panel data for provinces, cities and municipalities for 1995–2000, regression analysis of per capita local tax revenues on per capita household income[27] (as a proxy for the local tax base) and per capita IRA (as a way to check whether inter-governmental grants stimulates or substitutes for local government revenue effort) reconfirm the dis-incentive effect of the IRA on local tax effort in the post-Code period. The results show that LGUs which were "net winners" from fiscal decentralization tended to have lower per capita local tax revenue (see Table 21). This is the case for both the real property tax and the local business tax equations of provinces and in real property tax equations of cities. The coefficient of per capita IRA is negative and statistically significant in the local business tax equation of cities. These findings suggest that LGUs which received higher IRA (whether in absolute terms or relative to their expenditure responsibilities) tended to be lax in their tax effort. Thus, there appears to be a need to alter the IRA distribution formula so as to provide incentives for local tax effort.

As expected, the analysis also shows that per capita local tax revenue is positively and significantly related to per capita household income for both real property tax and local business tax for cities, municipalities and provinces alike in 1995–2000 (see Table 21). This finding confirms

[27] Personal income data are obtained from the Family Income and Expenditure Survey (FIES) of the National Statistics Office.

Table 21. Regression of Per Capita Tax Revenue of LGUs[a]

	Province		Cities		Municipalities[b]	
	PCLBT[b]	PCRPT[b]	PCLBT[c]	PCRPT[b]	PCLBT	PCRPT
Constant	–17.246	–17.980	–0.886	–241.829	–15.072	–16.392
	(–2.91)	(–3.82)	(–0.25)	(–2.25)	(–5.38)	(–5.26)
Density	–0.360	0.204	0.213	0.005	0.468	0.490
	(–1.48)*	(1.05)	(2.19)**	(1.35)*	(3.45)**	(3.24)**
PCFIESY	2.128	2.155	0.732	0.015	1.289	1.399
	(3.67)**	(4.62)**	(3.26)**	(6.68)**	(4.47)**	(4.36)**
PCIRA	–0.384	–0.163	–0.469	0.114	0.504	0.538
	(–1.03)	(–0.55)	(–1.63)**	(1.72)**	(1.74)**	(1.66)**
D1*PCIRA	–0.102	–0.070	—	–0.080	—	—
	(–1.70)**	(–1.45)*	—	(–1.36)*	—	—
X^2 (Chi-square)	4.83	10.66	40.78	22.13	25.77	23.69

[a] Numbers in parenthesis refer to t-statistics.
[b] Follows double log specification.
[c] Follows linear specification.
* Statistically significant at 10%.
** Statistically significant at 5%.

that local tax effort is largely determined by ability to pay. Given the wide disparities in the distribution of the local tax base across regions, this result further highlights the potential for regional inequality to increase with greater fiscal decentralization.

5. Agenda for Reform

5.1. *Expenditure Assignment*

Overall, the devolution of expenditure responsibilities to sub-national governments is consistent with the decentralization theorem. One important exception to the application of this principle in the Philippines is education. Although the construction and maintenance of school buildings was devolved to LGUs under the Code, the primary responsibility for the provision of education remains with the central government. In contrast, the experience in many countries shows that devolving education could possibly improve production efficiency and thus, a review of this specific expenditure assignment may be warranted.

Section 17(b) of the Local Government Code provides an unambiguous delineation of functions across levels of government, but Section 17(c) on nationally funded devolved activities and Section(f) on national government augmentation of devolved services obfuscates what initially appears to be a clear cut assignment of expenditure responsibilities.

There is need to revisit the 1991 Code in order to clarify the assignment of expenditure responsibilities across levels of local government. In particular, Sections 17(c) and (f) of the Code should be re-examined hand-in-hand with the review of the distribution formula of the IRA. This would require a careful re-assessment of the need for the continued funding of devolved activities by national government agencies as well as LGU budgetary support of local offices (and employees) of many national government agencies. The imposition of unfunded mandates that are not associated with compensating transfers to LGUs should be eliminated. The devolution of functions from the regional government of the ARMM to ARMM-LGUs should be encouraged.

Three major trends in LGU expenditure are a major source of concern. First, aggregate LGU spending on the social services sector registered a general upward trend in 1991–2001 when expressed as a percent of GNP and in real per capita terms. However, some stagnation (especially with respect to health expenditures) is evident in 1998–2001 when either of these measures is used. These movements are common across all levels of local government and appear to be related to the fiscal difficulties LGUs face when simultaneously, their IRA is not released in full, and they suffer from a decline their own-source revenue. This development is worrisome considering that LGUs are primarily responsible for the delivery of basic health services. It also highlights the need to design grants that will help ensure that LGUs have primary responsibility for delivering health and education services that are at least equal to minimum service standards.

Second, LGU spending on transportation and communication contracted from 0.5% of GNP in 1991 to 0.4% of GNP in 2001 despite the devolution of the responsibility for local infrastructure to LGUs. This decline masks even larger reductions in the infrastructure spending of provincial and municipal governments. These developments appear to be linked to the mismatch in the distribution of resources and expenditure responsibilities across levels of local governments. Also, given the robust and strong association between economic growth and infrastructure spending, they may be indicative of a widening of the disparities in economic development across levels of local government. This underscores the need to strengthen the regulatory framework and arrangements for LGU borrowing and to address the requirements for LGU capital investment financing in the design of inter-governmental transfers.

Third, personal services are the single biggest expenditure item at all levels of local government. While the share of personal services in total LGU expenditure contracted from 45.8% in 1991 to 37.5% in 2001 in the case of cities, it expanded from 41.6% to 45.1% in the case of provinces and from 46.1% to 55.3% in the case of municipalities. Because of these developments, there has been a squeeze on the capital outlays of provinces and both MOOE and capital outlays of municipalities. In this regard, there is a need to re-assess the compensation and position classification system, as well as the list of mandatory LGU positions provided for in the Local Government Code, in order to give LGUs more leeway in adjusting their PS expenditures. Also, a review of the cap on PS expenditures is in order. Existing practices and procedures that allow LGUs to comply with this requirement do not appear to be helpful in enabling LGUs to effectively control their wage bill.

5.2. *Tax Assignment*

The current tax assignment scores well in terms of the autonomy criterion. While the Local Government Code authorizes LGUs to levy several taxes, the more revenue productive taxes are retained by the central government. Even in the case of allowable local taxes, the Code seriously constrains the power of LGUs to set local tax rates. Thus, the link between LGU spending responsibilities and their taxing powers is weak.

Given this background, future Code amendments should focus on promoting tax decentralization. In particular, LGUs should be given greater discretion in setting tax rates by (1) raising the maximum allowable tax rates, (2) allowing LGUs to adjust the tax rates more frequently, and (3) relaxing the restrictions on the size of the tax rate adjustments that are authorized. More importantly, LGUs should be allowed to impose a surcharge (i.e., piggyback) on some central government taxes (possibly, the individual income tax).

Also, the tax structure prescribed by the Code for the local business tax should be simplified so as to accommodate a weak local government tax administration and improve taxpayer compliance. At the same time, support for greater computerization and capacity building for the staff of the tax division is critical.

Finally, the conduct of the general revision of the schedule of market values of real property might be de-politicized by lodging this activity with the central government. Such a move will not reduce the autonomy of LGUs, provided they retain control over local tax rates and assessment levels.

5.3 *Inter-governmental Transfers*

In the Philippines as in other countries, LGUs in the aggregate suffer from a vertical fiscal gap. Many types of taxes are either easier to administer at the central level or are deemed to be unsuitable for local government imposition because their tax bases are geographically mobile. On the other hand, the principle of subsidiarity implies that many functions are best assigned to local governments. To a large extent, this gap is addressed by inter-governmental transfers (specifically the IRA) and LGUs have been clamoring to increase the size of the IRA pool.

As indicated above, there is a mismatch between the assignment of revenues (local taxes plus IRA) and the assignment of expenditure responsibilities to the different levels of local government. The share of provinces and municipalities in total LGU own-source revenue has declined in the post-Code period despite their large share in the cost of devolved functions.

In this context, there is a need to re-assess the tax and expenditure assignment across different levels of local government. At the same time, the vertical imbalance should be addressed primarily through greater tax decentralization — the assignment of more productive tax bases to LGUs. Consequently, inter-governmental transfers could then be re-designed to help close the disparities in the fiscal capacities of LGUs as well as to ensure that LGUs get the appropriate financing to achieve minimum service standards for key basic social services.

References

Ahmad, E, D Hewitt and E Ruggiero (1997). Assigning Expenditure Responsibilities. In *Fiscal Federalism in Theory and Practice*. T Ter-Minassian (ed.), Washington DC: International Monetary Fund.

Bird, R (1999). Rethinking subnational taxes: A new look at tax assignment. IMF Working Paper No. 99/165. Washington DC: International Monetary Fund.

Capuno, J J, T C Manuel and M B T Salvador (2001). Estimating the IRA, Centrally-Provided Local Public Goods and Services, and Other Central Fiscal Transfers to Local Governments, Report prepared for National Economic and Development Authority with support from the Australian Government through the Philippines–Australian Governance Facility.

Celestino, A, N Malvar and R Zipagan (1998). *Local Fiscal Administration in the Philippines*. Manila: UP Center for Local and Regional Governance.

Jimenez, E, V Paqueo and L de Vera (1988). Does local financing make primary schools more efficient? PPR Working Paper WPS 69. Washington DC: World Bank.

Loehr, W and R Manasan (1999). Fiscal Decentralization and Economic Efficiency: Measurement and Evaluation, Report submitted to USAID Manila.

Manasan, R G (2002). The Role of Education Decentralization in Promoting Effective Schooling: The Philippines, ERD Working Paper No. 24, Asian Development Bank, Manila.

McLure, C E (1999). The Tax Assignment Problem: Conceptual and Administrative Considerations in Achieving Subnational Fiscal Autonomy, in www.worldbank.org/decentralization.

McLure, C E and J M Vázquez (1999). The Assignment of Revenues and Expenditures in Intergovernmental Fiscal Relations, in www.worldbank.org/decentralization.

Shah, A (1994). *The reform of intergovernmental fiscal relations in developing and emerging market economies.* Washington DC: World Bank.

Ter-Minassian, T (1997). *Fiscal federalism in theory and practice.* Washington DC: International Monetary Fund.

Appendix

Asian Development Conference 2003: Development and Decentralization in Asia

This appendix gives the details of the first Asian Development Conference, 2003, and supplement the book by offering a review of the whole subjects and the discussions by many experts from the international organizations and many countries' officials and economists in Asia. Varieties of their problems are surveyed and debated at the conference. First, the whole program is given and then follows the summary reports of the discussions by three moderators. The book adopted many contributions from Seminar A and some from Seminar B, so that the summary report of A is brief and the summary reports of B and C are detailed. Since many papers were not included in this book, the editors hope that the reader will recognize the remaining problems of *Decentralization* and pursue the studies further.

I. ADC Program

10–11 November, 2003
Venue: Kitakyushu, Japan
M: Moderator, Co-M: Co-moderator, S: Session, D: Discussant

Opening Ceremony & Welcome Remarks

Keynote Lecture: **Roy W. Bahl** (Georgia State U)
"The Promise and Reality of Decentralization in Asia"

Panel Discussion on Reality of Decentralization Policies in Japan

Panelists: **Kenji Araki** (The Decentralization Promotion Council, Prime Minister's Office), **Taku Kajiwara** (Governor of Gifu Prefecture), **oichi Sueyoshi** (Mayor of Kitakyushu City),
Coordinator: **Tatsuo Hatta** (U. of Tokyo)

(Continued)

Seminar A **⟪Political Decentralization⟫**	**Seminar B** **⟪Local Public Finance⟫**	**Seminar C** **⟪Urbanization Problems⟫**
M: **Eiji Tajika** (Hitotsubashi U.)	M: **Takashi Fukushima** (National Graduate Institute for Policy Studies)	M: **Hidehiko Tanimura** (U. of Kitakyushu)
Co-M: **Hiroko Kudo** (Waseda U.)	Co-M: **Motohiro Sato** (Hitotsubashi U.)	Co-M: **Peter J. Marcofullio** (UN U. Tokyo)
Seminar: A-1. **S1: Hee Joon Song** (Ehwa Woman U.) 'Decentralization and Local e-Government in Korea'	**Seminar: B-1.** **S1: Azmi Setapa** (Malaysian Inst. for Economic Research) 'The Perfomance of the State and Local Government Finance'	**Seminar: C-1.** **S1: Takeo Ihara** (U of Kitakyushu) 'Retrospect and Prospect of Urbanization Process in Japan'
D1: Shigeyuki Abe (Kyoto U.)	**D1: Olarn Chaipravat** (Fiscal Policy Res. In., M. of Finance)	**D1: Yung Joon Lee** (Pusan National U.)
S2: Jay N. Shih (Taiwan, National Ceng Chi U.) 'Administrative Reform in Taiwan: An Uneasy and Unfinished Political Task'	**S2: Mahfud Sidik** (M. of Finance) 'Indonesia's Imbalance: Fiscal Decentralization and its future direction'	**S2: Zuo Xue-Jin,** (China, Shanghai Academy of Social Sciences) 'China's Urbanization during Its Economic Transition'
D2: Yuzo Yabuno (Kyushu Univ.)	**D2: Peter McCawley** (Asian Development Bank Institute)	**D2: Masahisa Fujita** (Kyoto U.)

(Continued)

Seminar: A-2.	Seminar: B-2	Seminar: C-2.
S1: Toshihiro Ihori (U of Tokyo) 'Political decentralization in Japan'	**S1: Shin Saito** (Osaka U) 'Toward the Reform of Japanese Local Governments'	**S1: Sam Ock Park** (Seoul Nat.U) 'Over-concentration of Economic Activities in Capital Region and Regional Development Policies'
D1: Zong-Chang Peng (Tsing-hua U)	**D1: Dubburi Subbarao** (USA, The World Bank)	**D1: Lim Lan Yuan** (S. of Design & Env., NU of Singapore)
S2: Benjamin Diokno (U of the Philippines) 'Decentralization in the Philippines After Ten Years?'	**S2: Christine Wong** (U of Washington) 'China's Problematic Fiscal Decentralization'	**S2: Ming Sheng Hwang** (Nat. Ceng Chi U.) 'Private participation inter-city transport; and single-day access sphere'
D2: Shunji Asanuma (Hitotsubashi U)	**D2: Jung Hung Kim** (Korea Institute of Public Finance)	**D2: Pongsak Hoontrakul** (Chulalonglorn U.)
S3: Dana Weist (The World Bank) 'Thailand's Decentralization: Progress and Prospects'		**S3: Banupong Nidhiprabha** (Thammasat U) 'Sustainable Urbanization in Thailand'
D3: Nobuki Mochida (U of Tokyo)		**D3: Shoichi Yamashita** (The International Centre for the Study of East Asian Development)

(Continued)

Seminar: A-3. **S1: Bert Homan** (The World Bank) 'Managing Indonesia's Rapid Decentralization'	**Seminar: B-3.** **S1: Chu Wei Tseng** (National Ceng Chi U) 'Fiscal Decentralization and Local Government Finance in Taiwan'	**Seminar: C-3.** **S1: Eduardo T. Gonzalez** (Development Academy of Philippines) 'Managing Urban Decentralization'
D1: Sresh Narayanan (U. Sains Malaysia)	**D1: Jan P. M. van Heeswijk** (Asian Development Bank)	**D1: Peter J. Marcofullio** (UN U. Tokyo)
S2: M. Govinda Rao (National Institute of Public Finance and Policy) 'Fiscal Federalism in India : Trends and Reform Issues'	**S2: Rosario G. Manasan** (Philippine Inst. for Dev. Studies) 'Local Public Finance in the Philippines — balancing autonomy and accountability'	**S2: Bambang P. S. Brojonegoro** (U of Indonesia) 'Decentralization and Urbanization in Indonesia :The Concept of Metropolitan Area'
S2: Nguyan Khac Hung (Nat. Academy of Public Administration, M of Home Affairs, Vietnam)	**D2: Wang Tong** (State Council Office for Restructuring Economic System, China)	**D2: Kunio Yoshihara** (U of Kitakyushu)

Closing Ceremony & Closing Remarks

Observations on Seminar Series A	M: **Hiroko Kudo** (Waseda Univ.)
Observations on Seminar Series B	M: **Motohiro Sato** (Hitotsubashi U)
Observations on Seminar Series C	M: **Hidehiko Tanimura** (U. of Kitakyushu)

II. Some Comments for Seminar A: Political and Fiscal Decentralization

Hiroko Kudo (Waseda University)

Discussions in Seminar A on political and fiscal decentralization went on without exactly defining *decentralization*. It may be useful to compare it with synonymous terms like *devolution* and *delegation*. *Devolution* usually means the political power shift from the center (the State level) to periphery (local level) and often used in political rather than economic, fiscal or administrative context. In Italy, for example, *decentralization* is understood to accompany the gradual transfer of central government's tasks and functions to local governments, whereas the radical *devolution* of power was discussed by Northern League with creation of secessionist parliament as a political bargaining toward the coalition partners.

Delegation is used in more concrete context and deals with administrative functions or competence. Needless to say, delegation of the functions of the central government to local governments is possible without real *devolution* of power. In Japan, most local governments perform the varieties of functions delegated by the central government without any political devolution or decentralization. These delegated functions are fiscally guaranteed with the national treasury disbursements and controlled directly and exclusively by the central government.

Thus, decentralization clearly has something to do with power structure, administrative institutions, functions, decision-making process, service delivery, participation and so on. All these elements are involved in the concept of decentralization. How they are involved in decentralization must be clearly specified. Is legislative procedure decentralized? Or is the way of delivering public services decentralized? Is the decision-making of local expenditure items decentralized?

Next, for what decentralization is undertaken is also important. Is it for business corporations or citizens? This aspect has something to do with whom the decentralization will be beneficial for.

Thirdly, we must be clear whether we consider decentralization within the framework of unified State or go as far as the possibility of federal State. Federalism comes close to the political *devolution* mentioned above. Even in Japan there are arguments and some proposals that go as far as to decentralize the Japanese political organization into roughly 10 regions — called "Doshu-Sei", but the major discussions and the decentralization policies being implemented in Japan nowadays are within the given framework of the present political system.

Lastly, not only the benefit of decentralization but the cost must be considered. Usually it is argued that decentralization will bring the government closer to citizens and will make it respond and act more quickly to the needs of the citizens It will also activate civil participation and improve public service and so on. However, decentralization has also negative aspects. First of all, changing the power structure, administrative institution, functions, process, service delivery and so on costs a lot. More precisely, decentralization generates more decision-making units, and so it takes more decision-making time. All these would be calculated as new cost. The possible interference of the new decision-makers could cause corruption. Integration of new units may be difficult and become divisionistic. Decentralization might produce different standards for business practices and administrative processes in different locations, causing inconveniences for private businesses and citizens. The transaction cost might be larger in the decentralized states. These negative impacts accompanying decentralization should not be forgotten all together.

The reaction of Japanese Business Federation toward the argument of federal state has changed. In the 80's when the idea was first proposed, it was strongly against the concept. Nowadays, however, it is promoting decentralization, probably because the main concern of big businesses in Japan has shifted from the concern about the administrative cost to delivery of services for consumers. No doubt if better consumer services are delivered, decentralization is much more beneficial to the private businesses.

III. Summary Report of Seminar B: Local Public Finance

Motohiro Sato (Hitotsubashi University)

In Seminar B, six papers on local public finance were presented from Malaysia, Indonesia, China, Taiwan, the Philippines and Japan. They covered a variety of issues associated with fiscal decentralization, especially focusing on inter-governmental transfers and local own revenues. This report aims at summarizing the discussions with a view to identifying common policies and country-specific factors.

1. Common Policy Issues

1) Inadequacy of Financial Resources

It was addressed that the local governments commonly in such countries as Malaysia, Indonesia and Philippines were not adequately funded to finance their expenditure obligations. In the Philippines, for instance, unfunded mandates spread through mandated increase in public officials' salaries. Mismatch between expenditure responsibility and revenue assigned makes it difficult for those local governments to carry out their expenditure functions, leading to undersupply of key local services like education and health. It may be arguable that on statistics local governments in the aggregate have fiscal surplus. That is indeed the case in Indonesia and Malaysia. This does not mean, however, that local governments are granted abundant funds. It may imply rather that with their limited budgets local governments are forced to plan carefully their expenditure and/or transfers from the central government are not received timely so that they are simply delaying the spending on local services. Given the existing vertical fiscal gap with the central authority dominating major tax bases, local governments must rely heavily on inter-governmental transfers in conditional or unconditional forms. Although some economic rationale exists between vertical fiscal gap and normative roles in such transfers, the practice of inter-governmental transfers differs from the normative descriptions due to the lack of accountability and reliability, This situation substantially hinders efficient and effective fiscal management and policy implementation at the local level.

2) Inter-Regional Fiscal Gap

Not only inadequate funding but also fiscal imbalance across the regions matters in some countries. Fiscal decentralization has exacerbated further. In the case of Indonesia, for instance, an arrangement to share national resource tax revenue as a part of decentralization program benefited only the natural resource rich regions, leaving the natural resource poor ones with inadequate revenues. From normative standpoint, equalization grants should serve to lower such fiscal disparity. In Indonesia, there are such formula based on general-purpose transfers named DAU. In the Philippines, they are called IRA. Both of them are fixed to a certain portion of the central tax revenue: 25% of net domestic revenue in Indonesia and 40% of internal revenue in the Philippines. Observations reveal, however, that these grants are not sufficient to equalize fiscal resources across the regions. On the contrary, it is noted that often per capita transfer is positively correlated with per capita income, implying that richer regions get richer after transfers! In Japan, however, it is pointed out that general-purpose transfers called LAT excessively equalize fiscal capacities; such LAT dependent region as Okinawa becoming richer in terms of per capita government revenue after transfer than such fiscally independent region as Tokyo.

3) Financing Local governments

Revenue sources of local governments largely consist of (i) own revenue, (ii) intergovernmental transfers and (iii) local borrowing. In most countries, the central authority regulates or prohibits the last one, which Dr. Sepata from Malaysia challenges. He claims that bond financing could offer a solution to the finance of local governments. Although local borrowing can finance development expenditures like investments in infrastructure, caution is needed. As experiences in Latin America reveal, the central governments may ultimately bear costs of bailing out indebted local governments, which gives rise to moral hazard or the soft budget problem, because local governments may *ex ante* anticipate such *ex post* rescues by the central government.

The literature on fiscal federalism sometimes argues for a case in which the central government can raise tax revenues more efficiently and equitably, and fiscal vertical gaps should be filled through intergovernmental transfers. In practice, however, inter-governmental transfers are neither adequate nor reliable in such countries as Indonesia and Philippines. Moreover, abusing its spending power, the central authority often excessively intrudes into local matters, hindering local autonomy. Most paper presenters in Seminar B advocated more local autonomy in revenue raising to enhance local own revenues alongside with de-regulation of the central controls on local taxes. Japan is not an exception of this trend. There is increasing demand for devolving more taxing power to local governments as a part of the *trinity reform*.

Table 1 Local Revenue

	Benefits	Costs
Local Tax Revenue	Enhance local autonomy and fiscal responsibility	Exacerbate fiscal inequity and externalities
Inter-governmental transfers	Fill vertical and horizontal fiscal gaps Ensure national minimums	Cause excessive central intrusions into local matters/pork barrel politics May not be reliable/ accountable
Local Bond	Finance development purpose expenditures	Lead to ex post bail-out and the soft budget problems
Non-tax revenue: fees & charges	Satisfy the benefit principle	May be levied in adhoc/ discretional manners as unofficial policies

S. Saito addressed a concern, however, in the context of Japanese decentralization that horizontal fiscal imbalances may be exacerbated due to uneven distribution of tax bases for revenue side. In developing countries, moreover, local governments may not be skillful enough to administer the tax systems due to the shortage of human resources or managerial ability. Thus simple-minded attempts to mobilize local revenue will not be enough to meet the fiscal shortage of local governments. Of course, if managed properly, decentralization on revenue side may improve local autonomy and possibly fiscal accountability and to promote regional economic development. This has been the case in China after 1980.

Lastly, the formal authorities of local governments often do not match real ones in developing and transition economies with the relatively weak law enforcement. For instance, in China the central authority's attempt to re-centralize tax system in 1994 reform allegedly spread a wide use of informal instruments to finance local spending such as fee and charges levied on regional residents and businesses in adhoc and discretional ways.

4) Summary

Fiscal decentralization is gaining political support in most Asian countries but is not a panacea. A relevant question is not to initiate it but how to design it. It involves many dimensions on expenditure and revenue sides as well as a variety of ways to assign tasks or authorities to different levels of governments. We need to optimize, therefore, the design of decentralization by minimizing its costs and maximizing its benefits.

It does not mean that different governments can act independently. On the contrary, usually closer policy coordication is required in many fields such as economic development, welfare and education. Intergovernmental transfers can be a useful device to enhance cooperation. For that purpose, local governments themselves must mutually trust each other and be accountable. Such reliability is missing in newly decentralized countries like Indonesia and the Philippines.

2. Country Specific Issues

1) Malaysia

Economic development has changed the environments surrounding local governments in this country with increasing population in urban areas and their demand for better quality of public services. The local governments, however, are not granted adequate financial revenue sources to fulfill newly arising fiscal needs. A Setapa claims that local bonds in domestic and international markets could offer a solution, although accounting practice and transparency issues must be resolved. In addition, the central authority must not bail out the indebted regions so as not to cause the soft budget problem and harm macro-economic stability.

2) Indonesia

This country has undertaken a "big bang" approach for fiscal decentralization. It is attempting to radically change the inter-governmental relations by devolving more power and responsibility to lower level governments. It was once governed by one of the most centralized and authoritarian government but has been transformed into one of the most decentralized or fragmented nation. Two laws outline Indonesia's decentralization, Law No.22/1999 that underlines assignment of expenditure responsibility between the central and local governments prepared by Ministry of Home Affairs, and Law No.22/1999 that determines revenue assignment drafted by Ministry of Finance. The former does not clearly delineate expenditures so that ambiguity and uncertainty remain over which tasks to be carried out by which level governments or how much financial resources should be ensured to which expenditure. The latter stipulates an arrangement for tax revenue sharing but gives rise to horizontal fiscal imbalances, which needs to be reduced by the equalization grants. The general-purpose transfers called DAU are formula-based but have limited capability for equalization due to hold-harmless provisions that ensure previous year amounts of transfers to individual local governments. Moreover, local taxing powers are not sufficient to meet their newly assigned expenditure functions. The author argues that more tax autonomy be granted to regional governments, while strengthening equalization functions of DAU. He suggests "picky back tax" for personal income tax with tax rate locally decided but collection by the central government.

3) China

The presented paper discusses macro-economic effects of active fiscal policy developing simulation models called MCAFR.

4) Japan

Comprehensive reform of inter-governmental relations involving tax devolution, deregulation of the central control on local spending and reduction of inter-governmental transfers has been discussed in Japan. On statistics, Japanese local public finance may look decentralized on the expenditure side with local spending occupying about 60% of public expenditure. The practice is, however, that the local governments have been as agents of the central authority, implementing centrally decided policies. The central government is dominant on the revenues side, accounting for about 56% of tax revenue. The resulting vertical fiscal gap needs to be filled by massive transfers from the central to local governments in conditional and unconditional forms. Recently, such dependence on inter-governmental transfers not only hinders local autonomy but also give rise to moral hazard among grant receiving regions. Tax devolution and reduction in conditional transfers aim at enhancing local governments' discretions in their spending so as to fit local needs as well as improving their fiscal accountability. The problem is that due to uneven distribution of devolved tax bases, horizontal fiscal imbalance prior to transfer is exacerbated by this reform; along with decrease in transfers many local governments that have been fiscally dependent will be confronted with revenue decrease, which is confirmed by the author through a variety of simulations. Only Tokyo with affluent own revenue source will be a winner of this reform, generating so called Tokyo problem. On one hand, decentralization enhances productive and locative efficiency. On the other hand, revenue side decentralization may benefits only rich regions, the rest being left with lower revenue including transfers. One may argue, however, that in the status quo, fiscally poor regions receive excessive transfers, becoming richer than Tokyo after transfer, and thus reform bring about more equitable distribution of revenue across the regions.

5) Taiwan

As is the case in Japan, local public finance in Taiwan is characterized by a large vertical fiscal gap; the central government occupies a bulky share of tax revenue, about 81% in FY2001, whereas local level governments are in charge of about 35% of public spending in the same year. The consequence is that local governments are heavily dependent on inter-governmental transfers that take conditional and unconditional forms. General-purpose transfers in this country, called Centrally-Allotted Tax Revenue (CATR), has been tied to certain portions of major central tax revenues, 10% of central income tax and commodity tax and 40% of business tax, and so on. Reflecting different functions on the expenditure side, different allocation formulas of CATR apply to Metropolitan and county/city, the business sales are dominant in formula for the former and fiscal ability defined by difference between basic fiscal needs and basic fiscal revenues playing an important role for the latter. Supplementary to CATR, grants in aid are provided, taking a form of block grants aiming to finance certain local spending categories such as education and social welfare. Overall, it can be said that local governments do not possess sufficient tax collection powers with local discretions in raising own revenues being restricted by the central regulations. Recently, a policy change was made to promote local autonomy. In December 2002, local governments are authorized to levy special taxes and surtaxes on existing national taxes, though their discretions are still limited. To reform the funding and allocation formula of CATR and Grants in Aid, revision of the Law Governing Allocation of Government Revenue and Expenditure (LGAGRE) has been also proposed, but such a reform proposal is far from initiating a considerable fiscal decentralization.

6) The Philippines

The Local Government Code of 1999 determines the assignment of tax and expenditure responsibilities to the central and sub-national governments that are largely consistent with widely accepted principles of federalism literature. Closer look exhibits, however, that expenditures being not clearly aligned, the central government de facto retains its devolved functions, and that the local governments with their constrained control of local tax rates are granted only limited authority of raising own revenues. Weaker link between own revenue and public expenditure diminishes efficiency gain from fiscal decentralization, and lowers the incentives for local governments to be fiscally responsible. Both vertical and horizontal fiscal gaps are evident in the Philippines. The former is often exacerbated by the unfunded mandate such as mandated increase of officials' salaries. The horizontal fiscal imbalance is supposed to be dealt by inter-governmental transfers or IRA in this country. Its formula is based upon population (50%), land area (25%) and equal sharing (25%)m, so that it clearly does not account for inter-regional fiscal disparity. Evidence reveals that richer regions are treated more favorably, and that equal sharing component gives rise to pervasive incentives of local government to split own jurisdiction. Furthermore, Manasan points out that the IRA discourages tax collection efforts of transfer receiving regions.

IV. Summary Report of Seminar C: Urbanization and Decentralization

Hidehiko Tanimura (University of Kitakyushu)

In Seminar C, seven papers were presented from Japan, China, Korea, Taiwan, Thailand, Philippines, and Indonesia. This summary presents the outline of each paper and ensued discussions in each session. Although each country is in a different stage of urbanization in terms of its density, concentration, and hierarchy, there is a consensus that the proper management of not only its urban settlements but also its national urban system is essential for its socioeconomic well-being.

1. Urbanization in Japan and China

Takeo Ihara (U of Kitakyushu) presented a paper on the urbanization process in Japan. Based upon Leo Klassen's spatial cycle model of concentration, suburbanization, dis-urbanization and re-urbanization, Ihara attempted to clarify the process empirically in Japan and develop policy recommendations. His main findings were that the "regional cycle" hypothesis does not always hold in Japan. The phase diagram of the urbanization process, however, has advantages of describing urban development in Japan. Generally cities are undergoing relative or absolute decentralization as the suburbs continue to grow, although there are cities undergoing other aspects of the process. Medium size cities are at the stage of suburbanization, while large scale SMEAs are mainly at the stage of re-urbanization.

In phase diagrams, Ihara tested whether cities under the counter-clockwise movement of urban growth as predicted by the model. With cities of 1 and 2 million, he noted the irregular shape of Kitakyushu. He also noted that many cities hover around the first quadrant, suburbanization.

In terms of policy recommendations he said that there were recent distortions in the process within Japan that make a new phase or process likely. It seems that cities are ready to jump right from suburbanization to counter-urbanization. Moreover, social and demographic factors are more important than the stage of urban growth in predicting future changes. This has led him to suggest a research agenda that returns to understanding why people move and how cities grow.

Discussant Yung Joon Lee (Pusan National U) led the discussion, focusing on the size of population and its relations to the spatial cycle in Japan. He suggested a hypothesis that the stage of urbanization is related to the size of population with a particular urban hierarchy. He then presented the Korean case in comparison. (His discussion is summarized in Exhibit C-l.)

Zuo Xuejin (Shanghai Academy of Social Sciences) presented a paper on China's urbanization during the country's economic transition. He showed how China's urban share of population increased from 18.4% to 36.1% from 1964 to 2000. The main jump occurred between 1980 (26.23%) and 2000 (36.09 %). He noted that these data may not be representative for a variety of reasons, including definitional changes of the urban status. He noted that both large cities and small cities are growing more slowly than medium size cities in China. At the same time, the reasons for the slower growth differ from small to large. The barriers to migration and urbanization include attempts for cities to restrict migration. Cities are careful about accepting rural migrants due to the existence of large urban-rural disparity. This is because all the welfare programs in the country are run by localities (making them conservative in who they select as viable migrants). Interestingly, relationship between intra or inter-provincial migration and levels of unemployment within cities is not statistically significant. He suggests that these barriers should be removed to accelerate urbanization rates. China has inadequate aggregate demand. He believes that an increase in the urban population will help solve this problem by stimulating domestic demand to make the economy grow.

Masahisa Fujita (Kyoto U) was the discussant. He suggested that the recent information provided by the paper is helpful for those interested in development policies of China. For example, the paper explains the now common sight of beggars in Beijing, as the country has loosened its migrant policies and people are flooding into cities from the countryside. He also noted some different aspects of China's urbanization. First, there is a boundary problem of deciding what is urban and rural, as some of China's cities have boundaries that include large amounts of agricultural land. Second, he noted that the large difference in income typically increases rural to urban migration, but in China's case it doesn't exactly work that way even after the legal barriers are lifted. (As Zuo suggested cities can control migration to their individual cities).

Finally, he provided a lecture on the theoretical underpinnings for accelerating urban growth. He did this through the use of a chart that relates labor productivity changes to the changing ratio of rural and urban population.

2. Urbanization in Korea, Taiwan and Thailand

Sam Ock Park (Seoul National U) presented 'Over-concentration of Economic Activities in the Capital Region and Regional Development Policies in Korea." His main findings are; 1) there remains an over-concentration of activities in the capital region, and 2) more importantly while the difference between internet users between urban and rural are not that different, there is a significant agglomeration of Internet businesses in Seoul. Within the Capital region Seoul has 79.5 percent of the business to business electronic commerce (B2B EC) operating sites.

This suggests the calls for the 'end of geography' are inadequate, electronic spaces are still linked strongly with physical spaces. E-business still has a place-based component. Because of this situation, the government has emphasized the national balanced development. The main aim is to promote the formation of regional innovation systems (RIS), as the most important strategy. This R1S strategy for development in the current global knowledge economy includes attempts to:

- Promote region-specific clustering;
- Building habitat for innovation and entrepreneurship;
- Building collective learning and innovation networks;
- Building a stock of social capital; and
- Promoting local and global networks.

These general strategies were then translated into a set of specific recommendations for Korea.

Discussant Lim Lan Yuan (National U of Singapore) suggested that what Singapore has done provides an interesting point of departure for his recommendations. He went through the five recommendations in terms of Singapore's policies and found common ground in theory and opportunities for collaboration.

Ming Sheng Hwang (National Cheng Chi University) presented: "Private participation in inter-city transportation projects and single-day-access-spheres in Taiwan." Decentralization in Taiwan has been linked to the increase in the size of the single-day-access-sphere. He reviewed the transportation infrastructure development history within the country. In each case he identified the shrinkage in the "single-day-access-sphere. Before the Japanese arrived it took approximately 10 days to travel from the North to the South of Taiwan. The Japanese began a program of infrastructure development on the island including a railway, which reduced the North-South travel time to 10 hours. Travel time again was reduced by a high-speed highway implemented by the Taiwanese government to 5 hours, but this effort did not include private sector participation. A current project does include private-sector participation (BOT) will reduce the time of travel to 1.5 hours. It should be operational within a year.

Discussant Pongsak Hoontrakul (Chulalongkorn U) observed that the shrinkage of single- day-access-sphere may centralize certain functions and decentralize other ones. He suggests it is important to promote private participation to nurture market and openness for innovations. One of his concerns is how to assist the under-privileged in these attempts.

An interesting question was raised about impact of the high-speed railway on the relationship between Taipei and Kaohshung. Reference was made to the case of Osaka when Shinkansen connected it to Tokyo, which significantly lost its headquarter functions.

Banupong Nidhiprabha (Thammasat U) attempted to demonstrate how Bangkok was on a path of "sustainable urbanization." He argued that as the population grew around the city but did not do so much in the city, Bangkok had been less dense than most people thought. He defines sustainability in terms of the population density and its attendant problems. As a result of the de-concentration of the capital due to successful family planning, dispersing economic activities etc, the city is becoming more sustainable. Considerable discussions were made on the current environmental challenges in the city, including water supply, land subsistence and air pollution. The wrong pricing policy on artesian water and gasoline aggravates these problems. He concludes, nevertheless, that Thailand is on a "sustainable urbanization" path.

Discussant Shoichi Yamashita (International Center for the Study of East Asian Development) questioned whether the "sustainability analysis" can be applied to rural areas in Thailand. He analyzed the skewed distribution of GRP by area and population distribution in the country, showing also a map of existing and planned highways. These diagrams, he suggested, show that the merits of urbanization may not be felt at all parts of the country. Finally, he presented the environmental Kuznets curve and asked whether the city or the country will undergo that process.

3. Urbanization in the Philippines and Indonesia

Eduardo T. Gonzalez (Development Academy of the Philippines) presented: 'Managing Urban Decentralization in the Philippines'. From his analysis of urbanization and growth corridor success within the country he identified 6 policy recommendations

1. Top-down and bottom-up approach for urban development is needed;
2. The country should continue policies to pursue regional balance, but that these policies should avoid reinforcing current advantages of metropolitan areas;
3. Increasingly stronger competition amongst local governments translates into the need for control over the location and timing of growth and development;
4. Cities should diversify their economic functions and development profiles;
5. Cities demand fiscal autonomy making well-defined intergovernmental fiscal regimes;
6. Encouragement of human capital creation.

Discussant Peter J. Marcofullio (United Nations U, Tokyo) argued that it was essential to realize environmental challenges undergo a series of transitions as cities develop. At first, the primary challenges are those relating to the 'brown' agenda including water supply, sewage, and sanitation issues. As cities industrialize, they face the 'gray' agenda associated with industrial and auto-related pollutions. Cities in post-industrial societies are battling with the 'green' agenda challenges such as greenhouse gas emission, ozone depleting substances and non-point source pollution. While cities of the West have experienced these impacts in a sequential order, cities in rapidly developing Asia are confronted by a compressed and 'telescoped' form of transition.

Bambang P. S. Brojonegoro (U of Indonesia) presented; 'Decentralization and Urbanization in Indonesia: the Concept of Metropolitan Area'. Three years ago Indonesia implemented a "big bang" in decentralization policy, resulting in a 10 percent annual growth in new local governments. More municipalities, particularly outside of Java, imply the demand for increased and various services. The central government must use municipalities as the basic units of analysis and planning of economic activities and political administration and must consider their public services for evaluating them. He therefore recommended the formulation and implementation of the idea of metropolitan areas, which must be concretely introduced in law and more importantly to political willingness.

Discussant Kunio Yoshihara (U of Kitakyushu) observed that no significant improvement in the provision of basic public services in Indonesian cities had taken place whether they were under the centralized regime as before the 'Big Bang' or under the decentralized formula after it. Metropolitan form of government as suggested by Bambang must prove that it is effective in improving them.

4. Summary

1) Cities in Asia are experiencing a diversity of development paths in terms of economic development, population growth, and environmental challenges. In order for the nation's socioeconomic well-being to improve, it is essential to have a good management of not only its national urban system but also of individual urban agglomerations. It is suggested that the former should be primarily the responsibility of the central government, while the latter should be dealt with more effectively under the decentralized formula of local governments.
2) Management of the national urban system includes such issues as supremacy (as opposed to balanced urban hierarchy), rural to urban migration and its economic implications, environmental challenges, and research and development of technology as well as inter-regional transportation and communication infrastructure.
3) Local governments should be given responsibility and commensurate resources to manage their individual urban settlements, including the provision of basic public services such as health and education, and the management of municipal waste and other environmental challenges.

Author Index

Subject Index